AF490254

Dimes from Heaven Trilogy

Dimes from Heaven Trilogy

Dimes from Heaven,
More Dimes from Heaven,
Once Upon a Dime

by Monica L Morrissey

CONTENTS

CONTENTS

CONTENTS

More Dimes From Heaven, A Journey to Self Publishing

Once Upon a Dime

CONTENTS

Copyright © 2023 by Monica L Morrissey

All rights reserved. No part of this book may be reproduced in any manner whatsoever without written permission except in the case of brief quotations embodied in critical articles and reviews.

Because of the dynamic nature of the Internet, any web addresses or links contained in this book may have changed since publication and may no longer be valid.

I have tried to recreate events, locales and conversations from my memories of them. These memories are from my perspective only. Others may or may not remember them as I do.

First Printing, 2023

Epigraph:

"Yet winks from God are not communication to those who die; they are messages to the living, providing reassurance that the person who died has a role to play in the infinite plan and that those of us who are left have a continued role here on earth."
~SQuire Rushnell ~When God Winks

Acknowledgements

I want to thank my husband first. If he hadn't planted the seed about this story becoming a book, I might never have followed through with it. He always knew how sensitive I was but I never wanted to admit it. Thank you for loving me and understanding that I had to follow my dreams.

A big thank you to both of my children, Shamus and Patrick, for being who they are and helping me become a better person. I feel blessed to be your Mom. Thank you to the two women who love my boys, Emily and Heather. You both chose to love my kids and for that I am so grateful to have you as part of our family.

Thank you to my older sister, Debbie. You are always there for me no matter what. I know Mom and Dad are always with you too.

Thank you to Victoria Hill, who gave me permission to tell my story. You listened to my first draft (which sucked by the way!) and gave me the courage to face my fears. You took time out of your busy life to sit on my front porch, take a hike up Barr Hill and listen to my story. You weren't afraid to tell me the truth that I needed to hear. You gave me the confidence to continue writing, even when it was difficult.

Thank you to Tracy and Chelsea Collier. Tracy helped me to "show don't tell" in my writing; which is something I used to teach to my students. Chelsea- I loved how you turned into my teacher and I was the student. You both gave me great advice, especially when I was stuck. I feel honored to call you my friends, my soulmates.

Thank you to my dear friend, Tanya Barber, who helped me enjoy life everyday. Thank you for being there when my anxiety was at its most extreme. I had no idea how difficult writing was going to be. You were there to lend an ear and some advice. I am forever grateful for our friendship and our memorable trips to Wal-mart and Olive Garden with our husbands!

Thank you to Kim Knudson who helped me with editing. You were my editor in chief just like when our students wrote the Greensboro History books. You questioned me and made me explain things so that it would be easier to understand. I enjoyed talking with you during our many meetings!

Thank you to Wendy for reading my manuscript and giving me tips on how to organize my sentences. I appreciate your friendship and you support!

Thank you to all of the healers who have helped me work through so many different emotions and physical issues. Thank you to Betty who helped me work through my present life through past life regression work and EFT. My acupuncturist, Sarah, and my massage therapist, Liv, who both listened to me when I lost both of my parents. Along with helping my body heal from the stress, you helped me emotionally and I can never thank you enough. Thank you to Michelle, who helped me with my digestion when the medical doctors couldn't. You helped me find my "qi"(pronounced chee) when I didn't know it was gone. Thank you to Sierra who helped me find the pieces of my soul that I had lost throughout my life. I will never forget you saying, "Welcome back Monica." I felt it inside my entire body. Thank you to Grace, who first helped me heal after my back surgery. You gave me my life back. I am honored to now have you all as friends. Without you, this book never would have been possible.

Thank you to my new "parents" who make me feel loved everyday. I feel blessed to be a part of my Uncle David and Aunt Jean's life. You both helped me and Dad when Mom passed away. I know that my Mom and Dad are thankful for your continued support after they left us. Thank you to Eldon, who always reminds me how important God is in our lives and how God heals us. I am blessed to have you in my life. Thank you to Merrilee for caring for my father and adopting me after both of my parents transitioned to Spirit. When I receive love from the four of you, I imagine that you are also giving me love from my parents. You are my angels and I am blessed to have you all in my life.

Thank you to all of our friends who feel like family. As I danced with my son on his wedding day this year, I felt the love from all of you to my entire family. The Morrisseys feel blessed to have you in our lives.

Thank you to our Dimick Road family. Brian and I had no idea how special it would be to raise our family surrounded by all of you. I am so thankful that we moved to Dimick Road and our kids had such good people around them while they were growing up. You all are a part of our hearts forever and always.

Thank you to all of my students. Whenever I talk about "my kids", I would have to distinguish between my own children and my students. All of my students will always be "my kids" because I got to be a part of your lives for a time period. I loved teaching and our time together will always be a part of me. I love connecting with each and every one of you on Facebook or in person. I hope that some of you may write a book someday!

Thank you to Terhas, who said to me one time, "I love how your heart is so open." It's open with you Terhas, because I know that I can trust you and you won't hurt me. I'm not like that with everyone. Both of my parents loved you too. I look forward to reading your memoir someday.

Thank you to all of my colleagues, especially the ones who helped me during the time I lost both of my parents and the ones who encouraged me to write my dime story. I feel honored to work with you and know that you all are making a difference in the lives of many children. Thank you for choosing to be an educator. It can be one of the most challenging but also the most rewarding job you will ever have. To Sylvia, who, when I told her I was going to write a book, was just as excited as I was! You are a beautiful soul.

I know so many people who have been affected by the death of a loved one. I hope that my dime story will help all of us understand and know that our loved ones are near us every single day. I know it isn't the same living life without them, but I hope we all feel love in our hearts from Heaven.

Thank you especially to my Mom and Dad. I know you were with me every step of the way. It wasn't "goodbye" when you left me, it was "See you later."

There are so many people in my life that I am thankful for. This book was one of the most difficult things I have ever done in my life. It is most definitely my Baby and I hope you enjoy it as much as I have enjoyed sharing my story with you.

Note from the author:

I always knew that I had a deeper connection to something. I wasn't sure how to explain it and I didn't always know how to access it. Looking back now, I realize that I wasn't raised to explore or understand this connection and it went against everything that I felt inside. This story is my journey about discovering the world beyond the human experience and learning to accept my gifts and challenges as an empath. I didn't set out to write a memoir. I only wanted to write about the dimes. I didn't know that through the process of writing, I would heal from the inside out. Before I did that though, I had to understand my life from a different perspective. I had to step out of my anger and into my body. That's when I found the answers. This book shares the intimate details of how being an empath affected every part of my life, including food, relationships, and my internal messages to myself. The Liberty Head dimes helped me have "Freedom of Thought", which is the meaning of that particular dime. May you have Freedom of Thought as you read.

"A memoirists work is not just to transcribe his life, but to uncover meaning behind those life experiences for himself, and for his readers." ~ Joni B. Cole

Foreword:

I have been privileged to be a part of Monica Morrissey's healing journey for over a decade, ever since she sought me out for a past life regression some time ago. Years might go by between our times of connecting, but at crucial moments Monica would always show up to face herself honestly, dig deeply, and heal what needed healing so that she could claim more and more of her authentic self.

It is a joy to hold this book in my hands. How beautiful to see Monica not only claim the truth of who she is as an empath, but also share her story with the world. It is one thing to work deeply on one's own healing and become more whole, and I have such respect for anyone who takes this journey. It is quite another to have the courage to share this intimate journey through writing. We are so fortunate that Monica has felt this calling to share her experiences.

When Monica first told me the stories of the dimes, I thought, "These stories must be shared!" They are remarkable evidence that the love and connection do not end with physical death. As Brian Weiss says, only love is real. These experiences are a testimony to that truth. Inspiring, reassuring, tangible proof – I love these stories from Monica's direct experience.

While the "dimes from heaven" are the core of the book, the reader will find much more in these pages. Monica lets us into her life as she describes the challenge it has been to grow up as an empath in a family and culture where feelings were not affirmed or encouraged; where her gift of sensitivity was ignored and thus hidden for so long; where, at ag 50, "coming out" as her true self still feels perilous. How many readers will relate to this? Many, I believe. In my practice, I work with so many highly sensitive people whose lives have been marked by the fear of begin who they really are. This speaks to me personally as well.

And so this book is a gift to us all. The many authors who have helped Monica find her way are quoted throughout the book. Monica Morrissey is, after all, a professional educator and part of her mission is to share information and resources. Readers will benefit from the extensive bibliography at the end and will find much valuable and inspirational information.

We often hear that the two primary emotions which underlie all others are Love and Fear. Indeed, we can often feel how we vacillate between the two, longing to open our hearts but fearful of being hurt or unsafe. It is author Gary Zukav who added a nuance that I have appreciated: we either choose Love or Trust, or we let Fear and Doubt prevail.

I have been so moved by Monica Morrissey's honesty and vulnerability as, over and over, she faces her own fears and doubts and shares this part of the journey as well. It is deeply human and remarkably open-hearted. And then, despite the struggle, she finds ways to cultivate more love and trust and keep affirming what she believes and knows. Her process, described in detail in the book, is a real inspiration.

The world feels like a dangerous place for empaths and highly sensitive people. And yet the world so needs their gifts of sensitivity and spiritual connection. It is an act of great courage to bring a book like this into being. Thank you, Monica, for trusting us with your story and yourself. We are the richer for it.

Betty Moore-Hafter

Certified Hypnotherapist and EFT Master Trainer

Certified in Past Life Regression by Dr. Brian Weiss

https:/creativeeft.com

Author of *Freedom at Your Fingertips,* along with nineteen other World Class EFT experts

"I believe in Healing. I believe deeply that the key to healing our lives and achieving our goals is inside each of us. We can rediscover our "blueprint" for wholeness and well-being within the deep inner self. I think of myself as a companion on the journey, a partner in healing, and I approach that role with compassion and non-judgment. I bring to you my deepest listening and presence, and I trust your own healing process that is unfolding. This is a privilege for which I am very grateful.

Are You a Seeker Too? *In some ways, we are all seekers, aren't we? Seeking happiness, seeking relief from pain, seeking fulfilling relationships, seeking a satisfying life. I wanted to understand what blocks our wholeness and how we can heal and be more in alignment with our best selves, even when the going is rough and challenges and adversity come our way."*

Betty Moore-Hafter

I am forever thankful that I was able to work with Betty. May the readers of this book seek to find the answers within you. ~Monica

Preface

"The essential lesson I've learned in life is to just be yourself. Treasure the magnificent being that you are and recognize first and foremost you're not here as a human being only. You're a spiritual being having a human experience."
~Wayne Dyer

Over the past ten years or so, I noticed more and more people talking about signs from people who have transitioned to spirit. I wanted with all of my heart to believe in such a thing. A voice inside me questioned and doubted everything that I couldn't prove. *How could this be true? I wondered.* Ever since I was a little girl I wanted to believe that there was only good in the world and God would help those who were hurt. During some of the chaotic moments and events in my life, I lost pieces of myself. I was trying now, as I was about to turn 50, to discover where my soul's journey was going to take me next. My body was sending me messages to change and grow, but I struggled accepting myself. Through writing, I was able to dig deep, get clear, and heal in a very different way than I ever imagined. Through writing, I discovered I was an empath, something I knew very little about. It was my life lesson to learn to be me, exactly the way God made me. To do that though, I had to question the foundation of my childhood.

"Then I realized, what do they really know? This is MY idea, I thought. No one knows it like I do. And it's ok if it is different, and weird, and maybe a little crazy. I decided to protect it, to care for it. I fed it good food, I worked with it. I played with it. But, most of all, I gave it my attention." ~Kobi Yamada

Here is **my** story; the first "phone call" and the many dimes my father sent from Heaven.

Chapter 1: My Young Life

More Than a Dime

"I learned from my journey that a true seeker must go deep into his or her own consciousness to come closer to realizing the truth of our existence." ~Eben Alexander M.D.

Chapter 1 My Young Life

"More learning can occur when there are many obstacles than when there are few or none. A life with difficult relationships, filled with obstacles and losses, presents the most opportunity for the soul's growth. You may have chosen the more difficult life so that you could accelerate your physical progress." ~Brian Weiss

My first memory of talking to angels was when I was maybe 10 or 11. I can remember being so unhappy in my family that I started to "talk" to the lights floating outside my bedroom window. *Does everyone have a voice inside their head that speaks to them? Where does it come from? Does it only come from my brain? Does it come from someplace else? Do other people think about things as much as I do? I wonder as I speak to the floating lights outside my window. I'm on the top bunk, mostly because I am the "big" sister. If I didn't have to sleep on the top bunk, I never would have seen the lights. It's almost like they are talking to me, supporting me when I feel alone. Who are they I wonder? I feel like they like me.* During those years on the top bunk, I stared at the floating balls of light in the corner of the house every night. They were like bubbles that never popped. *Why would I think that I could talk to them?* Because of the dimes, I would begin to understand the **things we cannot see and my own connection to spirits.**

Some of my childhood memories are blank; blocked out. There were times in my life that were great and others that were more difficult. During the difficult times, I would put on a mask and pretend I was ok. I didn't have the strength to live like others. I was sensitive and didn't know how to express any of my feelings. For me, when my mother spoke to me about something I had done wrong, I didn't know how to recover from it. I would feel so bad. It was like the words got stuck inside my body and then I didn't feel good. I thought that because of the way she had spoken to me, she might not love me anymore. *My family didn't understand me, either. Most of the time I didn't know what to do. I wanted to talk about feelings and it seemed my parents wanted me to 'get over it'.* Because of this, I learned how to hide all of my feelings, stuffing them all inside my body and eventually this made me sick.

My cousin's husband says he thinks I was a UPS kid- dropped off in a family where I didn't belong. I laughed but knew how true this felt. *Anita Moorjani describes this feeling perfectly in her book, Dying to Be Me, "Why am I always different, wherever I go? Where do I belong? Why don't I feel like I belong anywhere?"* Although for different reasons, I think she understands how I felt. I believe she was confused because she didn't agree with all of the organized religious beliefs of her family and culture. This feeling seemed to create a war within her. *Does everyone feel this way? Does everyone want to belong somewhere? Why are there so many rules about believing in God? Can't we all believe in the same thing? Was my family the reason I needed to talk to the lights? Is this why I needed to know that someone else was out there, ready to love me for who I am?*

Growing up, I spent a lot of time outdoors. I loved to swim in the lake all summer and play outdoors in the woods. At my family's camp on the lake, I would catch frogs, fish, water ski and play out on the raft with my friends. The lake I swam in was filled with mud and seaweed, but I didn't care. Some girls I know wouldn't even go near a lake like that. I was a tomboy at heart and I remember wanting to live in the woods. For me, these times outside seemed magical. Growing up in the 70's, we would play outside until it was dark. We were up and down the street at different houses until the day was done. I loved to be outside.

Our family camp on Lake Elmore was a magical place for everyone. I learned to water ski when I was five years old. I still have the red, white and blue striped skis that I got for Christmas one year. I would go out in the row boat and fish with my Grandmother. At night, we played kick the can. My cousins had a camp three down from our camp so we would all get together to play when it got dark. The boundaries were the road, the lake and in between about five camps. I was one of the younger kids and I'm sure I was outsmarted most of time.

As an adult, I enjoy spending time outside- hiking, camping, or swimming. I once had a friend who I met in my late thirties, say to me, "With you, I have done the most things outside, without make-up, that I have ever done in my entire life!" Yup, that is me- an outside, no make-up kinda gal! Hiking and being in nature gives me time to think. I can start a hike ruminating on something going on in my life and by the end of the hike, I have worked through it. It's almost like when I work out and sweat on the hike it clears out the negative thinking. If only I could hike everyday. Of course, my favorite hike is Elmore Mountain, directly across from the family camp on the lake. When I hike that mountain, I feel like I am home. ***I feel connected.***

For people who know me professionally, they might wonder about the person I described. "What? Monica always shows up to school with her nails done, wears dresses and always looks great. She can't be a tomboy or a nature freak!" Truth be told, if I had a choice, I would be in yoga pants and a t-shirt every single day living out in the woods. For my profession though, I have to be able to get up and go to work every day. I believe that as an educator, I have to show up to work looking professional. Except for make-up- I still do not wear make-up. People will see my real face every day.

We had an electric player piano and a pool table in the basement at our house. All the kids would head downstairs to play. We would sit on the bench at the piano and sing along to songs like Mickey Mouse March, John Denver's Country Roads, Take me Home or If I Were a Rich man from the play Fiddler on the Roof. If we weren't singing songs we were playing pool, hide and seek or a variety of board games. Whenever I had sleepovers, we always slept in the basement. We always had to be super quiet. I was always embarrassed when my mom would holler down the stairs. When she flicked the lights, it either meant quiet down or dinner was ready. I was never sure which one she was going to say.

We had a sugar house out back and it was up to the kids to help gather the sap. We would ride all over to different sugarwoods in the back of a pick up truck. We had to carry five gallon buckets to gather the sap. There was one family in particular who always helped our family with making syrup. Having them there made it so much more fun. When it would get late in the spring, the sap would be yellow and sometimes we would find mice in the buckets. Although that part wasn't always fun, the best part was when the Mom of the family who helped us would bake maple biscuits. The yummy taste of maple syrup would make all the hard work worth it.

These recollections could go on and on. This is long before electronics took over our world. Of course, these are all great memories for me, but I felt lost in the crowd. I didn't feel like I fit in. I was too sensitive and had difficulty "being tough". These memories most likely create such a happy feeling for everyone who was there. When I think of the time spent with all the different families we were friends with, it was most definitely the best part of my childhood.

From the outside looking in, my young life most likely looked fine to most people. I was a pretty girl (at least that is what people told me- of course, I didn't feel 'pretty'), our family had lots of friends and relatives around, I got good grades, and had plenty of friends at school. Many people will reminisce about the fun times they had at our house and our family camp on Lake Elmore. To them, our family probably looked a lot like Leave it to Beaver. Everything was good on the outside and inside. To me, I knew that something wasn't right. I could feel it inside me. *Was it me or was it the family I was born into? How would I ever have the courage to look inside myself to find who I truly am? Sometimes I feel like I am fighting voices in my head, wondering if I am enough. How can I feel like I am enough?*

I spoke to lights. *Crazy, right?* At a very young age, my mother didn't understand who I was. Growing up, I always felt it was important to keep up appearances. It seemed important to my Mom to make sure people thought our family was perfect, a fact that would make me struggle to share any of my feelings with anyone. As an adult in my 20's, 30's and most of my 40's, this is how I would also live my life- thinking and worrying about what other people thought about me and my family. I knew I needed to learn that there was a different way to live.

I would never have dared to share this information with anyone- *and now I am putting all of this on paper! Somebody might read it, my truth would be revealed...my mother's voice worries me as I write. I am putting myself in a very vulnerable position, one which I had tried my whole life to cover up. I needed to learn how to live differently. Making mistakes was ok. Being imperfect was ok.*

"Owning our story and loving ourselves through that process is the bravest thing that we will ever do." ~Brene Brown.

Brene Brown, through all of her books, created such a different role model for me to learn to live differently. She talked and shared all of her feelings. This was something new for me. I thought I had to stuff all of my feelings to look tough. I thought I had to be different on the outside and couldn't share what I was feeling on the inside.

Growing up, we attended church, but I never felt God in our house. In fact, it was the opposite. For our house, I felt church wasn't about living with God's message; it was about putting on an air that we were a strong family. I felt that church made us look good. I remember the minister visiting my father, soon after my mother's passing. She tried to explain to me that she didn't really understand my Mom and that they "had an understanding". I got it. I knew exactly what she was saying. I had an understanding with my Mom also, and that was to not explore what made me who I am or to talk about any other "nonsense". Emotions, God and talking about our problems would all be off limits. *'Just suck it up and deal with it,' I would think to myself. I guess having four children to deal with, there wasn't much time to help me deal with my insecurities, or other such silly things, like not making the softball team. Why did I struggle every time my parents spoke to me about a mistake I had made? Why did I worry so much? As a child and a teenager, there were many things that happened to me that I never dared to talk to anyone about. I was always worried what other people would think. I did turn to God though. I thought He would always listen to me and love me. At least, that is what I believed.*

People have a lot of different words for God, Spirit, Jesus, etc. For me, God is a Spirit with an all encompassing positive energy field around everything in the entire universe. This includes everything on earth and beyond; plants, animals, things, stars, everything you can imagine. I don't tend to focus on structured religion with its many rules. I don't believe God judges us and we should feel bad about ourselves. This creates the negative voice inside us and separates us from loving ourselves. Spirituality is much more than organized Religion. For me, whatever words you choose to use are your business; for me it is a Spiritual Energy that is the basis of all life and beyond. It is the unknown, the wonder that can't be "proven" so to speak.

I remember one time my son asking for our whole family to be the "same" religion. He knew I was raised in a different church than my husband. I decided that if that was important to him, I would make that happen. I decided to convert. I remember being nervous to tell my parents. *Would they be angry with me? Would they understand that to me, it didn't matter what organized religion that my family attended as long as I was able to raise my kids believing in God?* When I told my parents, my Dad responded, "Well, I think we are all talking to the same person." *He got it. Now, if you are wondering what religion I am, I will ask you, does it matter?*

"As you learn about your energy on a soul level, you will encounter topics and information that feel right to you as a core spiritual truth and some ideas that don't make any sense at all." ~ Melissa Alvarez

Take what you want and leave the rest. For me, the dimes spoke to me, a true message from my Father, helping me understand that God is within me.

My Grandmother (my father's mother) and me on my wedding day.

From a very young age, I always felt the presence of God. It is difficult to describe; other than, I know that someone somewhere cares about me and everyone else on Earth. It isn't like one ultimate power, it's more like all the people in Heaven loving me. I feel it in my gut and my heart. I first felt this in church when I was young. My Grandmother (my father's mother) was close to God. She read the Bible everyday, wrote in her journal and only said nice things about people. Never would you hear her say anything bad about anyone. My husband's mother is very similar in this way and has taught me a lot about being grateful for everything in my life. I loved sitting next to Grandma in church; I knew she got it. I could *feel* it. For me, being in church made me feel safe. I loved singing songs and learning in Sunday School. I felt a presence that I couldn't explain. My heart beat better when I was at church. For me, it wasn't about the people in the church, it was what I felt inside. I knew that God was speaking to me. He was helping me in a family that I didn't understand. When I was young, I envisioned everyone together believing in the same thing that I believed.

The moment in time that I felt the most connected to God and my Grandmother was when she and I found about a dozen four-leaf clovers at our family camp on Lake Elmore. It was a sunny day and my Grandmother and I were sitting near the sandbox next to the lake. She found the first one and showed it to me. I couldn't believe it! I wanted to be like her so I started looking for another one. We kept finding more and more. It was magical. I had never even seen one four leaf clover, but we found a dozen. We took them inside the camp and put them in a book so they would dry and I would be able to save them. When I think of that afternoon, I can see the sun shining on my Gram's face and hear her laughing. She is my angel. *When I find four leaf clovers now, could they possibly be a message from my Gram, saying hello? I believe so.*

As a mother, it was always important to me to pass the belief in God on to my own children. I knew there would be times in their lives when they would need to turn to Him to ask for help. Life can knock you down and it's important to know how to pray for guidance. My kids believed in God long before the dimes. Although I brought my kids to church often, for us, God was more than attending church. God was there for you always and forever.

One of the more positive memories that I have growing up was going to see the group of performers called, "Up With People". Wow. Talk about energy. During their songs and performances, it felt like a tsunami of love crashing on the entire audience. I soaked up all of the positive energy from those performances and dreamed of one day being on stage performing with this group. It was like God was in the room with all of us. The excitement, the energy, the positivity- I absorbed the energy into my body like I was a sponge soaking up water. I felt amazing after attending one of these shows. Their motto is,

"In our ever-changing global world, hope is the foundation for uniting people and communities. This is the heart of Up With People."

I have no idea how this particular show was in our community back then, but it was. Now, their shows aren't even close to Vermont. If only I could attend one of these, and take a hike once a week, I would feel so much better!

Does it matter what others think? My anxiety goes up as I share about my beliefs in God. Being vulnerable is not my thing. I like people to think I have my life together. Well, Brene Brown sure did introduce me to being vulnerable, but writing this book feels like too much vulnerability.

"Daring Greatly means the courage to be vulnerable. It means to show up and be seen. To ask for what you need. To talk about how you're feeling. To have the hard conversations."~ Brene Brown.

I did not know how to even begin to do this. I keep writing even though I wonder...Should I be telling everyone all of this? Should I keep it to myself? What will my colleagues think? My past students? But the dime is the key. It helps me keep writing.

"When life calls us, that's when you have to answer," Louise Hay's voice echoes in my head.

Was I being called to do something? How would I know if this is what I was meant to do all along? A lot of people say that everything happens for a reason and the timing is always the way it is supposed to be. Was this true for me now? Was the timing exactly as it was planned?

There are many points in my life where I "checked out" and have no memory at all. During my teenage years, I would cry to a minister or guidance counselor; only to build my wall back up directly after letting them see my pain. I had no idea what the word vulnerable meant but I wasn't going to seem weak to anyone. I was unable to know how to deal with my feelings and had nobody to talk to. I was afraid that people might hurt me so I put up a wall to protect myself. It was like armor I put around my heart so I wouldn't get hurt. When I "check out" of my body, it is like I'm not present. My head is busy thinking about other things. It's like I time travel in my head. *How do I explain this to other people? I seem to spend so much time in my head instead of being present. Nobody will ever understand.*

I do remember one time when I was about 10 years old. I can recall some friends at school talking about doing something nice for their mother for Mother's Day. I decided I was going to get up early Sunday morning and make my mother breakfast in bed. I was so excited and thought it was such a fantastic idea. I was sure my mother would be so happy and proud of me for doing something nice for her. So, I proceeded to get out of bed around 7:00 that morning and went to the kitchen to start cooking some eggs. My mother heard me and came out to see what I was doing. I explained to her what I was doing and that I wanted to surprise her. She scolded me and told me to get back to bed this instant. It was "too early", she explained. I went back to bed, so disappointed. *How could she ruin my surprise? I thought I was doing something nice for her and she still spoke to me and made me feel horrible.* I remember lying in bed so mad that I couldn't get back to sleep. Then, about a half hour later, I get up out of bed. She comes out of the bedroom and tells me I can make her breakfast now. I refused. She had ruined it and I couldn't understand why she had done that. *My boys might sometimes wonder why I always appreciate everything they ever do for me. It's because of this story. When I tried to do something nice, I was not given the chance to show my mother love. I felt rejected and didn't know how to recover. I held that anger in my body for years.*

I remember another time when I was about 14 or 15. Well, I should say, I only remember the beginning. It was the first time I got drunk and don't really remember most of what happened. It was my cousin's wedding. One of my cousins or relatives started giving me drinks. They gave me rum and coke because it looked like I was drinking a regular coke. *Nobody would know that I had an alcoholic drink. I had never even tasted any alcohol before. I drank it like I drank a regular coke. I have no idea how many I drank and I have no recollection of the rest of the night. I know I didn't pass out. I have little blips of memories here and there. Laughing with my cousin. Arguing with my mom. And, at some point, leaving the reception.*

I had learned in Health class that alcohol is a downer or depressant. But when the alcohol first hit my system, I felt all warm and tingly inside. It felt like my body came alive and there was an electrical current running through my entire being. I didn't feel down at all and wondered why the health teacher had said alcohol was a downer. I had been looking for some-where to fit in my whole life. It seemed like alcohol helped me feel a sense of belonging. I felt connected to everyone who was drinking. But, ultimately this was a facade that clearly ended the next day. It was only a superficial feeling of fitting in. 

I have always wondered if I did something embarrassing that night. My mom and dad never talked about it with me. Ever. They obviously knew I was drunk. They had to. Why wouldn't they talk to me about drinking alcohol? As a young person who didn't ever drink much, my first time drinking would most definitely have an impact on my future

This ability to build a wall would be my protection when I was afraid to let any-thing or anyone come in or out. I stuffed all of my feelings and didn't like to talk to people about some of what was happening inside me. At many times, I didn't always love myself, something that Anita says is key to being able to live like there is Heaven on Earth.

"The only thing you need to learn is that you already are what you're seek-ing to attain. Just express your uniqueness fearlessly, with abandon! That's why

you're made the way you are, and that's why you're here in the physical world." ~Anita Moorjani

Anita received these messages from God during her Near Death Experience (NDE). Loving myself sounds so easy, yet is so difficult for me. I've always wanted to believe in myself and know that God is within me. I wondered how I would ever face my fear of loving myself. If God loved me, why couldn't I?

Recently a childhood friend of mine told me that he believes in signs from Heaven. This was, of course, after I shared about finding the dimes I believed to be from my father. He proceeded to tell me about a photograph being magnified so much that you could see a face inside an orb (a ball of light in a picture). *Were people starting to believe in this stuff? Were those floating lights outside my childhood room people? souls? Could my father really have placed those dimes in those exact spots? How could he do it without a physical body to set them there?*

"One of the newest ways in which angels are showing themselves to us is by appearing in photographs as orbs of light...The method works best when you hold the intention of seeing the angels while you're taking the photos." ~Doreen Virtue

While writing my dime story, I am on vacation with my husband in Florida. I decided to start writing as a way to try to heal my emotions. As I sit here on the beach writing this, my husband asks me what I am writing about. I answer, "Well, eventually it will turn into my dime story." He responds, "Are you writing a book?" I pause and say, "Maybe..." I get up to get a drink, thinking- what if he or someone doesn't like my book or doesn't understand any of it? My mother warned me never to write anything that would be embarrassing if someone saw it. My fear grips me. My gut actually hurts. Please- I pray- leave me to get lost in my writing so that I may find myself.

"How much we know and understand ourselves is critically important, but there is something that is even more essential to living a Wholehearted life: loving ourselves." ~Brene Brown

Chapter 2: Meeting Jesus

"The fundamental message behind every NDE is one of love, peace and compassion for others; their transformational power transcends cultures, faiths and creeds. It is a message we can all benefit from without having to come close to death."~Dr. Penny Sartori and Kelly Walsh

While writing this story, I am dealing with, yet again, another pain in my root chakra. The pain was different than my back surgery twenty years ago but it felt like the message my body was trying to give to me was the same. I've heard over the years that writing can be therapeutic. But, I also remember my mother's warnings not to share too much of myself with others. I decide to take this week, while on vacation to begin writing my dime story. Anita Moorjani says we have to heal from the inside out- we have to deal with our feelings before we can physically heal. I think what she means is that in order to heal, we have to feel God's love within us. God is the only one who can truly heal us, but we have to believe in the process and change our negative thoughts to positive thoughts. We need to pray for ourselves and through the power of prayer, we will be healed. We have to learn to accept ourselves as God made us. Anita's father and Soni, both of whom had died, communicated to her during her NDE,

"Now that you know the truth of who you really are, go back and live your life fearlessly!"

I wonder how to do that after having ignored my feelings for so long? I remember one time trying to use cream on my psoriasis and a friend laughed at me, saying,

"You're trying to heal it from the outside, not the inside." At the time that made no sense to me. I had no idea how to even begin to heal from the inside. *I had built a wall so strong, I couldn't even begin to tear it down. Now was the time to begin. I knew it would be the only thing that could heal me.*

It seems that sometimes our blessings have to come through pain. Through pain, we feel God nearby to help us through our trials.

Was the pain in my body and the trials I have been through actually blessings and messages from God? What if being born into my birth family was a time for me to grow? Would I be the same person if I hadn't had those experiences? Does it take everyone this long to figure out how to love oneself? Am I the only one who has a negative voice inside my head, speaking to me telling me everything that I have done wrong; ruminating on every little thing? I feel like I have two voices inside my head- one who is extremely critical and another that comes from someplace else. The one who speaks to me about following my dreams; or sending me random messages. Is this my intuition? Where do these messages come from? I knew I needed to listen to the voice who cheered me on, not the voice who doubted everything I had ever done in my life.

"Self doubt undermines the process of finding our gifts and sharing them with the world. Moreover, if developing and sharing our gifts is how we honor spirit and connect with God, self doubt is letting our fear undermine our faith."
~Brene Brown

I remember reading Louise Hay's book, *You Can Heal Your Life*, years ago when I had surgery on my lower back. Louise quotes *The Course in Miracles* saying that,

"all dis-ease comes from a state of unforgiveness, and that whenever we are ill, we need to look around to see who it is that we need to forgive."

Do I need to forgive myself or someone else? How will forgiveness help my physical pain? Have I been holding on to resentment and anger? Was this, in turn, making me ill from the inside? Will my inner voice help me discover my emotions that will in turn heal my physical body? Will I be able to change my inner voice and listen to God more?

Now, here I sit thinking- this is dumb to think that anybody would be interested in my story. 'I'm not a writer- never will be,' my negative voice sings to me. I hadn't passed the writing exam years earlier in college and forever after I was scared to write. Right now, the thought of sharing this with someone scares the living crap out of me. I will be rejected yet again and I will be a failure, not only as a writer but as a person. They will find out that I am not perfect. I make stupid mistakes all the time. People won't understand. They will talk about me. They...They...they....

As I write this, I worry about what others will think of my beliefs and ideas. Many people see me as a public school teacher, one who should not be talking about these types of things. One time a parent even mentioned the fact that teachers shouldn't be allowed to wear cross necklaces....as he eyed the cross necklace around my neck. *Really? I thought. Should I not get married either?* Spirituality, energy based healing, speaking to the other side and such nonsense isn't what teachers should be like. Remember-there is a separation of church and state; any of this may be seen as trying to influence children into believing in things such as Spirit, God, or souls living forever. I continue to write, knowing that in the end, I need to share my story and I am more than a public school teacher or administrator. I know too, that I am able to show up to work and by seeing a bigger picture, use my talents and abilities to make a positive difference in the work that I do. I like to think about sprinkling love wherever I go. *Is it important that I believe what I am doing comes from God? Yes. Does it matter that others know it is from God? Unfortunately, yes, as some don't believe in such a thing. Maybe I am the messenger. I have to accept that some will never understand.*

At various times in my life, I felt more connected to God and those times have kept me here on earth, even when I wanted to be in Spirit. I wanted to leave earth my first year in college. That year in college was difficult. In high school I hadn't been allowed to do much on my own. I was now living in a dorm, trying to grow up and make new friends. This is pretty darn hard to do when I felt totally alone and different than everyone else. I had nobody to really talk to about anything. I didn't grow up close to my sisters and I didn't feel emotional support in my family for the things I was going through. During high school, I had a few close friends who were a few years younger than me. They were my lifeline and helped me so much. But in college I was removed from the high school scene and felt weird going back for help.

Nobody else seemed to have the problems I was having. Why did I struggle so much? Please God, help me understand.

"When written in Chinese the word 'crisis' is composed of two characters. One represents danger. The other represents opportunity." ~John F. Kennedy

I dulled my pain and tried to fit in by turning to alcohol and drugs during my first year of college. In elementary and high school, I had what I call "automatic" friends. My family knew several families whom we did lots of things with on the weekends. We went snowmobiling, skiing, ice skating and lots of other fun things. These people were my automatic family friends because our families were close. I didn't have to do anything to be their friend. I was a part of the group. The other set of "automatic" friends I had were at school. I went to a small high school and my classmates were all super nice. I played soccer, basketball and softball. Although I wasn't that good, being a part of a team helped me have a core group of friends. I never felt close to many of my peers, but I always felt like I had a lot of friends. When I went to college, I tried to play sports. I thought it would work the same. Join a team, have some friends. I wasn't a very good athlete in high school and I never should have been trying to play college sports. If I wasn't able to play competitively in high school, it wasn't going to happen in college either. At the time, I had no understanding of this. I know it probably sounds dumb but never did someone say to me,(or did I think it myself!) "hey, you sat the bench mostly in high school, maybe college sports isn't for you." *I had no idea what to do with my time. Sports was how I spent my time and that was where I got friends so I thought that's what I should do.*

I soon felt like a failure and didn't know how to make friends. Instead, I turned to the crowd who drank and smoked weed, something I knew little about. I was trying to fit in somewhere.

Looking back, I'm not quite sure how I even got passing grades that year. I was lost but others thought I was fine. I am lucky that I lived through that first year. Often times during that year, I thought it would be better if I didn't have to live on earth. A voice inside my head would say, *"Just crank the steering wheel- hit that tree head on and then everything will be ok."* To this day, I don't know why I didn't do it, other than it wasn't my time. I think God had other plans for me. At the time it was difficult to believe that my life on earth was worth anything. Dr. Christian Northrup talks about jumping in front of a car in one of Louise Hay's videos. *I believe she understands. Someone so famous also thought it would be easier to leave this place. Wow... I didn't think famous people had negative thoughts like me. Especially Dr. Northrup- she is so positive!*

In college, I did find a few friends. I hadn't felt like I fit in anywhere my entire life. *Why would college be any different?* The biggest reason I felt like I didn't fit in during college was because I had missed the drinking age cut off. Right before I turned **18**, the law changed the drinking age from 18 to 21. That meant, since I was one of the youngest in my class (I started kindergarten when I was 4 instead of 5) and I had an October birthday, almost all of my peers were able to drink alcohol and go to bars. At that point, since I wasn't of age to drink, I wasn't allowed in bars. Now, I look back and most likely this saved my life. If I had easy access to alcohol at that time, most likely I would have OD'd on it (for those of you who were at the Van Halen concert in Montreal with me you know exactly what I mean when I write this.) I drank alcohol like water, just like my first drink of rum and coke. I had no idea how to pace my drinking so I drank way too much most of the time.

I used alcohol and marijuana to try to fit in, be cool and numb any feelings or emotions that I might have. *Why was I always so scared and unsure of myself? Everyone else seemed to have confidence. Why couldn't I?* One friend, in particular, invited me to her grandparents' house in Florida. Her grandparents would serve us alcohol by the pool. I felt so grown up. I didn't grow up around people drinking because of my Dad's heart attack when he was 46 years old. We would be sitting by the pool, and her grandparents would serve us beer in a frosted mug that had been in the freezer. For me, I had never experienced such a thing.

Alcohol and drugs made my anxiety and insecurities even worse. (I only smoked pot less than a dozen times, but I think it affected me way more than others.) Pot would make me nervous and paranoid. I only did it to try to fit in. Instead it increased that voice inside me; the one who criticized *everything* I did. I also didn't know when to stop. Because of this, I can barely remember some nights; especially one particular night at my friend's house. What I do remember of that particular night was meeting Jesus. *For real? a voice inside says. Who is ever going to believe that! Ha! Good luck with that one, my gut churns as I write. I remember listening to the soothing sound of Anita's Indian voice describing her near death experience in her audiobook, Dying to be Me. I think she will believe.*

I didn't believe it that night and have never told anyone about it until now. Many drinks later, I ended up in a spare bedroom, somewhere in my friend's house. Excited to be away from home, I was thrilled to meet her friends; hoping they would like me. Drinking gin and tonics, I was quickly drunk and passed out; well, sort of. My friend liked to smoke weed and laugh at everyone. Me, I barely even knew what weed was until I got to college. She loved to joke and laugh at things that people did- which didn't help my insecurities.

Somehow I ended up on the bed, where I passed out and rolled onto the floor. My eyes were closed but I could still hear the party. All I could hear was a sea of laughter. Everyone was laughing at me. My face was about an inch from the wall. I could have easily puckered my lips and kissed the wall. With a wave of fear gripping me, I wasn't inside my body anymore. I was floating above it and can see my body lying there on the floor. I remember hearing the buzz of the party, the music and seeing everyone in the kitchen laughing and enjoying the party.

That is when I met and talked with Jesus. Jesus was there to tell me it was ok. I was told that I had more time and to return to my body. I explained to Jesus that I did not want to return. This is what I dreamed of when I wanted to run into the tree. I wanted to stay in whatever place this was. It was easier here. I didn't think I would ever feel this comfortable. I don't remember much else, other than everyone laughing at me, as I was curled up in a ball on the floor next to the wall. I remember hearing my friend saying, "Look- she is so passed out!" *My worst fear coming true- laughing and making fun of me. I was frozen and couldn't respond. I did not have any control over my body. I couldn't move and I couldn't talk. I wondered if I would ever feel comfortable in my skin after this. Then everything went black.*

At the time, I thought it was a dream. *But, it felt so real. Was it a dream or was it a near death experience? Had the drugs and alcohol created a situation where my heart stopped for a few brief moments? Was this what Heaven was like? Whatever it was, I felt like it was a message from God. It felt real.*

I woke up the next morning in the same spot where I had passed out the night before. I was more at peace, not worried about approval from my friend. *What happened, I thought? Why was I so peaceful around these people? Usually I was a pile of nerves. Why didn't I feel that I needed to please them?* Everyone was laughing, asking how I was. I played along and never dared to tell anyone what happened. Heck- How could I? I would be even more humiliated. I had met Jesus, even if I thought nobody would believe me and they would all think I was crazy. *I had no idea at the time what to do with this information, but, inside, I knew I had spoken with Jesus and connected to the place I dreamed about.*

On my way home from Florida that year I got a ride home with Eldon and Joyce Towle, the family who helped us with maple sugaring. Their son and daughter lived near Boston, so they picked me up from the Boston airport. Their son was ill with cancer. I knew he was in the hospital but had no idea how sick he was. Yet again, my mother hadn't shared with me the details. Similar to my father, "feeling ill" instead of having a heart attack that almost killed him, I was told, "Their son is getting help in the hospital for his cancer." Back then, cancer wasn't as prevalent and I had no idea that it could kill a person.

I remember going to see him in the hospital. His son was about 2 years old at the time and he jumped right up into the hospital bed with his father. I had never seen a sick person who I knew personally like this before. He was lifeless. He didn't respond to his family. *What is going on here? I didn't know he was this sick. What are the doctors doing to help him? I wanted to run. Seeing him made it a reality and I didn't know how to deal with my feelings. I was scared.*

For some reason, I remember everyone else leaving the hospital room. I was alone in the room with him. I walked over to his bed, touched his hand and then bounced back away from him like a magnet repelling against the opposite ends. I remember his eyes. I saw death and I knew that he knew that I saw it. I wanted the others to be around so that I wouldn't feel this. I didn't want him to know that I saw him transitioning to spirit. It didn't even seem like he was in his body. *I had no way of dealing with this information at the time and looking back to that moment, I know that God was in the room with us. I believe God was taking him out of his physical body to embrace him so that he wasn't in pain anymore. But, for me, a confused 18 year old, I had no way to express any of this. For others, it was normal to see him like this. For me, I would be confused until I read many books helping me understand death and dying. He died the very next day, after my visit. I thought it was my fault. I thought he had seen death in my eyes and gave up.*

As I write this, my husband went swimming in the ocean and then asked me what I was writing, "anything about us?" What I think he meant was "anything embarrassing?" I explain that writing this is therapeutic and that I need to do this in order to heal my pain. After reassuring him that I am not writing anything embarrassing (at least not for him!), he responds, "Whatever helps you and makes you feel better." This is another reminder that God brought him to me soon after the night I met Jesus. I am so very thankful for the way my husband loves me and accepts me. He understands and accepts that I have a connection to God and that it is important to me. Will he still love me when he reads this? 'Yes,' a voice whispers, 'of course he will.'

I ask him if he wants me to read some to prove there is nothing embarrassing for him. He says, "No, you can share it with me when you are ready." A feeling of acceptance for who I am washes over my entire being. I thank God that we were brought together right after my first year of college. If I hadn't gone to the movies that night and met him, I'm not sure I would still be alive.

Many years later, God helped me get sober and I am happy to say that I haven't had an alcoholic drink in about 20 years. And, I never smoked weed again after I met my husband. For me, it is a black and white decision- absolutely no gray area. I don't drink or smoke and that is all there is to it. I don't need to alter my body to enjoy life. I used to think that confidence came from a bottle, now I'm trying to find confidence inside myself.

When I look, I see Him everywhere. While I write this book....did I say book? No way, anxiety and fear grip me as I wonder if this will ever turn into a book. I'm not important like Brian Weiss, Anita Moorjani, or Wayne Dyer. I remember my Mother telling me about Wayne Dyer once. Of course, I knew way more than my mother and anything she likes, I will not like. This was years before I would discover Wayne and be forever influenced by his positivity. Does my story reveal any important messages? Will people think it is very exciting?

I think of the people I have shared my dime story with, including a writing teacher who encouraged me to write about it. I tried and struggled; there was so much more to tell than "just a dime". How could I share everything with everyone? They might not believe me. They might criticize me. They might make fun of me or my family. But, how could I not share the story? The positives had to outway the negatives.

"In order to succeed at being yourself, build confidence, and overcome insecurity you must focus on potential instead of limitations. In other words, focus on your strengths instead of your weaknesses." ~ Joyce Meyer

When I moved back home in May, after my first year of college, I noticed the energy of the plants and trees around me. Springtime in Vermont is an amazing rebirth after a harsh winter. That year, I felt the plants and trees welcoming me home. Clearing out my body from the booze and drugs that year, I began to see life a little clearer. I felt the spring breeze and smelled the flowers for the first time in a long time.

Graduating from Johnson State
College!

Chapter 3: Faith

"For we live by faith, not by sight" 2 Corinthians 5:7

Believe what you do not see and see the possibility in all things.

I always wanted to believe in signs from Heaven. Some people talked about a rainbow being a sign from their Grandmother, a butterfly a sign from their mother. I hadn't really been taught that it was ok to believe in those things. Life tested my faith and my belief in everything. I have a sign in my house that says, *"THIS HOME BELIEVES"* To me, if I could teach my kids one thing- it would be this. Believe in Heaven. Believe in the signs. Believe in the unknown. Believe in a bigger purpose. Believe in miracles. Believe that there is good in the world. Believe in yourself. Believe that I am always with you. **Just Believe.**

"More than the other Divine guidance styles, claircognizants tend to waver when it comes to faith. When you're a thinker, it's easy to think yourself into a box of skepticism. Faith seems illogical and rests upon so many intangible factors." ~Doreen Virtue

I see God/Spirit everywhere. There is music playing as I eat my lunch on the patio of the condo. The ocean waves roll in and people splash in the pool. Coming from somewhere above me, the radio blares Christian music about feeling lonely in this world and God helping us through it.

I listen and know that it is a sign to continue to share my story. I listen to this song all the time. I can sing it by memory. I pay the Sirius radio premium each year so that I can listen to The Message every single day. I tried to live without it for a week and I hated it. Hearing this song playing now is a little unusual...*people at a condo in Florida playing Christian music? If I didn't have Sirius radio, I wouldn't know the song...interesting coincidence. Will there be more?*

I watch a bird creep around the corner of the fence. Our small condo deck is on the ground level; the bird about twenty feet away from me. He seems to think he belongs and makes his way around the corner of the building. Standing about **3** feet tall, he cranks his neck to look for something, maybe some food? Each step he takes, he looks around, shakes his feathers and continues his journey. *I wonder what message I can learn from him. It isn't important what I think of this bird. It's his story, not mine. Why should I judge him for not fitting in. Why is that important? Doesn't everyone* *want to feel like they belong somewhere? I know I do. For now, I remember that although sometimes I might not feel like I belong, it is fine to walk in that path; to not let fear or the belief that I don't fit in hold me back. The bird flies away and I wonder where life will take him next.*

I used to think poetry, messages, songs, etc. were dumb; especially things that couldn't be proven. Only for ~~dreamers.~~ *As I write the word dreamers, my pen runs out of ink and there is only the outline of letters, with no ink. Like a message so clear yet hidden. That specific word. Dreamers. The word dreamers looks like a ghost on paper. No ink, just a shadow of letters on the paper.* Speaking of dreamers and messages from God, was that a sign or do I ignore it? My brain trained for so long to not believe in foolish things, that it is difficult to believe in all the messages I encounter. *Am I a dreamer thinking anyone will want to read my dime story? Will it matter? I always doubt messages, but when people hear my dime story- everyone believes my father is sending messages from Heaven. Most people get goosebumps.*

One of the books I picked up at the bookstore on the way to the airport has some interesting things to think about. Brian Weiss helps me process where I am at right now.

"So many of our fears are based in the past, not the future. Often the things we fear the most have already happened either in childhood or in a past life. Because we have forgotten or only dimly remember, we fear that the traumatic event may become real in our future." ~ Brian Weiss

The words help me feel safe in the present moment. I know that my fear is from the past.

"If you are ruminating about the past or worrying about the future, you will completely miss the experience of enjoying the cup of tea. You will look down at the cup and the tea will be gone. Life is like that. If you are not fully in the present, you will look around and it will be gone. You will have missed the feel, the aroma, the delicacy and beauty of life. It will seem to be speeding past you.

The past is finished. Learn from it and let it go. The future is not even here yet. Plan for it, but do not waste your time worrying about it. Worrying is worthless. When you stop ruminating about what has already happened, then you will be in the present moment. Then you will begin to experience joy in life." ~Brian Weiss

This message speaks to my core being, my root chakra and my breath. A voice speaks, "Breathe every time you worry or want to be present." This helps me enjoy Florida, every moment I make a connection or feel my pen hit the page.

When I was writing this morning a neighbor posted a song on Facebook. The song was about wanting to be different. This is another song that I listen to all the time- I envision myself living differently, the way I was born to live. The way my soul wants so desperately to live.

I cried when I listened to the video. The song reminds me of two of my nephews. Tyler, who died suddenly in a car crash and Micah, his brother. The sudden death of Tyler is when I started learning about souls, spirit energies and connecting with people in Heaven. Soon after his death, a colleague introduced me to Brian Weiss. Brian Weiss was a skeptic. He was an atheist and a scientist. Then his first patient, Katherine, began opening a new idea to him. While Dr. Weiss had her under hypnosis, she remembered several traumas. She told him about things that happened to her in a previous life. When she came back the next week, her phobia was gone. It was like it had disappeared after the hypnosis. She had a fear of water. Poof- gone! *Could past life regressions really help people? Is this why some people have extreme phobias? Are they carrying it in their soul lifetime after lifetime? Am I holding pains in my body from another lifetime?*

Through losing Tyler, my family and I had to pray to help each other get through that time. I always say it is normal for a person to lose their parents. It's part of the way the world works. *But I don't think a parent should have to bury their child.*

If we are willing to listen, I believe God will speak to us in ways we might have missed otherwise. *Tyler still speaks to me.*

As I think about my fear of facing who I am and trying to let my positive energy guide me another Christian song plays from somewhere above me. It is a song about fear. It is a very clear message to me that in order to listen to my soul's calling, I need to overcome my fear. I need to listen to my faith instead.

A voice inside me says, "It's ok. Face your fear. You have support now and you know that Spirit is everywhere, helping you forgive and accept yourself." Why are all of these spiritual songs playing right at this moment in time? Never before did I hear this type of music playing in a public place. Or, maybe the signs were there but I wasn't listening. I was too caught up in life and society so I never noticed the signs. Maybe I was spending too much time listening to my ego, judging others instead of listening to Divine guidance that was there all along. Had I spent my life being busy- all the time in my head instead of being in the present moment? Would I be able to slow down and connect with Spirit? Would learning to be still help me connect to the "something else", I had always felt inside? Listen, I think. Have Faith, I think.

Wait, is Faith like the wind? The wind blows but one cannot see it. We all know the wind is there because of the effects it has on other things, like leaves and flags. You know it is windy by looking outside and seeing all of the leaves blowing on the trees. Is Faith like that? When I share my dime story, people get goosebumps. Are they feeling faith blow onto them like the wind hitting their skin? Will writing this story help spread Faith throughout the world? Listen to the wind. It has the answers.

"When angels or deceased loved ones come extra close, you can feel their presence. Many people I interview can recall when they sensed specific spirit nearby. Most say something such as, 'Yes, I could feel my mother with me the other night. It seemed so real, but I still wonder if I was just imagining it.'"~Doreen Virtue

This is Elmore Mountain. This picture was taken from the lawn of our family camp.

Chapter 4: My Experiences with Death and connecting with Spirits

"The word angel means 'messenger'. Angels bring messages from the Divine Mind of our Creator." ~Doreen Virtue.

"We are always loved. We are never alone." ~Brian Weiss

 I wasn't allowed to have pets growing up because I think my parents were worried that the pets would die and I might cry. I didn't attend many funerals before the age of 18. When I was 18, I went to a funeral for an older neighbor on the lake. I went alone and, much to my surprise, it was open casket. I didn't even know they did that. I was shocked to walk in and see the physical body. I felt a presence when I walked in but I was too shocked to even understand what was happening and had no knowledge about connecting with souls who had transitioned back to Spirit energy. Now I have a whole new definition of what death means.

Sometimes spirits give me messages in my dreams. Recently, a high school friend's father came to me in a dream. He said, "would you please let them (his family) know that I am really sending all of those messages. They don't believe in these messages." In the dream, it was exactly his face as I remember him. During the dream, he had looked deep into my eyes to make sure I received the message and would deliver it. Of course, this was after I had found THE dime, the key to me believing that I knew my father was connecting with me. My friend's father knew that I had to believe now and he wanted me to get the message to his family. My father and he were friends so it would make sense that they were sharing this new spirit communication system. When I messaged my friend, she was in tears and thanked me for the message. I have no idea what the messages were, but she said the timing of my message was so meaningful. *Synchronicities, like the friend posting the song on Facebook. Are they planned by someone else?*

My insecurities tell me I'm not really a medium or anything so don't bother thinking I am anything special. My anxiety goes up because I'm afraid people will think I am crazy and not understand what I am talking about. My family sometimes picks on me. I even say it myself actually! They call the healing, reading and work I do on myself, "voo-doo work". It's said with love, as they don't always understand what I am doing. But, at times, it gives me high anxiety because I am worried what others will think of me. What a lot of people don't realize is that I have read so much about soul work and connecting with Spirit, that for me it is the way the universe works. Everyone should know about this. I begin to wonder if all of the books I have read have actually taken the information from the Bible and translated it without an organized religion's focus tied to their name? What if everyone believed in the same things about God/Spirit and didn't have different churches? Would we all be allowed to share our beliefs?

Earlier this year I shared parts of my dime story with a colleague. I remember Michelle looking right into my eyes when she said, "You are an empath." *I thought, what? What does she mean? What is an empath? I don't really want to tell her that I don't know what she is talking about. Is that like a medium? I've been to mediums before but I don't think I hear messages from dead people in my head....or do I? What's the difference between an empath and a medium? I think about the mediums I have been to. They can "hear" messages "from Heaven" at any given moment. How do mediums know their thoughts are coming from Spirit, like the Spirit communication I had so clearly explained to my father? Isn't what we hear in our head our own thoughts? How do I distinguish my own thoughts from a message? And, if I am an empath, what exactly does that mean? Will people accept me if I am an empath? What will my family and friends think? I guess it won't matter because I don't think I can change who I am. I mean I am who I am, right? It's not like I have a choice.*

When I say spirits, I'm not talking ghosts, like the movies. I'm talking about an energy, a presence, a knowing. Something one can "sense" or a sign that reminds us of someone who has journeyed on. The kind of feeling that one has to have **faith** in order to believe it to be true. It's like the feeling of the wind on your skin; you can't see it, but you know it is there.

One of the first times I felt consciously connected to a spirit who was a relative was my Grandmother (my mother's mother). At the time, I was 21 years old, had no understanding of spirits and nobody to talk about my feelings. Most likely my Grandmother had an aneurysm or a stroke. I'm still not exactly sure which it was that caused her to decline so rapidly. My parents didn't share information with me about her condition- only that she was in the hospital. This was like when my father was in the hospital for the first time. I was about 13 years old and I was a candy striper at the hospital. I remember walking down the hallway with Dr. Blowers, a friend of my dad's. Dr. Blowers says, "Well, your father was lucky to survive such a massive heart attack. It will be a long road to recovery, but he can do it." Wait, *what? My father had a heart attack? My mother had only said, "Dad wasn't feeling well so he went to the hospital." Dr. Blowers had no idea that I wasn't told about my father's condition. The* same would be true when my Grandmother was in the hospital. I wouldn't be told any information- other than she wasn't 'acting right.'

I remember arriving at the hospital to see my parents standing in the room, away from my Grandmother's bed. I went right to her bedside, holding her hand, speaking to her; telling her how much I loved her. At the time, it was as if I was drawn to her like a magnet. But this time, instead of repelling, I was pulled towards my Grandmother. Even though she looked like she was sleeping, I know she was listening to me. When I spoke, she squeezed my hand and I know for certain that she heard me. *At her bedside* I felt my Grandfather standing right there with us. It isn't like I actually see his physical body. It is a sensation of energy, a moment in time where I feel the love of spirit through my Grandfather, someone who passed shortly before I was born. I didn't necessarily know it when it was happening, but as I write about it and think back to that moment in time when I was holding my Grandmother's hand, I can feel him there with us. Without proof, I never dared to trust my intuition. *What would people think if I thought that my Grandfather was there in the room? Was he waiting for her? Was she aware that he was there and it was safe to leave her body? Many thoughts cross my mind. Is this what it means to be empathic? Doesn't empathic mean you show a lot of empathy? Kind of like sympathy, but different? My mind still wonders.*

After my Grandmother passed away in February, my husband asked me to marry him. In the middle of a winter storm, he brought me to "our" hill, where we had walked on our very first date. When we were dating, we spent many nights walking that very hill. Spending the rest of my life with him would be a dream come true. God had brought him to me and he would be my rock, always accepting and loving me as I am. My parents asked us if we wanted to buy my Grandmother's house. At the time, we thought it would be better than renting. While we cleaned out the house, I felt like my Grandmother was there 24/7, supervising the entire project. This was ok when all of the family was there but when I moved in with my new husband, *you can imagine my confusion.* My Grandmother was a very proper woman, who refused to smile for any pictures. I sensed her energy in every room as we made her house our new home.

Well, as you can imagine, I had a difficult time, as a newlywed, enjoying my life with my new husband, with a Grandmother who I thought was watching my *every* move.....both day and night. Because of my embarrassment, I would suppress my connection with spirit. If I look back at that time, I remember being so happy living in her house and feeling her all around me. I can still feel her as I write this and I can envision myself inside the house where she was watching over me, not in a weird way but in a protective, loving way- you know? *A spirit kind of way.*

"And don't worry that Grandpa is watching when you shower or make love. These souls aren't voyeurs. In fact, there's some evidence that spirit guides don't see our physical selves on Earth; they perceive our energy and light bodies instead. So they simply understand your true thoughts and feelings during each circumstance." ~Doreen Virtue

I don't really remember when spirits first started visiting me. It would happen in that in between sleep and wake state- not quite awake yet not quite sleeping either. I would push them away, almost reflexively, *as if I was scared*. One time I had an awful experience- I envisioned 1,000 skeletal looking spirits - all wanting my attention, and heckling me. I did not understand what was happening and again, had nobody to talk to. I don't believe in Hell, I believe everyone crosses over into the light. But I do think there are some low energy spirits who are very troubled and try to seek someone who might be able to help them. I told them to leave me alone because I was sleeping; something that my family can tell you is a problem now. I never want to be woken up- I hate it! I have a lot of sleep issues (both going to sleep and staying asleep) so when I am asleep, I want to stay asleep. I didn't want whoever these people were to disturb me. A part of me really wanted to help them all. But, alas, that would be impossible. *How is it possible to help so many troubled people? Instead, I try to sprinkle love wherever I go.* I have now requested that only positive spirits visit me and that only love and light are welcome in my home. I have put up a positive light to protect myself and have never had the experience that I had years ago.

Now I get bearhugs, a feeling of heaviness or a feeling like someone is sitting on the edge of the bed. I still have difficulty understanding and accepting these feelings. *Is this what she meant when she said I was an empath? I don't understand how this all works.* In this state, I have a weird feeling engulf my body. I am separated from my body and I cannot control it. When this happens, I literally can't move. I feel like I am trapped inside my body. I can't escape, even though I feel like I want to. I want to run or get up out of bed. But, in that in between state of wake and sleep, it is like I am paralyzed. The only thing that I can do is breathe. I am unable to move. *I think back to when I had my near death experience. What was happening? Is this my soul that is disconnecting from my body? How do I get back to my body so I can move? It is the most unusual sensation for sure.*

I believe spirits can show in many different ways. Sometimes it is in a physical form and sometimes it is an energy; a feeling. The physical form comes in many different ways- For some, it is butterflies, dragonflies, sunflowers, or rainbows. For me personally, it is four leaf clovers from my Grandmother Palmer, dimes from my Father, pennies and rainbows from my Mother, GoodYear signs from my Father and Grandfather and the list keeps going on and on. (My father and grandfather sold GoodYear tires at the family business.) For me, it's real. It's not just cute and nice that I "think" that they are sending messages. *It really is them.* I know others who want to believe so much but doubt whether or not it could really happen. *When I begin sharing parts of the dime story, many people believe they are from my father. So many synchronicities happening all around me. I wonder if other people ever doubt their own beliefs? The conversations I had with my father before his death make the dimes so much more meaningful. Dad's spirit sending messages to me that I am not alone. The story of the dimes is so much more than the dimes. The entire story helps me understand and believe that our souls' journeys go on forever and ever.*

My Dad and I when I was young. I see Goodyear signs all the time!

I have attended many more funerals over the years. I cried with my family at my nephew, Tyler's funeral. The most difficult part of funerals for me now is watching my own children in pain. Tyler was killed on impact in a car crash, the result of his side of the car hitting a brick mailbox. Through one of his best friend's, Red Sox pitcher David Price, Tyler is remembered. *As I write, I cannot stop crying as I feel Tyler's strong presence encouraging me to tell my story. I wonder, was Tyler like me? Does he want to help the world be a better place through my writing? I know the answer, yes. He says, "Aunt Monica, tell your story. It's important and I am one of the keys to your story." These messages sometimes are so strong that I wonder where they come from. When I listen AND feel, they are overwhelming. A poem by Tyler March 7, 2001*

<u>His Road Not Taken</u>
Going along the path,
There's a split in my way
Which way should I chose?
I will find out another day.
The two paths are different,
I don't know which one to choose.
One seems to be very new,
The other has been stomped on by shoes."

After Tyler's death would come unexpected lessons for me. I was introduced to Brian Weiss and the idea of past lives, a totally new and different way of thinking about life and souls. *Could going deep within the soul to remember a past-life really heal the pains from this life? Were souls really floating around waiting to enter a human body to work out their lessons? Brian Weiss was shocked when his first patient was healed from exploring another lifetime. He was a skeptic, but his patients showed him that by going deep within the soul to remember, they could heal past pain.*

"Yet these memories allowed her to recover from her recurring nightmares and anxiety attacks in a way she'd never experienced." *~Brian Weiss.*

"The awareness that we have multiple lifetimes, separated by spiritual interludes on the other side, helps to dissolve the fear of death and bring more peace and joy into the present moment." *~Brian Weiss*

How would anyone else ever believe this? I wonder...

The year after Tyler's death, I would meet a medium for the first time to learn about what my life lessons were. She shared lessons that I needed to work on in this lifetime, all similar to other lifetimes prior to this one. I remember one of the first questions she ever asked me- "What do you do if you come to a tree or a rock in your path?" My answer- "go around it, climb over it, whatever I need to do to get to the other side!" She responded with another question, "How about taking a different path?" Oh- wow- that idea had seriously **never** crossed my mind! *I had no idea how to begin to take a different path. Was this book my new and shiny path? Would it help my soul discover a different way to live? Different than the way I was raised. Did I need to leave behind my childhood beliefs to create a new life- one filled with Divine Guidance on my new path?*

After I read Brian Weiss's books, I started reading Wayne Dyer's books. Wayne explains how important it is to find "one's true calling." He wrote The Shift and I literally felt my world shifting. So many other experiences help me begin to totally change my way of thinking about life. It was changing my brain. I had thought life was one thing, yet was slowly being introduced to many new ideas. Life was so much bigger than what I thought it was. I wasn't sure who to share these "New Age" ideas with. People wouldn't understand, like I felt my mother didn't understand. *People don't read as many books as I do. Everyone is so busy with life. I thought people wouldn't believe me. That is, until, the dimes started coming one by one. Then I would start sharing more and more, with anyone who had the time to listen. When I shared my story, people believed and even shared some of their stories with me. But, I never had time to tell the entire dime story. There was so much more to tell. How did this all fit in with all of these different ideas about souls, past life regressions, talking with people who had passed on.....How would I ever be able to explain this to others?*

Be in the now. Face my fears. Release old beliefs. Don't hold on to outdated thoughts. Ask God for help. Follow your dreams. Remember, your body is listening to everything you are thinking, a voice from within guides me as I write.

Tyler's friend, David Price believes that spirits are all around us. They were best friends all through high school and college.

"No one enjoyed David Price's performance in Tuesday night's All-Star Game as much as Tyler Morrissey did. He was in the upper deck. He was behind the dugout. He was behind the plate. He was even on the mound with Price. After all, as far as Price is concerned, he always is."~ *Gary Shelton St. Petersburg Times July 13, 2010.*

"Almost 3 months after Tyler's death, David felt Tyler's presence- helping David as he began his MLB career as a pitcher. This was something that Tyler always believed would happen to David and David knew that Tyler's spirit was right there with him every step of the way." ~ *Gary Shelton St. Petersburg Times July 13, 2010.*

BY MONICA L MORRISSEY

Just watch Price when he pitches for the Red Sox or previous games with Tampa Bay. Does he ever look up towards Heaven? Or tap his heart?

BY MONICA L MORRISSEY

Chapter 5: Before the Dimes

"We have so many more intuitive abilities that we know or use." ~Brian Weiss
"Information about our past lives and the spiritual dimensions can also be gleaned from other intuitive insights as well as from dreams, through meditation, or even spontaneously, as in deja vu experiences." ~Brian Weiss

The same year that Tyler died, 2008, my Mother almost died from congestive heart failure. She would be taken early in the morning in an ambulance to the hospital to find out that she needed open heart surgery to fix a valve in her heart. Later we found out that she hadn't been to the doctors in 33 years; the last time she went to a hospital was to give birth to her last child! My father had had open heart surgery three times, but she had never had surgery. She seemed to hate hospitals if she was the patient. She seemed fine if it was someone else.

I can remember the day right after her surgery. My mom was in an intensive care unit that included 2 patients and about 10 hospital staff. When my father and I walked in to see her, she was unresponsive. The tubes connected to her were helping her breathe. She was lifeless. I felt like she wasn't really there. The other patient in the room was a good distraction for both Dad and myself. Dad knew the guy. He joked around with my dad. Mom was heavily sedated and, although the jokes made Dad laugh, I'm sure he was struggling. It was easier for us to joke and talk than to really feel our feelings- scared to admit that we weren't sure if Mom was going to make it through this.

After our brief visit, we went to the waiting room. There we would meet the man's daughters. One of his daughters would come into my life later on to become the principal at the school where I taught 6th grade. This was an important time in my life as she basically kept me in the field of education; something that I had been thinking of leaving due to certain people in my career wanting to "get rid" of me. At the time, I doubted that I should even be in education and wondered what I should do with my life. I loved teaching all of my students but sometimes the politics of education can be a real downer. The woman I met in that waiting room would forever change the course of my life's journey. I would stay in education because of her encouragement. *Sometimes people don't know the effect they have on others. Did this woman know the difference she made in my life? Well, how would she ever know if I wasn't willing to admit this before?*

In the waiting room, introductions were made all around. This family knew my husband's family. Later, with the strain of the day, my sister-in-law took my father home. Soon, everyone else left too but I stayed a little longer. The small waiting room, located directly next to the doors of the intensive care unit, had changed from a busy, lively place full of friends and laughter to me sitting alone wondering about my mom. *As I sit here writing this, I feel goosebumps all over- a tingly sensation. Is this a sign of someone present helping me work through this- and write this book? Or sending me a sign that I wasn't truly alone in that waiting room after all? Does anyone else ever feel this type of 6th sense? How does one learn to believe in this stuff? What if someone laughs and says this is all hogwash? Will I always feel like I need to hide this part of me? Does this have something to do with being an empath? Why isn't there some sort of physical proof so that we actually see something? The dime....that was my physical proof, wasn't it? Weren't the goosebumps like the leaves on the trees? Was the feeling on my skin showing me that an energy was near?*

Within minutes of everyone leaving, the hospital staff started running through the doors of the ICU. One doctor looks at me as he goes through the doors. I see the fear in his eyes but am all alone with my worries. I know something is going on but am too scared to ask any questions. Is it my mother or the other guy? I sit quietly for what seems like a long time. A sudden stillness comes over me. I sit and wait. Finally, a doctor comes out to explain that Mom had "coded", meaning they had to "bring her back". I hear their words, yet it takes me a minute to digest the information. I feel dreamy, almost like I am hearing their words but can't really understand them. They ask me if I want to go in to see my Mom. I walk into the room to see Mom's body there, but she doesn't look like she is even alive. Without the distraction of my father, I see my Mother the way she is- empty. I almost run from the room. I think of the boy in the book *Heaven is for Real* by Todd Burpo and Lynn Vincent. In that book, the little boy was having surgery and almost died. He was able to see what was happening around the hospital during his surgery, like when I was watching the party even though my body was on the floor of the bedroom. *Did my Mom have any sort of out of body experience that she never spoke about? Did she know I was there? Was she still inside her body? I leave the hospital lost and crying.*

My mother did recover but she would need to go for another surgery years later to fix the valve again. Eventually she would try to eat better and ride her bike, but it would never be enough to battle heart disease. The doctors reported after her heart surgery that, at some point earlier in her life, she had a massive heart attack and only half of her heart was able to work properly. When the doctors suggested another surgery, Mom refused.

From that point on in my life, I began to take my parents to various doctors appointments. Although it was difficult to take time off from teaching, I felt it was important to spend time with and help my parents. It was difficult to be away from my own kids, who were in high school at the time. I know that I showed my kids how to take care of others by action, not words. When I lost both of my parents I remember my sons saying to me, "Mom, you sure are strong." *Believe me when I say, the only thing that got me through this time in my life was my faith and my belief in God. He helped me through it and I couldn't have done it without the support of my husband, my two sons and God.*

It's difficult to balance work, kids, ailing parents and have time to process all of the reading I was doing. At the time I began to work toward my Master's degree in education and I would not have the time to read anything for pleasure. My Mom was always difficult to deal with, and even more so when her health began to decline. But I accepted her for who she was and I have no regrets. I did my best to care for my parents. A medium gave me insight as to why my mother treated me the way she did. She suggested that Mom might be jealous of my connection with my father, *one that I feel went beyond this realm.* Once I saw that piece of the puzzle, it was clear that this had been impacting my relationship with my mother. I began to change the dynamic when I took care of my parents. I began doting on my Mom and asking her all sorts of questions; she loved to talk. My father actually glowed with happiness when I did this. It was amazing to see the change in both of them. This one little piece of the puzzle helped change our relationship during those last few years. Being able to see her point of view helped me understand our relationship. *But, when she was alive, wasn't able to connect with my father or my mother in the way that I wanted to.*

As I write this, I begin to wonder what my parents might think of this book. Are they with me now as I write?

This reminds me of being vulnerable, something I never really thought about until one of my professor's introduced it in one of my master's class. Thanks Jacqui! As part of learning how to be a good leader, she introduced us to the concept of vulnerability, or, basically, "being human"- not perfect. She introduced my class to Brene Brown. We watched her YouTube video about vulnerability. If you haven't seen it, go now and watch it! It will forever change your life. I began my understanding of being open to vulnerability. To me, it meant embarrassment. Things that I didn't want people to know about me. Things I wanted to hide from people so others wouldn't know that I wasn't perfect. Looking like the perfect family is what I had been taught. In my career, I had tried to be the perfect teacher. Now, those walls began to crumble. During this time, I felt that I had to be the strong one. *Sharing my story is going to make me vulnerable. This scares me so much. How will I ever get over this feeling so that others can hear my story? If I show vulnerability, will it help others?* In my Master's degree program I had to conduct an Action Research project in my classroom instead of writing a thesis. My entire project was about how making mistakes helps our brain to learn. This was ok for Math class, but I didn't want anyone to see my life mistakes. That would make me feel shame and embarrassment. I would be vulnerable, which was something that I didn't know how to do. I had to learn that some people would know and understand the love that I have. I know that whatever I do, if I do it with love, no matter how someone reacts, it would be ok. Being vulnerable was going to take a lot of courage.

I recall my work on Action Research for my Master's Degree. I was expected to read, understand and integrate several researchers. I didn't think I could do it, but my professor did. How does one integrate all of the research into one big project? I did it- Carol Dweck- growth mindset. Jo Boaler- growth mindset, brain research and teaching math. Etc. etc. I find as I write that I can compare my life to one big Action Research project too. I found things along the way that I learned and integrated into my life. Many different authors have planted many different seeds of knowledge. As I began to reflect on my journey, I realize all the authors who have guided me in my life. It was like Action Research for my soul's growth.

One of my main life lessons is to enjoy the journey, the ups and the downs. During Action Research and life, I wanted to finish all of my projects. At times, it was all so tiring. If I finished everything, then maybe I would be able to relax. Instead, I was like the energizer bunny- I would keep going and going. Having something completed made me feel like I accomplished something. *"Enjoy the journey,"* they suggested. *Did anyone know how difficult this was for me? I had to realize that life was about the journey, not the destination. Like Action Research for my Master's degree, I had been conducting my own research about life for years. So many teachers helped me understand that the work is worth it.*

As I worked towards my Master's degree, I took care of my parents during their last days on earth, and was still trying to raise my kids. I find it difficult to be in the present moment because I am always trying to finish everything before I can relax. I wanted everything to be completed. The estate, my degree, everything. I wanted to have some free time for me. I was taking care of everyone and studying all the time. I was so exhausted that it was difficult to function. My battery was empty. *As I write, I know I am also meant to share my stories to help others. I am not famous, but I have an interesting tale to tell.*

"Today is your life, Live with intention
Speak the Truth, Make mistakes

Take risks, Have an adventure
Embrace the Journey."
~**Anonymous**

Nowadays, sayings like this one are so common. People have these types of signs in their house, on Facebook, Instagram and everywhere. Growing up, these guiding quotes were never there for me. When shared they are a positive part of technology. I think about my journey in life. What have I learned? Have my experiences led me to believe certain things? Things that others will have no understanding because they haven't lived through my life? How can we all be more patient? How can we all help each other?

I remember another time sitting in the waiting room. This time I was with my mother while dad was having procedure done on his heart. I got a text message that my uncle, my mother's brother, had a heart attack and is on his way to the same exact hospital. *How do I tell my mother that while her husband is in surgery right now, her brother had a heart attack? I remember how long it took my father to heal from his first heart attack and I remember Dr. Blower's words, "He almost didn't survive."* I break the news to Mom and she takes a big inhale, covers her mouth and says, "That's how my father died."

Moments later, my uncle is wheeled in and stops to visit with us in the waiting room. *Can you believe it? They bring the patients right by where we are sitting in the waiting room? This is a huge hospital. I would think there might be a different hallway. Well, I guess it makes sense since we are in the wing where they do heart surgeries.*

My uncle was ok and later, he and my father try to convince the doctors that they should get a special price on their surgeries. Since they were family they thought it should be kind of like a buy one surgery get one free, like buying something at Price Chopper. Buy one heart surgery, get the other for free!

My Grandfather (my mother's father) died a few weeks before I was born. My mother had told me that it was difficult when I was born because he loved kids so much. Everyone knew that he would have loved another granddaughter. His name was Rudolph and I think how cool that name is. I wish I could have met him. I have no idea what that had been like for my mother. Had losing her father so young changed her? Did I actually not know my mother because I hadn't had her experiences in life? Had I been so busy judging her that I hadn't taken the time to learn what her life's journey had been like?

I'm thankful for the time spent with my Mom and Dad. I learned a lot about life and death during that time. Even though my mother didn't like to talk about personal things, my father and I talked a lot during our daily trips to the hospital to see my mother. During that time, I got a glimpse of some of their life stories. I began to understand that I knew little about their life experiences. *What made them who they were?*

Of course, the dimes from my Dad would teach me so much more.

-

Chapter 6: Messages and My Inner Voice

"This is very significant proof that our thoughts have powerful physical effects on our bodies and that we can't afford to ignore them." ~Dr. Christian Northrup (www.heartmath.org)

When I was first married, my husband asked me what I wanted for my birthday that year. I told him I would love a Mickey Mouse watch. I had been to Disney as a child and adult, and I had sung the song Mickey Mouse March as a child so much that I felt connected to that Disney character. I also loved the story of how Walt Disney got his start in creating his company. My husband went in search of a Mickey Mouse watch. Of course, this was long before Amazon Prime. He went to the local jewelry store and explained that he was looking for a watch for his wife. He was shown a few watches, mostly expensive. Then the clerk jokingly says, "Well, I do have this one Mickey Mouse watch." My husband's response? "Oh wow! That is **exactly** what I was looking for!" Perfect timing for the perfect watch.

As the pages flow, I am amazed at how therapeutic writing can be. My husband questions me again, 'What will people learn about me if and when people read this?' I share the part about him accepting me and how thankful I was to meet him at that particular time in my life. I begin to cry. I thank him for always accepting me for who I am. He asks me not to cry. I tell him I have been bottled up for years and need to let a lot of stuff go. This will help me in my healing. I begin to share some of my stories of other signs from above. He understands and leaves me to myself, allowing me time to write.

I often give other people advice. It comes naturally. I always want to help people. I have had so many different health issues over the years, it feels like I could help anyone figure out how to improve their health. I've also had so many events that have shaped my understanding about life- raising kids, losing my parents, executor of the estate, back surgery, getting sober. All of these things help me connect to stories from people going through hardships in their own lives.

I realize now that all of my advice that I have so freely given, is actually advice I should have given to myself. Most recently a woman, who has had difficulty carrying a baby to full term, confides in me. I tell her that I sense her great grandparents are with her and she needs to not only focus on the front of her abdomen, but also her back. During this trip, I realize that I also need to look at the possibility that my pain may be radiating from my back. I also feel like my Great Grandmother is around me, guiding me. Light bulbs! Fireworks! *I realize that all these years I was freely giving others advice, it was actually things that I needed to hear. I call this the Boomerang effect. I try to help others and it was actually the words that I needed to hear. Some people speak about projecting onto others what is going on internally with yourself. Boomerang. Right back at ya!*

I also wonder about the back metaphor. Did I need to look in the past (behind me) to find my answers? Would writing about this help me heal my past and help me move forward in my future? I had to believe that this was true.

I think of all the advice I have given recently. I tell new teachers to run, hike, make sure they take time to relax. I give Reiki to the teachers. I know that maybe if I went and got Reiki from someone, maybe I, too, could heal. Essential oils- I teach others about them and forget to use them myself. Emotional Freedom technique (EFT tapping)- I brag about how well it works for stress, but rarely use it myself. I told a Tracy's daughter, Chelsea, that she should write a book.... And now- here I am. *I find it easier to give advice than to receive it myself.*

I hear voices of all of the advice through the years- me telling others what I think might help them. Now, I see the voice was trying to talk to me. You see, I have an insatiable desire to try to help others. It's like I absorb their energy and want them to get well. It's difficult to explain but I love helping people. Even though I know many alternative ways to cure illnesses and heal, I don't use them on a regular basis. I might use them on vacation or in the summertime but they were not part of my normal routine. When teaching, I was "too busy" to do them. I liked to get to school early in the morning so there was no time for exercise or to prepare meals. After school, I had meetings or was too tired. So, out of 12 months during the year, I was only using these tools for about two months total. I tried to do these things only when I was on school vacations. It's difficult for me to balance work and take care of myself. *Instead of preaching about it, I needed to take my own advice for once. Boomerang. Right back at me.*

My husband and I take a walk on the beach. We are both lost in our own thoughts. We talk about life and the people in our life. Friendships, divorces, deaths. We think a lot of people we know most likely have insecurities. I say that I think at some level we all do, starting to admit my own insecurities. Admitting my insecurities would make me vulnerable, something I knew little about in my life growing up. So many messages coming to me as we walk and talk. I begin searching for dimes along the beach, wanting a sign to help me feel that I am walking my true path; something to give me the faith to believe. "That isn't how it works", a voice tells me. "You don't need physical proof. Faith is knowing He is there, even when you are unsure", the voice continues to explain. I stop looking for a dime. One will show up if and when it is the right time. I need to understand that the messages I am receiving while writing are from Spirit, not necessarily from my brain. Sort of like an internal guide inside me.

A baby girl in a bright pink hat waves to me as we walk. So precious and new, reminding me that souls come to Earth when they are ready. Some people believe that we choose our parents before arriving on earth. *Did I choose my parents in order to learn the lessons I needed to learn? What was I supposed to learn?* Babies have God within them. This is why it is such an amazing feeling holding a baby. I smile at her and continue walking and thinking.

I begin talking to my husband about all of the students I have had over the years. It wasn't about the great lessons in Math or Geography. It was me caring about each and every child. Remembering, that when each student was born, their family and friends went to the hospital to hold that new baby. They all deserved to be treated with love and kindness. I tried to learn about each student; making connections with them and discovering what they loved to do. I helped them be present in the classroom; creating a safe environment for them to learn. I encouraged them to share about whatever was worrying them and then focus on their learning. I always enjoyed helping students grow and learn. They all knew I cared. I knew about growth mindset long before Carol Dweck's research proved that positive thinking worked. I had to believe in these kids. Carol Dweck calls it growth mindset, but I call it Faith.

We plan and God laughs. Oftentimes, people use this phrase. For dinner that night, my husband and I can't decide. Do we want to eat outside or inside? We go back and forth. When we arrive at the restaurant, the hostess says we have an outside table right now or an inside one in about a half hour. "Ha!" I say to my husband, "We thought we had a choice when we really didn't. God decided where we should be- not us!" We both laugh on our way outside for dinner.

Teaching has been my entire life and, for most people who know me, that is all they really see. What if I decide to share this book with someone and decide I want to write about God and teaching? Will I be judged as a public school teacher? One who believes in God and weird things about souls returning to earth to grow and learn. Who knows? I think of the many doctors who were scared to share their beliefs, especially with their colleagues in the medical world. People like Brian Weiss, Judith Orloff and Christian Northrup. I am an educator who worries what other educators will think. My insecurities flare up right along with my physical pain. I continue to write. Brian Weiss says,

"Are you afraid of your reputation, afraid of what others think? These fears are conditioned from childhood or before."

Right, my fears do come from a childhood of feeling insecure.

"Love dissolves fear." ~Brian Weiss

Songs about fear play over and over in my head.

I remember Wayne Dyer commenting on something about spiritual beings...

"You aren't your work, your accomplishments, your possessions, your home, your family... your anything. You're a creation of your Source, dressed in a physical human body intended to experience and enjoy life on Earth." ~Wayne Dyer

I describe to my husband my hot flashes, another part of my life that is changing the way I live. "I don't know how to dress anymore," I explain. What I am really trying to say is, "I don't know how to move forward in my life- to live differently." See, I have been in both emotional and physical pain for years. I cannot ignore it any longer. I explain to my husband that during a hot flash I have to have a lot of patience, basically stopping time and making me fully present in the moment. Hot flashes are forcing me to be present in the moment.

"Research into the physiological changes taking place in the perimenopausal woman is revealing that, in addition to the hormonal shift that means an end to childbearing, our bodies- and, specifically, our nervous systems- are being, quite literally, rewired. It's as simple as this: our brains are changing. A woman's thoughts, her ability to focus, and the amount of fuel going to the intuitive centers in the temporal lobes of her brain all are plugged into, and affected by, the circuits being rewired." ~Dr. Christian Northrup

I had never really experienced anxiety, other than not feeling confident, which I think is very different. I didn't know that anxiety could come with hot flashes. This was so different. This anxiety was an anxiety where I wanted to crawl out of my skin. I couldn't control it and I didn't know why or when it would come and then it would be gone. I remember students who tried to describe their anxiety. I couldn't truly understand until I felt it myself. *Why was God doing this now? Was this part of some plan to help my soul grow? Why couldn't I relax and enjoy life? Why do I feel compelled all the time to keep learning?*

"Instantly I comprehend the truth of these thoughts. Reality is the present. Dwelling in the past or future causes pain and illness. Patience can stop time. God's love is everything." ~Brian Weiss speaks to my soul.

Why does someone else's writing in a book seem so much more powerful than me sharing my story? Why do I feel Brian Weiss's words are more important than my words?

A man speaks to us as we are walking on the beach. "People used to wear pigtails in the 50's. You don't see that much anymore, you know?" We stop and for a brief moment, I sense my father's presence. This often happens when I talk to older gentlemen. I tell him that I am glad I could remind him of those times. I love wearing my pigtail braids!

I go for a run- my mind won't stop. I need to get back and write everything down. It's like a dam has opened and I want to catch every single drop of water all at once. What if I forget some of the thoughts I have when I am running; all that water slipping through my hands. The words gone before I can put them on paper; only traveling through my mind but I couldn't catch them quick enough. I must try to slow down and enjoy the process, like real life action research. There are no deadlines as time marches on. "The dime story is always within me," a voice assures me.

I'm in no hurry when I run. I'm not tracking myself on a device and have no idea how far or how long I run. I run, turn around and come back. A few people say good morning and a few of the other runners nod their head in my direction. I stop and do some yoga on the beach. I am breathing in the air from the ocean as the waves roll in. How exhilarating! I am trying to be confident. I have been doing yoga since I started my new job a year ago and I know how to do some poses. I falter on one pose, wondering if anyone saw me and possibly judged me about my yoga. I am trying to steady my pose when a woman walks by and says, "Good place to do that." Her words are not lost. I remember them quite clearly.

I hear Anita Moorjani's voice,

"The only way to heal the physical body is from within. It isn't from food, medical techniques. You and you alone can heal yourself."

Can this be true? I wonder how.... I think what she means is that I need to feel God's love inside me. I need to listen to the positive voice, not the doubting voice. The choice is mine.

This is exhausting. When I eat healthy foods and am open to receiving messages, signs consume me more and I find God everywhere I turn. My intuition is turned up on high. I sit on our patio after our walk. My mind is full of thoughts- how will I possibly remember them all? I can't seem to write fast enough. The caretaker of the condo is walking nearby, spraying something between the cracks of the cement. I say, "Good Morning!" He jumps and says, "Oh! I was talking to myself. So much on my mind to remember. I have to get it all into my brain, you know what I mean?" as he points to his head similar to the way the Wizard of Oz scarecrow does when he says he doesn't have a brain. Yeah, I think, I know exactly what you mean. Seriously? How does this guy say exactly what I was writing about? I don't even know him! Is it a sign from God? I have so much to write about and yet I haven't even started sharing about the dimes. This story is so much more than the dimes. I worry that when I start to talk about the dimes, the story will unfold yet I might not have looked inside myself enough to be healed. I have so much to share! But, who will want to listen?

Day by day, wave by wave, trying my best to stay in the present moment, as that is where there is Heaven on Earth; or, at least that is what Anita says can be true. *I drink my probiotic. Will it help heal my gut? Can I truly digest all of the information I am receiving this week? Am I healing through the writing and the healthy food I am eating and drinking? A voice inside tells me this is what I need to do. How do I know if this voice is coming from Spirit, like intuition or something? Is this something to do with being an empath or is it my brain? I find that if I don't listen to the voice, I will hear the message more than once. For instance, someone mentions cutting down on their coffee. Ok, that's fine, but then another message comes about coffee. Usually by the second or third time, I know it is not just coincidence. I am meant to hear the message- like a tape replaying over and over again in my head until I listen. The universe speaks to us. What does Anita say about food? She thinks it doesn't matter, but my mind says- use both ways to heal. Heal with food and through emotions. I will continue this journey with both and have faith that I will be healed.*

Most people might not know by looking at me that I struggle with food and my weight. At one point in my life I lost almost 60 pounds. At 5 ft 4inches, I was close to 185 pounds. It's not that I want to be toothpick skinny; I don't want to keep gaining weight. It seemed that no matter what I did, I kept gaining more and more weight. I saw women all around me happy with their bodies, no matter their size. For me, it isn't about dieting to the point that I don't enjoy life or that everything I eat is either good or bad. I wanted to enjoy life and not feel like I was on a diet. Health was my goal so that I could enjoy the next step of my life's journey. I wouldn't be able to do that if I kept getting fatter and fatter. I want to be me in a regular sized body. *Would I ever be able to do this? Was I scared of being fat like my mother? Would being fat lead me to heart disease, like both of my parents?*

I don't think my Mother was scared of dying. She always said she didn't want to be in a nursing home, where others would have to care for her. It made sense towards the end that she didn't want medical help. I believe she knew exactly what she was doing when she wouldn't get help that year. Right before Thanksgiving of 2014, I watched her as she began to take on fluid from her congestive heart failure. When confronted, she refused to talk about it and eventually told me that she, "wasn't going to be in the hospital for the holidays." I had no argument for that. I understood and tried to help her and dad during the next month as much as I could. At this point, it was difficult for her to think straight. We had sold the family business and, ever since then, she didn't know what to do with herself. My Grandfather had started that business in 1933. My parents had owned and operated the business together for many years. That was her life and I think she didn't know what to do with herself without her work. She enjoyed seeing the customers who all had become friends over the years.

I remember being extremely patient with her while I helped her buy Christmas presents- a scarf for every girl in our family. We bought them the day before Thanksgiving, when I drove her and my dad to the city of Montpelier. Dad needed to renew his license (he probably shouldn't have been driving but I did not have the nerve or heart to tell him) and Mom had a JC Penney coupon she wanted to use. These scarves were one of the last personal gifts she would ever give to all of us girls. I remember walking with her in the store that day. She stopped about every 10-15 feet to breathe. She looked at me and stated that she needed to go slower. I gladly slowed down to walk with her, while dad waited in the car. *Patience. Slow down. Be present. All lessons I need to learn again and again.*

In early December of 2014, I called a few of my Mom's close friends to share my concerns about her declining health. I was worried something would happen to her in the night and my Dad would try to get help, but it wouldn't be quick enough. I was scared she might die right in their bed. Thoughts came back from the last time she was rushed to the hospital with congestive heart failure. My husband tried to warn me that maybe I shouldn't be calling everyone, but I listened to my intuition, the voice inside- *was this God's way of speaking to me? Does God speak to empaths somehow?* Those friends were so grateful for my phone calls. These friends reached out to her in her last few days. Whether it was a phone call or bringing Mom some of her favorite soup on her birthday; it meant a lot to Mom and to them.

We had a great day celebrating Christmas that year with Mom and Dad. We set aside the Saturday after Christmas to have an afternoon with only desserts, no big meal. My father loved desserts! I stopped by one evening prior to our visit. Dad asked me when those presents we got were going to be wrapped. Mom had said she would do it and I didn't realize that it was too much for her at the time. This would be the last time I would see them before our Christmas celebration. Well, I guess I could do it right now, I suggested. I was worried about stepping on Mom's toes, not wanting her to lose some of her independence in life. Although it was late and I wanted to get home, I got out all of the supplies and started to wrap the presents.

While wrapping, I listened to my parent's banter about dinner. At that point, Mom wasn't really able to prepare dinner; something she had always done. Dad began to get his own dinner, eating something that Mom did not approve of. She often told him what to eat and what not to eat. Mom prepared herself an apple and cheese. She brought her plate into the dining room, where I was beginning to wrap the presents. She sat down, breathing like she had climbed Mount Everest. She wasn't even able to talk. This is how congestive heart failure works. The heart valve doesn't work properly, allowing for the extra fluid to be dumped into the lungs. The person feels like they can't breathe, fooling them into thinking that they will get better if they could breathe.

"But I trust in you, O Lord; I say, 'You are my God.' My times are in your hands." Psalm 31:14-15

I wonder how much longer she has left? Why won't she go get help? My thoughts wander as I wrap the presents she is to give to everyone in a few days. I try to be present but I'm always thinking about things in my head. Why am I like this? Always thinking of the next thing I have to do. Difficulty being in the moment. I guess when I was younger it was always easier to be in my head than my body. This was a skill that I was super good at. It helped me be able to ignore my feelings.

When we celebrated Christmas that year, my sons would have their picture taken with both sets of their Grandparents, not realizing later how much those pictures would mean to all of us. My boys were lucky to have two sets of Grandparents for their entire childhood. I wish all kids were able to feel the love from a Grandparent. *A Grandparent's love feels like love from God, a voice whispers. Anything given by a Grandparent is also filled with love. The most significant dime was given to my son, from his Grandfather. Without that dime, I never would have written this book.*

"Our thoughts are silent words that only we and the Lord hear, but those words affect our inner man, our health, our joy, and our attitude." ~ Joyce Meyer

Chapter 7: Come What May

"You cannot control what happens to you in life, but you can always control what you will feel and do about what happens to you," ~ Viktor E. Frankl

"It is now well documented that the electromagnetic field of the heart is 5,000 times more powerful than the electromagnetic field of the brain. And that is why, no matter what we think, what we actually feel is what matters most. Every time. No exceptions. You might be able to fool your brain, but you can't fool your heart." ~Dr. Christian Northrup, from www.heartmath.org

I never felt like my Mother gave me her approval for any of my accomplishments. When I would talk about my son hitting a double in a little league all star game, she would change the subject. I would talk about my new job; she would talk about a customer from their business. I never quite understood this part of her. As I reflected on my relationship with my mother, I watched as she slowly began to slip away from us.

What would my life be like without her? I had spent most of my life angry with her. Would all my pain and feelings disappear when she was gone? Would I ever be free to be happy with myself as I was? Did I need my mother's approval to make me whole? I know how important it was to face my feelings because I didn't want to end up with heart disease like my parents. And, if my feelings were what was going to determine this, I needed to work not just on being healthy, but dealing with my own internal pain. I was fighting an uphill battle. I had dreams of playing with my grandkids. I didn't want my kids to have to take care of me when I was ailing, like I had with my parents. I needed to get healthy by eating better, exercising and dealing with my feelings. It had to start now or else it would be too late.

I bought a ring the fall of 2014, when I saw my parents' health worsening. It said "Come What May" on it and was meaningful to me because I thought my parents might not make it through the winter. *Should I listen to my intuition? What if I was wrong? Was my intuition part of being an empath? Could I have a sense of what the future might hold? Wasn't everything in God's plan?* I knew that whatever happened, I was going to need to pray to be able to get through it. I was going to have to take it as it came, whatever that may be. As the common sayings go, "what will be will be" or "it is what it is". Whatever "it" was, I was going to need God's help.

On Dec. 30th, 2014 my father panicked. Mom wasn't "acting right". He told my sister and uncle that somebody had to come over right away; he didn't know what to do.

This same situation had happened previously in the summer as well. He phoned people to come over to help. When I arrived at their camp that day, Mom was belligerent and not cooperating with the rescue squad *or anyone*. She had diabetes and her blood sugar was dangerously low. After her heart surgery, she had been diagnosed with Type 2 Diabetes. She tried to manage her insulin levels with medicine, but not usually with food. I tried to help her learn how to eat healthier, but she would only make small changes, not big changes.

Last summer at camp, after trying to get her to cooperate, I told her that it was morning and it was time for her orange juice. She always had one small glass of orange juice every morning with her coffee. We even put it in a small cup. She was in bed and I got into bed with her. I remember the look in her eyes as I held her tight with my arm around her neck, hugging her and began pouring the orange juice into her mouth, which she barely opened. On some level, she knew to trust me; but, at the time, she was out of her mind. I remember the look in her eyes. *Was she going to trust me? She wouldn't listen to anyone. She wouldn't cooperate with anyone else.* She drank the little bit of orange juice and it helped. She was then able to walk to the car to go to the hospital. *I don't think Mom remembers what happened, but I knew this was one of the only times in my life where I was able to help my mother. Most of the time she seemed to refuse my help and love.*

When my uncle called me that December 30th, I was already on my way to my parents' house. I was planning on stopping by for lunch on my way through town to an acupuncture appointment. When I arrived, Mom was in the bathroom and Dad quietly reported that she had been there most of the morning. Dad greeted me with tears in his eyes and I wasn't exactly sure what I was going to do. I had phoned the doctor's office, to report her condition. The receptionist was a member of our extended family and I knew she couldn't talk to me about Mom, but I could talk to her. I explained to her that Mom had been taking on fluid since Thanksgiving and she wasn't acting right. I told her I would be in touch after I visited. She would wait to hear from me and was ready to help.

I had brought my lunch and began preparing my parents a lunch also. Mom demanded that her soup be in a coffee cup, not a bowl. *What does it matter? I thought to myself. Whatever she wants I thought, but nothing seemed to make her happy.* She wasn't sure what Dad should eat, seeming sort of confused. In and out of the bathroom she went. She tried to eat, but then ended up back in the living room. Dad and I finished eating and now they were both sitting in their recliners in the corners of the living room. *That's when the scene unfolded. A conversation that had been put on hold until after the holidays. Now was the time for us to face Mom's reality.*

Mom said to me, "I don't know why you had to rush right down here". I stopped dead in my tracks, at the edge of the living room and proceeded to throw words right back at her, "I don't have any idea what you are talking about. I am on my way to an acupuncture appointment. I stopped in for lunch to see you both."

That is when I stopped, thought and glared back at my mother. I was standing with one foot still in the living room and one foot in the room that would be my escape route out of the house. The board that separated the two rooms was a nice piece of cherry wood from my Great Grandfather's farm. *Was he there helping me help my father and mother? I wonder as I write.* I looked back across the living room at both of my parents sitting in their recliners on the other side of the room. *Should I stay or should I go? Which foot should I follow? It would be so much easier to walk away. I knew it wasn't ok to take the easy route. My father needed my help and my mother didn't seem to want my help.*

My Mother hadn't told anyone that she was ill. She didn't want to go to the hospital; she had already told me that. But, the holidays were over and it was time she got some help. Her eyes met mine. *Should I continue to my appointment or face her right now and demand she go to the hospital? What should I say to her? I'm the child. She is the parent. I shouldn't speak back to my parents, right? Growing up that hadn't worked for me. Was I going to be able to face the mother who I felt did not understand me?*

I stood still and thought to myself, "*I guess it is now or never so here goes nothing! Time to face this*"- something I rarely felt the courage to do with my mother. The words I spoke next came from the positive voice inside me- the one that isn't afraid to speak the truth- no matter what it is. I began to explain to her that we all cared about her. She wasn't used to hearing this. "*You want to know what is happening? That man (my Dad cried as I pointed towards him) loves you very much. We all want you to go get the medical help you need. In fact, a lot of people around here love you very much.*" The voice inside me at that moment was the positive voice, my intuition guiding me, telling me what I needed to do at that particular moment. Switch the argument and fighting to love and caring. That's the answer.

These words were rarely spoken when I was growing up. My whole life I had been searching for my mother's love. I had held onto my anger and even though I had tried over the years, I hadn't showed my mother much love. *If I showed my mother that I loved her, would she, in return, give me the love I so longed for?* She agreed that it would probably be ok to call the doctor's office.

I sat on the couch and called the doctor's office. "*Hi. This is Monica. I'm sitting here with Mom and she isn't feeling very well. We thought maybe she should see the doctor today.*" The secretary knew the situation so I didn't need to explain further. With that, she gave me two options. I could come now (which meant I would miss my acupuncture appointment) or at 3:30, which meant I could still go to my appointment and then come back later to take her to the doctor. At the time, I felt like I made a selfish choice, but now I see that it was meant to be. I had listened to my intuition and made the choice that would, in the end, be the best choice. That afternoon would be the last time that my Dad would be able to talk with my Mother. That afternoon they talked about a lot of things. Later, I would learn my mother gave me her "approval" that afternoon.

When I arrived back from my appointment, Mom was sitting in the chair in the dining room, the spot where she always put on her shoes. Dad, with tears in his eyes watched as Mom tried to put on her socks and shoes, unable to bend over. I helped her. One sock. One shoe. Other sock. Other shoe. *Role reversal again. I felt like I was the parent caring for the child.* She had trouble standing up; Dad and I helped her. Out of breath from the exertion of standing up, my parents kiss and say I love you to each other. This scene was rare in my family. Growing up, I never really saw my parents be affectionate with each other. I helped Mom put on her coat, then went to move the van so that it would be easier to get her into the car. They had a precious minute alone. It was difficult getting Mom into the car. I helped her so that she could sit on the seat, but it left her legs sticking straight out of the van. Her legs were so swollen with fluid, her knees were barely able to bend. I backed up the seat and one by one, lifted her legs into the car by grabbing the top of her pants. I was so focused on getting Mom into the car, I have no idea what it must have felt like for Dad to be left alone in the house; watching me load her into the car and worrying about his wife of almost 60 years.

We made it to the doctor's office; Mom greets our relative and the doctor as if this is a normal appointment. The doctor seems shy and asks Mom what is going on. Mom doesn't give a whole lot of details. *I think about the past month. We had to buy her bigger pants because of the fluid. She doesn't even eat much but she keeps getting bigger. She can barely walk she is so out of breath. Should I tell the doctor about her legs not bending when I tried to help her in the car? I don't want to embarrass her, but I think her condition is pretty serious.*

The doctor does the usual blood pressure check and makes small talk about the weather. At one point in the conversation, Mom had almost convinced the doctor that it would probably be ok if she went home. I remember thinking, *"Oh, My God, what is going on here? Am I crazy? What about getting her heart checked out or possibly staying overnight to be monitored?"* I tried to listen to my intuition and allow the doctor to help us, but I also needed to make sure he knew how bad she really was. She wasn't acting like she had been at home with Dad. *How would I make sure she got the proper medical help she needed?*

Finally, they both agree that maybe she could spend one night and see what happened. *Phew, I think.* We wheeled her over to the emergency room to be admitted to the hospital. The look on the nurse's face when she took a quick peek at Mom's legs was all I needed to see to know that Mom was right where she needed to be. Her skin was so tight it looked like her skin was about to pop open. Mom would be given medicine to begin to try to get rid of the fluid.

Mom and I talked about everything and nothing all afternoon while we waited for a hospital room. She asked me about school and our plans for New Year's Eve. There were some distractions, including one of my students in the ER with his brother, who had broken his arm skiing. Mom would get to meet him and she loved that. I remember her asking him if I was a good teacher. What was he supposed to say with me standing right there? We had what I call "surface conversations". Talking about things that don't matter much. No deep conversations like, *"What if I might die? Or What about Dad?"* We talked more about the weather and people who worked at the hospital. That's the way my Mom was with me.

After settling Mom into her room and stopping by to visit my Dad, I went home. I wish I had stayed that night with Dad, but it wasn't meant to be. The phone rang at 4:00 AM at his house. He was disoriented and confused- trying to hear without his hearing aids. He couldn't understand why someone was asking him if he would need the police to give him a ride to the hospital. From there, the phone calls would bring everyone to the hospital to find that Mom had "coded" and they had done life saving techniques until the family arrived. She was breathing but nothing was happening "neurologically" speaking. The decision was made and we were guided to let her go; a decision that haunted my father. He thought we had made the wrong decision to let her go. He was scared of death and had fought his own heart disease for most of his life. Mom and Dad had a secret code when he would have his heart surgeries. The secret message would be three squeezes or 3 movements of the arm or hand. Three squeezes meant that they were still alive and responding. To them it meant, "don't give up on me." Because Mom's arm had signaled (she had slammed her arm down), he thought it was a message from her to not let her die. In the moment, I felt that Mom didn't want all of this attention around her and she didn't want to live like this. It was like she threw her fist in anger. To Dad, it was a totally different sign. I wouldn't discover this until later; Dad never shared this at the hospital. His experience was different than mine based on our differing views.

We all congregated in the ICU hallway while the hospital staff removed the machines that were keeping Mom alive. *What does one say during a time like this? To me, the memory is a blur. So much to think about.* The family gathers around her bed. With all of the machines gone, Mom was barely breathing. We all talked to Mom and told her it was ok. Within minutes, her heart stopped beating and she took her last breath.

I can see her taking her last breath and then my eyes immediately focus on my Father. Sitting in his wheelchair, crying uncontrollably. I had never seen my father like this. *What should I do? How do I take care of him?* My adrenaline kicks in and I know that this will be very difficult for my father. Decisions will need to be made and my father will need help. *My life was about to change and I was about to discover some hidden coins, which would begin to uncover my true beliefs about life and death; helping me to heal from the inside out.*

My strength would be tested many times and, in due time, my father would help me to have faith in believing that people can really connect with people who have died. There really is a spirit communication available to those who want to use it. Would my mother contact me now? Would she be different as a spirit? Would I be able to forgive her? Did she try her best with what she was given? Were my expectations too much for her?

"Holding onto anger is like drinking poison and hoping the other person will die." ~Buddha

Anger and resentment eat away at my insides every day, if I let it. Now she is gone, what will happen to my anger? How will I be able to avoid heart disease? That is one of the first questions doctors ask you, "Any heart disease in the family?" Yeah- both my parents....Turning 50, I was wondering how to live differently to avoid the emotional pain that affects my physical body, possibly following in my mother and father's footsteps of heart disease.

This is me hiking the mountains
in North Carolina.

"I didn't get to grow up and pull away from her and bitch about her with my friends and confront her about the things I'd wished she'd done differently and then get older and understand that she had done the best she could and realize that what she had done was pretty damn good and take her fully back into my arms again. Her death had obliterated that. It had obliterated me. It had cut me short at the very height of my youthful arrogance. It had forced me to instantly

grow up and forgive her every motherly fault at the same time that it kept me forever a child, my life both ended and begun in that premature place where we'd left off. She was my mother, but I was motherless. I was trapped by her, but utterly alone. She would always be the empty bowl that no one could fill. I'd have to fill it myself again and again and again." ~Cheryl Strayed

Chapter 8: Time with My Dad

"Regardless of any overt risks we may have for heart disease (such as poor diet or lack of exercise), the seeds for potentially developing heart disease later on are sown the minute we learn to start shutting down our hearts to avoid feeling disappointment and loss. Whether or not heart disease eventually results has a lot to do with how well we learn how to feel and express our emotions fully and name the needs they signify." ~Dr. Christian Northrup

Faith in God will heal me. I think as I envision a healthy heart within me.

Had my father's heart been broken since that first heart attack when I was 13? What broke it? Would he be able to heal it this late in life? Would losing his wife break his heart even more or could he be able to live differently now to change his path? Even though diet and exercise are important, how was I going to learn to be able to express my feelings? When I was studying for my master's degree, information about the newest brain research fascinated me. Would I be able to change my brain in time to avoid heart disease? There were so many connections that were hard wired into my brain when I was young, how was I going to reprogram them? How long would it take to make them a habit? Where do I even start?

"Every thought of yours is a real thing- a force." ~ Prentice Mulford (1834-1891)

When I was young, I would get home from school and my go-to snack was Sprite and Cheez Doodles or pretzels. My Mom kept a large supply of soda on hand all of the time. On top of our fridge a variety of different salty snacks would be piled high. Fritos, pretzels, Cheez Doodles, Doritoes, Cheetos and more. We never had any fruit out on the counter, ever. Once in awhile there would be an apple or an orange in the fridge, but we were never encouraged to eat them so they would get soft and nasty. There wasn't as much of a focus on eating healthy when I was growing up; or, at least, not in my family. My brain was hard wired into thinking this is what a person ate when transitioning from school to home. As an adult, I attempted to change my habits to make more healthy choices. I was undoing years of conditioning around food. *My writing seems to flow better when I eat healthy but, so do my emotions. Why is this a problem? Well, because I don't know how to feel my emotions and I don't know what to do with them. Eating carbs or junk food helps me to not feel anything, kind of numbing me and making me feel safer. It actually closes up my throat so that I am not able to breath deeply. When that happens, I lose touch with my center. I lose touch with my inner voice that seems to come from someplace else.*

"Your life's journey has been perfectly designed for you soul's growth. Embrace every lesson and every moment."~ Dr. Judith Orloff

Recently I saw a sign at a farmer's market. It read, "Eat like your life depended on it." I thought, that makes a lot of sense. *Then I thought, "Think like your life depended on it." How do I change every negative thought into a positive thought? Start small, one thought at a time. I am writing a book and it is going to be a good book. There, my anxiety begins to subside. Not gone, but it's a start.*

After my Mother died, I decided to take a leave of absence from teaching to care for my father. This was a very difficult decision as I loved my new job as a middle school Math teacher. The Curriculum Director told me, "I have never met anyone who regretted taking time to be with their parents." Over the next few months, my life revolved around Dad. This meant I didn't take the time to grieve for my Mom. I was too busy caring for my Dad around the clock since he had taken a bad fall the night my mother died.

Trying to console my father was difficult for me. I was consumed with taking care of my father, funeral arrangements, and paper work involved with my Mother's death. He had lost his wife, his true love of almost 60 years. *How could I possibly help someone through this? Especially my father.* I thank God everyday for Dad's best friend, Eldon, arriving to stay with us. He would help my father, as he had lost his wife a few years before. The support was invaluable. I didn't know much about grief and Eldon explained the different stages. I printed information about the stages of grief for my dad to read, but ultimately it was this friendship that would help him get through that first week without Mom. Our families were so connected over the years. It was like I had another Father that week.

I remember serving these two friends dinner. Dad wanted to pay for the flight to Vermont. Eldon had flown up from Florida in the middle of winter to be with Dad during this time. During dinner, he looked across the table at my father and said, "I really don't want you to pay for my flight. You have to understand that our friendship is priceless to me. You can't put a price on it. If you want to do something with money, give a donation to the Lamoille Area Cancer Network, in honor of my wife." With tears in his eyes, my father agrees. We were eating lasagna, both men were missing their wives and thankful for their friendship. I can feel the energy of tremendous love these two men had for each other and their families. *This is what is happening as I unfold my story. When I write and think back to some of those moments in time, I sense a strong energy. At the time, I thought it was the love between these two men. Now, I understand that it was more than that. It was both of their wives, in the room with us. I can feel it as I write.*

We had many laughs and many tears that week, reminiscing. We cried because my Mom wouldn't get the medical help she so desperately needed. We laughed when Eldon told me how fast he ran down the grass bank at camp after I had knocked myself out by skiing head first into the dock. He was so scared. For me, all I remembered was I was skiing on one ski for the first time and I wanted to try to spray my brother sitting in the boat near the dock. The next thing I knew, I was lying down in camp with something on my head, listening to his daughter whine that she didn't want to go home. I remember all of my early life memories of playing Barbies, swimming and such. I did all that with her; she was my best friend. Along with reminiscing the fun times together, Eldon taught me how to put toilet paper on correctly, that OJ is served with ice and when you have a chocolate dessert, you serve white milk or, if you have a white dessert, you serve chocolate milk. It was a time to grieve, laugh, heal and begin to process a new way of life. For my father, life would be different without his wife by his side. I would move back in to the home where I grew up to care for my father for as long as he needed me.

I would begin sharing some of my insights about life, afterlife, signs and such with my father. He slowly started to feel it. A tipped lampshade? He thought it was my Mom doing that. I was told to straighten it out immediately. He would say that she didn't like it tipped. He thought she was still angry all the time, like she had been the past few years. When she was sick over the last few years, it was difficult for her to think clearly. Oftentimes, she would be difficult to deal with. It wasn't her fault. Her mind wasn't able to work like she wanted it to. One time she said, "It's like my thinker doesn't work anymore." *I can imagine how difficult it must be growing old. We begin to lose pieces of ourselves.*

I tried to explain to him that Heaven was different. All human problems were gone. I'm not sure he ever quite understood.

"Pain, like fever, is a symptom. It is also a vital component of the human experience." ~Margaret A. Caudill M.D.

When I was trying to heal my root chakra (the area at the base of the spine that relates to your sense of security and safety) after my back surgery in 1996, the traditional medical doctors were unable to help me. They removed a herniated disc on my right side at the L5/SI joint. It was perhaps the worst, but eventually the best time in my life. I didn't heal as expected and went in to a deep depression. My kids were one and three at the time and I was unable to care for them. This literally broke my heart as I loved being a Mom. I was barely able to function and losing my job became a strong possibility. I looked to the doctors for help and they wanted me to take some pills to "relax me". I remember the pill well. It was called amitriptyline. I took one pill and proceeded to be "out of my mind". I remember screaming- yes screaming at my older son. I remember my promise to myself that when I became a mom I was going to mother my children differently than the way I was mothered. I can't remember what I screamed at him for but no three year old should have to endure that type of treatment. I realized what I was doing as I had an out of body experience. I watched from above as I screamed at my son. *Would I let others ever treat my son like this? Absolutely not. So, why was it ok for me to do this? It wasn't.* After I screamed at him I walked back to the kitchen, took the bottle out of the cupboard and dumped the entire bottle of pills down the toilet. Never was I going to let this happen again. I then walked back to my son, scooped him up in my arms and rocked him in a chair. I prayed for God to help me find a different way to heal my pain. Luckily, soon after this I was introduced to alternative healing techniques; such as massage therapy, Reiki, and chiropractic care. *The only problem was once I learned about these ways to heal, I only did them when pain was interfering in my life. I did not practice them on a daily basis.*

The answer to my prayer came soon after that time. There happened to be an evening meeting in town on how to manage pain. I have no idea how I found out about it, but I went and began to learn how to deal with pain in a very different way. I learned about our body's natural relaxation response. When we breathe from our belly, our body automatically relaxes. After that one meeting, I began trying alternative methods of healing. This included Reiki, massage, acupuncture, network chiropractic and learning to breathe for meditation. The worst part of my life had turned out to be the best thing in the end. I learned how to care for myself in a very different way.

While trying to heal recently, I was given the drug amitriptyline again by another doctor. The urologist told me that it would help relieve my bladder pain. I was told by the doctor to "Just keep taking more and more until I don't feel the pain anymore". At this point, I hadn't slept well in months and was desperate to sleep. I followed the doctor's orders. It didn't work. *Was I surprised? Well, not really.* I decided to stop taking them. *Did I need to revisit what I had learned from my back surgery years ago? Was this God's message to me that I needed to keep searching for different answers to help myself heal? Was I going to finally have to get honest with myself and admit that I didn't love myself? How would I do this? I had read all of the books and inspirational quotes that explained that positive self talk was important to my healing. I had all of the tools, how would I be able to begin to use them wholeheartedly in my life? How would I change my daily life to include these?*

"Let go of the difficulties from your past, cultural codes, and social beliefs. You are the only one who can create the life you deserve." ~from The Secret by Rhonda Byrne

I sneeze all the time. If anyone has ever heard me sneeze, they know that I don't sneeze one at a time. I do little ach-oos over and over again; sometimes 5 or 6 times. I'm not sick when I sneeze. I'm not even stuffy or having an allergy attack. When teaching, I used to joke with my students, saying, "I think I am allergic to you." Actually, I began to think that I was allergic to certain foods. That is, until I read Mallika Chopra's book, Living with Intent My Somewhat Messy Journey to Purpose, Peace and Joy. She was Deepok Chopra's daughter! *How could her life be messy? Didn't having a father like hers make it a given that she too would automatically be perfect? I mean, Deepok must have taught her so much. Imagine having a father like that! I think that might have made my life so much easier.* Then, I read her book and found out that she, like me, was finding her way in the game of life. But, one thing stuck out for me in her book. She was about to meet Eckart Tolle and had been sneezing for hours before the meeting.

"It hits me that while I sat with Eckhart, I didn't sneeze at all. I was feeling truly peaceful and in the present moment." ~Mallika Chopra

Wait, could her thoughts have been making her sneeze? For me, was it my thoughts or the actual food I was eating? Again, I think of Anita Moorjani talking about emotions being stronger than the food we eat. I begin tracking my thoughts when I sneeze. Oh my....yes, it's true. Every time I sneeze, my thoughts were something like, "I shouldn't be eating this cookie. It's going to make me fat." Or "You need to make a better choice. Say no to the social pressure of having cake. Why aren't you stronger?" Could this really be? Was I seriously allergic to my thoughts and not whatever was in the cookie or cake? Sometimes, it wouldn't be about food, but a general negative thought. I begin the slow journey of changing my thoughts into positive thoughts and I sneeze less and less. Instead of thinking I shouldn't be eating some things, I bless the food and am grateful for all food I am given. Changing the hard wires in my brain became a full time job. I think of my father as he wants to work on his physical body like a car engine. I had to feed my engine the fuel it needed to run the way it was meant to run. For me this meant eating God's food from earth, not man made processed food.

"Any time you look at yourself with critical eyes, switch your focus immediately to the *presence* within, and its perfection will reveal itself to You. As you do this, all imperfections that have manifested in your life will dissolve, because imperfections cannot exist in the light of this presence. Whether you want to regain perfect eyesight, dissolve disease and restore well-being, turn poverty into abundance, reverse again and degeneration, or eradicate any negativity, focus on and love the presence within you and perfection will manifest." ~Rhonda Byrne

Well, I didn't need "perfection"; any improvement would be great! *Would I be able to make these new wires a permanent part of my brain? Would changing my inner dialogue from negative self talk to positive self talk heal my physical pain? It's been two years since I read Mallika's book. "Think like your life depends on it." The saying repeats over and over in my mind. I knew I had to believe that God was inside me, healing me with my thoughts.*

"Recognizing emotion means developing awareness about how our thinking, feeling (including our physiology), and behavior are connected... I have seen no evidence in my research that real transformation happens until we address all three as equally important parts of a whole." ~ Brene Brown

My father heard me speak of alternative ways to heal over the years. He wanted to try them, but never had the chance or never dared to. While staying with him, I asked if he wanted to try Reiki or acupuncture. He did! *Would I be able to share alternative healing techniques with my father? He wanted to try other things to heal. He was nervous and had so many questions.*

I called up a friend and asked if she would be willing to come to my father's house to give him a Reiki session. My Dad was nervous and asked a zillion questions. Our conversation went something like this:

"Would it be like a massage?" *No, she puts her hands on you but only touches you. No pushing into your muscles.*

"Will it hurt?" *No, you might feel hot or cold.*

"What does hot or cold mean?" *There is no science to Reiki. It is energy based healing and I can't really explain it to you. You have to feel it and then see how much better you feel after. It works better if you relax and believe that it will help you.*

"How will I know if it worked?" *You'll enjoy the experience and hope that it helps your pain.*

And the questions went on and on like a three year old asking Why? He wondered how his human engine would heal with this type of servicing.

My Dad's first Reiki session goes very well. He sleeps better that night and can't believe how relaxed he felt. He describes the sensation in his legs. "It was like she took all the energy out of my body and it shot down my legs and disappeared right out my feet. How does that work?" It wasn't like a car engine where one knew that when someone changed the oil, the engine would run better. This was an energy that you couldn't see or explain. *You had to believe.* I smile and know that some of the energy and emotions stored in his body for years was released. His engine had been partially cleaned out. After that first session, he kept asking when, "hot hands" was coming back. He couldn't remember her name but knew her hands were hot.

When Dad receives his second Reiki treatment, I remember back to a guided visual meditation I had during a training for Reiki. It was about a year after my back surgery. I remember the vision clearly. I was told to envision my favorite place and imagine myself there. I was in such a relaxed state that my inner mind took over. *Was this the voice inside my head that came from somewhere else? Had I tapped into it during the meditation?* I was swimming like a loon. I dove deep down in the water and shot across the lake. When I popped up out of the water, my Grandmother Palmer (my father's mother) was there, ready to embrace me in a God Love hug. She wasn't like I remembered her. She was much younger. I remember that hug as my father receives his Reiki. *I wonder where my father's mind goes when he gets Reiki? Does he fall asleep? Does he have any visions? I never told anyone about my vision of swimming deep in the water. Would he dare to say anything if something happened in his mind during his treatment?*

Dad had a few more sessions with her and then his nerves got the best of him after a treatment. At one point in the session, he said that his heart felt funny. He was worried that whatever she was doing was going to be bad for his heart. His heart doctor had reassured him that Reiki was good for him and that it wouldn't "hurt" him. Dad wasn't convinced. He decided to stop having Reiki but started asking about acupuncture.

I set up an appointment with my acupuncturist to come to the house for a home treatment. This would be the same person who had supported me when I lost my Mom. Dad had questions. I was only able to explain some of the answers to him. Sarah decided to do a small, short treatment for his first time. Dad reported that it was hogwash and he didn't feel a thing. "I'm not spending money on that. It didn't do anything!" This would be the end of his trying alternative therapies. He would go back to the Western medical world to try to help him deal with his ailments. *If only he had been able to experience this years ago. Would he be happier? Would he have been able to live longer? I wanted to help him, but it was ultimately his choice whether or not to try alternative healing. I couldn't make him do it.*

While living with my father, I noticed how different our diets were. For awhile, my Dad received the Meals on Wheels program in town. They would deliver a meal every weekday. While I was making vegetable soup and eating fruit, Dad was giving all of the vegetables in his meal to me. He wouldn't eat butter, but would eat margarine. I realized as an adult, I had changed my eating habits so much compared to what I had eaten when I was young.

Dad with a cat
on his left
shoulder and a
bird on his right
hand.

BY MONICA L MORRISSEY

While living with my father that winter, I had talked about the possibility of getting a cat. Years ago, when my Mom was sick the first time, my younger son had said to me, "Mom. I don't want to be mean or anything and I don't hope that Grandma passes away. But, if she does, can we get Grandpa a kitty?" See, my Father loved visiting our home because we always had cats at our house. I talked about adopting a cat and my father would brush me off. He bragged about the picture of him when he was a kid. He was holding a cat in one hand and a bird in the other hand. I knew he would love having a cat. This cat would become the angel Dad needed in his life.

I found an older cat and the rescue adoption process began; with the understanding that if it didn't work out, the cat would move to my house. When I think of the word rescue, I originally thought that we were rescuing the cat. *But I think the cat rescued Dad.* Once that cat moved into Dad's house, that cat never belonged to me. Once the cat was comfortable (which took so long!), she was our entertainment and Dad's angel. Dad was more patient waiting for the cat to settle in than I was. She had stayed in the bathroom for days, only daring to go between the bathroom and the cat litter box. You could tell she had had a traumatic experience and was very scared.

Here is Dad's "pet" bird on his head!

This is the cat Dad and I adopted. Her name was Missy.

It was so exciting that first night she made a trip to the living room. Dad and I were sitting in the recliners in the corners of the living room watching TV. Missy, the cat, does a loop around the middle of the house. We almost missed her as she scooted around the corner near the TV. Then she would walk by his chair, eventually working her way to his lap; a perfect friend. Dad considered her a sign from Mom and would share this with a few people. That cat cheered Dad up so much. He was so proud to tell people about "his" cat. He especially liked to watch her eye his "pet" squirrels outside of the window. Birdseed in his bird feeder was actually meant for the squirrels too.

Dad talking to
the cat, Missy.

While looking outside towards the bird feeders that year, our family sees a red cardinal. My mother has red cardinals all over her house. *We wonder, was this her watching over her house?*

I think my father talks to the cat about my mother. I'm not sure, but it feels like he thinks he is connecting with Mom. I wonder if he thinks there is a way to connect with people who have passed on? Is this part of being an empath? Was my father also an empath? Or an animal whisperer? He always joked with my sons that when hunting, my sons should "talk" to the deer.

When Dad was young, he signed up for the Air Force instead of going into the army. He wanted to serve his country. He went to basic training in Texas. Soon after he left, my mother was very sick with rheumatic fever. He was worried about her and the doctors weren't sure if she was going to make it. He came down with his own illness during basic training. He went to the infirmary and they tried to treat the illness. They did not have any luck and one of the doctors decided he needed to go home to be looked at by another doctor. The doctor gave Dad an honorable discharge and my father came home to my mother in the hospital. She did survive but it was touch and go for awhile. I talk with my father about how different our life might have been had he stayed instead of being discharged. He says, "I had never thought about it before." *I wonder to myself, Seriously? Other people don't think about these things? Why am I the one always thinking of how our life journeys are sometimes determined by one single decision or event? What events brought my mother and father together? What happened after he was discharged? This doctor will never know how much this one decision would affect so many lives.*

"No matter what he does, every person on earth plays a central role in the history of the world. And normally he doesn't know it." ~Paul Coelho

My Dad shared lots of stories during our time together. Even though he missed my Mom, he always kept his sense of humor. He sometimes would get short with me, stating that "this wasn't supposed to be a fun time." This was a sad time for him as he missed my Mom dearly. For my family, though, we heard stories that we never got to hear.

When I needed to prick his finger to take a little blood, guess what finger he offered? Or how about the time I had an appointment and my older sister, Debbie, kept asking if he was ready for breakfast. He kept saying no and then the minute I walked through the door, he said, "good thing you are home. She wouldn't feed me!"

Once, while eating dinner, I casually asked him, "Where did that clock come from?"

His response was not what I expected. "That damn thing near killed you!" he replied. "What?" I ask, totally confused.

He repeats, "That thing damn near killed you- you don't remember that? I guess you wouldn't. You were quite little, I guess," he says with a laugh.

I can imagine it in my head as he proceeds to tell me that I was learning how to walk. I was pulling myself up using a bureau. We were at the camp on Lake Elmore. He watched in slow motion as the bureau, with the clock on top, came tumbling down on top of me. He thought it was going to kill me and then proceeded to tell me that the clock had come with the camp, the camp my Great Grandmother had purchased in the 1940's. I now have the clock in my house and my son owns the bureau, a gift from his Grandfather. Stories we had never heard before helped us through our grief.

A touching story about Mom's last birthday was one of the most memorable stories he shared. This would be **8** days before my mother died. When they were headed to bed one night, Mom said to Dad, "You know. I really liked the flowers you got me today but what I really want is a hug." It meant a lot to Dad because my Mom never usually asked for things like that. My Mom didn't really express any emotions around me. My father knew that I was posting some of these stories on Facebook. One day he says to me, "Post that story. It's a good one."

"Each of us takes in at the cellular level how our mother feels about being female, what she believes about her body, how she takes care of her health, and what she believes is possible in life. Her beliefs and behaviors set the tone for how well we learn to care for ourselves as adults. We then pass this information either consciously or unconsciously on to the next generation." ~Dr. Christian Northrup

I wonder if my mother had asked for more physical affection, would she still have died of heart disease? Wouldn't it also have helped my Dad's heart, too? What made her this way? Was it when she almost died from rheumatic fever? Was she so affected by her own father's death that her heart never recovered? Was she always scared that my father would die, like her own father had with his heart attack?

One of the stories Dad told during our time together was about the last afternoon Mom and he had together. They were able to talk about what would happen if she passed. Looking back at the decision I made that afternoon, I can see now that it was meant to be. If I had taken her earlier to the doctors, they wouldn't have had that precious time together. During that afternoon, after I had spoken to my Mom that we all loved her and wanted her to get help, she said to my dad, *"Don't worry. Monica will take care of everything."* Of course, I would not learn this until after my Mother had transitioned to spirit. *I had finally received my mother's approval and now she was gone; only here in spirit.*

Often times, my Dad and I were able to telepathically send messages to each other. I know- visions of Star Wars, the Jetsons or some futuristic alien entered your thoughts. We would be sitting watching TV and I would say something about a doctor's appointment tomorrow. He would respond, "How did you do that? I was going to ask you about that!" He would do the same thing in return. *How does this work I wonder? Is this part of the empathic stuff that Michelle was talking about? How can people talk without words? How can Dad and I hear one another's thoughts? It's as if*

I was reading his mind and he was reading mine. Words not spoken but sent in energy. Was this similar to faith being like the wind? Could we blow our thoughts to each other without speaking the words out loud?

Weeks turn into months, all of us on edge thinking that Dad was going to go next. He had been fighting heart disease for **33** years and was now making comments like, "Now, I see why some people don't want to be around anymore." I knew he missed his wife and didn't like life without her by his side. When he would get like this, I'd call the minister for a visit. She always helped him. I never listened to their conversations and oftentimes I wondered what they talked about. I know that through her, he was connecting with God.

During this time of stories and visitors, I adjusted to living with my father. We made plans for his estate, my father receiving advice from my Mom's brother and my Mom's cousin. He wouldn't make any decision without the advice of my Uncle. *Even when Dad was transitioning to spirit, he would need my Uncle's approval that it was ok.* My Uncle was my Dad's connection to my Mother.

It was a cold winter that year and we stayed inside for most of it. My Dad had taken a bad fall the night after my Mother died, so it was difficult for him to get around. I would ask him often if he wanted to go outside for a walk. I knew he wasn't able to, but I liked to joke with him. He would always respond, "I guess not today. Maybe tomorrow." One time I responded, "You always say that. Tomorrow never seems to come." He smiled and said, "I know, that's why I keep saying it."

"Yesterday is history, tomorrow is a mystery, today is a gift of God, which is why we call it the present" ~ Bill Kean

BY MONICA L MORRISSEY

Dad sitting outside on his walker chair. This would be in April on one of the few sunny, warm days.

Chapter 9: Unexpected Surprises

"Be miserable. Or motivate yourself. Whatever has to be done, it's always your choice." ~ Wayne Dyer

When I was living with my Dad, we had visitors almost everyday. He loved seeing everyone and it brightened his days. My Uncle and Aunt visited us the most. Dad and I loved it when they stopped in for coffee and donuts. Dad liked to talk with my Mom's brother to get his advice on everything. Dad never had a brother so Uncle David was as close as he would get. I was able to spend time with them; something I hadn't really done since I was young.

One lazy Saturday afternoon, my husband, Dad and I are watching TV in the living room. We were the only ones at the house. Dad says, *"I have a coin collection. I think I know where your Mother and I hid it."* It was like a surprise adventure. He couldn't quite remember the exact location and didn't quite know what would be in the collection. My husband and I look at each other, grin and the search began. We go into the office, where we would uncover the collection in the bottom of the cedar chest. Before we actually get to the coin collection, we are distracted by some books located on top of the coins. Much to everyone's surprise, I pull out two books about sex- one a basic chapter how-to book and one a black and white picture book with drawings. Copyright about 1941.

The two books that were on top of the coins.

We all burst out in laughter as my dad clutches his forehead, puts his head down and avoids eye contact with me. I don't usually talk about sex with my father. Although years ago, when my father had a massive heart attack and almost died, he and I watched a movie together at the hospital. The topic was about life after a heart attack. There was a sex part and I was about 13 at the time. We were both silent and then I remember my dad saying, *"Well, I didn't know this was going to be in here."* I think he was thinking the same thing when we discovered books about sex instead of the coins he was envisioning.

The discovery of the sex books would only be revealed to certain visitors when Dad gave me the cue- a smirk and a wink. I would go get the books. I would never say a word unless I got the cue from Dad. We had some good laughs with some of his visitors. So, if you were one of those visitors, consider yourself lucky. When we found them, I assumed the books belonged to my parents. One can only imagine how surprised I was when he shared with a visitor that the books actually belonged to his mother, my Grandmother. *"Oh dear!" I thought, as my Grandmother often said. My Grandmother even had notes on certain pages in the book. Thoughts of my worries about my other Grandmother watching me when I was first married flash across my mind. Well, I guess people have been having sex for a long time.*

After the initial laughter about the book discovery, we did uncover some containers with coins.

While I am writing, fear takes over me. I only have 2 days left of vacation. Can I really write a book in a week? Can I heal from the inside as Anita suggests? Am I writing this to share and, what if I share it, but am told it isn't good enough for a book? I have been writing since Sunday; today is Thursday. I don't want to do anything but write; even though we are on a beautiful beach on the ocean. "Stay present in the now," Eckart Tolle speaks to me. Feel where your feet are, hear the birds, the traffic, the slam of the door. My heart beats faster as I think there is no way I can tell the entire dime story in the next two days. But I want to. I speak to my fear and admit it will be ok if the story isn't finished in a week. Who writes a book in a week anyway? Signs from above take time. I now understand when writers talk about being driven to write. The words come and I don't want to stop. My faith pushing me forward, becoming stronger than my fear. I do know that when this book becomes a movie, it will have to be a musical because of all the Christian songs that guided me during my writing. My story is inspiring.

I remember when I bought my first Christian CD. It was a TV commercial where you could call the number to buy the CD. I called and ordered it, something I never usually did. The CD was called, I Can Only Imagine. Of course, this was long before the internet or Amazon. I remember another song on the CD was a song that my sons sung at the religious school they attended when they were young. It was about our God being an awesome God. These songs I sang over and over again. I had never listened to such inspiring Christian songs. I had only sung hymns in church. I loved those but these made me feel good inside when I sang them. *An awesome God? Wow, that's pretty awesome!*

I remember the night I went to see the movie, I Can Only Imagine. I didn't cry during the movie but I felt God inside me like when I was in church as a child. I had gone to the evening show with a friend and arrived home around 9:30. I was sitting on the couch chatting with my husband and I got a text message from my son. It was 10:00 by then and he usually didn't text me that late. He shares with me that he and his then fiancée thought Grandpa (my father) had sent a message to them. They had named their new rescue dog, Cooper. When they were in the basement with friends, his fiancée looked up and said, "Shamus, look at your Grandfather's sign from the family auto repair business- Cooper Tires." I cried. His text was perfect timing. I was so uplifted by the movie that this felt good inside, too. *My son believed in signs from Heaven. I had done my job as a Mother. My son would be able to face anything in his life if he believed in God and knew his angels were always with him. One of his angels was most definitely his Grandfather. He knew parts of the dime story, but he didn't actually know the entire story. Writing this book will help even my sons know the whole dime story.*

I pull out a container of coins and a leather pouch with bills. I have no idea what to do with all of this. *"Are they worth anything?"* I question my father. He has no idea but suggests maybe we should sell everything. I think otherwise. We discover Canadian bills and coins. I learn that some of my father's family came from Canada; a fact I had never known before now. We don't tell anyone about our little scavenger hunt and finding. I begin sorting and documenting the inventory; hiding it when any visitors arrive. I would be sorting the coins on the table and quickly put a tablecloth over them to hide my project. The coin collection overwhelms my father but I continue to try to organize the collection. We invite a coin collector to the house to help us sort out the valuable ones and those that could be *considered worth nothing, basically "a dime a dozen."*

I begin to devise a plan; convincing dad that we should divide the coins between his kids and grandkids. He closes his eyes. The work makes him feel tired and over-whelmed. I begin to see patterns in the numbers. **8** Grandkids **4** kids. 12 of these, **8** of those, **4** of this coin and so on. Everyone's coin collection begins. Over the next few weeks, I begin to show him how I am organizing them. He again throws up his hands and says, "ok, whatever." *These coin collections are going to be amazing, I think. I can't wait to give them to everyone. Even if the coins aren't worth anything, they are so cool to have. The Grandkids will be so excited. Imagine having an 1898 coin given to you by your Grandfather! Now, that is a special coin to keep forever. It isn't worth money, but it sure holds a lot of love.*

While sorting, I suggest buying wooden boxes for the coins and a frame for the silver certificates. We had some oddball items in the collection that were worth a little bit of money. Dad wants to sell those and use the money to purchase the boxes and frames for everyone. Dad is from a generation where he didn't use any money from his savings account for projects like this. He would get the money for his project some other way. The items we sell are a unique $4 Canadian bill, a dime worth $80 and a few other coins. Dad doesn't think anyone should get these because then it would make the collections different. Making sure that everyone had similar collections was important to him. We drove to Burlington, and he went into the coin store to sell a few coins and the Canadian bill. Most of the coins don't have any value; they were neat to have.

The coin collection was one of Dad's projects for me as I was there day in and day out. He began to trust me more and more as I showed him that I was able to keep this secret from others. About the same time, he started asking for a shot of Canadian Club

(CC) and ginger ale to help him sleep. After my father's heart attack in 1982, he never drank much because he was always worried that it wasn't good for his heart. After checking with his favorite heart doctor, he was able to enjoy some cocktails, which helped him sleep. Although, I never could get them exactly how he wanted them. One night the CC would be too strong; the next night there was too much ginger ale. We laughed as he gave me that sideways smirk while he complained the drink mixture wasn't quite right. I never said a word to anyone. One time Dad mentioned his evening cocktail to my husband, who had no idea what he was talking about. I looked at Dad and said, "I haven't said a word to anyone, including my husband."

With this new drink at night, he shared with me the story of his father, in the hospital sick with bladder cancer, and struggling to eat. My Grandfather's doctor prescribed him a shot of whisky, something one nurse did not agree with. It helped him eat, which in turn helped him stay alive. My father spoke to the doctor about how this particular nurse had spoken to my Grandfather about his *"prescribed"* shot of alcohol, which in turn caused the doctor to speak to the nurse. My Grandfather would never be bothered again about needing a drink to help him eat.

I did enjoy spending time with my father during this time, but I was always on edge. I was always worried that my father was going to die next. He wasn't able to do much during the day and eventually wouldn't be able to go out much at all. Winter is difficult in Vermont and we had many cold days that winter. The coins gave us something to do during those long days.

**"Heaven may speak to us through a loud, disembodied voice outside our head; a quiet inner voice inside our head; a conversation that we 'happen' to over-hear; or by hearing music in our minds or over and over again on the radio."
~Doreen Virtue**

Was this voice from Spirit within me all the time? Is this why songs continue to play inside my head? Why I hear songs all the time that send me messages? How do I begin to listen? I have so many things I need to change in my life. How will I ever be able to do them all? I need to change the way I eat. I need to change all of my negative thoughts into positive thoughts of gratitude. I need to stop talking negatively about other people. I need to do these things on a daily basis.

"By getting in touch with your true self, you will harness the powers of intuition, insight, imagination, creativity, and intention. These are the qualities of your soul." ~Deepok Chopra

I read Susan Pierce Thompson's book, Bright Line Eating. She talks about changing our habits and how much willpower it takes. She also thinks that flour and sugar are extremely addictive for some people. Her "bright lines" for sugar and flour are similar to my black and white view of alcohol. She believes that she shouldn't have any sugar or flour because they are like drugs. She cites evidence based on scientific research. I have my own research that I did with my own body and I know pain is sending me messages. *Would I be able to follow her food plan- eating three meals a day of whole foods? I tried and I failed. I felt like I needed less sugar from fruit and more protein. I had to have protein to feel good. It grounds me and I am better able to focus. I am more in touch with my intuition as my story unfolds. The more I listen and figure out what works for my body, the better I feel. I had to stop listening to all the advice on the internet and Facebook and decide to listen to my body instead. I need to use the tools I had collected from a lot of experts and just be me. I need to do it my way.*

"To learn to trust my body, I need to tune in to its signals, so I decide to follow a simple approach my father outlines. Before eating, he suggests, practice STOP, for Stop what you're doing; *Take* a one-minute breathing break, inhaling and exhaling and paying attention to the breath; *Observe* your hunger, rating it on a scale of one to five, with five being famished; then *Proceed* with awareness." ~ Mallika Chopra

I had to solve this puzzle. It was imperative if I wanted to be able to enjoy my Grandkids someday. I had to solve this for myself and only I could do it. I had all of the necessary tools. I needed to put them in place. This was real life learning in action. My intuition would tell me that writing about the dimes would help me own my story, admit my imperfections and move forward in my life. This, along with a particular type of dime given by my father, would set me free. God would help me heal through telling my story. Just like the coins being a surprise, I might be surprised to find the answers in the most unlikely places. Just like my parents hadn't told me about the coins, were there other things that they hadn't told me? Did I need to discover the answers for myself?

I remember having a conversation with a friend about how difficult it is to watch your children struggle. We both thought it would be awesome if we were able to share the lessons we had learned during our own struggles so that our children wouldn't have to go through so many tough times in life. *That isn't how life works though. Each person has to learn by growing and accepting our journey. Even someone like Deepok Chopra's daughter had to learn it herself. Parents can't do the work for the child. They can only be there to help support them when they need the support.*

"Owning our story and loving ourselves through that process is the bravest thing that we will ever do." ~Brene Brown

The coin collections were almost ready to give to everyone, but Dad had one more idea. Those particular dimes. He said, "you know- the ones that are different? They have a different head on them. I think they might be called Liberty Head dimes." Would these dimes help Dad heal his heart? Would these dimes be able to heal me? Would they help me change my internal programming? Would this be my parents helping me find my way in this journey of life? If I was willing and ready to listen, I know the answer is yes. My faith believes that they are here with me helping to write this book, the biggest, unexpected surprise of all.

This is one of the boxes with a few coins that were given to Dad's kids and grandkids.

Chapter 10: A Liberty Head Dime for Everyone

"Everyone must leave something behind when he dies, my grandfather said. A child or a book or a painting or a house or a wall built or a pair of shoes made. Or a garden planted. Something your hand touched some way so your soul has somewhere to go when you die, and when people look at that tree or that flower you planted, you're there." ~Ray Bradbury

I remember my husband telling me that when the kids were little, he used to walk around the house at night and look in the windows. It gave him a different perspective and made him thankful for his house and family. I tried it recently. I thought of people looking at me from the outside. *What did they see? What would I see if I looked from outside myself? What would I tell myself? From the outside of the house, I can only see parts of the inside, not the whole thing. I think of judging others from the outside looking in. I don't know everyone's story from the inside. I can't see inside the whole person when looking from the outside. Will people look at me differently now that they have seen inside me? I have shown them some of my world from the inside. I think of the two voices inside me and wonder how to treat myself with kindness, no matter if I'm looking from the inside or from the outside. I think of my mother. I really didn't understand who she was and why she was the way she was. Like the coins in my parents' house, I had no idea what my parents hold inside. I had no idea their experiences in life and how those shaped who they were and why they were like that.*

"If you change the way you look at things, the things you look at change."~Wayne Dyer

My family has many of my father's belongings to help us remember him. When we were building my son's new house, we put up my father's flag on the Fourth of July. The flag was the last item that we removed from my Dad's house. These physical things help make it feel like he is nearby. Both of my sons have several signs from the family business. Cooper tires. Goodyear. Raybestos Breaks. *And of course, we all have our dimes.*

One afternoon, as Dad awakened from his nap in his recliner, he says, *"I have an idea for those dimes that are different than a regular dime."* Ok, I reply. I am curious to see what he wants to do with the dimes. He went on to explain that he wanted to take the Liberty Head dimes and put them in a necklace for everyone."Could we do that?" he asks. I assure him that we can figure it out. My brother's girlfriend made jewelry and was so excited about the project. She and I agree that everyone will treasure their new dime from my dad.

Plans were put into place. We ordered the dime holders and chains. I continued to work on the coin collections and eventually everyone (my siblings and all of Dad's grandkids) would receive their dime necklace and personal coin collection from Dad. *The dimes from my father have only begun, I think as I write. I had no idea at the time how much this one dime from my Dad would mean to all of us.*

I walk down to the beach after taking a few minutes to do Yoga; taking care of my physical body. *I wonder- can I heal my physical pain through writing about my experiences, my connection with spirit? I hear many different voices in my head all saying, "YES!YES! You can and you will!" It's like I have cheerleaders inside me.* My acupuncturist says digestion is sometimes about digesting information. When too much information is given, our body has difficulty digesting it all. I think she is referring to my Master's work in Education and losing both of my parents in a short amount of time. In the past 4 years, I had received my Master's degree in Education, along with my administrator's license. I had lost both of my parents and was the executor of their estate, which included cleaning out and selling three properties. I had learned so much about myself, but I knew there was more to learn. *But was she also suggesting that my gut was directly in contact with my brain? Weren't they two different parts of my body? When I go see a brain doctor, they don't talk about my gut. And when I go see someone for digestive issues, they don't ask me questions about my brain. How were these two things related?*

I feel my mom is even cheering me on. I wonder how this all works. Was she sending me messages to listen to the positive voice inside me? The one that comes from someplace else?

While caring for my parents, I was raising two boys through the ages of 18-21, not exactly an easy task. I wanted to be there to support their transition to adulthood. I wanted their experience to be different than my experience. I wanted them to know I loved them more than anything. I knew they were testing their independence but I also knew they still needed me. When my kids were at this age, I would place myself in the kitchen or living room during that "in between" time. For those that understand this age group, there is this time period when they come home, shower and then head out to see their friends. This is the time you see them the most during this stage in their life. Before my Mom died, I would try to make sure I was in the house at that time as much as possible. Boys are different than girls, or at least my boys were. They didn't talk as often as I think girls do. I could sometimes tell when something might be bothering them. Sometimes I would ask, "what's up?" or sometimes I would be there in case they wanted to talk. When I had this sixth sense, and I was home in the kitchen, they would open up about something that was bothering them. We had some nice heart to heart conversations about a lot of things in life. Although they had some life challenges during this time, my husband and I were there to help them get through it. *They also knew that I believed God would help them and we loved them unconditionally.*

I wondered what my boys thought of me. Was I a good Mom to them? Would they hold resentments about some of my mistakes I had made as a mother? I had most definitely done some things as a mother that I wasn't proud of. Raising kids is hard. I think of how life has changed since I was a young mother. Now, with the internet we have so much more information. I had no idea how to be a good mother. I knew that I loved those two boys and that's all that mattered. I wonder what it was like to be a mother in the 60's or 70's, like my mom. I'm sure life must have been really different then too. Did my mother do the best she could with what she had been given? Just like me? Would life be different for my kids when they became parents? Would each generation change and grow more and more?

"When you judge another, you do not define them, you define yourself." **~Wayne Dyer.**

Was I a reflection of my mother or was she a reflection of me? Had she passed on her own insecurities? Had I absorbed them somehow? Again, there was no way to determine this. I would never know her internal voice. I only know my own.

"Who tells you who you are?"~William Sloane Coffin

One time a medium I met with explained that life can be played in a variety of ways. She asked if I thought I was in the *'game of life'*. I wasn't clear what exactly she was asking. I thought I was in the game. *I mean, I wasn't dead so I must be living life as life was meant to be lived, right?* She then proceeded to help me envision a baseball stadium. Where was I in the stadium? *I said, "I was watching the game."* Yup- during my life I was only watching the game. I wasn't involved in the tough at bats with some curveballs being thrown at me.. Sometimes I would watch from the sidelines, cheering others on. When it got hard on the field, I would jump to the highest part of the stadium to watch from far away. When I was younger, I jumped out of the stadium with alcohol. *She told me I had to be all in if I was going to grow my soul. I remember thinking, ugh- that sounds too hard. Visions of wanting to hit the tree with my car in college seemed so much easier than being in the game. Would she think writing this book was me in the game, playing my hardest? I sure thought so...This was hard. I felt like I was being called by God to keep at it. Would I be successful? I hoped I would be but I had to have lots of falls. Brene Brown calls them facedown moments in her book Rising Strong.*

My mind continues to race. The thoughts unending. As I hear children on the beach, I wonder if I will ever finish this story. I know the answer. Life is a continuing journey that never ends. The words keep coming and it is difficult to turn off, as I try to let go, taking breaks throughout my days at the ocean. My head hurts but I continue to write my story. Will the story make sense? I have taken so many detours along the way. Will someone pick it apart- like my college essay so many years ago? Tell me things don't make *sense. Suggest putting this here and that there. I don't want anyone to change my story. As I continue to write, I know this is the journey I am meant to be on. I know that through this I will heal. I also know that this is **my** story. I will need help but will listen to my intuition the entire way and "Thy will be done."*

You can't trick God. I listened to Anita's book Dying to be Me and read Louise Hay's book, You Can Heal Yourself. I tried to tell God that I loved myself. This way, he might heal me. It didn't work. I prayed and the more I tried to convince Him of this lie, the more pain I was in. I told him this so that either 1. It would be true (oh, how I wished for this!) or 2. He would believe me eventually (and I would be healed from my pain). Neither of these happened. My pain would endure. I needed to face my insecurities; healing them through writing. Many years ago, in pain from back surgery, I was first introduced to Louise Hay- You Can Heal Yourself. I have tried her first activity in the book. Look at yourself directly in the mirror and say to yourself, "I love you." Do you know how difficult this is? Try it! I remember thinking it was as stupid as dreaming. Until I can do this with truth, God/Spirit/the Universe will not believe me. I am trying this again and I still struggle with it. I try to look past my skin, and speak to my soul. God will know when I am actually telling the truth. When this happens, I will feel God inside me and I think He will heal me.

Part of the problem is that when I attempt to love myself, I feel like I am being selfish. I worry that people might judge me. I worry that it might seem like I am egotistical. *Why do I think this? Do others feel this way too? I wouldn't want other people to treat me without love, so why wouldn't I treat myself with love and kindness?* I remember when I was a teacher I told students that I might send them to the principal if a student said a put-down to himself or herself. They looked at me funny and said, "Why?" I responded that I don't let anyone treat any of my students poorly. *They thought it was ok if they weren't talking to someone else, but that isn't true. I wanted to change their negative self-talk. I knew I needed help with this so I thought maybe others did too. My inner voice seems to be more negative than positive. This needs to change for everyone!*

"Do you not know that your body is the temple of the Holy Spirit Who lives within you, Whom you have received from God? You are not your own...So then, honor God and bring glory to Him in your body." 1Corinthians 6:19-20

I needed to understand that I had let the stress of life affect my body and it was time to open my heart, ask for help and heal.

Brene Brown shares that Rising Strong is,

"The goal of the process is to rise from our falls to overcome our mistakes, facing them is what brings more wisdom and whole heartedness into our lives."

I realize that I don't know my Mom's story. I don't know why she was the way she was. I felt like she taught me how to sweep emotions under the rug. That way if they were hidden, nobody would notice. Instead, what ended up happening was I thought my emotions weren't all that important. She would compare our problems to other's and they seemed to have it far worse than us. She explained that I should be happy for all of the things I had in my life. Sure, I get the gratitude thing, but I also needed to learn how to work through my feelings. Instead of learning to admit my feelings, I would learn to get really good at story telling. When I had problems in my family, I was taught that if I ignored them, eventually they would go away. I was taught how to be "tough" and keep going. Another thing I got really good at was blaming my problems on other people. I didn't have to admit any wrong doing if I had enough of a story to blame someone else. *What made my mother this way? What was her early life like? Did she have two voices inside her like I do? She hadn't ever really shared her feelings. She didn't like to talk about things when she was here and now she was gone. There seemed to be no way for me to find any answers. Had I been too busy looking at the outside of my mom and forgetting to look inside myself? Were the answers really inside me instead of from my mom?*

While staying with my Dad, we found a photograph of his Mother, my Grandmother. The photo was a tiny one like one gets at a photo booth. My Grandmother was around the age of 20 in the picture. She was talking on an old fashioned phone. Her middle finger was positioned in a certain way. *Was my Grandmother giving the camera the middle finger, just like my Dad did when I needed to draw his blood? It sure looked like it!* We laughed often at that picture during those months. The symbolism of the phone suddenly makes me think- *Was this a way for my Grandmother to send a message to me that she is using some sort of spirit communication system? Did she teach my father how to use it? Was she trying to call us this entire time? Was she calling me now? I was ready to pick up the phone and listen.*

My Grandmother (my Father's
Mother) talking on the telephone.
She was probably about 20 years
old in this photo.

Dad starts giving the coin collections to everyone. We document everything in the boxes and frames. Silver dollars- not worth anything but cool to have, a variety of quarters, and 1898 (the year my Grandmother was born) half pennies from Canada. The collections for every- one all similar. A little note is attached to each collection, documenting the coins and a note with love from your Father/

My Dad with both of his parents.

Grandfather. The dime necklaces are a hit; Dad wears his to church the first day he attends since my Mother's passing. Greeted by so many people in church, he is over- come with emotions. Mom was always by his side at church. Now life was different with her not there.

Did wearing that dime help him face going to church without his wife by his side? Can an object like that actually have power? Was she sitting in church with him that day? Was that the breeze we felt that day?

I started wearing my dime necklace every day and it helped me to ask God for guidance during this difficult time in my life. It wasn't like I wasn't praying before, but for some reason, this dime made me feel more connected to God and my intuition. From the outside, I had a dime that I wore around my neck, but I felt something on the inside when I wore it. To others, it would only be a necklace. To me, it was so much more. This wasn't any old dime. This was a DIME because it had been given to me from my father. For my kids, it was a DIME because it was given to them from their Grandfather, with the same love God gives to all.

My Dad before he went to church. He is wearing his
dime around his neck.

Chapter 11: Thy Will Be Done: A Summer on the Lake

In my life, I have to pray to God a lot. When I was young, I talked to God about my emotions and problems. Then, as an adult, I consulted with Him about life decisions. I clearly remember one conversation with Him at Caspian Lake in Greensboro. I had graduated from college and was searching for the perfect job to begin my teaching career. I was twenty one years old, about to get married and I knew I needed some help. I had several interviews and, by the time I got to the Greensboro interview, I was exhausted from the stress.

The afternoon of my interview I drove to the beach at Caspian Lake. It was the first time I had ever been there and I thought the lake was beautiful. I parked my car and looked out at the lake. The water seemed to calm my whole body. The sun was setting and shining on the lake. I wondered if this was where I was meant to be. Then I said a very different prayer. I asked God to put me where He thought I belonged. I asked him to guide me in my decision. Then I drove to my interview at Lakeview Union Elementary School.

The interview in Greensboro was the only interview where I intentionally asked God to, "place me where He thought I should be." The other interview conversations with God that I had were more like, "Please let me get this job." These prayers were more like wishing on a star. There is a big difference in asking for what we think we want or need versus asking for His will to be done. *This one decision would determine so much of my life. It would determine our family friendships, the neighborhood where our children would grow up, my education career and so much more. I taught at Lakeview for 24 years. I loved all of the kids and their families over the years. When I changed jobs later to teach at the local high school, I even started teaching my second generation! Looking back, I know God placed me exactly where I needed to be. Just like he brought my husband to me at the right time in my life, he brought my husband and I to Greensboro and East Hardwick, Vermont so we could raise our family here.*

"The goal of the rumble is to get honest about the stories we're making up about our struggles, to revisit, challenge, and reality-check these narratives as we dig into topics such as boundaries, shame, blame, resentment, heartbreak, generosity, and forgiveness." ~Brene Brown

The first night that I didn't stay with Dad, he takes a fall. *"Don't tell Monica,"* Dad instructs my brother, who is staying with him. Dad didn't want to "bother me". An hour later, *"you better call Monica"* he tells my brother. His stay in the hospital gives me a reprieve from caretaking. I realize that I can't keep doing this. It's too much for me. Eldon had warned me of this the first week after my mother's death. He said taking care of someone takes a lot out of a person. I knew eventually this time would come. It was here. *I asked God for guidance.* I knew my father didn't want to go into a nursing home but I knew that I could not keep going at this pace. I went back to teaching full time and trying to care for my father nights and weekends. This was an impossible task for anyone. Often times, I would be called away from school with something that my father needed me to help him with. Immediately after school dismissal, I would drive to Dad's house to care for him. Other people did try to help. *I didn't know what to do, but I knew that I had to do something. Decisions needed to be made, and Dad would begin to discover the changes in his life were actually better than any of us anticipated.*

It wasn't easy breaking the news to my father. Basically, he had two options- 1. Nursing home (which he did not want to do) or 2. Hire full time care. I took a day off from school to meet with Dad, his minister, the social worker and a hospice nurse to discuss our options. Dad decides that it is ok to admit him into the Hospice program, not an easy decision for sure. Dad never showed any signs of dementia or other failings so he was able to talk about everything with the social worker. I had brought Dad to all of his doctor's appointments and had been hearing the doctor talk about shutting off his defibrillator for months. For my siblings, this would be the first time they heard about this idea. Shutting off his defibrillator would be part of being under hospice care. It meant that we were not going to be doing any more 'life saving techniques' to save Dad's life. Dad had been fighting to stay alive as he had heart issues for about **33** years. It was difficult for all of us to let that fight go. Dad was proud of that defibrillator. He had to have the batteries replaced. Most people who had a defibrillator didn't live that long. The doctor explained that his heart was extremely weak (like pumping at about 15%) and if the defibrillator did try to restart his heart, it would be excruciating pain for Dad and most likely would not save his life for very long. *His heart was too weak. I wonder beyond the physical pain and problems with his heart, what were the emotions that created this disease for him? For him, he truly thought his engine would be able to be fixed by the medical doctors, the mechanics of our bodies. My Dad always trusted them. The doctors were telling us otherwise. He was not immortal and years of heart problems had led him to this point. The medical doctors could only do so much.*

Being an empath, I had learned, meant that I was able to feel what others were feeling. I had looked up the definition:

"A person thought to have the ability to perceive or experience the emotional state of another individual. *'He was also something of an empath, intuitively* *alert, it would seem, to what was going on behind those faces" (Roberta Smith)'* **(retrieved from** *http://www.yourdictionary.com/empath)*

Had my father's heart taken on some of the pain of others? Was being an empath how my father and I were able to send telepathic messages? I looked back at all of the parts of my life when I had tried to help others. Was it because I felt their pain so deeply? Had I taken on their hurts into my physical body? I remember back to the Up With People concert from when I was young. I remember thinking that I had absorbed so much positive energy… was this what being an empath meant? I could "feel" others, both good and bad? I knew that accepting this gift from God would have to be part of my healing. Along with gifts, I would also begin to learn that being an empath affected my food choices, my thoughts, my weight…everything I had struggled with my entire life.

I felt the pain my father had as he was facing death. I felt that his fear was sometimes stronger than his faith. He seemed to have doubts about Heaven. He wanted to know how it worked before he had to go there. Just like Reiki, his questions would go unanswered. He would have to wait to see for himself. *He would need to believe in God. I couldn't help him. This was his journey. He had to be in the stadium for this game.*

We hired around the clock care to begin. For me, this would mean I could be his daughter again, not his caretaker, planner, cook, etc. I would be able to visit and help him with this huge transition. He was happy to be able to stay home but so nervous about all of these new people in his home. He had difficulty remembering everything. He thought these people weren't going to know what to do or let him do what he wanted. He struggled to understand how it would all work. Little did he know, that some of these people would be able to comfort him since he was still grieving. He didn't know that he would make so many new friends. He got to share about his life and got to know them during their long nights of conversation. God had answered our prayers. These people, who my family cannot thank enough, thank me for sharing my Dad with them. They miss him dearly and believe that he is always around. *When I share parts of my dime story with these people, there is no question that he is here with us.*

When I was in the third grade, a fourth grade girl followed me into the bathroom. She peeked over the bathroom stall and began talking to me as I was peeing. I was so embarrassed that someone was watching me pee. She began talking about another girl and how much she hated her. I joined in with her, agreeing with every bad thing she said about the other girl. This was what I had learned from an early age. I believed this girl and I would most likely be best friends because she and I hated the other girl. That's what happened with my Mom and I when we talked about others. We bonded. My brain had been conditioned to believe this and I had been programmed like the child who automatically looks both directions when crossing the street. It was a part of me, like a habit.

When I walked out of the stall, the other girl was standing right in front of me. I had been framed and had no idea. The other girl slapped me across the face hard. I'm sure she also said something to me, but that part I don't remember. This memory is very clear to me. Did I go tell a teacher? Absolutely not. I had been the one who did the wrong thing. I had gotten what I deserved. I shouldn't have been talking about that girl and agreeing with the person. She wasn't a bad person. The only reason I did it was to bond with the other girl. *Is this happening nowadays? You bet. All over the internet. It is so much easier to talk about people on a computer than face to face. Things are written on the computer that people would never say in person.*

Why is this important? Because it is difficult to change the neural connections in my brain. It takes a long time. For me, because this has always been a part of my memory, anytime I start talking bad about someone, I get a sick feeling like they are right behind me, ready to slap me across the face. *Has this happened since then? Yes, Well, not the slap, but getting caught? Absolutely!*

Brene Brown explains that humans love to tell stories. Part of the reason that we tell stories, she explains, is that after telling the beginning, middle and end of a story, our bodies release dopamine. We were built to tell stories, especially emotional ones. *Is this why I agreed with the girl in the bathroom?* The only problem was, I learned at a young age to share stories where I would try to convince others that I was good and the other people sucked. I was taught that I could bond with my mother and others better if I told a story about how awful another person was. I wouldn't admit how I was hurt. By telling a person my side of the story, I felt closer to them and they would be on "my side" instead of the "bad person's" side. I would turn them against the other person. I was really good at avoiding my feelings and being pissed off at others.

"Almost everyone that I have known or have interviewed will say that it's always easier to be pissed off than to be hurt or scared." ~Brene Brown.

As I slowly began to make changes in my life I found myself getting ill when I started talking badly about others. Making life changes can be a slow process, but I tried to admit the way a situation made me feel instead of always trying to blame the other person for my problems. I was good at fabricating the story to make sure I looked good. I learned that by talking badly about someone, it would make me feel better than someone else. *When I was a kid I never really thought much about it because it would make me feel like I was closer to my mom. Now I see how it divided us all. Instead of being angry with the person, I now try to admit that what they did hurt me.*

I tried to be more like my Grandmother- looking for the positive instead of the negative. I have to admit this is hard stuff. I wasn't perfect but I was beginning to make the changes that would hopefully last a lifetime. I had to override the negative voice and make the voice from God bolder and louder.

I often share parts of my dime story (as I have come to call it) with others; at work, on Facebook, with friends. But, there is so much to the whole story; I can never tell the entire story. I can't start with the secret stash of coins, the necklace from my father and make it to all of the different pieces and parts of the story. *This is not just a story about a few dimes.* It's about faith, connecting to spirits, healing through emotions, loving one's self, finding myself and so much more. *Would sharing my story of finding myself help others? How can one believe in all of these things? How can we prove what is happening? How can we prove that it is a sign?* My Dad once said, (while sitting outside on the deck at camp), "How do you think it all works? Who is 'turning the knobs up there'? I think about someone and then they drive by. How can that work?" Dad wanted to believe that something bigger than us was helping everyone here on earth. *Is my Dad suggesting that God is turning the knobs- making all of what we call 'synchronicities' and 'coincidences' happen? He discovered it after he transitioned to spirit. I notice the word "coin" in the word coincidence again. Was that a sign or some weird thing that I shouldn't even think about? I mean, my entire story is based on coins and coincidences.*

Squire Rushnell calls them "God winks"-

"You're about to confirm something you have suspected all along: that co-incidence-God Winks- are little messages to you on your journey through life, nudging you along the grand path that has been designed especially for you." *~Squire Rushnell*

About the time we started around the clock care for my father, my mother showed up in a dream. I was worried about leaving my father to attend my niece's wedding. I would be gone for about 5 days. After four months of caring night and day for my father, how could I possibly leave him with his new caregivers? In my dream, my Mother and I were at a wedding and I couldn't find my father. I desperately wanted a picture with my father. My Mother appeared in the dream, wrapping me in a hug (which was NOT normal for my mother!) and said, *"Your father can't make the wedding. He will be fine." Was this a message from my mother telling me it was ok to leave Dad behind with his new caregivers? He was so afraid of the changes. How could I go away for 5 days when he was just beginning to get to know his caretakers? My Mother had spoken to me in a dream? How could she? She was so much younger than I remember her. She had laughed at me when I told her that in the dream. She laughed and said, "Everyone is young here." How could this be? How do I believe when she never once showed signs of faith? Was she telling me to believe now? Was she supporting me in my life, making up for all the years I didn't feel supported?*

"Picture your brain forming new connections as you meet the challenge and learn. Keep on going." *~Carol Dweck*

My brain was beginning to change and believe that my Mother had not only changed, but she was helping me now more than ever before.

I went to the wedding and Dad called to tell me that I knew two of his new care-takers. Their children had been in my class years ago. *Can you believe it? I thought. What are the chances? It had been more than 20 years since I had their children in my class. And now these people were helping me with my father. I had come full circle with these people. First, me caring for their children and now they were helping to care for my father. Had God helped "turn the knobs" to bring these people back in my life to help me in one of the most difficult things I had ever been through?*

We moved Dad to his camp on Lake Elmore in early June. He had mixed emotions about this but, in the end, was happy that he was able to stay there for the summer. When I would visit, he would obsess about a variety of things. He would say things like, "I think there is an animal in the ceiling. There is a stain and I think the animal died and is still in the attic space. I have to move home." We would look and couldn't find anything. Another thing would then become the focus. "I don't think the caretakers want to stay at camp. We should move back home." Every single caretaker would share with me how happy they were to be taking care of my father on the lake. "My chair isn't the right height. I need someone to build it up so I can get in and out of it better." This was something we were able to fix for him. There were some things we were able to help him with, but sometimes it was something he had to work through.

All in all, it was a great summer at camp. We celebrated my sons' birthdays with lobster. Since their birthdays are both in July, we always celebrated at camp each year. This night would be the last time I took pictures of my Dad with my sons. I can't remember all the jokes that night, but it sure was fun to see my sons with their Grandfather.

Merrilee and my Dad on the pontoon boat.

My Dad got to take his favorite caretaker, Merrilee, out for her first boat ride on a pontoon boat. The cat spent one night at the house and then joined him at camp. She was so therapeutic for him! Many nights spent looking at the lake, with the cat in his lap, reminiscing about all of the memories over the years

I stop writing to swim in the ocean, dance around the stingrays, realizing I have been writing for about five hours, only stopping to drink and eat very little. I usually read during my vacation. I even brought five books. Once I opened the door to write, the messages kept coming. I'm digesting all of the great spiritual teachers as I'm learning how to digest food differently. Susan Pierce Thompson teaches that we should eat without multi-tasking. Even though my mind continues to want to pick up the journal and pen-I refuse. I need to eat with intention- asking the food to nourish and heal my body. My beliefs about food are changing slowly. Food needs to nourish my soul. Anita says it does not matter what we eat, we have to love ourselves and feel God within us to be healed from any disease. I feel my gut begin to listen.

"...you may be among those who have experienced the tremendous frustration of trying to explain to doctors that your pain is real and it is persisting, even though all your tests come back negative, that there is no medical explanation for your continued suffering, that surgery should have worked, or something similar." ~ Margaret A. Caudill

I felt I was now in a similar spot in my life as when I had my back surgery in 1996. I had been to several medical doctors pleading my case that something was wrong. I had to solve this in a different way if I was to be healed. Again, traditional medicine wasn't working. What alternative methods would help me? Would writing be able to heal me? Would unraveling my story help remove the physical and emotional pain from my body? Would it be like peeling an onion? Each layer being removed with the story unfolding? Until there was only the inner core of the onion, like my soul? Would I find my soul through writing and sharing my story?

"Change happens when the discomfort of the familiar outweighs the fear of the unknown." ~ Louie Schwartzberg and MJRaval.

I had to feel the discomfort first. It would take me a long time to look for other ways to find peace. I think this book is the answer, but the dimes would lead the way.

When I return home after my vacation, I have several appointments with healers whom I hope will be able to help me. Unlike traditional doctors, one will do a past life regression therapy, combined with EFT (Emotional Freedom Technique) and the other is a naturopathic doctor. I hope they will be able to help me. I know that I will need to unpack my emotions in order to heal. I will need to change the way my brain is wired. I know what I need to do, now I need to take action and do it. Easier said than done. Tomorrow needs to be today.

My husband and I on top of a mountain in North Carolina. We spent our twenty fifth wedding anniversary hiking in North Carolina and Tennessee. We were able to meet Dad's college roommate while we were in North Carolina. I called my Dad whenever I was on top of a mountain, even in North Carolina and Tennessee.

I remember that summer at camp with Dad. I climbed lots of mountains that year and called my father every time I reached the top of a mountain. *Things can change so much from even a decade ago. As a child, I never would have thought it was possible to talk to someone from on top of a mountain. Communication systems. I wonder what they will be like in another ten years.*

I often climbed Elmore Mountain (directly across the lake from camp). When I hiked Elmore Mountain, I would sit on a rock and say, "Dad, wave to me! I'm on top of the mountain." He would tell me he was waving and he could see me up there. I would look down at the camp, where I spent most of my childhood. I hiked first thing in the morning and then stopped in for coffee to check on him. *Dad loved to pretend to wave to me. I loved being able to talk to my Dad on top of a mountain. Calling my father from the top of a mountain would not have been possible ten years ago. People might have laughed at such a thought. What communication systems would we have in another ten years? Will we be able to talk to people in Heaven easily? I felt connected to him as I prayed for his health.*

I spent a few precious nights at camp with him. Waking up on the lake is one of my favorite things in this life. I wake up early and drink my coffee out on the porch. As I look out at the lake in the morning, it was as smooth as glass. Calm and clear first thing in the morning before any boats, wind or people disturb the water. I remember back to my childhood, taking a bath in the lake with Ivory soap (because it floats!) and begging Dad to take us skiing before the wind made ripples in the lake. I wanted to have a smooth ski before anyone else made waves on the lake. I see myself playing out on the raft with my cousins and friends. We played on a rectangular raft. It wasn't the usual raft; it was about a foot wide all around the perimeter of the rectangle. There was a large hole in the middle. We would run around it, sometimes sinking it on one side. Little did I know that this raft was actually a raft from World War II; there used to be a net in the middle. *Was life like that? We didn't really know and understand things until we were adults? Would my memories from growing up on the lake always be inside me? Were the outer edges of my life solid and a net in the middle to catch me if and when I needed it? Was God my safety net?* I enjoy the peace and quiet before the day begins.

The biggest topic of conversation when I visited Dad was what Merrilee was cooking that day. Many people who knew my parents knew that Mom didn't let Dad choose what he wanted to eat. This was one of the things that I wanted Dad to feel like he had some control over. At this stage in his life, he didn't have much independence so I wanted him to be able to feel like some things were in his control. Every caretaker was trained to write a list of all of the food choices that were in the fridge. Then, upon given the list, he would choose a little of this, a lot of that and some of the other things. He really enjoyed his desserts. One of the first days Merrilee was there, she sent me a message- *"Your father wanted a brownie with peanut butter with his coffee this morning. I hope it was ok- I figured he was a grown man and he could decide what he wanted for breakfast. I wasn't going to tell him no!"* And, so it began- Dad ordering lots of desserts and he got to choose to eat whatever he wanted. Many desserts were eaten before his meal. His favorite dessert was the ginger snap cookies made with his mother's recipe.

I think to myself- this is so different than what I am experiencing right now with my food choices. Sugar bothers me. Makes me feel awful. Most people love it but I always feel horrible after I eat it. I begin to choose my treats wisely, depending on how they make me feel. Will I have to go 100% sugar and flour free as Susan Pierce Thompson suggests or will I be able to do more like 90%-10%? Only time will tell. Although Susan feels that sugar and flour cause food addiction (and, for some, it may!), and elimination is the only way to food freedom, I find that I can't do it. I don't want to feel bad if I have a toasted marshmallow (my absolute favorite treat in the world!) at a campfire. Every time I have a negative thought about food, I switch my thinking and bless the food. I am thankful that God has given me such wonderful gifts. One step at a time. One prayer at a time. One meal at a time. I will listen to the voice inside me that helps me love myself as I am.

My husband interrupts my writing. He says, "Are you going to publish that?" I respond, "I have no idea who to share it with." "Maybe you should have been a writer," he suggests. I cringe...What? Me? "Do you know what I am writing about?" I ask. "No," he says.

"It's all focused on the dime story, but it is so much more than that. Everything I have learned over the years. It's so big. I'm not sure anyone will believe in what I am writing about. Look at this," as I fan out the pages of a nearly filled journal. As we talk, I notice a small wire cable above us at the condo. It goes from one balcony all the way across to another side of the condo, crossing over the pool area. It's tiny and it disappears in

the sunlight. Sometimes it is visible and sometimes it isn't. I say, "that wasn't there last night." "Yes, it was," laughing as he disagrees. "That cable has been there all the time."

Has my ability to write and listen to my intuition been within me all this time? Were the answers inside me all the time, but I wasn't looking the right way to be able to see them? Like the sunshine blinding the cable, had I let my anger and resentment blind me from seeing myself? I didn't think my ability was there. Just like the wire cable above. The analogy is not lost.

"You must change your focus and begin to think about all the things that are wonderful about You. Look for the positives in You. As you focus on those things, the law of attraction will show you more great things, the law of attraction will show you more great things about You. You attract what you think about. All you have to do is begin with one prolonged thought of something good about You, and the law of attraction will respond by giving You more like thoughts. Look for the good things about You. Seek and ye shall find!" ~Rhonda Byrne

I have been a writer all my life but I didn't see it before? My mind questions myself. I can turn this story into a book. People around the world will hear my story. This book is created with love for everyone.

The words to my favorite song come to my mind. This is the song I want played when I transition to spirit. **Let there be peace on earth by Jill Jackson-Miller and Sy Miller (1955)** I sing the words in my head.

The last picture I have of me with my Dad is from the pontoon boat ride with Merrilee and a neighbor from camp. Dad and I shared lots and lots of camp stories while on that boat ride. We laughed and it was a moment in time I will always treasure.

On the boat ride, my Dad shares that his Grandmother bought our family camp in the 1940's for about $500, along with about 5 building lots directly to the left of the Elmore beach. She bought the lots and then sold them, thinking they weren't worth much. *As I remember him talking about this, I can sense an energy around us. Was that my Great Grandmother? Was it Spirit? Why can't I see anything? Why isn't there proof instead of "just a feeling"? The breeze on the lake is gentle and feels good on my skin as we tour around the lake on the pontoon boat.*

August brought another month where Dad slowly declined.

The voice inside me is still thinking about my husband's casual comment about me being a writer. Processing the possibility excites and scares me at the same time. Is my story good enough? Will anyone want to read it? I remind myself who I am writing for-myself. A voice repeats, "Write, digest the information and it will help you heal." My pen continues to call me. In a hurry, I continue to tell my story. I am reminded of a book I once read, Life's Golden Ticket. It explains that we are all given a ticket to live our life from our soul. The ticket is from the Creator (God). We have to figure out how to use it. In the book, the character reflects on his life so far and the lessons he has learned along the way. I think of my life lessons and where I want my life to go next. How do I want to live?

I was finally ready to take a chance, take a risk and speak my truth. The ticket was available to me now and I was ready to use it. My ticket is this book. I need to publish this.

"You can live more fully. You can love more completely. You can make a greater difference." ~ Brendon Burchard

I think about Carol Dweck's growth mindset research. Would I be able to practice what I preached? I tell students all the time that I believe in them. Could I believe in myself and my ability to write? I knew I had to. I had to use that Golden Ticket I had read about years ago. I thought about my own children and other teenagers, most likely struggling with the same two voices inside. *Would this book help them? Would admitting I have anxiety and insecurities help people talk about it more? I believe it had to. The voice inside giving advice throughout the years, boomerangs back to me. When I think of giving advice to others, it is always a caring, loving voice. I need to talk to myself in that same voice.*

"Mindset change is not about picking up a few pointers here and there. It's about seeing things in a new way. When people...change to a growth mindset, they change from a judge-and-be-judged framework to a learn-and-help-learn framework. Their commitment is to growth, and growth takes plenty of time, effort, and mutual support." ~Carol Dweck

Was growth mindset like faith? If I didn't have faith, then I would have a fixed mindset. I would only believe what science was able to prove. I knew there was more to life than what the eyes could see. I had to believe that my faith was stronger than my fear. My faith would lead me in the next journey of my life. Faith was my Golden Ticket. I never would have guessed that this would be my path. I was an educator, not a writer. I had to accept that "Thy will be done" was in God's perfect timing. It wasn't wishing on a star, like how I used to pray. It was accepting the opportunity given to me.

Dad at camp with his cat, Missy, on his lap.

I knew that camp was exactly where Dad needed to be that summer. The lake, the mountain, and the family camp were all a part of him. *He was connected.*

Chapter 12: Transitioning to Spirit

"For change to occur, you must start where you are. Recognize the value of each incremental step instead of just focusing on the outcome you want." ~ Louie Schwartzberg and MJRaval

I remember a conversation I had with someone years prior. She had shared that she felt like she was an orphan because both of her parents had passed away. She went on to explain that it was really weird and she didn't know what to do. I wondered about the word orphan. I always thought of the word orphan to mean a child who had lost their parents somehow. *Wasn't losing my parents as an adult a normal part of life? I understand I will miss them, but isn't that the way the world keeps going on and on? Would I be lost without both of my parents? I had turned into the parent while caring for my dad. I had to organize the household and make sure everything was running smoothly. When did the roles change and what would happen when both of my parents were gone? I don't think I felt like an orphan, but, then again, growing up I didn't think I had much guidance and support. I had been given food, water, shelter, clothes, but I felt like I never got the emotional support I needed. And, if emotions affected my physical body, how was I going to avoid heart disease and all of the other physical problems that could arise? I wonder if the reason people feel like an orphan is because we all feel like a child inside, no matter what our age. Would the child inside me feel like an orphan after my father died?*

I remember the morning well. I phoned camp before I left for work to check to see how Dad's night went. The previous day Dad had a bad cough so I was concerned. Congestive heart failure, like it did with my mother, was affecting my father's breathing. The gentlemen caretaker who answered reported that Dad had an "ok night." It was the same gentleman who was excited a few nights prior that the cat was now sleeping with Dad. I felt that the cat sleeping with him meant he was close to transitioning. I had heard about cats at nursing homes. The cats seemed to visit the people who were about to die. That same night Dad had woken up confused, thinking there was a boy in his bedroom. *I knew intuitively that the young boy was his Grandfather. Of course, there is no proof when I am in touch with energies. It was just a "sense" or a "hunch". I was scared to share that idea with anyone. Who would believe such a crazy idea? But I knew it was true. I felt it. It was in the breeze that summer day.*

Dad had some pretty tough days that summer. He asked a lot of questions, like: "When are all of these people going to stop coming and I just get to live by myself?" or "How much money did all this cost?" or "Who was going to take the boat out of the water?" or "What if the cat gets outside?" He would get stressed and we would call the minister for another visit. This always seemed to help him. Luckily, he believed the cat was his angel, helping him.

I phoned camp at around 7:00 A.M. that morning and was given a reassuring, "all is fine." My gut told me different, but I still went to work. This week was inservice- the teacher prep week before the students would arrive for a new school year. As I walked up the stairs at school, I reminded the principal and guidance counselor that my father was still not well- therefore I might not be able to meet with them about the Math classes they wanted to talk about. They had heard this before, but I knew this time something was different in the way I said it. *I had a feeling.*

Sure enough, about fifteen minutes later, the phone call came through the school landline. Merrilee was frantic. Dad had a coughing spell so bad he couldn't breathe. I could hear the fear in her voice. She had called the hospice nurse but didn't know what to do. As I walked outside to go to my car, a colleague hollers, "Hey- how come you get to leave? That's not fair!" Barely looking up in my haste, I respond, "My dad is not well." *He feels it in my words and sees it in my face.* He instantly apologizes and continued to apologize for months afterwards. He had no way of knowing how ill my father was. I knew he could see the panic in my eyes, unspoken fear being sent through the air.

That day would have been Mom and Dad's 60th anniversary. *Was his heart breaking? Was he ready to be reunited with her? I had heard about things like this happening, but hadn't really put the pieces together, until I was on my way to camp to see my father. This was their anniversary. He missed his wife. His heart was literally breaking.*

I don't remember the drive to camp but my adrenaline kicked in and I began planning. I was in my head, not paying any attention to driving. Oblivious to the road, the cars around me or the houses I pass. I knew the road by heart. I was driving to the place I spent most of my childhood. The nurse would arrive about the same time as I did. *Would we need a hospital bed? Would we need to move Dad back to his house? How bad was he? We had been worrying for almost 8 months. Was it his "time"?*

We pack everything to move Dad back to his house. The last thing we would pack up was Dad. He walks up the hill from camp, using his walker. We lock up the camp and begin the drive to Morrisville. *Just me driving my Dad in his van. What will we talk about? I can sense that he is scared.* He is having difficulty breathing and he is coughing a lot.

One of the projects I asked Merrilee to help dad with was to choose who got some of his furniture. He refused. He told Merrilee, "My wife said to let them fight about it after we're gone." I wouldn't discover until later, but Merrilee, instead of agreeing with him, (bless her!) responded, "Is that what *you* want to do? What does your heart want to do? What do you **feel** in your heart?" During the drive down to Morrisville, I brought this idea up again. We had just passed the round barn and the *dimes came to my mind.* I explained to my father that a bureau given to you by your father or grandfather was more than just a bureau. Similarly speaking, *"A dime is just a dime, but, a dime from your father or grandfather is a DIME!"* Jackpot. He got it. He understood the importance of giving furniture instead of all of us wondering his wishes and/or fighting like he said my mother suggested. He would make the decision of who got which piece of furniture. **A bureau would be more than a bureau!!** It would be a bureau from your Grandfather. A desk would be more than a desk. It would be a desk from your father.

When we arrived at his house, Merrilee, Dad and I sat in the living room. My father was sitting in my mother's recliner and Merrilee and I were on his couch. Dad had requested "cowboy" beans from the local brewery for lunch. As he tried to eat, we created an organized list of furniture to be given to his kids and grandkids. Dad began to decide piece by piece or set by set. Four antique pieces would go to his four children. When Merrilee said a piece or set of furniture, he would say the name. Grandkids were a bit more challenging for him to keep straight, but we managed to write who got what furniture. One of the funniest parts during this time (which was difficult because he was going downhill so fast that day), was when he suggested giving my son the dining room table and chairs. *"Don't you think his 'wife' would like that?"* He repeated this 2 or 3 times. At the time, my son wasn't married. We joke and say that Dad knew he would marry her someday! They got married on **8-18-18**.

Soon after finishing his wishes for the furniture, and signing the paper, he began going downhill fast, barely able to talk without having a coughing fit. All of his Grand-children and my siblings would come for dinner that night, *everyone understanding that he was most likely transitioning to spirit soon. My family all prayed.*

Most likely he had a stroke in the night. We tried to comfort him as much as we were able and were very thankful when the nurse arrived in the morning. Many people stayed to help us during the next few days. *I had never watched a person die like this before. It was a difficult transition for Dad. Was he stubborn? Scared? I knew he didn't want to leave because he didn't know what Heaven would be like. Maybe it would help if we tried to explain that Heaven wasn't as far away as he thought it was. Would that help him? This initiated the "talk" I would have with my father. I know he was listening but was unable to respond.*

It went something like this:

"Hey dad- there is this new communication system you haven't heard of yet. It's a new Spirit Communication system. It's where angels in heaven can talk to humans on earth. It's awesome and works well. You won't really be away from us. We will be able to talk all the time. I can talk to you and you can talk to me. We will always know that you

are here with us. It's kind of like a new telephone system (my dad was a mechanic and always had to understand the details of how things worked). It works so well you will be able to call me anytime and I can call you too! Mom has already tried the new system and she is excited for you to join her. Your Mom is there too! Your Mom is waiting for you." I told him over and over again that his Mom was there and he would be able to talk to us from Heaven. "*You can send messages anytime you want and we will all talk to you too,*" I whispered as he moved his head slightly. *I wondered if he could hear me? If only I had read the book, the first phone call from Heaven by Mitch Albom, I would have added, "the end is not the end."*

Spiritual songs soothed him during his last night and morning. His caretakers, myself and my siblings played Christian songs on the iPad. Those songs helped all of us as we said goodbye to an amazing man. Songs like Amazing Grace soothed him while his body fought the good fight.

Recently, I was shopping at a mall. I remember hearing a conversation between 2 kids as they walked the opposite way I was walking. I only heard a small part but wondered what they might be thinking about. One said, "I wonder what it is like to die." *It made me wonder- was this kid an empath too? Why would they say something like that?* He went on to say something like, "I am not talking about a gross kind of death. But, you know, what will my life be like after I die?" I remembered back to college when I dreamed of leaving earth. *Did young people have a sense of what Heaven was like? Was this kid an empath like me? He seemed to have a sense that there was something beyond this time. What if all of society knew that there was more to being human? Would we cherish each day instead of running around being busy all of the time? Would it slow us down and we could learn to take care of ourselves better? What would Heaven be like for my father? Did he have reason to be scared?*

That Friday morning, my siblings, friends and caretakers all gather around. We had been up for the past two nights, hospice nurses in and out at all times. Dad had made some good friends with the caretakers who we hired to help him over the last few months. A few of them stayed to help us. They had been through this before and knew what to do. I was so grateful for not only their care, but their friendship during this time. We knew my father was close. To me, it wasn't 'death' as many people describe. He was changing his form. He was getting rid of the human, physical body to trade it in for his soul spirit, where he would move on to be with God. *He would become an angel and help us with our human experiences. I wonder if he will be able to connect with us like I promised him. He had 79 good years and was now going to be reunited with the love of his life, my Mom.*

Many messages came to me during those last few hours. I was listening to my intuition and, even though my father was dying, I was trying to only think positive thoughts. *We all knew this was coming. It was even harder to go through. I didn't know how to do this. My mother had left us so quickly. This was so different.*

I got the feeling that he didn't want me by his side. Not knowing if he didn't want me there when he passed, I took a walk out into the kitchen to get a drink. I had heard people say this before- that someone had waited for a person to leave the room before they died. *Was I that person for my Dad? Did he want to do this without me? Did he want to be with someone else for his final moments on earth?*

A thought came to me- I told my brother's girlfriend that I thought Mom wanted her to go talk to Dad. My Mom loved her and thought the world of her. She looked at me and asked, "How do you know that?" I said, "I don't really know. I just feel it and had to tell you." Laughing as I shrug my shoulders. *Was it really a message or was I just making up a story in my head? I didn't know but I did know that the message wouldn't stop until I shared it. Repetitive thoughts....were they a voice from spirit?* She went over to my father while I stepped outside for a moment.

My Uncle, (my mother's brother), was in the driveway. There were so many people around, he hadn't gone into the living room to see my Dad. I spoke right to his face, a voice inside me begging me to speak the words, "Get back in there and tell him it is ok to leave us. He wouldn't do anything all these months since Mom died without your blessing. You are his only connection to Mom. Get back in there and tell him it is ok to leave now. Do you understand me?" He laughs and follows my orders. I stand there not even knowing where those words just came from. These voices inside my head once again guiding me during one of the hardest things I have ever been through in my life. Was this something to do with being an empath? Usually my voices had negative and fearful thoughts. What was this all about? Was I supposed to listen to them?

I go back into the house. We had decided earlier to give Dad some morphine to help him transition. He didn't like morphine normally because it gave him halluci- nations. When I spoke with his heart doctor about morphine and dad's concerns, we both agreed that at this point, it would be ok. I return to his side to continue giving him some more morphine. When he was close to transitioning to spirit, he yelled out "MOM!" several times. Because he had had a stroke, it was difficult for him to speak clearly. *But there was no denying what he said when he hollered this. I believe my Grandmother, my father's mother was there welcoming him into another realm.* He breathed his last breaths with many of us standing around his bed. He had listened to my Uncle's advice one last time. His body now empty; his soul continuing on, like a motor that will run forever.

The house empties slowly after they have taken my father away. I stay with him until they take him. After three long days with very little sleep, I go home, blurred by the reality of it all. Both of my parents are gone and the reality of it hits. *So much to do and so little time to grieve. Am I an orphan now? I had been parenting my father for months. I hadn't felt like a child anymore. Now, I felt like I had more angels watching over me.*

That was a Friday, with the first day of school approaching on Monday. I had missed the entire week of teacher prep and inservice. I wanted to be there to greet the students as the first day is always the most exciting day of school. I have time. The funeral is not for another week. Just as the colleague who questioned me walking out of inservice, another colleague innocently says before school starts that morning, *"Good morning! How is your Dad?"* I froze. How do I tell her? Poor thing! *"Well, ummm. He passed away on Friday."* The reality hitting me as I state it out loud. She feels awful (Sorry!) and I continue to try to make it through the rest of the day. I am so thankful that I worked with such a caring team that year. I was able to walk out of school that week and not have to do sub plans. The team took over my classes which helped me so much. I will never be able to re-pay them for the help they gave me during this time of my life. Only a teacher can understand how important this team was to me. Teaching is not a job where I can be out anytime I want. There always needs to be plans in my absence and the kids miss their teacher. People talk about middle schoolers and how difficult kids this age can be during that stage in their lives. During this time of my life, I had the most caring middle schoolers ever. They helped me through several tough days.

I listen again to Brene Brown, Into the Wilderness. She speaks of divisiveness, trust, boundaries. She makes statements based on data and research. I think of my life, have I actually been collecting research to guide me in my journey? Have all of these messages led me to where I am now? Is my research valid? Does my story have any merit? Will I ever be able to connect with my Dad like I promised him? Will all of this information help me evaluate my life and be able to move forward? Will I be able to find my soul's calling? Will I feel like an orphan now that I lost both of my parents? Why did I have to lose them both within an 8 month period? Was this all part of God's plan? What would I do now?

"There is sadness that the relationship was not as good as you would have liked it to be, plus the sense of loss that there is no longer the opportunity to put it right...If you had a relationship like that, then forgive yourself. You were only one part of that relationship and can't take total responsibility, especially since you were the child, not the responsible adult." ~www.griefandsympathy.com

Had I tried to connect with my father and mother the best that I could? Did it matter anymore? Would they trust me to take care of the estate the best way I could? Would they connect with me using the "Spirit Communication System" I had explained to Dad? Time will tell.

My Dad on my wedding day.
Forever he is smiling and winking.

Chapter 13: The First Call from Heaven

"The living can't speak to the dead." ~Mitch Albom

I absolutely hate conflict of any kind. I always try to make everyone happy and am, at times I think, too kind. I live in a small community where we only have a few restaurants. Recently, my husband and I decided to go out to dinner at the last minute. We walked into one of the restaurants, were seated and then nobody came to ask us for our order. After about 10 minutes, I looked at my husband and said, "How much longer are we going to sit here without service?" He agreed that it was weird that we hadn't been served or even offered drinks yet. The restaurant wasn't very busy and there were three waiters and waitresses just standing and chatting. My husband looks around at the situation and, within 30 seconds of my statement, stands up, and is clearly ready to leave. We walked out of the restaurant and went across the street to another restaurant. We walked in, saw some friends and sat ourselves down at their table to join them for dinner. We didn't even ask. We just plopped ourselves in the booth and started talking. We then ordered our meal and had one of the best nights ever. Although we were friendly with this particular couple, they weren't normally someone we would go to dinner with. This night was significant. It was one of the first times I walked away from something that I felt was negative. What happened was we found something much better. At the end of our dinner, the couple shared with us they were celebrating their 45th wedding anniversary and were very happy that we had joined them. *Interesting to think that we would have missed out on this had we not taken a different path.*

I had decided to take a different path in the woods instead of trying to climb over the rock, making life more difficult. Because I had walked away from what wasn't serving me, (literally not being served at the restaurant) I learned that I needed to walk away from more things in my life. When I chose to do this, I would find love in unexpected places, just like the lovely anniversary dinner we had with friends.

I remember a phone call from someone who I thought was a good friend. She was apologizing to me for being jealous of me losing weight and me having two jobs. *Wait, what? I thought- am I supposed to feel bad about this? I supported her when she was trying to lose weight and I encouraged her to search for her passion in life. Why would* *she tell me this? My response to her was, "I just want you to be happy." Remember in my childhood? I truly wanted everyone in this world to feel God's love and be happy. I wasn't prepared for what came next. Her reply back to me, "I **am** happy. I'm happy **whenI'm not with you.**"*

"Knowing the world 'out there' reflects your reality 'in here.' The people you react to more strongly, whether with love or disgust or hate, are projections of your inner world....Use the mirror of relationships to guide your evolution." ~ Mallika Chopra

Was I unhappy with myself? Was I a reflection of her inner world or was she a reflection of my inner world? Either way, I had to walk away. We had so much history together but I needed people around me who loved me. I needed to protect myself from people who didn't show me love. I needed to choose who I wanted to be around based on what I received in return. I needed to walk away from people who didn't reciprocate my love. That's hard. Especially when you have spent so many years together making family memories. My outer world had to match my inner world. I was in the ballpark playing the game and I didn't want this to be a part of my game. My intuition told me it was imperative to my soul growth to walk away from this toxic relationship. I needed to choose my friendships by the way they made me feel. Just like food. Take a taste and if doesn't feel right, walk away. I also knew that my inner world needed to include God. If it did, then He would give me the signs I needed to understand how to live better.

"Love your enemies, do good to those who hate you, bless those who curse you, and pray for those who spitefully use you." ~Luke 6:27-28

I have a sign in my bathroom that says, "Do all things with LOVE." It is my guiding star helping me navigate life's journey. As long as I always do things with love, then I know that no matter what others think, I did my best. Life was giving me chances to show that I was in the stadium now. I was playing the game instead of watching and letting the game happen. I was ready to make the plays and protect myself from people who hurt me. I wasn't going to jump out of the game with alcohol or food. I wasn't going to numb my emotions. I was ready to face them. That comment from my "friend" was a gut punch and when I looked back at the relationship, I had been sucker punched for years. The difference now? I wasn't sweeping all of my feelings under the rug. I was facing them head on. And I was deciding to take another path.

Seven days after my father's death, I climb Elmore Mountain by myself; taking the day to grieve. I need to do this before we have to say goodbye to him. I park in the parking lot near the entrance to the trail. A family (a grown couple and their parents) begin to hike at about the same time as me. I feel safe with them around as sometimes I don't like to hike alone. I sense a connection but don't recognize them. I pass them easily, saying hello as I pass. *My mind races. I worry about what I am going to do when I get to the spot where I used to call my dad and ask him to wave to me. I can't call him today. He won't answer the phone. I keep putting one foot in front of the other, asking God for help.*

I think of Cheryl Strayed as she hikes,

"The father's job is to teach his children how to be warriors, to give them the confidence to get on the horse to ride into battle when it's necessary to do so. If you don't get that from your father, you have to teach yourself" ~ Cheryl Strayed

Had my father given me the confidence to be a warrior? What does that look like? Was it now up to me to teach myself, using the lessons I had learned from all of the challenges of growing up in my family?

My cell phone rings and I am reminded of a medium who says that talking to spirit someday will be as easy as speaking into a black box, referring to our cell phones. No cord. No physical connection; But you really can talk to the person on the other side. Kind of like the "Spirit communication system" I had explained to my father. I share the news of my father's passing and the details of the services with my dear friend, Peggy. I cry and tell her that I don't know what to do when I get to the top of the mountain. She says, **"You will know when you get there."** *Not helpful, I think. Not helpful at all. I like to know what to do. I like predictability. I like to plan my life ahead of time and not leave it to chance.*

Hiking is my thing. I love the woods. I love the way it relaxes me and clears my mind. While I am crying on the phone, the family from before passes me. I know they see me crying. I cannot hide it from them. *It's almost as though they know that today I need someone there.* I finish the conversation and begin hiking again. Soon, I pass the family again. They are all out of breath on the rock stairs in the trail that seem to keep going up and up. Often times, my friends and I joke that the stairs are either stairs to Heaven or Hell- however you wanted to think about them. For me, even though the walk was steep and challenging, they always made me feel good. For some, they felt like hell because there were so dang hard to get up! *I always chose to think of them as stairs to Heaven- they always led me to the top of Elmore mountain, where I feel connected. I also only believe there is Heaven after our human life. There is no hell; only regrets for mistakes one might have made during their lifetime. Souls will get another lifetime to grow.*

I say hi again as I go past them. They say, "go ahead!" Before long, I make it to the rocks, where I used to phone my dad. I sit and cry. *I can't call him. He isn't at his camp down below the mountain.*

The family arrives shortly after and I begin to apologize for crying and ruining their beautiful hike. I explain that my dad died last week and I always used to call him from this spot. I point out our family camp where he would pretend to wave to me. *I think to myself- do they really care? Why do I share so many intimate details with strangers? I could just sit by myself and then head back down the mountain, not sharing my thoughts. Why do I always feel the need to connect with people?*

I find out this is the first time they have ever hiked Elmore Mountain. I share that this is my home where I grew up. My Great Grandparents even used to own the town store! They offer me a hug and I accept, apologizing for being sweaty and smelly.

Then, the younger gentleman approaches me and asks, *"Do you have faith?"* I begin to crumble. *"Yes, if you only knew how much!"* I begin crying harder.

*"Well, I am a minister. Do you think we could say a prayer together **from your father?"** This guy has no idea how much this means to me right now. How would I ever be able to explain it to him? How would he ever understand how perfect his timing was? How can I explain about the "Spirit Communication System" I had told my father about? Would anyone else think this was my father's way of calling me? He was using the phone system, where I had said, "It works so well you will be able to call me anytime…"*

I honestly don't remember the prayer because I cried even more. I sobbed loud up on that mountain, because I knew that even though I couldn't call my dad that day, **my dad had called me.** Just like Peggy had said in the phone call, *"You will know what to do when you get there."* God was there on that mountain with me, bringing a minister to me, Dad using the Spirit Communication System I had explained to him when he was transitioning. He knew how to use the spirit lines of communication to be able to talk to me. There is no doubt in my mind that he called me that day on the top of the mountain. This wasn't like Mitch Albom's book, The first phone call from heaven, where I could actually "hear" my father's voice, but I know that God had arranged this minister to be on the mountain that day so that my father would be able to send me a message that he is always with me in spirit.

I was shaking and sweaty. I didn't know any of these strangers but they had answered my prayer, asking for guidance on the top of the mountain that day. They had helped my Dad phone me. Eldon told me he calls these *"God moments." This was only the beginning of those moments.*

I feel God as I write. I can remember that day, holding hands with a stranger on the mountain while he said a prayer. As I write this, my crown chakra is so open that I feel lightheaded and free. I'm sitting near the pool and I have to work to ground myself by looking around me. When I am like this, I feel like I am in two worlds. I feel the energy around me. All of my angels helping me write. To ground myself, I focus on 8 things directly where I am. This helps relieve my anxiety. It helps bring me back to reality.

Dad's funeral was on a hot day and the ceremony was long, fulfilling his wishes with a lively Amazing Grace and a proper farewell from the Free Masons. As I held my family, spoke at the service, listened to the minister tell everyone that Dad believed the cat was his angel, lowered him in the ground with a ginger snap cookie and ate desserts before dinner at the church reception, *I knew that his physical body was gone.* Anita's voice speaks to me, almost like my father is speaking through her,

"That body whose hand you're holding isn't the real me. We'll always be together, connected through all of time and space. Nothing can separate us. Even if I physically die, we'll never be apart. Everything is perfect, just as it is. I know that now, and I want you to know it, too." *~Anita Moorjani*

It is difficult to explain what life is like after taking care of someone full time. I had so much time that I didn't know what to do with myself. The estate work would soon begin but I was so used to always being worried about my father's care. My adrenal glands were shot and I found it difficult to relax. My nervous system would take years to recover. I was used to being glued to my cell phone, just in case a call came and something bad had happened to Dad. I was on edge 24-7 and now he was gone. The estate and my school work for my Master's degree took priority for many months. There is so much paperwork to be completed

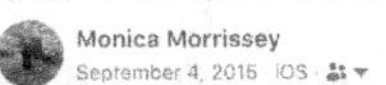

My Facebook post from the day my Dad "called me" from Heaven.

when someone dies. By Thursday of the next week, I was exhausted. I had been attempting to go to school, helping the team teach when I was able. Family dynamics made it a challenging experience for me. *I decided I needed a break. I needed to try to connect with my father, ask for his help with everything I was dealing with. I needed him to help me. I needed to know that what I was doing was ok. I prayed to God to help me.*

Dad's obituary:

"James Howard Palmer died peacefully in his home on August 28, 2015 surrounded by his family and close friends. Jim was born in Morrisville, Vermont on November 28, 1935, the son of Howard and Ruth (Mudgett) Palmer. Jim graduated from Peoples Academy and later Franklin Technical Institute in Boston. He married the love of his life, Deanna Smith, on August 25, 1957. After graduating from college, he began working for his father at Palmer's Service Station, a business which his father had started in 1933. There, he learned the invaluable art of exceptional customer service and auto repair. Jim enlisted in the Air Force but was honorably discharged for medical reasons. Upon his return, he rejoined the Palmer family garage where he eventually took over the family business as manager and owner...

Jim and Deanna cherished their summers on beautiful Lake Elmore at the Palmer family camp, which was purchased by Jim's Grandmother in 1941. They especially enjoyed hosting Sunday breakfasts, cooking pancakes, eggs and bacon.....oh the many pounds of bacon...over an open fire for 75 plus people! Hosting the Allen Family Reunions was a favorite for everyone. Jim and Deanna made the Palmer family camp feel like home to all who came to visit. Jim worked his entire life to make camp into what it is today. Jim was able to continue to live at camp this entire summer due to his very dedicated caregivers who became like family.

Jim and his wife enjoyed many trips with friends and family, including trips to Puerto Rico, Hawaii, and Rome. Jim treasured the Florida vacations with the Hale & Towle families. Jim and Eldon Towle would make sure to bring their home made syrup when they went on vacation. He loved to be surrounded by his family and friends, often snowmobiling, waterskiing, many hours spent sugaring, and listening to the kids sing along with the player piano.

Community was important to Jim. Throughout the years, Jim served on the school board, select board, Morrisville Rotary, was a founding member of the Morristown Rescue Squad, a member of the Freemasons and was a church officer for the First Congregational Church. Beginning at a young age, with his Mother, Ruth, his church family was an important part of his life.

Jim had many important people in his life. Growing up, he spent many hours with his cousin, David and a good friend of the family, Gloria Wing. While running the business, all of his customers and business associates became his friends. Jim and his good friend, Eldon, solved many of the world's problems while their wives were shopping. Anyone who met Jim, instantly became a good friend.

A heart attack early on in life made it so Jim had to retire sooner than he expected. This opened up the opportunity for Grandkids to come over anytime. For many years, it was Grandpa's Daycare and taxi service. Each Grandchild held a special place in his heart. His heart attack was actually a blessing for both him and his grandchildren.

Jim loved each and every caregiver that he had over the past four months. They helped him so that he could stay in his home and the camp on Lake Elmore where his friends and family could come and visit him anytime. Jim was very thankful for the care that Merrilee Perrine, Home Health and the company,Love Is, provided. He held a special affection for one particular caregiver, his precious cat, Missy. She was a rescue cat who became his Guardian Angel. "

I realized that since my father had been in the customer service business, I had watched him try to please everyone. The many customers throughout the years loved my parents dearly. Happy customers meant more business, right? What I didn't understand was that it's impossible to make everyone happy and this wasn't my job in life. As I learned about being an empath, I realized that my whole life I had wanted to help everyone. This is why I gave so much advice all the time. Letting that go was going to be so important to my health and well being. *Will my dime story be the way I can help people without making myself sick? Will it help some more than others? Is it worth the risk? Free will and free choice will determine everyone's path. Either choose the one that looks fresh and new or the path that has been stomped on by shoes.*

"Don't try to win over the haters...You are not a jackass whisperer."~Scott Stratten

Chapter 14: The First Dime from Heaven

"The definition of *coincidence* found in the *American Heritage Dictionary* is 'A sequence of events that although accidental seems to have been planned or arranged.' This definition, of course, begs the question, 'Planned or arranged by whom?' Most people will answer, 'By God, that's who.' Whatever you call the creative life force, it seems to be not just an architect of the past but of the very minute-by-minute present of our lives." ~Squire Rushnell

Was Squire describing the same thing my Dad had wondered about when he had questioned, "Who do you think is 'turning the knobs' up there to make all of this work?"

I was lucky that I didn't feel like an orphan after both of my parents were gone. I had Eldon who I started calling Dad as he always felt that I was like another daughter to him. Merrilee, who had taken such good care of my Dad, told me straight out that she loved me so much that she was adopting me. So now, I have people who I call Mom and Dad. I can call them anytime. They are not the traditional parents, but I sure do feel loved. I am also extremely lucky that my Aunt and Uncle became a big part of my life. We had connected after my Mom had died and I enjoyed getting together with them. Through these 4 people, I learned more about my parents. They shared stories when we got together and I am so thankful to have them in my life. I could tell that my Uncle loved his big sister a lot.

It had been exactly two weeks since my father had transitioned to spirit and a week since Dad had "called me" on top of the mountain. I took a day off from work. Before I would tackle the paperwork and phone calls, I hiked Elmore Mountain again. I was determined to take time by myself to clear my head. There was so much to do for the estate and I needed to be able to think. I wouldn't be able to call my father today when I reached the top of Elmore Mountain. He again wouldn't answer. I called him often this summer telling him to wave to me from his camp below on the lake. I hadn't figured out a way to call Heaven yet. I know for sure he called me last time, but what was I going to do today? I couldn't expect another miracle like last time. Last time, Peggy had told me that I would know what to do when I got to the top of the mountain. Today would surely be different.

"But ask the animals and they will teach you, or the birds in the sky, they will tell you; or speak to the earth, and it will teach you, or let the fish in the sea inform you. Which of all these does not know that the hand of the LORD has done this? In his hand is the life of every creature and the breath of all mankind."
~Job 12 7-10

I felt so alone as I climbed the mountain; deep in thought as I walked. I wanted to believe that my Dad was helping me climb the mountain every step of the way. I could feel it in the wind and wondered where the animals in the forest were. It was the end of summer. Soon the leaves would be falling and the snow would blanket the forest.

I made a plan on the last few steps toward the rock where I would sit to call my father. I always knew the last part of the hike was when I would see white birch trees. I remembered this when I was a kid climbing the same trail. I always liked to know when I was almost there. The trees opened up and I could see the sun shining on the white birch trees on either side of the trail.

I decide to phone Merrilee. She always answered anyways. When I phoned her, she and I both agreed that we missed my dad a lot. I paced while on the phone, trying to calm my nerves. As I walked towards the rock where I always sat to call Dad, I couldn't believe my eyes. *How could this be? How does a coin, this particular coin, land on top of the mountain, exactly in this spot? Was my father grinning like this was some sort of game to him? Could he really do things like this from Heaven? Did he leave physical evidence as a sign that would only mean it is from him?*

"Merrilee, you will never believe what I found on the ground, right here." I can't even believe it as I try to put words to what is happening. It feels surreal. I have nobody around me this time on the mountain. She says, "I can't believe it." The rest of the conversation is a blur as I feel my father's energy all around me, enveloping me in the biggest hug I have ever received.

"Your dad knows how you feel, because he's able to read your mind and heart from his vantage point in Heaven." ~Doreen Virtue

A voice whispers to me, " Yes! It is me! I figured out that Spirit Communication System that you whispered in my ear the day before I left my body. You know- where you said I could call you and you could call me anytime? That new spirit phone system. Isn't it great? We really can connect from here. Remember how I called you last week? I didn't have the faith that it would work, but now I know it to be true. You told me my engine would still be running- this engine is so different! I'm not in any pain and I know my engine will run forever."

I was not expecting another sign today. *The last one was so clear but this one? How could it be? I can see my Father grinning, thinking that he really figured out the system I had whispered*

A picture of the dime I found on top of Elmore Mountain.

into his ear, shortly before transitioning. Of course he figured it out- he loved stuff like this!

If my father had read Mitch Albom's book, the first phone call from heaven, he might have been able to tell me more about heaven. Something like:

"In heaven, we can see you...We can feel you...We know your pain, your tears, but we feel no pain or tears ourselves...There are no bodies here...there is no age...The old who come...are no different than the children...No one feels alone...No one is greater or smaller...We are all in the light...the light is grace...and we are part of...the one great thing." ~Mitch Albom

I pick up the dime and so begins me sharing my dime story with others. I do not even remember walking down the mountain. My thoughts engulf me. I wonder how this could even happen. *How will I be able to explain this to people? They won't know the conversation I had with my father before he passed. They won't know about the minister I met last time, helping my father "call me".*

This verified what I have felt my whole life but never felt confident to let other people know about my connection to Spirit. People get shivers and goosebumps when I tell them about it. **I just know.** Dead pen again! When I write the words "I just know"it is again in ghost letters.

I know that every time I run out of ink, it is a sign from God and my father to continue to write this book, this story, to share with others. He always wanted proof of how this all works, now he is continually sending me messages and signs, giving me the courage to share this with the whole **world....** Really? Three dead pens in a matter of a few days. The words **that** disappear on the page have been, "I just know", "world" and "that" Pretty soon, I will have to really search for a pen as I am running out of pens! I feel a sense of peace as I receive this message to share my **story.-** yes another dead pen. I am using my markers that I color with and slowly, one by one they die on certain words.

"I just know"

"World"

"That"

"Story"

A message. I am open to receiving messages, guiding me in this journey.

I still have that dime that I found on the mountain that summer day. It is now in a necklace that I can wear whenever I want. It will forever remind me that Dad is around- a physical reminder that we can connect with Spirit. As we clean his house and camp, dimes start appearing everywhere. The entire family would begin finding dimes. I remember my husband, while helping clean out the family camp, threw a bunch of dimes at me. It was almost like he was scared of them; like my Dad possessed the coins. *I laugh inside. Angels aren't creepy like ghosts. They are around to help us. If only everyone would believe this.* Cashiers, low on change, would give me all of my change in dimes. 30cents- three dimes 60 cents- 6 dimes. *But, this story is so much more than dimes. The dimes make it real.*

"True self-confidence is "the courage to be open—to welcome change and new ideas regardless of their source... Real self-confidence is not reflected in a title, an expensive suit, a fancy car, or a series of acquisitions. It is reflected in your mindset: your readiness to grow." ~Carol Dweck

Can dimes from my Father in Heaven help me to be ready to change my mindset? Choosing confidence instead of anxiety? Can I turn my negative thoughts into positive thoughts? Can I listen instead to my intuition and the many messages from God? Can I change the patterns and the neuro connections in my brain? It's like trying to make railroad tracks go in a different way. The metal of the tracks making the patterns so strong it is difficult to bend them.

"God Bless the Broken Road that led me straight to you."~ Rascal Flatts

Yes, my whole life I felt I was on a broken road. Now, the road was going to be different. God was inside me helping me heal and showing me signs that I was on the right path. God was sending me messages to write this book to share with the world. If I thought of myself as a messenger helping the world, my fears disappeared. I was on my own shiny new path, determining day by day how to love myself for who I am. My Mother and Father were helping me.

Chapter 15: Messages

"Your winks from God can be something of a riddle, something ironic, or just something triggering a smile and a shake of your head. But, when they happen, _you_ know- it's a little message to you." ~Squire Rushnell

Sometimes when I am driving, I can drive and not remember any part of the trip. I seriously keep the car between the lines and don't even notice the other cars in front or behind me. I am either thinking of something from the past, most likely ashamed or feeling bad about something or thinking of something in the future, most likely worrying. People will tell me all the time that they waved to me and I didn't see them. It's like I'm in a different world. This is what my life felt like sometimes. A blur. I was driving, but wasn't paying attention to anyone or anything around me. That's what the next few years after my parents died felt like. I was driving, but not stopping to enjoy life.

I knew my father was with me the entire time I was dealing with his estate. Many times I had to pray for guidance during difficult times, similar to what I did when I was caring for him. When I prayed, it calmed my mind and I knew that I was following his wishes.

My father owned **3** properties. We closed on the last property of my father's estate the day before our now annual vacation to Florida in April. Most of my responsibilities as executor of the estate were over. By now, I was close to finishing up my Master's degree. For the next year and a half, action research would consume my life. My work was like a scientist doing an experiment. Read, reflect, test, read, reflect, test...repeat. _How do I know if I did it correctly? Who would guide me in this journey? Our professor explained that we needed to trust the process. Our answers would come through our work. Learn through the process. I didn't like that. Along with a plan, I liked to know where I was headed. How could I drive if I didn't know my route?_

I liked to have things completed. Finished. Over with; so I could relax. Was action research like our life? Read, reflect, test? Are we all here to learn lessons in life? How can we know if what we believe is true? How will we know if we have learned the lesson? As I continued my research, I compared action research to life's journey- full of questions and always searching for the answers. The more knowledge we have, the better able to navigate life lessons. How many books had I read about past life regressions, being healthy, *loving myself and messages from Heaven? Too many to count! I had to learn to enjoy the journey because there really is no finish line. Life is never done.*

One of the books I had to read for college was called, Make Just ONE CHANGE Teach Students to Ask Their Own Questions. Of course, the book was supposed to be for my classroom teaching practice. But what ended up happening was I began to think about all of life's questions. *What was my purpose here? As I turned 50, what was left of my life and how did I want to spend it? What did God have in store for me? Would I be able to plan things or should I let God decide my path? Was my path always going to be predictable or was it going to take different roads that I couldn't even imagine? Writing a book was never something I thought I would do. Teaching, real estate and being a mom and a wife had been my entire life.*

As part of my reflections on the research I was conducting, I learned things that would apply to my life also.

"Time in between does help your thoughts take a different path and that is ok. Reflection helps all learners and researchers. Enjoy the process." ~Monica Morrissey

I realize that in taking the time to write this book my thoughts have taken several paths. I have gained new insight about my gifts and challenges. I have discovered that I am an empath. I have realized that my faith is truly stronger than my fears. I still have many questions, but I am slowly being guided to the answers.

"Who looks outside, dreams; who looks inside, awakes." ~Carl Yung

My younger son and I decide to go to a Red Sox game in the fall the year after my father died. Our neighbor's daughter, Samantha, had died suddenly and we were all in shock. She was 27 years old. She was fine one day and not the next. I had even said hello to her in the grocery store the day before she died. She looked fine. Our family talked about how a life to 100 years old was not promised to everyone. None of us knew how long any of us would be around. We knew our life journey was God's decision

Samantha loved sunflowers. I love to plant them in my garden to remind me of her.

We weren't going on our annual family trip that year to Boston because my husband was helping my older son and his girlfriend build their new house. With winter coming, they needed to finish up the house. Patrick and I decide that we could go without them. Realizing how short and unpredictable life can be, we decide to go to a Sunday game and take Monday off from work. ***The memories are what stay inside of us when a loved one goes to Heaven.*** We decide spending time together at our favorite place in Boston is worth the money and the time.

Patrick and I head to Boston to see Big Papi play one of his last games at Fenway. While he was driving my car, he says, "Hey Mom, your mileage is **5,555** miles. Isn't that cool?" *I wonder if I should share that Spirits or Angels show us they are around through numbers? Would he believe me or just think I was doing more "voo-doo stuff"?* I decide that we have plenty of time to chat in the car and it was a great discussion starter. *I so want my children to understand and have faith in the Spirit Communication System available to everyone.*

"Every thought you think creates your future." ~Louise Hay

I begin to tell Patrick that some people believe that repetitive numbers can be a sign from Heaven. Silence. *Explain more, I think.* My number is sometimes repeating ones. I see them all the time. Often times, I can look at the time and it will be 1:11 or 2:11 or 5:11 and so on. I believe that an angel is around and they are trying to send me a message. His cousin Tyler's number is 8. I share that I see those a lot too. He immediately thinks of his Grandfather, his most current angel. He looks at me with wonder in his eyes. I wish I had access to some books or a website to look up what a 5 means. Then I could help him understand what the message might be about. I know he will never Google such a thing. But the seed has been planted. I have given him something to think about and ponder. *Stay in the moment. Don't think about the past and don't worry about the future. Enjoy the time with your son. My inner voice reminds me of how important this is.* After chatting for several minutes, the subject changes and I wonder if he believes.

"1- Stay positive . Think about and focus upon what you like, not what you dislike, fear or what you are worried about…your thoughts create!…

5- Change is in the air! Call upon your angels to help manifest positive new changes in your life…

11- Honor your intuition, it's right on! Keep your thoughts in alignment with your dreams and intentions for the future, and release any doubt or nervous energy into the light. 11 is a powerful number of dreams, intuitive illumination, and connection with spirit." ~retrieved from https://www.ask-angels.com/spiritual-guidance/angels-and-numbers/

During dinner before the game, Patrick says, " Hey Mom- Guess what time it is?….**5:55!**" *Is he beginning to believe in the power of numbers being a sign from Spirit?* The game continues and we have a great time. Big Papi doesn't bat but we still enjoyed the baseball game. When the game is done, Pat says, "Mom, did you notice all the 5's? In the 5th inning, they scored 5 runs and they won the game by 5." Patrick automatically thinks it is his Grandfather. I know now that my Father was only beginning to send signs to Patrick. Although we were watching the baseball game at our favorite ballpark, I felt like Patrick and I were also playing the game of life. We were learning how to navigate life with our angels in Heaven cheering us on. Shortly after this trip, Patrick got a new job. After he got the job offer, he said, "Mom, I think Grandpa helped me." *I respond, "of course he did."*

If the dime on the mountain or the dimes we find throughout the years wasn't enough to make us believe, my father would eventually connect with Patrick for **THE dime** *that would make this book possible. As I write, my body heals. Telling my story for me and others gives me a sense of peace. If my story can help one person, then it is worth it. I have surrounded myself with other people's words, but never my own words. Will my words now help me? Daring to share is forever changing my life.*

My son, Patrick, and me at the Red Sox game.

Chapter 16: Life Marches on

Messages from Dad through a Medium

"'I am a noticer,' he said. 'I notice things that other people overlook. And you know, most of them are in plain sight.' The old man leaned back on his hands and cocked his head. 'I notice things about situations and people that produce perspective. That's what most folks lack- perspective- a broader view. So I give them that broader view...and it allows them to regroup, take a breath, and begin their lives again.'" ~ Andy Andrews

I had a good collection of tools in both my personal and professional life that I had collected over the years. Books I had read, conferences I had been to and general life lessons learned through some of the more difficult times in my life. I remember taking a group of teachers to a conference. During one of the breaks, a young teacher looked at me and said, "This is such a good conference." I agreed. Then Ryan looked at me again and said, "None of this is new to you, is it?" I smiled. "No, it's not," I said. After 27 years of teaching, I had lots of experience but also didn't quite know how to share the knowledge I had gained over the years.

I had a lot of life experiences too that had helped me grow as a person and a teacher. I had changed so much compared to the person I was during my first year in college.

I was lucky that my Master's program was built with constructivist values. During my studies, I wasn't told what to do and believe, I was encouraged to "find my passion". We read books like, A More Beautiful Question, Make Just One Change, Strategic Inquiry, and Leading with Soul, An Uncommon Journey of Spirit. I wasn't just learning to be an administrator, I was discovering why I wanted to be a leader. I learned to not only think about what great leaders are able to do, but to

"...develop a life and livelihood that center on meaning, purpose, joy, and a sense of contribution to the greater community." ~ Bolman & Deal

*Wait, what? I just wanted to finish my Master's program. This wasn't about finding myself. Just complete the work, get the degree and possibly get a new job. Not only did I have to think about why I wanted to lead, but the program forced me to dig deeper into **my** why- almost like **why am I here on earth kinda why**. It was as if they were asking me to think about why God would want me to be a leader? Wait, they were mixing religion with school, weren't they? Can they do that? But it wasn't like organized* *religion, more like spiritual religion. Can I really think about my educational journey as a spiritual journey too?*

During this time, I discovered Simon Sinek, who wrote the book, Start with Why. Because of my previous readings during my Master's work, I was curious to learn more. *Had I discovered my passion? Was this work inspiring me to peel the onion a little further and get to the deeper understanding and answers to my life's journey?*

"Leadership is not a rank or position to be attained. Leadership is a service to be given."~ Simon Sinek

Was I only getting my Master's degree to "move on up" or was I ready to be a true leader dedicated to the hard work of the people? Was writing this book helping me lead in a whole different way than I imagined? Had I found my calling? Something that I never saw coming? Is this what God had been planning all along? How would I know?

When I became a Real Estate Agent I learned that teaching and real estate are two very different professions. Well, at least in the sense that the day to day work is very different. One is sort of predictable and the other is not. With teaching, I couldn't predict what the students were going to do, but I could predict my schedule. There was a rhythm to the year. Begin the school year at the end of August, and end the school year in June. Work every weekday for the most part from Monday to Friday, 7:00-4:00ish. I had lunch at the same time every day and I could plan on the day ending around 3:00 for the students, but the planning would never end. It was predictable.

When I started real estate, that was the first thing that I noticed. It was unpredictable. I had to learn to adjust. I would go to the office in the morning with nothing on my schedule, and then all of a sudden have several phone calls and appointments. So many that it would be 4:00 and I had not even eaten my lunch. For a girl who was used to eating at 11:30, whether I was hungry or not, this took some time to adapt. Being a teacher, I could always plan on who my students were for an entire year. For real estate, I had no idea who my clients were going to be and no idea if the deal was going to go through. For real estate, I had to learn that the universe would help make the match for someone to be able to leave one house and go to another at the exact time that someone else would move into the house being sold. There had to be someone behind the scenes guiding the perfect timing. I wouldn't be able to control it. I would be there to help the deal go smoothly, but ultimately the transaction would be out of my control.

In teaching, I was constantly planning. It was my job to make sure every lesson went smoothly and the students got what they needed. I was in control for all of the planning in my classroom. *Was being a realtor supposed to teach me to believe in letting the future unfold instead of trying to control it? Was it forcing me to feel out of control so that I could learn ultimately that God is in control?* I had a difficult time adjusting because real estate was different than teaching in so many ways. *I had to learn to let go of the outcome.*

I grew up thinking that people who believed in such things as mediums, after life and such were not very smart. Well, maybe not that they weren't smart, but the way my mom would roll her eyes sent a message that it was sort of dumb to believe in such "nonsense". As I slowly began learning about a variety of different beliefs, I wondered if I would ever truly believe in some of these things. One medium in particular sure did change the skeptic in me. With organized religion, I felt that God was always there. With Mediums and past life regression work, it was unpredictable and I never knew what was going to happen. *Did I have the guts to take a risk and find out what life might be like when I changed my thinking about these things? Would I believe that God would help me along this new path? Would it challenge me to change my beliefs? Would I ever truly believe?*

A friend of mine was going to a group event. A medium would be speaking in front of a large group. Some people would be "read" and others might not. Being "read" meant that someone from Heaven wanted to send the person on earth a message. The medium would be the messenger. I met Tracy and Chelsea for dinner and then we went to the event. All day long, I had been thinking about my Dad, the dimes, and the mountain. I felt him everywhere. I even found a few dimes and a penny. I prayed that Dad would come through for the event. When we arrived, we sat in the very front row. When I sat down, I sat down next to two other friends, Samantha's Meme and Aunt Ellen. I felt awful. I had been wishing for my father to send messages through the medium but these people were in a lot more pain than I was. It had been over a year since my father had passed and losing a parent was a normal part of life. It had been only a few short months since Samantha had died and it wasn't normal to bury someone so young. *Please, I thought, send a message from Heaven to them instead of a message from my father. I'm sorry for being selfish today. They need this way more than I do.*

The medium was not what people envision when you think of a "typical" medium. I'm actually not sure what people think someone should look like, but according to my mother, they were all "crazy" people. The medium had tattoos, swore like heck, and basically did a comedy act along with her readings from Heaven. At the beginning of the "show", she told us if we didn't like the word fuck, we might want to leave right now. This was not the place to be. The first person I remember her reading was a young woman who had lost her dad. The medium got it right that one of the reasons she was so upset was that she was getting married and her dad wouldn't be able to walk her down the aisle at her wedding. *See, I thought. I was selfish in my wish to have my dad send me messages today. I was able to have my dad walk me down the aisle at my wedding, he got to see my kids grow up and I was almost 50 years old when I lost him.*

Does anyone see a pattern here that I was taught at an early age? I was comparing myself, my loss and my grief to someone else's loss. Mine wasn't "as bad" as the other person's grief or loss. What I had learned when I was young was that my emotions weren't important because they weren't "as bad" as someone else's. Comparatively speaking, *should I not be upset that both of my parents had died? Should I numb my feelings and know that others had it much worse than me so I should be fine? (this is what was programmed in to me at a very young age) We all felt the pain of losing someone we loved and all of our emotions mattered.*

The medium was receiving messages from heaven to the woman sitting directly behind me when, out of the blue, she says, "A dime a dozen." I think of my dime on my neck, grab my necklace, and look up at the medium. She states it again, "A dime a dozen." Her eyes meet mine as she sees me holding my necklace. She walks closer to me and says, "Is that a FUCKING DIME?" In this event, the audience is only allowed to say yes or no because she does not want us giving any more information. I say, "yes," in one of the quietest voices I have ever heard without it being a whisper. She went on to give several bits of accurate information. It went something like this:

"Was your father a jeweler?"

"No." *but it was his idea to make the necklaces. I wasn't able to say this but she was stuck on this idea that he made jewelry for a living. He didn't, but I think he wanted credit for the necklaces being his idea!*

"He had lots of properties. He was proud of those properties. It was almost like he had struck oil in Texas. 3?"

"Yes, 3 properties"

"Why Texas? I see some sort of military uniform."

She allowed me to say more than yes. "He was in the air force and stationed in Texas for basic training."

"He seemed to have rose colored glasses on most of his life. He wanted everything to be good but couldn't quite seem to view life with some of the dysfunction that might have been a part of his life."

"Yes."

"The dimes aren't worth anything though, correct?"

"Yes." *Well, I think. No monetary value, but I wouldn't ever give it away or sell it. This dime is from my father, so it means more to me than money. I wish I could tell her about the dime on the mountain.*

"Well, that makes sense, a dime a dozen!"

She went on with a few other connections but said she had never had a clear message like that with so many meanings attached to it.

She went on to give other messages from Heaven that night. It seemed like I connected with almost every story in the room. One person's sign from Heaven was a four leaf clover. *A message from my Grandmother too?* Another person's sign from Heaven was a rainbow. *When my husband drives and I look out the window at a road sign, if I look just right at night, I can see a rainbow. After my Mom died, I envisioned her saying, "I know it is quick and short, but it is your sign to believe." I have no idea why I thought that, but that is what I would think. I thought it was a sign from my Mom.*

"The pendulum of the mind alternates between sense and nonsense, not between right and wrong."~Carl Jung

I was born in October and I am a Libra sign. Libra, according to the Zodiac signs is represented by a scale, with both sides distributed evenly. This is both a blessing and a curse. I see both sides of everything. I want balance everywhere I look. *Can my beliefs be balanced? Can I believe in mediums, past lives, and healing from God all at the same time? I think back to one foot in the living room where my parents are sitting and one foot ready to leave. Have I always had one foot on earth and one someplace else? Is this part of being an empath? Or is it something else?*

I stop writing to sit by the ocean with my husband. I tell him that I am thankful for his support this week; it means a lot to me. He responds, "I want you to be happy." My reaction is not like the punch in the gut when I told someone the same thing. I cry because I know what he said is true and I accept his love. We go swimming in the ocean, on our last day of vacation.

I went to see a hypnotist who was trained by Brian Weiss. In fact, I have gone to see her several times. I was so scared that I wouldn't be able to relax so that I could find another lifetime, my childhood conditioning so trained to not believe in such things. I was fascinated by all of Weiss's books, where people were healed through a past life regression therapy session. I decided to try it. In one of the lives that I remembered, I was starving in a basement. My parents decided it was best if they ate the food available instead of giving it to me."It was better this way," they told me. *Was this my food issue? Did I always feel like I could never fill myself up? I hated to go long hours without food. Was my soul programmed from this past life?* When I 'died' in that lifetime, the hypnotist asked me what I saw or felt. I explained that my Grandmother (my father's mother) was there to wrap me in a big hug. I was enveloped in pure love. This was exactly what had happened to me during the meditation in my Reiki training. My Grandmother told me, "This time wasn't about you dear. It was about your parents." *Could this also be a message that my relationship with my parents in this lifetime was about them and not me? Would I have a parallel life soul lesson? How does one believe in such 'nonsense'? Seeing mediums and doing past life regressions was so different than worshipping in church. I seemed to actually connect with something more.*

My son, Shamus and I at the Patriot's game.

A year after going to the baseball game with my younger son, I had the opportunity to go see a Patriot's game with my older son and his fiancée at the time. The Patriot's were playing the Tennessee Titans. Our family was always involved in baseball, with both boys playing since t-ball. We loved to attend Red Sox games. As a family, we never really watched much football. At the football game, I asked my son how he got interested in football. He explained that it was the trip to Tennessee when him and his Dad went to visit my husband's brother, Tyler's father. His Uncle John took him to see a Tennessee Titan's game. We thought it was interesting that the Patriot's were playing against the Titans while we were at Gillette Stadium. While we were talking, he said maybe Grandpa was here. I said maybe even Tyler. *I cherish these types of conversations with my kids and am so glad that they are open to understanding our connection to Heaven.* Later on that week, we found out that Tyler's father was also at the same game!

After my father passed away, we sold all three properties for the estate. One of the first properties to go was the family camp on Lake Elmore. I hadn't told my Father when he was alive that most likely it would be too much for me to be able to afford to keep the camp. It needed a lot of work and it would be difficult with multiple people owning a property. This bothered me a lot and I felt sick inside. For weeks, I prayed to my father for forgiveness. He, like Mom had, came to me in a dream. It was so real. He was sitting with me on a couch. He was younger, like my mom was in the other dream I had months prior. He handed me a photo album, opened up to the page where there was a picture of him cooking bacon and eggs on an open fire at camp. He cooked Sunday morning breakfasts for about 75 people when I was a little girl. I immediately wake up from the dream and think, *What was my father's message? A voice from within says,* **"You will always have the memories."** *I think of my trips with Patrick and Shamus. Making memories helps us feel close to our loved ones. This was what life was really about. It wasn't about things, it was about people.* I begin to tell people about my dream. *I believe my father forgave me for selling the camp. I felt he understood.*

BY MONICA L MORRISSEY

I recently drove by my father's camp. The new owners had torn the camp down the year before, leaving only the foundation in the ground. They had built a beautiful new house on top of the old foundation. The foundation was built when I was a kid about 10 years old. We dug it out by hand. With help from another family, we had taken each load of dirt out of the cellar by wheelbarrow.

This is a picture of the camp from sometime in the 1940's.

My Father's camp before they tore
it down.

They tore down everything my father had built. They only left the foundation. I felt horrible yet again. *Had my father really forgiven me for selling the camp? He was always so proud of the camp he had rebuilt over the years. Seeing the camp gone made it real. There were now new people living there making new memories.*

I drove by this new house where my family camp used to be but it was not a camp any longer. This place looked like people could live there year round. It was beautiful- gray vinyl siding with pretty white trim. I decide to stop by to see a relative who lives at the other end of the lake. When visiting, Marion says, "Oh- did you see your father's camp? Isn't it beautiful? I think your father would be smiling and so happy that they used that foundation and made that camp, well really a new house, look so nice!" *I was floored. Wait, what? She was thinking in the positive, not the negative. Wow, I think, imagine having her for a mom growing up! Would I ever be able to reverse my internal programming to think in the positive? I knew I had to in order to be healed. Be easy on yourself, I think. It will happen but you will need to work at it! All of my horrible feelings wondering about my father's forgiveness disappear. They are replaced with him smiling at me.*

"The simple things are also the most extraordinary things, and only the wise can see them." ~Paull Coelho

I was so good at giving others advice about chasing dreams and finding their true calling. I would try to inspire them but I realized that I wasn't making the changes in my life. I knew that I needed to take a risk and follow my dreams. My true calling was coming in unexpected surprises. The dimes were leading me in a different direction.

"This is what we call love. When you are loved, you can do anything in creation. When you are loved, there's no need at all to understand what's happening, because everything happens within you." ~ Paul Coelho

Chapter 17: THE Dime

"I'd finally come to understand what it had been: a yearning for a way out, when actually what I had wanted to find was a way in." ~Cheryl Strayed

Looking back, I am thankful that I was introduced to God and attended church as a child. For me, it will always be a part of who I am. There was never any question for me and I never doubted the fact that there is some sort of God or Spirit that is more than the physical human life we all experience. *What I doubted the most were signs from Heaven, including the inner-most voice inside me. I wasn't sure if the messages were real or if I was imagining them.*

"Like a wink from your grandfather, these winks are communicating God's message to you: 'Hey kid, I'm thinking about you- right now." ~SQuire Rushnell

When I turned 20 I remember a conversation I had with God. I told him that he wouldn't "see me" for awhile in my twenties. I explained that I wouldn't be attending church for awhile but, "most likely" I would be back in my thirties. Why I conscientiously thought this, I have no idea. When my father wasn't able to attend church, he would always say, "pray for me". I thought the same thing and hoped that someone would pray for me. I guess every 20 year old thinks they know everything and it is part of the breaking away that everyone needs to go through. For me, the game of life gave me some challenges before I hit the thirty mark. I had back surgery when I turned 27, then went into a deep depression and realized that I was trying to numb both my physical and emotional pain with alcohol. There was no where else to turn but to God. I did attend AA meetings at first to get sober, but in a place where I thought there were "automatic" friends, I felt out of place yet again. I was able to get enough tools in my toolkit to be able to get sober and free, but I never felt accepted by the people there. I had to take care of myself and my family first and foremost so I instead went to counseling for years. I was slowly digging myself out of the hole I had dug. I was learning to play the game in the ballpark with some tough at bats but I had God by my side. I was learning to take a different path instead of trying to go through the rock. I feel that now I am at another turning point in my life. *Was I going to take the path all shiny and new or the path which had been stomped on by shoes? Would I be able to make the changes I needed to make?*

I spend so much time in my head thinking about how I feel or how other people feel. I can sense how someone feels before they even speak to me. I know if someone is scared, mad, or happy. For me, emotions affect everything I do. I reflect on different things I have learned along the way and the idea that I am an empath. "Think like your life depended on it." Emotions, including faith, are the one thing that Science can't take into consideration when looking at the results of some medical or educational experiments. For instance, medical science will conduct an experiment to show the results of some new promising drug for heart disease. They can track everything except the emotions of the person. The drug might work on some people, but it might also be about their thoughts. *Have they ever asked the person if they believe in God? Would this have an affect on the experiment?* Emotions are the one variable that you can't control in an experiment. The same thing is happening in education. The government wants "research based" programs to be used in schools. The research doesn't take into account that we are spiritual beings having a human experience. The spiritual part is what controls our emotions. No one program will ever work for everyone because we are all unique human beings, caught up in our own thoughts and emotions. *Did I think like this because I was an empath? Could I really feel others' emotions? Hadn't I guessed some of my students' thoughts when they were nervous or scared? How would we be able to design a research project about sensing the things we cannot see?*

"Eventually I learned to sense these fields, intuitively, without having to use my hands at all. To a psychic, a person's energy field is as real as the scent of her perfume, her smile, or the warm red color of her hair. This work had validated what I felt for a long time. There was more to human beings than their physical qualities, a palpable essence extended outward. Before I had no way to confirm what I sensed to be true. But, now another missing piece of the puzzle was falling into place."~ Dr. Judith Orloffe

Judith uses the words "psychic" and I think back to what my mother told me about "those" types of people. They are kind of, you know, crazy. *But what if I was one? What if I was one of the crazies my mother talked about all the time? Did being an empath make me a "psychic" and, if it did, what exactly did **that** mean? I most definitely was able to feel people's energy as Judith describes. Maybe I was taking on my mother's feelings. Was I just like her? Was I always worried what others might think of me? Was I worried about "keeping up my appearances"? What did I need to do differently? How would I take responsibility for myself instead of blaming her? Had I been so focused on her that I forgot to admit who I am? I struggled with being a public school teacher who also believed in God. My anxiety was my insecurity about myself and who I was. Especially admitting that I am an empath. Time to get honest with myself.*

Two years after my father's death, my younger son was continuing his search for a home to purchase. Most of the houses in the area were either too high priced or needed too much work. I was finishing my Master's work, finishing up my 27th year teaching and beginning a new job as Curriculum Director. I had a two week vacation before I would start working full time. In my new role, I would have to work all summer; something that was new to me after so many years of having the summer off. I was in the middle of an intense online law class for administrators, but knew that this two week window would be the only time I could help my son look for a home to purchase. We scheduled some showings with a friend of mine, Brenda- a Realtor whom I had worked for previously. We schedule three showings on Friday night, the first two houses are not even ones that I would want him to buy. When we go to the third house, it was perfect for him. The house itself was a mess, but we could see past that. *Of course, my fears appear. Is this too much for him? Is the land too wet? I sense my son's stress and wonder if this is what we should be doing. I reassure him that we are here to help him but I think this is a good fit for him.*

The contracts are drawn up and negotiations begin. Over the course of the next two months, we would go back and forth about details of the house, including the septic system, the deck railings and other such things. At times, we weren't sure if the deal would go through. Eventually, the closing was scheduled for August 31st. This would be about two years after my father's death and it happened to be the first day of school in my new district. This would be the first year that nobody would miss me on the first day of school!

On the morning of the closing, I stop by one of the schools during their opening day activities. Excitement in the air, marking a brand new school year. Goodbye to the summer days; hello to learning. I leave the school and begin the commute to my new office. As I fly out of town, around the corner, I realize that I am going a little too fast for this particular sharp corner. I'm in my head thinking of not being in a classroom this year. I'm also nervous about the closing today. I'm driving but I'm on automatic pilot, just like when I was driving to my father's camp the day his heart was breaking. The car behind me thinks that I am going too fast too. I realize it is a sheriff's car when I see his blue lights. I pull over. I was in my head driving; in another world. I fumble with my words, "I have no idea why you pulled me over.....Oh, I was speeding?" I had no idea what the speed limits were on my new commute. He was about to let me in on that secret. "Do you have something on your mind?" he asks. I nervously spit out- "I have a new job, it's the first day of school and my son is closing on his house today. My car is loaded and I have a lot to do." I know that a closing can have things go wrong, even at the last minute. As a realtor, it was always a concern that an attorney would find some legal problem and the deal wouldn't go through. I can't find my registration as he asks me if I have even been pulled over. "No," I respond, "except for once when I had a light out." He gave me a nice reminder to slow down because he would hate to have something happen to me or anyone else; explaining that even a small car like mine can do a lot of damage.

A warning, in more ways than one. A warning about the speed limit, but also a warning for me to get out of my head and back in the present moment. This is always a challenge for me. I'm either in the past or the future, and rarely enjoying the moment.

I needed to learn to enjoy the cup of tea, as Brian Weiss suggests. It's also a warning that life is short and I need to think about how I am living my life. *What daily choices are you making that will make your life the best life possible? Use that golden ticket.*

I have difficulty finding time to exercise. Well, I guess I have the time but I prioritize and don't put exercise first. I remember one time asking a student, whose father was a doctor, how his father had the time to run everyday. I knew that a doctor most likely would have long hours and would most definitely be tired when he got home. I did not expect this response. He said, "You find time to eat, don't you? Well, your body needs exercise and food so why not find time for both?" Although I had all of the tools about exercise, eating healthy, meditating, praying and so on, I hadn't been taking the time during the day to practice them on a regular basis. Until I do, I most likely won't see a change in my life. *How will I be able to do this? What will it take to "motivate me"? A voice whispers, "take your time. Start small." How will being in the moment help me heal? Will it help me enjoy life more?*

"I don't live in either my past or my future. I'm interested only in the present. If you can concentrate always on the present, you'll be a happy man. Life will be a party for you, a grand festival, because life is the moment we're living now." ~ Paul Coelho

During the walk through the house the evening prior to my son's closing, the place was a disaster. It was still being lived in (most of the time during a walk through, houses are empty) and it was filthy dirty. *What if they didn't clean it out in time for the closing tomorrow?* I was so worried about whether or not this was a good choice for my son. He, on the other hand, took a walk outside to the apple trees on the front lawn, picks up and bites into an apple. As he approaches, he says, "Everything looks good to me!" I know he is dreaming of the deer who might be eating those same apples later in the fall. Brenda laughs and tells me that she knows we are going to find a dime here somewhere. *Maybe, I think.*

The closing goes smoothly and we begin moving him in right after. The house is very dirty so I begin scrubbing down the kitchen. The reality that both of my children are now homeowners hits me as I clean. They worked hard and were living close by each other. I work on setting up the kitchen. After hours of scrubbing, I go to vacuum the bedroom, making sure the carpet is clean before they come back with the bed. The previous owners had a large breed dog and a cat. Pet hair is everywhere. I am vacuuming every edge and corner where the hair has been accumulating for years. I am inside the closet, on my hands and knees vacuuming when a dime is caught where the closet door is attached to the floor. With the light from the window shining in on the dime, I take a photo to post

My son, Patrick, and me on the day he moved in to his new house! (Before I found the dimes)

on Facebook. Brenda, our Realtor and friend, comments on my post, "I KNEW IT!" Soon after, I find a penny. This, I feel, was my Mom. Everyone would be focused on the dime. Some of my friends on Facebook had heard about the dime on the mountain and here was another dime!

The dime I found in the closet at Patrick's new house.

"He has made beautiful everything in his time. He has also set eternity the human heart; yet no one can fathom what God has done from beginning to end. " Ecclesisastes 3:11

Was this really another dime from my dad? To go with the rest of my collection? Did he need God's help arranging for me to find the dime? Was he sending a message to my son that he was here with him?

It's now the last day of our vacation in Florida. I stop writing to run on the beach. Grounding me and making sure that I don't float away; so caught up in my writing. I needed to take a break. I try to breathe in the smell of the ocean and absorb the sunshine. I search furiously on the ground for a dime. He must be here. I see many seashells about the same size as a dime, but no dimes. I'm afraid that I won't remember every single message that is coming to me now. I envision the caretaker pointing to his head, saying, "I'm trying to remember them in my brain." I worry that if I do decide to make this into a book, the signs won't be seen as fitting into the dime story. I think they do. The dime story is so much more than the dimes sent from Heaven.

My husband arrives and, noticing I am almost out of pages in my journal, asks if I am almost done. I shake my head no. Then he says, "Well, I guess you'll know when you are done." The waves roll in, the seagulls squawk and people continue up and down the beach.

"So we fix our eyes not on what is seen, but on what is unseen. For what is seen is temporary, but what is unseen is eternal." ~2Corinthians 4:18

I think back to the conversation with a stranger on the beach. I had shared with him that I was stepping out of my comfort zone to write a book. He will be a part of the book. He shares with me that he was saying a prayer on his walk and decided to stop and talk to me. He tells me he is no minister, just a man living the life Jesus speaks of in the gospel of John. He says, "I'm not sure what religion you believe in, but my guiding religion is the Roman Catholic Church." I laugh and share that I converted to be a Catholic because my husband's family was Catholic. I tell him that my father told me that, "We are all talking to the same guy." We finish up chatting and he blesses me. Even though he wasn't a minister, he reminds me of the time on the mountain when my father "phoned" me. No, the dime story is not finished. The dimes will never be done as this story will be passed on and on. When people find a dime, they will know that someone from Heaven is with them.

"Allow me to change your doubts into questions." ~William Sloane Coffin

Writing the dime story was a process to accepting myself. It will help me heal. I continue to feel the need to write my story; asking for answers. Answers are given; whenever I listen and when the timing is decided by the universe to be perfect. Messages from angels can be almost anything. *While in the pool, a woman says, "Hey Ty!" in the same southern drawl that sounds like my sister-in-law calling to her son Tyler. But, Tyler isn't really here, or is he? I check the time. 5:55. Oh yeah- that is when angels are around my son, Patrick.*

"Each of us has a destiny, and there is absolutely no excuse not to fulfill it. We cannot use our weakness as an excuse because God says that His strength is made perfect in weakness." 2 Corinthians 12:9

"We cannot use the past as an excuse because God tells us through the apostle Paul that if any person is in Christ, he is a new creature; old things have passed away, and all things have become new." ~2 Corinthians 5:17

Could this really be true? Would God's strength help me continue to write this book, be healed and learn to live life a different way? Was I going to lead in a different way than what I imagined when I had received my Master's degree in education to become an administrator?

"Yes," my angels respond.

"Stop your inner critic dead in her tracks and tell the lies to get lost because you are enough." ~Robert Jones

I work so hard the first day cleaning my son's new home that I am physically exhausted. We leave our son alone the next day to settle in and enjoy his new home without Mom and Dad around. The next day, my husband and I go to help him with a few things around the house. My son and husband go to the roof to work on the chimney and I begin to clean the nasty carpet in the spare bedroom. I know my son didn't really understand how dirty it really was.

As I clean, I continue to worry. *Was buying this house too much for my son? Did I guide him in the right direction? Will he be able to afford it? Would my father have approved of the purchase of the house? Would my father have liked it here?*

God Grant me the Serenity

To accept the things I cannot change

Courage to change the things I can

And the wisdom to know the difference.

~Reinhold Niebuhr (1892-1971)

We had made the decision to purchase the house and we were blessed with resources to help him if he needed more support. He would be ok. This was the perfect spot for him. *The positive voice inside me trying to convince me. If only I would listen...instead of feeling anxiety and worry within my entire body.*

Again, making sure to get every edge of the carpet, I am almost finished vacuuming when I notice I didn't really get around the spot where the cable cords come up through the wood flooring. I go back to the spot and notice a coin. I think it is a nickel. It is tucked down in the hole in the floor, next to the cords. I pull away the vacuum; afraid that I might vacuum it up. *I'm not sure I can get it. It is really jammed down in there. A nickel, my mind thinks. Not really too important if I can't get it.* **I could just leave it there.**

Finally, it comes out and I hold it up to look at it. This is not a nickel. This is a dime, but not like the dime I found the other day in the closet. This dime is a very **particular** dime.

This dime is the **same dime that was in my father's collection. A Liberty Head dime.** Instead of having Franklin D. Roosevelt's profile, this type of dime has the Liberty wearing a winged cap, symbolizing **"freedom of thoughts."**

This is the very exact type of dime that my father had made into necklaces for all of his family. The year on the dime was 1936, one year later than my father's birth year. I run out to my son and husband who are on the roof. I holler up to them, **"I found a LIBERTY HEAD DIME! You know- the kind that was in my dad's collection. It's exactly like the one in our necklaces. You cannot call me crazy anymore!! This is proof- for sure!"** They look down at me from on top of the roof. *They have to believe now, I think. My Father gave me the biggest **'God Wink'** if I ever did see one!*

I think, just as Neale Donald Walsch does in his story about his NDE when he said,

"Am I being played here? Is somebody kidding me?" Then the other voice inside him speaks, 'That is not necessary. Your truth will never be forgotten. It can be neither proven or disproven. It simply is.....Nothing matters.'"

I wonder, does it matter if anyone believes my story? Does it matter if I share it? Will people believe that my father was using the 'Spirit Connection System' I had explained to him? Had he placed a physical object yet again for me to discover?

Was my father helping God give me the signs I needed at the right time? Was my Dad helping God control "the knobs" he wondered about when he was here on earth? Did all of my angels in Heaven who I envisioned as cheerleaders help show signs to me? Did everyone have people in Heaven helping us navigate life's journey? Showing everyone, or at least those who want to believe, that there is something bigger than us?

"We are not thinking machines that feel, rather we are feeling machines that think." ~Antonio Damasio

These are the three coins I found
while cleaning Patrick's new house.

My son and husband look down at me as I scream at them. *What should I do with this dime?* I take a picture and post a picture of the dime on Facebook. One of the first comments was, *"Seriously?"* Yeah, I think. **Seriously. This is serious. This is a sign like no other sign.** *Nobody can argue this sign, I think. Nobody understands the conversations I had with my father. This story is so much more than dimes. It is a story like no other.*

My son was the best man for his older brother's wedding this year. His speech made me laugh and cry. The one paragraph that meant the most to me was the following:

"This summer my brother and I were riding around some back roads, talking about our lives, and he said something I will always remember. He said, 'Just be yourself. Don't ever try to be anything but yourself.' Shamus has lived his entire life by those words. For anybody who knows him well, they know he is a goofy, good hearted, out going guy. And I respect him for that, because he is always himself." ~Patrick Morrissey 8/18/18

I am ready to take my sons' advice. I mean, I am who I am, right?

Epilogue More Than a Dime

"It's all fine and good to imagine what life would be like somewhere else. It takes some courage to leave and go somewhere new. To head out to the great unknown. But what happens if upon taking the first step, something goes wrong? Maybe it was a bad idea to leave in the first place? Maybe it's best to turn back and stay put? After all, the devil you know is better than the devil you don't. Or, maybe if you have the right people with you, they will give you the courage to keep going." ~Simon Sinek

One might ask~ Is this the end of the dime story? The title of the dime story is More Than a Dime because the story is about so much more than the dime. For me, the dime was the key to me believing everything that I had learned and experienced over the years. It was also a sign to keep learning more about myself. When I shared my dime story with people, they were always touched, most of the time people got goosebumps. *What was this all about? When I began to write, I realized that this story is so much more than dimes.*

The people who I shared my dime story with encouraged me to keep writing and are my tribe. They are the ones who love me just as I am. They help me believe in myself and know that the risk is worth it. Once I decided that my story was "More Than a Dime", I couldn't turn back no matter how much anxiety or fear I had. I knew that it would be worth it.

I listened to **Jason Gray's song "I Will Rise Again"**. It helped give me the courage to continue writing.

Just like new life in the spring starts again after a cold winter, I was ready to start a fresh new season of life. I will rise again each day, navigating life, wherever it brings me. *Thy Will be done.*

Dad's funeral

Here is what I read at my Father's funeral:

August 29, 2015

Jim Palmer to most of you. Dad to us four kids. Grandpa to all of his grandchildren. There are so many things to talk about when I think of our Dad. His kindness, his sense of giving to others, his love for our Mother, his love for his kids and his grandkids, his love of his church family, his faith in doing the right thing, his hard work, his sense of pride, his humor, his knowledge of how things work, his curiosity, his interest in getting to know other people, the way his face would light up when visitors came.

I was able to get to know my Dad over the last few months more than I ever knew him in my entire life. I always knew our Dad was special, but I really learned it this year. We all got to hear the story about when he asked Mom to marry him, it was going to either be her or the Volkswagon car. He couldn't afford both, but would take her if she was interested. Well, luckily she was interested!

I can't really explain my Dad's sense of humor. He would tell a story and it would be so funny. Then, I would try to retell it and it just didn't work. I think it had something to do with the twinkle in his eye and the smirk on his face. It was also the way he worded it, it always came out so that we would all laugh. Even though he missed Mom every day, he learned to enjoy having all of us around. We got to hear stories we had never heard before. I think my two sons will always remember the "boy scout juice"- as he told them how to light a fire in the furnace. He said, And then it goes "boom". Well, probably they don't want you doing that these days. Or how about hide the thimble with the Grandkids. They were looking and looking and Grandpa says, "I ate it!"

Dad learned early on he probably shouldn't speak in inappropriate language. One time while working on a car, he was not speaking in very good language, he came around the corner to find the minister there. Another time, while playing over a bank near his house, his Mother came out and said, "You know I can hear very clearly everything you are saying." Whoops!...

Dad loved each and every one of his kids and Grandkids. Each of you held a special place in his heart. Even though his heart attack kept him from working at the garage, it was actually sort of a blessing. It meant that he was home and ready to babysit any Grandkid that needed a place to be. He was ready to pick up kids after school at any-time. He was ready to go play outside with them. ....I get asked a lot what my two sons are doing. When I tell them that Shamus is an Auto-Tech, I also say that I might have been a carrier of the Auto gene, but I never was able to use it in my life. It went straight to Shamus. When I think of Patrick, he is very similar to Dad when he is curious as to how things work. Dad was always about problem solving....

To us he was Dad, but to many of you, he was Jim Palmer, owner of the business Palmer's Inc. He loved all of his customers over the years, his many employees and enjoyed getting to know business associates from all over...There are so many memo-ries from Palmer's Inc. that it is difficult to put into words. We all grew up playing in the tires, watching Dad work his magic on cars, and helping whenever we could. Pumping gas was always a part of our teenage years and this is where we all began to meet the many customers who loved to go to Palmers.

I cannot express our thanks enough to Merrilee Perrine and all of the caregivers from Love Is. They all made this past year the best that it could be. He enjoyed getting to know each and every one of his caregivers. You all helped him through the difficulty of losing his wife. He had a whole new set of friends that he could share his life with. He always felt so proud to introduce his new friends to people stopping by to visit. I know his favorite was Merrilee- oh how he picked on her! He was so excited when she started to cook for him. Well, one day she made some cookies and when she brought them out, he was surprised by the size of the cookie. He said, "Well, now THAT is a cookie. I guess I won't need two or three. One will be just fine." If only you could have seen the expression in his eyes to go along with his words- that is what made us love him. A big thank you to everyone who helped this past year to make it so Dad could stay home. It was definitely a team effort with all of us kids, grandkids, cousins, relatives, friends, home health, Love Is and the doctors who still made house calls. Marisa and Alden visiting every week to help him was so appreciated. This helped him so much. Uncle David and Aunt Jean visiting for coffee every week. These visits helped him feel closer to Mom. With everyone working together, Dad had a great 8 months. People always told Dad how lucky he was to have everyone here to help him. I'm sure all the caregivers, friends and family can agree that we were the lucky ones.

Dad's church family was so important to him. His Mother was the person who taught him about Faith and then it trickled down to all of us. Church was always a big part of all of our lives and it sure has helped us get through the rough spots. We thank him for teaching us about his faith and we thank all of the people in the church whom he cared so much for...The joy on his face that day was priceless, talking with his church family. He especially enjoyed Ray's weekly visits. He could always count on Ray coming by to visit him. He loved that Ray felt like family.

This past year Dad learned a lot about technology. He was a regular check in on Facebook, learned the fastest way to get anything you wanted was through Amazon Prime, Facetimed with Monica on the beach in Florida, Facetimed with Melissa and Ray at their wedding, watched UVM basketball games on his iPad. Now his connection with us is through all kinds of signs. The Spirit Communication system is working for him now. We all know he is around us.

It was great to have Dad at camp this summer. We all learned to take the time to be with you because we didn't know how long you would be with us. Our hearts are now empty but it is filled with great memories... Camp has always had so many memories that we will keep with us. Deb learning to ski with one ski before you- sorry but you were dropping the wrong ski. Me- first time on one ski and I tried to splash Brian but ended up crashing into the dock. The many hours all of us begged to go skiing. The Sunday breakfast. Nothing better than a 100 or so people and scrambled eggs and bacon over an open fire. Elmore will forever be a part of all of us and all of the many families we were connected with. There are just too many families to mention here but so many people have shared their memories of good times with our family. You all know who you are. We are all thinking of you when we remember our Mom and Dad and how much they loved all of you. Especially Eldon, who now has lost his best friend, who was more like a brother. We are thinking of you today.

While taking care of my Dad, we all experienced his way of thinking. His biggest question was always, "How is this going to work?" This question was used all the time, when he was trying to figure out how his care was going to happen to getting showers from the Home Health nurses, to how he was going to live at camp full time. His mind thought like a mechanic his entire life. It was the way he was wired. He thought maybe another surgery on his heart might keep that engine going just like an oil change or a new transmission on a car. If they could just keep working on it, it would run forever. That is the goal of every mechanic. Keep that car running. I know your car is still running, just this time you are in spirit form and now your engine will run forever. Thanks for being there for me at the top of the mountain yesterday.

Part 2 Who am I and why am I like this?

"Life is not primarily a quest for pleasure, as Freud believed, or a quest for power, as Alfred Adler taught, but a quest for meaning. The greatest task for any person is to find meaning in his or her life." ~Victor E. Frankl

Most of the dime story was written while on vacation in Indian Shores, Florida. My husband and I vacation there in April to get away from the long winters in Vermont. This year I was in a lot of pain and the doctors couldn't figure out what was causing my pain. I hadn't slept for longer than 1 to 2 hours at a time for many months. I decided that I needed to try to figure out how to solve my medical problems. I understood that emotions cause physical problems in our bodies from years of reading books like Louise Hay's, You Can Heal Your Life and The secret language of your body: The essential guide to health & wellness. Normally when I go on vacation, I read books. This time, I would begin to write my "dime story". During the process of writing the dime story, I realized that it was so much more than a dime. The dimes were a powerful message to me from Heaven. Heaven was trying to get my attention so that I would have a deeper understanding. Through writing this book and consulting with five different doctors, I am finally on the road to recovery. My pain could not be healed with medicine alone. I had to do the emotional work and alternative healing too. *I had to learn to accept and love myself, especially the fact that I am an empath. Discovering I am an empath, changed my perspective and my writing.*

I never understood writing and how it might help me. I didn't understand people who said things like, "the words seem to come from somewhere else." When I started to write, I experienced this for the first time in my life. When I let go of the beliefs instilled in me since childhood, I was able to connect with my soul. When I did this, it opened up a whole new world for me. It was like the universe heard my thoughts and knew I was ready.

While writing, my crown chakra was so open I had to work at grounding myself. There are seven energy systems in our bodies, starting with the base of our spine to the top of our head. They are all associated with different colors and meanings. Here is a list: 1. Root chakra (red), base of spine 2. Sacral chakra (orange), just above the base of your spine 3. Solar plexis(yellow), the stomach area 4. Heart chakra(green), over the heart 5. Throat chakra (blue), throat area 6. Third eye chakra (dark purple), a little above the eyes, in the middle of your forehead 7. Crown chakra (light purple). My favorite color is purple and it is because when my crown chakra is open I feel connected to my intuition and the spirit world. When I am in this place, I feel absolutely wonderful and pain free, but I have to ground myself. Grounding is about connecting me back to earth. The best ways to ground myself are meditation, swimming or being in nature.

"As you journey to your destiny, you will occasionally find yourself at a crossroads in your career- a new path will suddenly appear, taking you into a whole new direction...Regardless of the circumstances, one thing is certain- you will feel uncertain." ~ SQuire Rushnell

Turning 50 affected me in a way I was not really prepared for. It wasn't a typical "mid-life" crisis. I didn't want to go buy a convertible. It was a reflection of where I have been so far in this life and what I want to do next. As I was reflecting on my life, I thought of my own children. My husband and I now have the "empty nest". I enjoy the freedom and have more time on my hands. My children don't need me as much. I had no plans whatsoever to become a writer. It wasn't even on my radar. I thought writing was for "other people". Once I decided to turn this story into a book, I knew I was on the right path..

"In fact, I believe an awareness of our diminished time on this planet offers the advantage of urgency." ~Joni B. Cole

Had I taught my own kids enough about life? Had I shared with them my stories and my beliefs? Had I let them make their own choices in life to learn their lessons?- which surely would be different than my lessons. What had I learned from them? What would they do when I was gone? Would they make some of the same mistakes I had made? Would me sharing what I had learned about life help them navigate their lives better? What was I going to do with all of the free time I had? I had always worked and enjoyed being a Mom. I didn't like to sit around and do nothing. I wasn't that type of person!

Losing both of my parents within eight months of each other, I realized I had raised my own children very differently than the way I was raised. I had tried to give them the support they needed to navigate life in a different way. I had taught them about God, faith and gratitude. I showed them that I not only cared about them, but I loved them unconditionally, very similar to how God loves them. No matter what happened or the choices they made, I would always love them. I might not always like the decisions they made, but that would never change my love for them. I taught them to love others and be kind. *It was important to me!*

I am an empath or a highly sensitive person (HSP)- whatever you want to call it. All my life I had just wanted to be "normal". Knowing and understanding what it means to be an empath helped me learn to accept myself. This meant accepting that I needed to take care of myself and that this did not define me. In education we talk about students who have Autism, but we don't say Autistic students. Autism does not define who they are. The same is true for an empath. I am a person who is an empath, not an empathic person. This has two very different meanings. An empathic person can feel what the other person is feeling because they have felt the same thing in their life. For instance, someone who has lost both of their parents can understand and feel empathy for me because I lost both of my parents. An empath is a person with an intuitive ability to know the mental or emotional state of another individual. Some dictionaries mention it to be "paranormal" ability instead of intuitive ability. *My worst fear coming true- being different and not normal!* I choose to define it as an intuitive knowing, rather than something weird out of a Sci-fi movie.

When I started reading about empaths and highly sensitive people, I remember thinking, "Oh my! There are other people in the world who are like me!" My nervous system is built differently and I have the ability to take on other people's emotions. After learning about empaths, I didn't feel like such a freak anymore. There are other parts of my life that are affected. I have food sensitivities, sleep, addiction, and anxiety issues to share a few. Awareness and knowledge is important. I wasn't aware that I was an empath so I was confused most of my life. I hope by sharing my story it will bring awareness to our world, especially in education. I want people to understand what it is like to be an empath. Teachers and parents need to understand that a child's emotions are critical to the learning process. It is difficult to learn if a child doesn't feel like he or she belongs.

This next section of the book is about my healing journey. Writing my dime story helped me become aware that I was an empath. *What did this mean? Did being an empath affect my entire life story? How would I need to change my life in order to stay healthy? By doing so, would I then be able to accept myself and heal my heart so that I would be able to avoid heart disease? How can I learn to change my internal dialogue?* Chapter by chapter, I will share how coins and coincidences help me find healing and peace.

Chapter 1 My Young Self

"We are programmed to attend to, store, and recall negative information over positive information, so much so that, according to one famous finding in the realm of relationship psychology, it takes at least five positive interactions to make up for just one negative one." ~Joni B. Cole

When I originally wrote chapter one of this book, it didn't look like the chapter you read. I spent a lot of time blaming and being angry at my mother. It was easier for me to remember the negative than the positive parts of my childhood. I don't want to seem ungrateful for my childhood because I know there were a lot of things I was grateful for. When I went to rewrite the first chapter, I had a lot of knowledge about what being an empath meant for me. I realized that the reason I didn't fit in to my family was because I was extremely sensitive and an empath. This made childhood more challenging for me, even when to others it seemed like I had a great family. By looking from the inside, instead of focusing on the outside, I was able to see how accepting myself was one the most important parts of my soul's journey.

In 1996 I had back surgery to remove a herniated disc at my SI/L5 joint, at the base of my spine. Although the pain I was having while writing this book was different, it was in the same general area. I was having bladder issues and was beginning to go through menopause. Not exactly something I am excited about sharing in a book with the world- but here I am! Louise Hay says that emotions cause us "dis-ease." If you look up the emotional message that is connected to sciatica pain, you will find things like, "...weren't able to express our true feelings or fears, we don't feel safe or secure." (retrieved from https://ravenstarshealingroom.wordpress.com/2017/03/26/the-metaphysics-of-sciatic-and-peripheral-pain/) It goes on to say that because of this, a person might become shy or reclusive. That was me! As a child, I was scared to share my feelings and became the quiet kid. I was lost among the crowds and wasn't sure of myself.

As an empath, I physically absorb emotions of the people around me. Imagine I am sitting outside in the sunshine. I can feel the warmth of the sunshine in my entire body. Now, imagine that sunshine being another person's energy. The person is sitting next to me and I absorb their positive feelings and it feels just as good as the sunshine on my face. This was like the Up with People concert! I actually feel good inside because the person near me is happy and is showing me love. I feel it physically and emotionally, just like the sun makes my body feel warm inside. Now, change the scene to sitting outside in the snow. It's cold and my body temperature starts to go down. I want to get warm, but I can't. This is what it feels like to sit next to a person who has negative energy. I feel it on the inside of my body, physically, as if the emotions were my own. Without the necessary skills needed to understand and separate from those feelings, the person's energy affects me just like they were my own feelings.

I have difficulty with my own feelings because of how I was raised. We didn't talk about feelings and I stuffed them all inside. But now enter all the feelings of all of the people around me every day. I can't always distinguish between what are my feelings or the person's emotions next to me. And all of these feelings get stuck inside my body and can make my body ill. This is what it is like to be an empath. I never knew this about myself and I never had the words to understand what was happening. Brene Brown says that the emotion that is most contagious is anxiety. I was "catching" that a lot these days. Once I was aware, I would start to distinguish what were my emotions and what emotions belonged to others. I am slowly learning how to stop absorbing feelings and emotions from everyone else. I separate myself and try not to let any negative energy from others inside my body. Of course, the people with sunshine always feel great but I had to learn to leave the ice cubes alone!

"We actually feel others' emotions, energy, and physical symptoms in our own bodies, without the usual defenses that most people have" ~Dr. Judith Orloff

I'll give you an example that happened to me recently. I was at a meeting with about fifteen people. The presenters were sharing their work and then asked us to turn and talk to our neighbor. During the presentation, I seriously wanted to fall asleep. It wasn't because I was bored or hungry or hadn't slept well the night before. I had no idea what was happening. I thought I might have to get up and take a walk just to stay awake. The presenters asked us to turn and talk to the person next to us. I turned to the person next to me and we began chatting. She was pretty upset about the presentation and thought it was a waste of everyone's time. I immediately recognized that my "sleepiness" was me absorbing her negative energy. I quickly used one of my new strategies to block the negative energy and then I was wide awake!

I can't watch scary movies, which includes the news. If I'm not careful, I will absorb all the negativity from the TV, newspaper or radio. Today's media is so divided, especially on governmental issues, and I don't know what is the truth anymore. I simply cannot partake in the conversations. Being a Libra, I want balance and in today's media there seems to be no common ground. It physically makes me ill. While healing and writing, I shut my TV off more and more. I discovered I was much happier this way. If we think about how life used to be about one hundred years ago(or more!), our human systems were not built to take in so much information, especially negative information.

I'll use another example to try to explain how an empath is affected by having a different nervous system. I watch The Big Bang Theory on CBS. There are so many times in my life where I wish I could be like Sheldon- who does not seem to care how other people feel. But that isn't how I am built. It's almost like I am the exact opposite of Sheldon when it comes to my feelings inside. I worry about how people feel all the time and I intuitively sense other people's feelings- whether I want to or not. It isn't a choice. Information about feelings come through as an energy from others. It makes it so I am in my head worrying about how they feel instead of being in the present moment. For instance, someone might say something like, "I'm not sure about this idea." I receive all sorts of feelings with the message like, "I'm actually really angry". It's like my intuition is talking to me adding information to what the person is saying. This can be a dangerous place to be in because I might be wrong if I don't check in with that person about how they are feeling. I might "read" their emotions incorrectly and then it might cause unnecessary problems. I have learned to check in with people and not take on any emotions that aren't mine.

Sheldon and I are similar in the way that our senses can get overloaded. Too many lights, smells, and sounds can most definitely overstimulate me. I hear people talk all the time about going to concerts to see different bands or singers. For me, that is a nightmare. Not only the crowds, but the noise, sounds, smells, and lights overstimulate my sensitive body. That is not my idea of fun at all. How would I rather spend my time? *On a beach or camping in the woods.* That is my idea of a great vacation! The biggest difference between the two vacations? People and nature.

I don't want to be around so many people that I become exhausted. Being outside in nature always recharges me. Most likely when I was young, playing outside helped my nervous system stay regulated.

Another thing that I learned was that empaths try to protect themselves with fat. It is like the weight I gain acts as a buffer to protect my body from absorbing another person's feelings. Once I learned the strategies to protect myself, I no longer needed the weight to protect myself. If you want to learn more, check out Judith Orloff's book The Empath's Survival Guide.

Don Miquel Ruiz wrote a book called The Four Agreements. The Four Agreements are the following: "1. Be impeccable with your word. 2. Don't take anything personally. **3. Don't make assumptions** and 4. Do your best." I find it important to note these agreements here because I want to make clear that as an empath I am never one hundred percent certain that my intuitive feelings coming from others are true or not. I never assume they are without verification from the other person. Learning about the Four Agreements changed my life, especially in my job as an educator. By not taking things personally and not assuming things, my relationships with parents, students, colleagues and friends have most definitely improved. I try to understand other people's point of view without absorbing their feelings or feeling defensive.

When learning about what it is like to be an empath, I learned about what some people call "narcissists" or "energy vampires". I'm not talking about the vampires in the movies, but people who have no sense of empathy. They don't have the capability to understand what it is like to be an empath. I have met many energy suckers in my life and am thankful that I was able to learn from them. At times, I tried to help some of them but realized that I had to let them have their own journey. They are not mine to fix. If I'm not careful about the people I am around and I happen upon an "energy sucker", they can drain my energy and I am left feeling awful. I had to learn to protect myself from some of these people.

"Happiness is the choice I make today. It does not rest on my circumstances, but on my frame of mind...In cultivating the habits of happiness, I attract the people and situations that match its frequency. I smile more often, give praise more often, give thanks more often and am glad more often. For such is my choice today." ~Marianne Williamson

I think back to my young self. We didn't have Facebook and I never heard uplifting phrases like this one. The negative self talk had been overpowering my entire life, and I hadn't realized it.

Shortly after my trip to Florida, I discovered Judith Orloff Md. She was key to discovering myself as an empath or a highly sensitive person. Through reading her memoir, I found a lot of similarities in my own life. Dr. Elaine Aron was another doctor who had a lot of research and information about HSP's. According to Dr. Aron's research,

"If you find you are highly sensitive, or your child is, I'd like you to know the following: Your trait is normal. It is found in 15 to 20% of the population–too many to be a disorder, but not enough to be well understood by the majority of those around you." (retrieved from https://hsperson.com/**)**

Dr. Aron used much of Carl Jung's research to help her with her interest in highly sensitive people. As an educator and a parent, I notice more and more children who seem to be highly sensitive. Each generation changes and we are talking more and more about feelings and emotions. Compared to my childhood, the conversation has changed from "suck it up buttercup" to "what's happening and how can we help?" Of course, there always needs to be a balance and not swing too far in one direction. Acceptance and understanding are the two things that helped me the most.

In Chapter one, I described things like: overly sensitive, liked to be outdoors, felt different than everyone else, and sensitivity to medicine or alcohol. All of these I discovered were true for empaths. Another clue was my sleeping issues. I had to learn to accept myself as an empath and figure out the gifts and the struggles. I had to understand that most people won't understand because they aren't born this way. *"I mean I am who I am, right?" I couldn't change who I was, even if I wanted to. And, there was no possible way for my parents to understand my needs when they were raising me. I knew they understood now. I could feel it. My parents were good people. They tried the best that they could!*

"I feel it is so important not to have judgment and fear towards myself. When my inner dialogue is telling me I'm safe, unconditionally loved, and accepted, then I radiate energy outward and change my outside world accordingly. My outer life is actually only a reflection of my inner state." ~Anita Moorjani

"Intuition was a gift I had to grow into." ~Dr. Judith Orloff

I remember the first time I heard that I should embrace my gift of being an empath. This was extremely difficult for me. Every day seemed like so much work. I had to learn not to take on other people's energy. I had to learn to meditate after working all day. I had to remember to exercise and get proper nutrition. It was exhausting. *But was it worth it? I had to believe it was. It was part of my healing.*

I am so thankful for people like Judith Orloff, Anita Moorjani and John Holland who shared their struggles with accepting their intuition and gifts. As I tried to learn and accept my intuitive abilities, words like 'psychic' took on new meanings. I wasn't a crazy gypsy lady.

"The well balanced intuitive doesn't wear long white robes or carry a crystal ball. She doesn't grab your palm in the middle of the supermarket and insist on giving you a reading. Nor does she blurt out unsolicited information. She's an ordinary person; the most remarkable thing about her is that she appears un-remarkable. Her power is internalized, integrated. She doesn't have to flaunt it. As she uses her gift discerningly, radiating an understated sense of calm, we see

before us someone with no need to glorify herself, someone who is profoundly simple." ~Dr. Judith Orloff

"She turned her can't into cans and her dreams into plans." ~Kobi Yamada

The more that I wrote, the more that I felt like a door to a secret vault inside me opened up. I wanted to share my story with others in the hope that what I had learned might help others. Through writing and reflecting, I was able to discover who I was and accept myself. Most people won't understand what it is like to be me. (about 80% in fact!) *Do you see any similarities in my story? Might you know an empath or a highly sensitive person? If you are an educator or a parent, do you identify with me or do your kids have similar traits? How would you help an empath?* It is especially important to nurture children who are highly sensitive or empaths. Looking back over the years, I most definitely had some students who have this gift.

"Security is mostly a superstition. It does not exist in nature...Life is either a daring adventure or nothing." ~Helen Keller

Helen's words help me share what it is like to be an empath.

How did I know I was an empath? Every single questionnaire I answered came out 100% yes. Questions like Do you have difficulty sleeping? Do you sense how others are feeling? Do you get exhausted when there are a lot of people around? Are you sensitive to loud noises? Are you sensitive to certain foods? Are you sensitive to prescription medication? Do you eat to cover up your feelings? **Every single question from every author I read, I scored 100%.** Normally in school, I always liked 100%. This time felt different. I knew that my awareness was only the first step to acceptance. If you want to look at a quick reference (without reading a whole book)- check out this website: https://exemplore.com/paranormal/What-is-an-Empath-Traits-signs-solutions Remember that I can relate to every single thing on this list.

According to some people, there are different types of Empaths. Vik Carter mentions six different types in his book *EMPATH 16 Simple Habits* to protect yourself, feel better and enjoy life even if you are highly sensitive. He identifies the following types of empaths: emotional, physical, intuitive, geomantic, plant and animal.

"Empaths are likely to have varying paranormal experiences throughout their lives as well, including near-death experiences (NDEs) and out-of-body experiences (OBEs)." ~Rebecca. Retrieved from https://exemplore.com/paranormal/What-is-an-Empath-Traits-signs-solutions

I shared a few of my out-of-body experiences in my dime story. (trust me- I have more!) I was always scared to talk about them with people. When I started talking about these experiences, I found a lot of other people had them too. I think back to my younger self and wish I had been able to talk with someone about these times. Hopefully, my book will begin to open up this conversation and people won't be afraid to talk about these types of experiences.

There are things I love about being an empath and things that I hate about it. I love being able to listen and follow my intuition. I know and understand we are souls having a human experience. As a teacher and a Mom, I have been able to use my intuition to help students and my own children. The challenges are learning how to care for my body out of necessity. I don't have a choice if I want to feel good. I will share some of the things that work for me, but every empath/HSP has to discover their own strategies.

About ten years ago, I learned about self regulation. I had some students in my class who needed help organizing their bodies to be ready for learning. I learned that, "A child with self -regulatory skills is able to focus his attention, control his emotions and manage his thinking, behavior and feelings." retrieved from https://day2dayparenting.com/help-child-learn-self-regulation/ When I looked back at my childhood, I realized that I had self regulated myself by playing outside, and especially swimming all summer. Empaths love the water and I was blessed with living on the lake all summer long. As an adult I read the book, <u>Last Child in the Woods</u> and was forever changed. Everyone needs time in nature. There is something about the energy of the woods and earth that helps our nervous systems. We were not meant to live inside all the time and/ or spend so much time on electronics. Without exercise and nature, our bodies are not regulated to work properly. That's why hiking helps me so much. Unfortunately, I live in a climate where it isn't always nice outside and sometimes I don't go outside enough. As an educator, I find that some kids aren't outside enough and this may be why kids are struggling in school. It seems like kids today don't have a way to regulate their bodies. Because I grew up outside, I think I was able to learn better in school. As an adult I think I tried to regulate my body with food. If I was feeling tired, I might reach for coffee or a sugary treat to help me focus. Eventually, those were too much for my sensitive system. I had to learn to regulate my body in a different way.

"When you are connected to the Divine part of yourself, you are aligned with the power of pure positive energy. And that pure positive energy creates a magnetic field that draws in more pure positive energy." ~Dr. Christian Northrup

When I use the word God, I am referring to a positive life energy force coming from an all encompassing Spirit. Like the wind, we can't see it, but we can feel it. This connection with my subconscious mind is part of my regulation. By connecting with this part of me, I am better able to regulate my fight or flight mechanism of my nervous system.

I talk a lot about the two voices inside my head. One voice comes from my subconscious, a direct connection to God/Spirit and the other voice seems to come from my consciousness or ego, a direct connection to the way my brain is wired. I have heard many people say that ego stands for "edge God out". Ego is what I use to rationalize life. I take information into my brain, synthesize it and then create stories in my head based on what I have told myself to be true.

"The ego is responsible for our personal will- the part of us that must be developed enough to get up every morning and go to school and do homework

or get up off the chair and exercise. Without personal will, absolutely nothing of value ever gets accomplished." ~Dr. Christian Northrup

My conscious mind is very different than my subconscious mind. Here is a perfect example of how my brain (ego) thinks differently than my soul (divine guidance).

Over the years I have experimented with Angel Cards. While writing this book, I found in one of my journals a reading from the card deck, Life Purpose Oracle Cards by Doreen Virtue.

My question was, "**Why am I here?**"

There are many ways to choose which cards are meant to answer the question I ask to the universe. I choose these cards by using a pendulum. I first spread out the cards and then hold the pendulum over each card, one at a time. When the pendulum begins swinging, I choose that card. Clockwise means yes and counterclockwise means no. If it doesn't swing, then it means no also. I usually do a past, present and future card to answer the question I asked.

Here are the answers I received. At the time they made absolutely no sense to me. Now, they have a much deeper meaning.

Past- "Creative Expression- Your soul longs to express itself creatively."

Present- "Builder- Your innate ability to build and create brings you a deep sense of accomplishment."

Future- "Spiritual Teacher- You heal with your classes, sessions and seminars."

I remember the reading and thought that I was not a creative person because I couldn't draw. This was my conscious brain talking- creating something based on past experience and knowledge. I believed ceativity was for art class and I most definitely was not an artist! *I understand now that my subconscious was speaking to me that I was creative in a very different way. I am most definitely feeling a deep sense of accomplishment as I write and have no idea how this book will change my life. I look forward to the unknown instead of trying to plan every detail. Just like the unpredictability in my job as a real estate agent, I know the universe is working to guide me in a whole new direction. I wonder what the classes, sessions and seminars will be? Because of the dimes from Heaven and this book, I have faith that Divine guidance will help my soul express itself and my brain will not get in the way. I believe that "positives outweigh the negatives."*

"When you choose thoughts that are aligned with your true nature instead of based in fear, you are always going with the most empowering options." ~Dr. Christian Northrup

An example from chapter one was my need to blame someone for what I thought was a tough childhood. That's my ego and my brain talking. My soul is more in tune with my heart and this book came from my heart. Once I looked at my childhood from my soul's perspective, I realized that I hadn't accepted myself.

Last year I watched the movie Resilience, which brought to life the research around the ACE study. ACE stands for Adverse Childhood Experiences. The research showed ten categories of experiences that affect the health of a person. In many cases the higher the score, the shorter life span for the person. Doctors were beginning to speak out about how our emotions and feelings affect our physical bodies. As an educator, I am ready to begin this discussion and how it impacts our schools. I want to bring this to light and change the educational frontier to address this need.

"When you surrender to what is and so become fully present, the past ceases to have any power. You do not need it anymore. Presence is the key. The Now is the key."~ Eckhart Tolle

Being a highly sensitive person comes with both gifts and challenges. I have to take care of my body or "machine" in different ways in order to keep my nervous system and my internal dialogue in good working order. I learned through trial and error what worked for me. I learned that being an empath helped connect me to God in a way that I always knew was possible. Through accepting myself as an empath, I began to get in touch with this part of myself. This part had been buried for a lot of years. By writing this book, I am beginning to accept myself and share my story.

Chapter 2 Meeting Jesus

, if you or anyone you know is having difficulty, call the National or Local Suicide Prevention Hotline at 1-800-273-8255 and find resources at https://suicidepreventionlifeline.org/ I don't believe that suicide is the answer to anyone's problems. This was a very difficult chapter to write. I am truly amazed that I have actually lived to be as old as I am. There were many times that I thought I wanted to leave. I'm so glad that didn't happen. I know that I turned to alcohol to try to numb my feelings and help me survive in many different social situations. I was able to laugh at myself if I was drunk and pretend that I didn't care. It helped my anxiety, which, at the time, I didn't even realize I had. When I was in college and throughout my life, I did not talk about anxiety or my feelings. I just smiled and pretended I was ok. **During my research about highly sensitive people, I learned that our nervous systems are extremely sensitive to alcohol and all types of drugs- including medicine.**

I remember the moment the doctor said I needed back surgery right away for a herniated disc in my back. My world turned upside down with that one statement. I was at a really great point in my life- other than my pain! My kids were one and three and, most importantly for me at the time- I had lost ALL of my baby weight! I was so proud of myself. I had gone to Weight Watchers and thought I had solved my weight issue forever. I was back down to my "normal" weight. Then I had back surgery. I was a Mom, wife, daughter, teacher. I had things to do and people to take care of. Back surgery took all that away from me and made me feel like nothing. I could barely be around my kids because of their energy. My back hurt every minute after surgery- worse than before the surgery. I had to move home and stay with my parents. I had to learn to accept help instead of being able to help others. I think the worst day for me was when I realized that I had to rely on other people. I had warmed up a piece of pizza for lunch and after eating, went to throw some of it away. I dropped a piece of pepperoni on the floor next to the garbage. I couldn't bend down to pick it up. My body would not allow me to do this. I cried. I had made a mess and couldn't even take care of myself. My identity at the time was consumed with taking care of others but this forced me to be the recipient instead of the giver. I went into a deep depression and had to crawl my way out. It forever changed me. I felt the pain I had while writing this book was a way for me to learn some of the same lessons I had learned after my back surgery. I had to learn to listen to my body or the pain would get worse and worse. I had to take better care of myself every single day.

My near death experience (NDE) in college most definitely was something I had never spoken about before. After reading about Anita's NDE and several others, I was aware that this was what happened that night.

Chapter 3 Faith

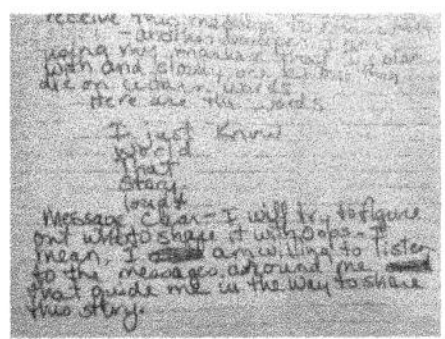

This was my journal where I started writing. The pen died on the words "I just know" ,"world", "that" and "story".

I cannot even begin to explain all of the "weird", "crazy" things that happened once I started writing this book. I started documenting them immediately after my trip. During the story, I felt the many different ways the universe/Spirit sent me messages. The songs were unending, especially while I was in Florida. I could rationalize that I hear a lot of uplifting music because I listened to the Christian station on Sirius XM radio. But, the fact that I was surrounded by all of these same songs- at the condo, on Facebook, etc.- I believe that was Divine Guidance speaking to me. I believe that I was so busy with life- my new job, losing my parents, and helping others that I wasn't always taking the time to notice messages from God. I had to learn to quiet my mind. The way I was able to get back in touch with Spirit was to be still- to learn to breathe, relax and make good choices of whole, real food. (more on this later!)

Faith is something I feel with my entire body. It is inside me. I felt it as a child and I still feel it today. I feel it when I quiet my mind and surrender to God's will. It's when my rational mind let's go of all of my beliefs and I am in the present moment. Just like the bird at the condo, I am who I am and I am where I am at in the present. No judgments. No preconceived ideas that I don't belong. Nothing. I just am. I imagine myself as a newborn baby- pure and beautiful. Every single part of myself. Even the things I don't like about myself. Everything is just as God made me.

"Meditation is simply a state of being in which the active mind slows down. It will bring you to a place where you can shut down. It will bring you to a place

where you can shut down your mental chatter and become more aware of the subtle energies inside of you." ~John Holland

There are many ways I learned to quiet my mind. I sit quietly for at least five minutes and focus on my breath. I have to do this everyday to feel the benefits. By quieting my mind, my entire body relaxes and I feel very different. I am more present. I am more in line with my Spirit and my soul. Food affects my connection too. The more real food I eat, the more I am connected. The more processed food I eat (anything man made), the more "fuzzy" my brain feels. I don't think about things the same way and I am more apt to judge and be negative. Another way to quiet my mind is to exercise. I had to learn that exercise was what my body needed and not think of exercise or eating healthy as a way to get skinny. As an educator, I am passionate about doing more of this type of work in classrooms and with adults in the workplace. When adults are more relaxed, we are better equipped to handle the stress at work. And, when students are able to slow down and regulate their body, they are better able to learn. We live in such a busy world. I believe daily Mindfulness techniques should take priority for everyone.

My faith continues to be strong and it helps me every single day. Without it, I'm not connected to myself and I feel absolutely alone in a big world. I pray every day for myself and others.

Chapter 4 Death and Spirits

I am still learning about my connections with Spirits. I know that I can sense things that I can't see. It is like a psychic feeling or a sixth sense. At times I feel great about this and at times, it scares me. I understand now that this connection with Spirit is not about being an empath. It is something else I will continue to learn about. This connection is what makes me who I am and I am learning to accept that part of myself.

I am not sure why my mother didn't share information with me about my father's heart attack. I tried to put myself in her shoes and know that she did the best she could with what she was given. She might have been scared and worried that my father would die like her father did. She would be left alone to raise four children. I think that major life events like this always change us and nobody can truly understand until we live through it ourselves. Even then, everyone's situation is so different that it is impossible to all have the same experience.

I have had difficulty sleeping for years. I need the room totally quiet and no movement around me. I can't sleep with a dog, a cat or even my husband. I used to be quite embarrassed about this and didn't want anyone to know. Now, my husband and I joke about it with friends. Even though we are laughing, I sometimes feel awful about it. When I began reading about empaths and sleep, I realized that this was why I couldn't sleep. I was an empath and empaths struggle with sleep. There were other people like me out there.

"I personally have certain requirements when it comes to sleeping well. First and foremost the room must be pitch black with no visible light. Secondly, I require it to be deadly silent so you can hear a pin drop. And finally, I need my own bed." ~Marianne Gracie

I remember the night I read this. I told my husband, "It makes me feel better knowing that I am not some sort of freak! There is a reason I have so much trouble sleeping. I am an empath!" Of course, he would have no idea what I meant when I said that. Just reading this information helped me feel like I wasn't alone. I sleep in a totally dark room, with earplugs, a facemask and the door closed so I won't hear anything. I also learned how important sleep was for an empath's health. During the time I was in pain in the story, I wasn't sleeping and it was affecting my entire nervous system. When I healed and began sleeping again, I felt like a new person!

"Do you know what happens when you decide to stop worrying about what other people might think of you? You get to dance. You get to sing. You get to laugh loudly, paint, write, and create.You get to be yourself. And you know what? Some people won't like you. Some will laugh or mock or point out flaws...but it just won't bother you all that much." ~Doe Zantamata

Well, for me, I might not necessarily be dancing or singing, but I am sleeping! I find so many people nowadays struggling with sleep. I always wonder if they tried sleeping like I do, would it help them? With a good night's sleep, I am better able to handle what life throws at me.

Past life regression work is a healing technique that I have used to help some of the physical and emotional pain in my body. These regressions aren't just a therapy session. While writing this book, I was able to meet Brian Weiss. His story is so inspiring because he was a psychiastrist who did not believe in anything that wasn't science based. If he hadn't followed his intuition, I might not be following mine. I was able to say to him, face to face, "You changed my life." I meant it. He said to me, "Thank you for telling me that and thank you so much for coming today." It was genuine. He knew that by following his internal voice, he had changed my life. It didn't matter that he had changed thousands of lives. It mattered that he had changed my life. *That is what is helping me write this book. Can I change just one life? If so, then daring to share my story is so worth it. My story only took a few messages from Heaven. What will it take the next person? And the next? We all need to share our stories to heal the world, a voice encourages me.*

I remember the phone call from my sister-in-law about my nephew, Tyler. It was before cell phones so I answered the land line. My kids had friends over and I remember looking at all the kids as I walked to the garage, searching desperately for my husband. I was hearing the words and hoping for something different. As I listened to, "Tyler was in a car accident," I was hoping to hear, "he is ok. Banged up and in the hospital, but he will be ok." That is not the information I received. It was, "he died." My husband looks at me with fear in his eyes. He can see it in my eyes even before

I hand him the phone. The kids all followed me to the garage. They are aware that something big, and most likely bad, is happening. I break the news to all of them. *How do I even explain something like this to my kids? I can't even understand it myself. We are all in shock as we sit down to talk. The rest of the day is a blur. I know we make plans to fly to Tyler's home town and we buy our boys their first suit to wear to the funeral. My kids would be so much younger (12 and 14) than I was when they attend their first funeral. I remember holding them as we cried together. As a Mom, I wasn't sure how to help them but I did the best I could.*

It was on the trip to my nephew's funeral a colleague recommended that I read Brian Weiss's book, <u>Many Lives Many Masters.</u> It was 2008. I was in the lobby of the hotel checking my email on the hotel's computer. A colleague had sent an email asking if I wanted to order a particular book to help with a class I was teaching. I responded something like this, "I'm sorry. I can't deal with this right now. I had to fly to Tennessee because my nephew was killed in a car accident. I'm not sure when I will be home. Thanks, Monica". She responded something like, "I'm so sorry to hear about your nephew. I read a really good book called <u>Many Lives Many Masters.</u> I think it might help you." The seed had been planted and forever my life would be changed by this one person daring to share information about souls, spirituality and healing through past life regression work. For me, it was foreign to have a professional colleague share such a new age/spiritual book. But it wasn't spiritual like religious. It was different. I don't know why but on the way home in the plane, I had the book <u>A New Earth; Awakening to Your Life's Purpose</u> by Eckartt Tolle. Eckartt introduced me to thinking more about why we are all here on this planet- like where I ask myself, *"Like why am I here on earth kinda why?"*

"What a liberation to realize that the 'voice in my head' is not who I am. 'Who am I, then?' The one who sees that." ~Eckartt Tolle

I have had the opportunity to work with Betty Moore Hafter (author of the foreword!) who was trained by Brian Weiss. I was able to access some past lives during several sessions. I am so grateful for this experience.

I remember the first time I ever tried a past life regression. During a regression, it is similar to a meditation where I close my eyes and a voice directs me through the process. First, the person directs me to relax every single part of my body, one part at a time. Then I visualize walking through a door and down a path. It is like I picture a movie in my head. Here is the story I thought about. I walk down a path. I am wearing leather sandals and a robe. My mind wanders and I begin to judge my thoughts. *I was scared that I wouldn't be able to do this because I wasn't sure I believed that this would work.* There are many other people at the place I am walking towards. There is a wooden cross, similar to the one Jesus was crucified on. *My brain thinks "What is going on? I couldn't be Jesus in a past life! But there were so many similarities!"* I ignore the thoughts and I continue walking. There are a lot of people screaming. Although I can't hear what they are saying, I can sense they are very angry. There are others dressed like me. At the end of the visualization, the voice directs me to skip to the end of this person's life. How did this person die? I proceed to talk about the pain in my wrists as someone nails me to the cross. As I die in this past life in my mind, I see my neck flail as the pain is released from my body. Then I am with God.

What? I'm sure you are questioning the truth of this story. Trust me. So did I. After the meditation, I was brought out of the hypnotic state and to the present moment in this lifetime. Were there any similarities in this lifetime? Only if I want to believe, I think to myself. I have had two wrist surgeries and continue to have pain in my wrists. *Was this left over from another lifetime? I would never be able to prove it to anyone, but what if?* I feel that I might be 'crucified' for being a public school educator who believes in God. *Well, maybe not crucified, but most definitely fired if I started teaching about my beliefs at the public school where I was a teacher or an administrator.* I had a difficult time accepting this experience as one of my past lives. That is, until one day a coincidence happened.

I had a difficult time believing because I felt like it was Christ's story and I knew I was most definitely NOT Christ in a past life. I did not know anyone else who was crucified on a cross. A few weeks later, my husband was channel surfing and happened to stop and watch a documentary about a religious community in another country. I stopped whatever I was doing to watch as they sacrificed people on crosses, just like Jesus. I remember clearly thinking, "Oh, someone other than Christ was crucified on a cross? I had no idea!" I was meant to see that 5 minutes of the TV show to help me trust that my story was real. *This one event would encourage me to go deeper and explore this alternative healing technique for many other pains in my body. It isn't like the pain goes away instantly but over the course of months it gets better and better until it finally releases from the cells in my body. Based on Brian Weiss's research and my own experience, I believe our body holds the pain in our cells from past life trauma.*

"I didn't realize yet that thinking is only a tiny aspect of the consciousness that we are, nor did I know anything about the ego, let alone being able to detect it within myself...The egoic mind is completely conditioned by the past. Its conditioning is twofold: it consists of content and structure." ~Eckhart Tolle

In my past life regression, I can hear my ego questioning everything that I was thinking. My ego wants to tell me it is my imagination running wild, but my subconscious wants to believe.

I am always amazed at the people I meet- both in and out of my profession. I always wonder what type of experiences brought each and every person to where they are in life. I wonder why they believe in this or that. Everyone brings to the table something different when talking about issues affecting our world. I'm sure that by reading this book, people will most likely think differently about the person who they thought I was. They might understand me or they might judge me based on what I have shared. Once introduced to new ideas, I knew my life had changed and everything up until this point helped me understand my path.

Chapter 5 Before the Dimes

It is normal for us to want to break away from our parents. It's part of our development. At age two or three, a baby starts to test the breaking away from his/her parents by walking further and further away. Then at about thirteen, we begin to realize that we don't have to believe everything our parents believe. Then at eighteen, we feel invincible and don't want to listen to most of our parents' advice. Since I was little, it seemed that my soul's quest was to always go against my mother- at every single age and stage. It was like I was born to live differently. I held on to things that happened to me as a child and tried to prove that I was right and she was wrong. I held on to my anger from her telling me to go back to bed on Mother's Day. I was never open to any of her attempts to connect with me. I built a shield to protect my heart from being hurt again. For example, when she tried to get me to watch Wayne Dyer, I wasn't receptive because I felt like she had hurt me before and I was trying to protect my heart even when I didn't need protection anymore.

In many parent-child relationships, a lot of people think the parent is supposed to teach the child. This is for things like learning to play baseball or learning how to cook. Nowadays, it seems the child is teaching the parent lessons. People are more open to talking about their feelings now more than when I was growing up fifty years ago. Each generation seems to be evolving more and more. We are changing the way we live by listening more to the children. My own children continue to teach me everyday.

Certain people I have met over the years have had an incredible impact on my life and it seems they might never know it. It can be a quick conversation, a professional relationship or a close friend. Certain things that people say resonate with me and guide me along in my life. I feel blessed and grateful for all who have entered my life to teach me things. Yes, even the negative people. They teach me who I don't want to be. These people help me look inside myself to see where I might need to be healed. I bless them and move on. Life is too short to stay in the negative. I truly want them to be happy.

That first video on vulnerability opened up new doors in my life. It triggered a domino effect for me to learn more and begin to admit my own insecurities. Brene Brown helped give me the courage to dive deep into myself to heal and then share my story. She helped give words to my feelings, validating them and helping me face them. By sharing stories about her life, she helped me know that emotions and feelings were ok. They were part of being human. It was ok to be angry with my mom but then I had to learn to move beyond the anger.

Chapter 6 Messages and my Inner Voice

How about that guy working at the condo? I still have visions of him pointing to his head and saying, "I have to remember them in my brain." It was one of those "weird" or "crazy" things that began happening to me as I began to write this book.

Because of these signs, I knew that my soul was meant to write this book. I had to be willing to listen and move forward. When writing, I felt connected to the Spirit within me. Through eating clean, taking care of myself and opening up my heart, God guided me in the right direction. Just like God placed my husband and I outside the night we went to dinner, I would be placed with an opportunity to share my story.

I knew about the many stages of child development through my education to be a teacher. I hadn't studied much about adults though. I was not aware that menopause was anything but hormones and hot flashes.

"Uncertain as I was as I pushed forward, I felt right in my pushing, as if the effort itself meant something. That perhaps being amidst the undesecrated beauty of the wilderness meant I too could be undesecrated, regardless of the regrettable things I'd done to others or myself or the regrettable things that had been done to me. Of all the things I'd been skeptical about, I didn't feel skeptical about this: the wilderness had a clarity that included me." ~Cheryl Strayed

I didn't realize that in menopause, along with the hot flashes, would come anxiety and an increase in my intuitive abilities. I would discover ways to help my anxiety. One was to be in nature as much as possible. The second was eating healthy. The third was making sure to exercise every single day, just like the doctor in the story. The more I did these things, the less anxiety I would have.

"We form at age 30, we transform at age 40, and we transmute at age 50." ~Barbara Hand Clow

I felt like I was in the middle of a life review, like in the book Life's Golden Ticket. Because of this, I experienced all of the emotions and feelings from everything that had happened to me in 50 years! I tried many supplements and medicines to try to feel better, but, eventually the thing that would help my anxiety and pain were writing this book and literally rewiring my brain. Like I thought in my younger years that I could find confidence in the bottle of alcohol, I thought I could heal my anxiety, menopause, and digestive issues with herbal supplements or a pill. That isn't how it works. Some medicine and supplements did help, but I had to do the tough emotional work too. *Through writing my story I was able to accept myself. Would I have written this story without the dimes? Most likely not. Would I have found another way? I have no idea, but am happy to be on this journey.*

"Research into the physiological changes taking place in the perimenopausal woman is revealing that, in addition to the hormonal shift that means an end to childbearing, our bodies-and, specifically, our nervous systems- are being, quite literally, rewired. It's as simple as this: our brains are changing. A woman's thoughts, her ability to focus, and the amount of fuel going to the intuitive centers in the temporal lobes of her brain all are plugged into, and affected by, the circuits being rewired." Dr. Christian Northrup

If you are over 40 and have not read Dr. Christian Northrup's book called *The Wisdom of Menopause; Creating Physical and Emotional Health during the Change,* do it now.

When I was in my twenties and had sinus infection after sinus infection, I went to an allergist to try to find the cause of all of my colds. I remember getting those results and as the doctor spoke to me, I remember thinking "hell no!- I will never live like that!" The tests revealed I was allergic to dust and basically everything outside, including trees, grass, pollen, everything. His advice was that I should buy an air conditioner so that I wouldn't have to open my windows, take medication every single day and I shouldn't be swimming, camping or doing other outdoor activities. Basically, give up my lifestyle and all the things that helped regulate my body. I turned to other answers, which included making my own herbs from weeds. I hoped that the herbs would heal my body so I wasn't having allergic reactions to the environment. Looking back, I wonder if these environmental allergies were related to my gluten and dairy sensitivities and, most likely had affected my breathing. By eating these foods, my body's immune system wasn't as strong. At the time, I ate a ton of wheat products! *I'll never be able to prove it because most medical doctors don't look at food as the culprit for many diseases or allergies. Was the flour producing more phlegm and affecting my immune system? I may never know the answer but today I can say that eating less flour definitely helps me breath better.*

When I eat gluten, dairy or a few other foods, I have to do what I call a recovery plan. I need extra vitamin C. I need to go have some lymph drainage done by either a massage therapist or a chiropractor to open up my ability to breathe correctly. I have to eat lots of vegetables and make sure to get extra sleep. No big deal, right? Well, I can usually handle eating those foods once in awhile but I can't do it for days. My body needs whole, healthy foods- no processed or man-made foods in order to feel good. I need a lot of protein in order to feel like my gut and brain are functioning properly. Many authors note these same things for empaths or a highly sensitive person(HSP) (Dr. Judith Orloff, Marianne Gracie, etc.).

"Patients who suffer from these chronic inflammatory disorders feel their symptoms not only come from the gut but also from the brain, in the form of fatigue, "brain fog," and chronic pain." ~Dr. Emeran Mayer

Another thing that happens when I eat wheat, dairy or other processed food is I get brain-fog and it increases my pain. When I eat these things, I am ok if I have a little bit. If I am free of these foods, my pain level decreases immensely and I am able to focus better. I can also access my "inner voice" better. When I say inner voice, I mean I feel more connected to my inner self, my soul or my subconscious. It's the same way I feel when I hike. Eating the foods God gave us and being on the earth, feeling the energy of nature are some of the best things for my body.

I recently heard a mother and daughter talking about food. It was the day I had worked on this part of my book. It mimicked exactly what I was trying to write about. Here is the conversation I overheard:

Mom: "Oh, you can't eat that because of your diet, right?"

Daughter: "Mom, I'm not dieting. It isn't that I can't eat it. I choose not to eat it."

Mom: "But, you can't eat it right? Are you still trying to lose weight?"

Daughter: "Mom, I am not trying to lose weight. I am trying to be healthy. I choose not to eat white flour and sugar. It's not that I 'can't' have it. It isn't a diet. Do you understand that?"

Mom: "But, you won't eat it right? I was going to cook lasagna. But, you can't have that right?"

Daughter: "Mom, I don't eat things with white flour. I eat whole foods. You know, like fruits, vegetables and meat. I can eat something else. It's fine."

I felt this person's pain. She felt like she had to defend her choice to eat whole foods. *Why do I have to explain this to everyone? Why is eating 'differently' such a weird concept for everyone? Whole, real foods should not be what people consider different! Why don't people understand that our society is eating way too many flour products? Why aren't people eating the food that God gave us? You know- the things that grow on the Earth. Why do I need to explain my choices in eating real food? Food needs to be from earth, not a science lab. I noticed a big change in my taste buds once I turned to real food. I was busy eating things because they tasted good- like sugar, bread, etc. Once I removed those from my food choices, vegetables and fruit tasted delicious!*

I am always amazed at our grocery stores. Most of the "food" items could live on a shelf for close to fifty years. The only place I should be buying 'food' is on the outer edge of the store. One trip around the store- go down the produce aisle, the meat aisle at the back of the store and the dairy/egg aisle (which now includes almond and coconut milk!). Then I should be done shopping. Everything else in the store are 'food-like' items. They are things that man created using some food and chemicals. I don't have to read the label on a banana because it is real food. If I can't pronounce the ingredients, then the item is not food. For the most part, I have to go shopping every single week because the food I buy will spoil and I will need more. But that's ok with me because I know I am eating food that doesn't include chemicals.

My body is like an individual science experiment. I can read about how nuts are really good for me. So, I try eating nuts for snacks. Well, when my body doesn't like certain nuts it shows me by affecting my breathing, my skin(I get itchy) or my digestive system. I have to listen to my body and stop listening to all of the advice everywhere. Sound simple? It's not. I struggle with it every single day. I actually ask my body before I eat if it really wants me to eat whatever is in front of me. My gut will tell me with just a sensation. We are all so different and our food journey needs to be our own science experiment. Food affects everyone differently because it isn't just about the food, it's our thoughts that affect the entire body.

I read the book The Mind-Gut Connection while I was writing this book. In chapter one, the author speaks of treating the body "like a machine". I knew I had stumbled upon exactly what I had been thinking about for years, especially after the conversation with my father. It was like my father was sending me messages about taking care of my machine in a different way. *"This is important. Listen up and make the changes,"* the voice inside me said. *Was it from my father? Was it from my internal voice- the one who wants me to be me?*

"The machine model was useful in medicine for treating some diseases. But when it comes to understanding chronic diseases of the body and the brain, it's no longer serving us." ~Dr. Emeran Myer

This quote explains my beliefs that our thoughts affect our "machine." Through my healing over the years, I have more luck with alternative healing than I ever did with medical doctors. I continue to do a mixture of medical and alternative ways to heal, but ultimately it is Reiki, Network Chiropractic Care, massage therapy, acupuncture and looking within myself which heals me the most. Eating real food helps my body to function better, but I still need these other therapies.

"But regardless of what supplements you take and what kind of exercise you do, when all is said and done it is your attitude, your beliefs, and your daily thought patterns that have the most profound effect on your health." ~Dr. Christiana Northrup

Our internal thoughts are the most critical part of enjoying our human body.

Was I able to make the changes I wrote about in the dime story? I am trying the 90%/10%. I eat clean and healthy 90% of the time and will enjoy treats about 10% of the time. I thoroughly enjoyed my cake, maple cream pie and gluten free pizza on my 50th birthday. Even though the processed 'food' they use to make gluten free pizza affects me- it isn't as bad as flour based pizza. Will I eat cake at every birthday or anniversary party that I go to? Probably not. This is partly because I would be eating cake and treats so much that it feels like I have to go into recovery mode almost all the time.

Chapter 7 Come What May

"I was standing with one foot still in the living room and one foot in the room that would be my escape route out of the house."~Monica Morrissey

This sentence is how I have felt my entire life. I have always felt that I have had one foot on earth and one foot in Heaven. I had to learn to connect my experience on earth and my experience with Spirit. This part of me is my highly sensitive system. I would much rather spend my time with God and my angels than deal with some of the pain on earth. I had to learn to do both. *I always felt this inside but never wanted to share it with others because I thought people would think I was crazy. I still have one foot in both worlds, but I am working on balance. I have to balance both my root chakra and my crown chakra.*

I have been reading about how our emotions affect our physical body for over twenty years. I was amazed when I began talking to people that most were not aware of this information. I might mention reading a book from Hay House and so many people had never heard of Louise Hay or Wayne Dyer. I realized how lucky I was to have this knowledge but I also realized that it was my path and my path alone that would determine if I would be able to incorporate this into my life. When I began to tell people about my book and how I was using a self-publishing company developed by Louise Hay from the Hay House Foundation, it was clear other people didn't read as many books from Hay House that I did. Sharing my story would be like that one colleague who decided to share Brian Weiss's book with me when Tyler died. That one thing would totally change my life's journey. *Writing and sharing this book would also be one of the most daring things I could do as an empath! When I am ok with "Come What May", then I am in a good space.*

Chapter 8 Time with My Dad

Healing using Alternative Methods

I find it very interesting that I have to call this type of healing "alternative" instead of traditional. These should be called traditional methods because cultures around the world have been doing this for years! In America we have developed a medical system focused on using a pill or a drug to "fix" the problem within the body. "Alternative" methods try to get to the root cause of the problem and help the entire body- not a piece or part of the body.

"Bodily symptoms are not just physical in nature; often they contain a message for us about our lives- if we can learn to decipher it." ~Dr. Christian Northrup

Remember the phrases, "Eat like your life depends on it" and "Think like your life depended on it"? Those phrases are how I began to heal my body. While writing the dime story, I didn't share that I took a break from technology that week and it was a shock to see how this simple change affected my physical body. I discovered that I was "tech sensitive". After discovering I was an empath I knew that technology was affecting my nervous system more than the average person. When my father was sick, I had to be glued to my cell phone. Now that I didn't need to be next to my phone all day and all night, I realized that with every vibration or notification I received, it was stimulating the fight or flight response in my body. With every vibration, I worried that something bad had happened. I had been so busy over the last few years that my nervous system was depleted and overloaded. Removing technology helped me learn to go within myself and still my mind.

"Medicine and science never paid much attention to the malfunction of the brain that was the primary cause of all these problems."~ Dr. Emeran Mayer

I was first introduced to trying to change my thought patterns by a chiropractor who I went to before my back surgery. I had a lot of ear and TMJ pain. I remember she would send me home with positive quotes to read. Something like,

"I hear with love. Harmony surrounds me. I listen with love to the pleasant and the good. I am a center for love." ~Louise Hay.

After my back surgery, I would discover that these were from Louise Hay's book, <u>You Can Heal Yourself.</u> This was the book that included the mirror activity where I had to look in the mirror and say truthfully, "I love you." Over the years I have looked up many symptoms to find out the message behind the pain. For instance, the 'cause' for ear pain was:

"Anger: Not wanting to hear. Too much turmoil. Parents arguing" ~Louise Hay.

Louise then has a positive thought to go along with the cause. Here is another one. Cause for Colds (respiratory illness):

"Too much going on at once. Mental confusion, disorder. Small hurts. 'I get three colds every winter,' type thinking." ~Louise Hay.

The positive thought to go along with the cause for colds is:

"I allow my mind to relax and be at peace. Clarity and harmony are within me and around me. All is well." ~Louise Hay.

I wonder if she is trying to say that we don't "catch" colds but we "think" colds? Think of all of the people who use wipes everywhere they go because they are so scared of germs. Not that we don't want to wash our hands, but could we possibly "catch" colds with our thinking?

As a teacher over the years, I have been sick a lot. I tried an experiment. Instead of worrying about all of the germs in my classroom, I began saying to myself and everyone, "I have been teaching so long now, I have built up my immunity and I tend to stay healthy!" I wanted to see what would happen. My words were important. Here is another internal voice I had tried, "I have been teaching so long now that I don't get colds anymore." The first voice is positive (healthy) and the other voice was negative (don't get colds). According to the book <u>The Secret</u>, the universe didn't hear the **"don't"** in "don't get colds. It heard, "get colds" because the universe is **always** positive. Nowadays I cringe when I hear someone say, "there is a virus going around. I hope I don't get it." *Do I still get colds? Absolutely! When was my last cold- most likely the last time I thought, "Oh my goodness- I hope I don't pick up germs from that sick person."*

In my new role as Curriculum Director, I wanted to share some of these ideas with teachers. The idea was that if teachers understood how our thoughts affect our learning, they might understand how important it was for educators to address students' emotions along with learning the curriculum. I organized a profession development day to show the movie <u>Resilience</u> to the entire staff at both schools in my district. The movie brought to light the ACE (Adverse Childhood Experiences)study. The ACE study identified ten different childhood experiences that affected a person's health, even into adulthood, including their life expectancy. Finally, there was a medical study that proved our emotions affect our health! My personal passion was now a part of my professional world. The seed had been planted and I would be able to encourage educators to learn to take care of their own bodies so that they were ready for the challenges of teaching. I introduced essential oils and Reiki to some teachers. I introduced EFT (Emotional Freedom Technique) tapping to people. I realized that I was now able to share my personal passion with others in my professional career. Teaching is sometimes exhausting but by learning how to take care of ourselves, we would be able to keep educating the next generation.

The seed had also been planted to begin doing mindfulness activities as part of the curriculum. If students were emotionally and physically regulated, then they would be ready to learn.

Reiki

"Reiki is a Japanese technique for stress reduction and relaxation that also promotes healing. It is administered by 'laying on hands' and is based on the idea that an unseen 'life force energy' flows through us and is what causes us to be alive. If one's 'life force energy' is low, then we are more likely to get sick or feel stress, and if it is high, we are more capable of being happy and healthy.

The word Reiki is made of two Japanese words - Rei which means 'God's Wisdom or the Higher Power' and Ki which is 'life force energy'. So Reiki is actually "spiritually guided life force energy." `Retrieved from https://www.reiki.org/faq/whatisreiki.html

When I was healing from my back surgery, I went to a free Reiki clinic. The first time I ever received Reiki, I fell asleep. My body was so depleted back then. I was in a lot of pain from my back and I had two little kids. It was a difficult time in my life and Reiki began to help me. I was trained to a level II Reiki practitioner. I did the training mostly to be able to give myself Reiki. Giving Reiki to others helps me feel better too. I cannot explain what happens during Reiki, but there is most definitely a healing energy that occurs. For me, it makes me feel better and relaxes my entire nervous system. *When I shared Reiki with others, I got comments like, "I feel like a totally different person!" I have had Reiki practitioners who were better than others but I am so glad to have Reiki in my life.*

Years ago, I had the opportunity to have a photographer take my picture with a special camera that would show my "energy field". In other words, the picture would show colors surrounding me. The camera would leave the lens open a little longer to pick up on the subtle light energies surrounding me. This is called a person's aura or energy field. I always felt this and could sense people's aura, but didn't really understand much about it. As an empath, I learned how to control my aura, where I could extend my energy and I could draw back my energy. Depending on how far I extended my energy would determine whether or not I picked up someone else's energy.

These pictures would be my physical evidence that I was always searching for. I wanted something to help me understand what was happening so that I would be able to "verify" auras to other people. Here is a link to the website where the photographer explains the colors surrounding me. https://aurainsightsauraphotography.wordpress.com/2011/08/17/aura-photos-of-before-and-after-reiki-1/

The photographer (Ramona from Aura Insights) said things like, "angel guides who surround her", "psychic ability", "open mind", and "intuitive abilities". The photographer took pictures both before and after I had Reiki.

According to this photographer, the white symbolized angels and spirit guides surrounding me, letting me know they are with me to help me.

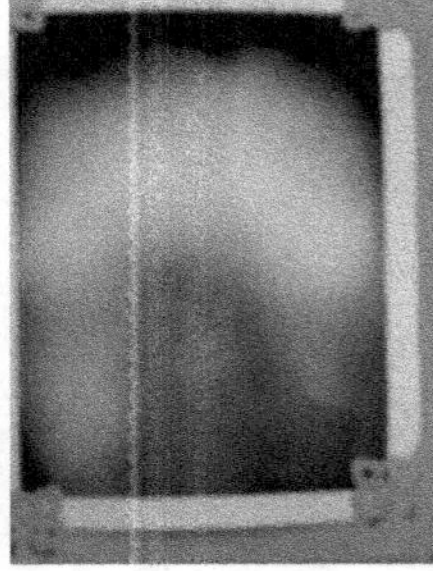

Here is the picture from before I had Reiki.

After I had Reiki, she wrote things like, "the session appeared to open her up to allowing even more psychic energy in!" The bright purple color had opened my crown chakra. This is my connection with Spirit, the part of me that wants to be in Heaven. This is something I have felt my entire life but didn't have words or knowledge to describe it.

This aura experience would be three years after Tyler had died and I had

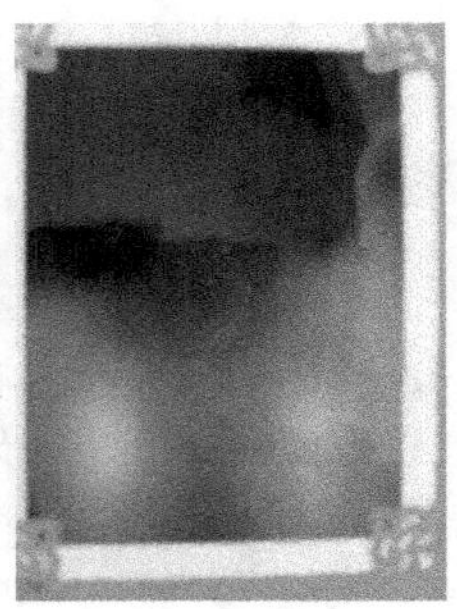

Here is the picture after I had Reiki.

only begun to read books by Wayne Dyer and other authors. It would take me years to understand and change my thoughts about what words like psychic and intuitive really mean.

For a long time, I blocked this connection. I knew that I could sense energy around people but this experience validated that a person's essence goes beyond their physical body. While writing this book, I am now trying to get back in touch with this part of myself. The photographer writes, **"In both her throat and heart area she shows purple, which just emphasizes how she uses some pyschic ability when she communicates with others, and it comes right from her heart."** For people who know me well, I most definitely wear my heart on my sleeve. It goes right along with the part in the story where I say, "Do all things with love." A colleague who I used to work with said something to me when I saw her recently. I gave her a big hug and she said, "I always feel better when you are around." This meant a lot to me as it was quite the opposite comment I had experienced with that friend years ago. This person felt my love. This person knew me and knew that I only wanted the best for her. She knew my energy was filled with love. I won't be able to be a "jack-ass whisperer" but I will be able to be a "love- whisperer" for those who want to receive love. When I started sharing about my book and being an empath, most people weren't surprised.

It was almost like everyone around me knew and understood my sensitivities before I understood them.

I am a Facebook user. I love it and hate it at the same time. I love the connection with friends, family and past students whom I don't get to see very often. I love watching my students and their families grow up. I love the inspirational quotes and posts from positive people. One post is very clear in my mind, "Just because you think it, doesn't mean it's true."~ author unknown. This kinda messed with my head. Until then, I believed everything I told myself. Then I started questioning every thought I had. Every feeling I had. I realized that most of my thoughts were related to my emotions and my life experiences. The reason I hate Facebook is because some people tend to only look at other people through their own experiences. I can never understand someone else's story because I haven't lived it. And nobody knows my story because they don't know all of my experiences. *For anyone who knows me, were you surprised by anything you read in my story? I think even my family didn't know some of the things I shared! Imagine a world where we all accepted each other and respected that we don't understand because we don't know the life of the other person. It's like we can only see in the windows to a person's house. We don't see everything inside.*

Here is my understanding of the nervous systems. The parasympathetic part of our nervous system is the "rest and digest" part. The sympathetic nervous system is the "fight or flight" part. Meditation helps the parasympathetic nervous system calm and relax the body. My sympathetic nervous system had been running the fight and flight in my body for about the past 4 years. It's meant for danger such as tigers and bears. We either decide to stay and fight or we run like heck to save ourselves. I learned at an early age to avoid things, thus activating the flight part of the nervous system. During the time I was caring for both of my parents, the sympathetic nervous system was working overtime and the parasympathetic nervous system was only relaxing during the few times when I was praying. I had to learn to relax. *Ultimately, this was part of my "cure" for all of my ailments throughout the years. I had to learn how to breathe and deal with my emotions instead of trying to get a pill to fix me.*

I was lucky enough to learn about Emotional Freedom Tapping (EFT) from the same person who helped me with my past life regression work, Betty Moore-Hafter from South Burlington, VT. (She wrote the foreward to this book!) EFT is so simple and easy. Anyone can learn and it is so helpful for dealing with and releasing our emotions in our bodies. It will help with any type of stress. I remember one time I had a really bad pain in my neck on my way to work. I tried to figure out what was bothering me and instantly I thought of someone at work who was a "pain in my neck". I tapped out how I felt about what had happened the day before at work and was able to go to work pain free. It relieved the pain in my neck and the anger from the day before. I was able to go into work with a whole new attitude. I even had a great attitude with the person who I thought was a pain in my neck!

Learning to relax sounds really simple but to a workaholic like myself, it's difficult. I have a hamster wheel inside my head that will not stop. As a teacher, I was always thinking of lessons and strategies to meet my students' needs. I wanted to be a creative and good teacher. I rarely used my plans from year to year because technology was changing and I wanted my students to love learning. I didn't want old, outdated lessons.

What I didn't understand, was that I needed to quiet my mind to help me find my inner, positive voice. This voice was also the voice that would help me step out of my comfort zone and write this book.

Remember the doctor in the story who made time to exercise? Well, everyone needs to make time to be quiet too. Our bodies need it- just as much as we need food and exercise.

I started small. I learned that it was important to do this every single day. The length didn't necessarily matter. It was that my nervous system got to relax on a regular basis. I am still learning and know that this will forever be a part of my life. *I wonder what our society would look like if everyone did this? What if we shut off our computers each night for thirty minutes and just focused on our breath? Would everyone sleep better? Would people treat each other better? Would everyone be less stressed? Would the fight or flight part of the nervous system be relaxed? Breathe, a voice reminds me.*

Chapter 9 Unexpected Surprises

Just to clarify- the books we found were not porn, as we think about sex books to-day. One was a chapter book, explaining the how-tos of sex- in full length paragraphs. The picture book had black and white drawings portraying different sexual parts of the human anatomy. The copyright dates were the 1940's.

I share the story of my Grandfather having bladder cancer because, embarrassing as it is, that is where most of my pain was while I was writing this book. In my bladder. I even had surgery to make sure I didn't have bladder cancer like my Grandfather. It was the Urologist who told me to keep taking more and more of the medicine. That one doctor wanted me to take a pill to cover up the pain. I can remember another doctor telling me once, "we don't have muscle relaxers, we have brain relaxers." Basically, by using drugs to "cure" me, this doctor was covering up my symptoms.

I was diagnosed with interstitial cystitis. I was encouraged to eat lots of flour products and little fruit, along with increasing the medicine. The thought was to have a low acid diet. Of course, looking back, I see that because I was an empath and sensitive to those foods, this was the absolute worst thing I could eat.

I had looked up to see what Louise Hay said was the emotional trigger and the positive affirmation for bladder pain.

"Bladder problems- Anxiety. Holding on to old ideas. Fear of letting go. Being *pissed off... I comfortably and easily release the old and welcome the new in my* *life. I am safe."*

No big surprise here, right? Just think about my entire story- the release and letting go of old ideas.

In this chapter, I introduced the idea of sugar and flour being addictive for some people. I had read David Gillespie's book *Sweet Poison Why Sugar Makes Us Fat* and most recently had tried eating like Susan Pierce Thompson's book *Bright Line Eating* suggests. I am still amazed that people are unaware of how broken our food system is. People do not understand how most Americans seem to be eating too much sugar and flour. This idea was first brought to light in the book *The Saccharine Disease* by Surgeon-Captain Cleave. This doctor began the conversation that it was sugar causing most of the illnesses in the 20th century. When I read Susan's book, she pointed to brain research which showed that sugar is more addictive than cocaine. I remember reading about a rat study where the rats got fat from eating too much sugar or flour. I began to say mantras in my head, "I will not be like the fat rats. I will not be a fat rat."

Mainstream media doesn't show us this information because so many companies might go bankrupt if everyone stopped eating sugar and flour. Now, let's just be clear here. I am not talking the whole "carb" debate. I am talking about flour and sugar, which both look similar to cocaine when chopped up into a fine powder. Flour is sugar in disguise because our body turns flour into sugar. Both create havoc with my digestive and respiratory system because my system wants whole foods from earth. This is what happened to me- I was eating way too much processed foods and not enough foods from earth. Along with having a highly sensitive system, I had been overloading my system for years with "food like" man made products. When I clear my system of flour and sugar, I breathe better and my stomach feels better. That's my test. Clear and simple. 90% of the time I won't have this type of food, but 10% of the time I will thoroughly enjoy them! I am lucky that I don't feel that I am addicted to flour and sugar like I was to alcohol. But, I constantly have to monitor it. I focus more on protein, vegetables and fruits. There are so many different programs and diets out there. I am choosing to focus on "if it grows, I'll eat it". And, I listen to the person who has the best advice for me- my body.

Chapter 10 A Liberty Head Dime for Everyone

"When you judge another, you do not define them, you define yourself." **~Wayne Dyer.**

We all have our own stories and our own internal voices. My stories determine how I respond to everything in my life. I always try to remember that I can't see inside the whole person to understand why they do the things they do. Writing this book is like opening up the windows to my life. We are all doing the best we can with what we have been given. Everyone is allowed, "freedom of thought", which is the meaning of the Liberty Head dime.

My sister, Debbie and my niece, Melissa and I on vacation.

Chapter 11 Thy Will Be Done: A Summer on the Lake

Eating well most definitely helps me feel connected to Spirit. I am able to receive messages when my body is functioning properly. I didn't realize how cloudy and disconnected I felt until I really started eating healthy. It usually takes at least one entire week to begin to feel more connected. This was the only way I was able to write this book. If I had food that didn't make me feel good, my thoughts were clouded by my ego and my writing was fake. When I reread sections written with ego, I had to go back and rewrite them. Basically when I ate crappy foods, I had crappy thoughts and those turned up in my writing.

"The beginning of freedom is the realization that you are not the possessing entity- the thinker. Knowing this enables you to observe the entity. The moment you start watching the thinker, a higher level of consciousness becomes activated." ~Eckhart Tolle

I reflected on my eating habits a lot during my vacation in Florida. I realized that I inhaled my food very quickly. I asked myself, *Why was I like this? Why was I always in a rush to gulp my food down?* I realized that my eating habits over the years were always hurried because I always had something else to do. As a teacher sometimes my lunch period would only be ten minutes due to emergencies or a student needing extra support. I realized this was how I ate all of my meals- in a rush to finish. I began observing other people eating. They took their time. Sometimes it might take twenty or thirty minutes to eat their meal. They would stop eating to talk. I ate and continued talking while I chewed. I seriously did not stop eating once I started. I needed to slow down everything in my life- from eating to walking to writing- everything- Just like the Sheriff reminding me to drive slower.

As a teacher and a Mom, I felt like I never had enough time to get everything done. Instead of being in the present moment, my head was always in the next moment or a past moment. The business manager at my new office had a sign posted in her office that read, "The quickest way to get something done is to do one thing at a time." ~ author unknown Seemed pretty simple! I thought I was one of the best multitaskers around. What I didn't realize was that by multi-tasking I wasn't in the moment. Looking back, I wish I had spent more time enjoying every day and every moment. *I couldn't go back in time but I could try to be more present in the moment with everything I did- even eating.*

"If you hold on to the hurt feelings, your energy will get drained. This makes it important to realize that you have the power to forgive others and feel better yourself, as a result." ~Vik Carter

Drinking lots of water is also important. I don't drink seltzer water very much because the carbonation affects my nervous and immune system. My body doesn't process it very well. I remember taking my Praxis exam to become an administrator. When I finished the exam, the gentlemen at the desk said, "Well, now you can go home and enjoy a glass of wine or a beer." I replied, "Thanks, but I don't drink alcohol." He apologized. I'm not sure why people say that. There is no need to apologize. Not drinking alcohol is my choice and I am happy with it. Anyways, he said, "Well, then, maybe enjoy a Coke or a Pepsi." I thought of how much sugar was in those drinks. Should I tell him I don't drink soda because of the sugar and carbonation? I did. He looked shocked. I didn't drink alcohol or soda. He looked at me and said, 'Well, what do you drink?" After my coffee first thing in the morning, I drink water with lemon or lime every day. It's the only thing my body really needs in order to function properly. *I don't think this made any sense to him.*

Chapter 12 Transitioning to Spirit

Thank you, God, for guiding me in helping my father transition to Spirit. I know You were with me helping me follow my intuition the entire time. I also know that when my dad left his physical body, he was changing form; he wasn't really gone. His soul continues his journey.

Chapter 13 The First Phone Call from Heaven

"Once an empath has better insight into people, places, events and situations that drain energy and ones that energize them, it becomes much easier to be selective in their day to day life." ~Vik Carter

I used to have a pair of boots that were my absolute favorite pair. They were tan colored, soft suede leather and they fit perfect. They had great arch support and went with a lot of my outfits. One year I didn't take very good care of them. They ended up getting wet in a pool of water from the melted snow. It ruined the leather. I tried and tried to fix them. Nothing worked. I couldn't wear them anymore. I wanted to go back in time and make sure to take better care of them. Of course, this was an impossible task but I still dream of those boots. The company doesn't make that particular boot anymore. I sometimes feel like this with relationships and some decisions. I made mistakes and didn't take good care of some of the relationships with people in my life. I did things that most likely damaged it forever. I couldn't go back in time and act differently. I had to move on and hope people would forgive me for some of my mistakes. I'm a different person now. I'm not the person who didn't understand how important it was to forgive and forget. Life can be like that- you have regrets and you want a re-do but time marches on. I was moving forward.

I used to be a planner. I planned everything and knew exactly what I would be doing each and everyday. When I started writing, I began to let life happen. When I did that, surprises came every day. My son would text me and and say he was stopping by my house. When I had thought I would be alone for dinner, he and his wife stayed for dinner. We ate something totally different than what I thought my dinner was going to be. I thought I would be eating leftovers alone. Unexpected surprises seemed to appear every single day. It was better than what I expected. I realized that I cannot plan everything in my future. I knew that I could set goals and work towards them, but ultimately it was God in the driver's seat. Just like being on the mountain. I had decided to hike the mountain, but God had planned something for me when I reached the top. Even this book wasn't planned by me. I never wanted to be a writer. In fact, as a teacher I didn't even like to teach writing!

I knew when Spirit was giving me messages during my writing. When this happened, it was like my linear brain (ego) let go. When my messages were coming from Spirit, I didn't know how to spell words and I didn't know how to use punctuation. Normally I am an extremely good speller and because I was a teacher, I was really good with punctuation. That part of my brain would shut off and I spelled simple words incorrectly. Wayne Dyer points out that there is a difference when you write from your soul versus just typing. I felt the difference as I continued to write.

"Start listening to the voice in your head as often as you can. Pay particular attention to any repetitive thought patterns." ~Eckhart Tolle

Chapter 14 The First Dime from Heaven

This is me with my Uncle David (my Mother's brother) at my son's wedding.

Writing this chapter was surreal. I can picture myself on the mountain, all alone on a sunny fall day. I know I was crying but had so much on my mind that I was barely in the moment. I can picture that dime in the dirt. I am glad I was on the phone with Merrilee because I was able to share with her one of the most precious times in my life. I knew this was my father reaching out to me. It helped guide me when taking care of his estate. I decided to make another necklace with that dime. Forever it will be with me and part of the reason I wrote this book.

The dead pens were an amazing way to send a message. I had to be ready to listen to all of the signs. I had spent a good part of my life covering up this part of me in order to survive in a tough world. *I had to believe and feel connected to Spirit in order for the universe to begin sending the messages.*

Chapter 15 Messages

Numbers continue to show me signs every single day. There were too many to put in Part II of the book. I highlighted all of the 8's in the story because that was Tyler's uniform number.

Chapter 16 Life Marches on

My son and I marching at the rehearsal for his wedding on 8-18-18.

This book is most definitely one of the biggest unexpected surprises of my life. I never dreamed I would ever become a writer. Once I started writing, I truly felt my soul opening up and I began to heal through the process. Without my Master's classes, I'm not sure I would have done this. The professors who worked with me forever changed my life. Not just with new credentials so I could get a new job, but they helped me discover my why- like "Why am I here on earth kinda why."

The camp foundation was the only part that was saved from our family camp. I think of foundations like childhood. My foundational beliefs were part of who I am, but I am constantly rebuilding them. I can change my body and my thoughts. I don't have to carry with me all of the parts of a foundation, but it does give me a starting point for life. I have the ability to change my life whenever I want. Sometimes it can be slow changes or I can tear it all down and start totally new. It's my choice.

I had a foundation of God within me from my childhood, but because organized religion had taught me some things, I wasn't always sure of myself. I had to let go of some of my childhood beliefs to understand that it was ok to believe in the things that I was being exposed to. Especially being an empath. My foundation was that I knew we were all different but I never knew about empaths or highly sensitive people. Now that I know, my life can be a new adventure!

The dreams I shared in the dime story helped me so much during those stressful times when I was worried. While writing this book, I happened to see one of my mother's cousins, Mary Redman. She was a tutor at the school I worked at. I hadn't seen her for years. She asked how everything was going and then asked about the family camp. When people do this, I always feel bad that we had to sell it. Mary remembers all of the Allen family reunions we had at camp with all of my mother's cousins and kids. The reunions are always a precious memory for everyone. So, instead of being negative, I shared the story of the dream I had where Dad showed me the photo album. I wanted Mary to know that we will always have those memories. Then she shared about one of her dreams.

Mary's husband, Paul, had passed away a few years ago. (I think it was when I was living with my Dad.) Mary shared that Paul organized a lot in the house so when he was gone, she had to figure some things out herself. She went to the bank to open the safety deposit box and didn't realize that Paul had the other key she would need to open the box. She went home and searched all over, including the desk where he kept everything. She got so angry and frustrated that she screamed and said, "Paul, you need to tell me where that key is right now!" She went to bed that night and he came to her in a dream, just like my mom and dad did with me. Mary told me that he laughed at her just like he always used to do and then said, "Mary, you know right where it is. It is in the drawer of that other table." Mary woke up, walked over to the drawer and there was the key. *Even though I know she misses her husband, I also saw the smile on her face. I know she felt he was connecting with her from Heaven.*

Chapter 17 THE Dime

"Being is not only beyond but also deep within every form as its innermost invisible and indestructible essence. This means that it is accessible to you now as your own deepest self, your true nature. But don't seek to grasp it with your mind. Don't try to understand it." ~Eckhart Tolle

Can you believe it? The EXACT type of dime from my father's collection? I found three coins in that house. First, a regular dime, then a penny and then a Liberty Head dime. At times, it feels surreal. Other times, I feel both of my parents nearby. Writing this book was most definitely a journey of my soul.

"You need to trust that there are parts of the creative process you cannot see, parts that work in mysterious ways, guided by whatever you want to call it- your unconscious, your muse, your higher power. You need to remember this because, with faith, you will find a way to do the work necessary to manufacture meaning out of material. Without faith, another unfinished project is likely to end up in the abyss of your bottom drawer." ~Joni B. Cole

While writing this book, I had to go within myself to find out why I had such a difficult time dealing with my mom. I realized that it wasn't her. It was me. I was built differently and none of us understood it because we didn't have the information. Not only am I an empath absorbing other people's feelings, but I am intuitive or psychic. I am still on this journey to discover exactly what this all means. I am not hiding this part of me anymore. I am learning to accept that because of my system being built differently, I have to take care of myself every single day. I have to use all of the skills I have learned. From meditation, to eating whole foods, not judging others, praying for those who hurt me, listening to my body and much, much more. Forever and always, life will be More Than a Dime, but the dimes showed me that we are connected to another realm, one that we can't physically see but we can believe in it just like the invisible breeze that blows the leaves. It's the life essence and energy that guides us in this spiritual journey as a human being.

One of my favorite things to do now is to drop dimes and pennies wherever I go. I imagine that when I drop a dime or a penny, I am sprinkling love. I imagine the person picking it up and feeling a bit closer to their loved ones in Heaven. Dropping dimes helps to heal my heart.

A few years before my parents passed away, I gave them one of the best gifts ever. Instead of a Christmas present, I gave them an Advent Story Calendar that I created. Every day for December they would open up a different envelope in the box I made. Inside the envelope was a story written by myself, my siblings or their grandkids. The story was a favorite memory about my parents. Here was one of mine:

"I loved having Christmas downstairs. Of course, at first, it was very important that Santa have a chimney where he could come into our house. It was always cozy to have the fireplace going and especially putting in the things that made the fire have different colors! It was always fun to open all of our presents down there. Of course, I thought I was dead meat when I got caught sneaking down to see my presents in the middle of the night. The biggest joke was definitely on me since I never knew it was DAD who set the traps, including the tin cans that made a loud rattle sound. I thought I woke up everyone in the whole house! I loved the year I got my new water skis because I knew then I could be like the "big kids"!

~Monica"

The Advent Story Calendar helped us all remember the positive memories. It's so easy to blame and focus on the negative. This idea was the best thing at the time for Mom and Dad. I'm happy that my parents were my parents. It made me who I am today. Whenever I see people who knew them, they always remind me how kind my parents were.

A young mother and friend recently wrote a post on Facebook and I felt it would be a perfect ending for my book. Here is what she said:

"Talking with a coworker yesterday about an activity she had planned with her kids for this weekend. She excitedly said "I am the best mom ever" and paused, looked at me and continued with "for my kids, and you are the best mom ever for your children." We both kept working, but I couldn't help but reflect on what she had said. How much truth was behind her words? These days it is so easy to become discouraged as a mother. Maybe you weren't able to breastfeed your child as long as you had wanted, your body just didn't cooperate. So maybe you had a c-section and had hoped to have an all natural birth. Only got 6 weeks maternity leave where some mothers are lucky enough to stay home and watch every second of their child grow and learn. I could go on and on but the point is as mothers we give so much of ourselves for these tiny little people, who steal our hearts at first sight. We put ourselves last, lose countless hours of sleep, drain every ounce of our bodies, and I'm sure I'm not the only one who feels like they just aren't enough at times. But we are! We are mothers! We grow people, and that's pretty freaking amazing. We are the best, and there is no doubt about that! I hope my mama friends who read this smile and reflect on how amazing you really are. And I hope you never forget, YOU are the best mom for your children! ❤" ~Kayley Griffin

We are all perfect- exactly the way we are. I know I am doing the best I can with my life and so is everyone else. We are also trying to be the best parents we can. Are we all perfect? Absolutely not! We are all humans doing the best we can.

When I began telling my dime story and began sharing about my book, people from all over began sending me pictures of dimes and telling me stories about connecting with people in Heaven. The dime made them think of me but more importantly, it made them happy, which is truly what I want for everyone in this world. I love hearing stories from other people. It connects us.

Elmore Mountain will always be a
part of me.

"At midlife our hearts ask us to wake up and live our personal truth so that there is a seamless connection between what we say we believe and how we actually live our day-to-day lives." ~ Dr. Christian Northrup.

In order to heal, I had to learn to connect my gut, my brain and most of all, my heart.

When I left Lakeview Union Elementary School to take a job at Hazen Union as a Middle School Math teacher, a colleague gave me a book. The book is called *Miss Maple's Seeds*. Inside the front cover, she wrote, "Monica- For all the 'seeds' you nurtured into 'beautiful plants'- Best Wishes on your new endeavor. ~Carrie ;) " When she wrote this, she would have no idea that her niece, Samantha, who passed away so suddenly would be planting a sunflower in my garden each and every year. I hope this book has planted some "seeds" of thoughts. I wish everyone the best as we all discover our life lessons and some sort of connection to the universe. Here are some of the authors who planted seeds in my mind. Check out my Resources to see all the authors who planted seeds in my mind!

How does all of this relate to education? We have an educational system built on a factory model that teaches to the linear brain. As humans, we have a need to learn how our hearts affect our ability to learn. Kids cannot learn like a robot. We need to be able to teach to the heart and the brain at the same time. We need to teach students how to regulate their bodies and deal with the stress they feel inside. By remembering our human characteristics, educators will be able to help children grow and develop into happy, healthy citizens. We will be able to help them get over their fear of making a mistake in front of their peers. We will be able to teach them about how our bodies function to better support them in the classroom. Might this topic be another book?

Resources/Bibliography

When I was young, I never wanted to read. It wasn't until I discovered Judy Blume's book, Are You There God? It's Me, Margaret that I started reading. After reading this book, often times I would think, " Are you there God, it's me, Monica." As an adult, I never read much until that first Brian Weiss book led me to Hay House Publishing. I had found "my books". These were all about real people with real lives. These books helped explain what I felt inside. They put me in touch with God in a different way than organized religion did. Of course, a few beach romance novels here and there were always a good way to relax, but I wanted to read about real people with real connections with God.

As Brene Brown so nicely says, **"As neuroscientist Antonio Damasio reminds us, humans are not either thinking or feeling machines, but rather feeling machines that think."**

These books made me think about my feelings. They all have helped me grow as a person.

Here are the many resources that I have used to guide me in my journey of life. Happy reading!

1. *A course in miracles: Combined volume.* (2007). Mill Valley, CA: Foundation for Inner Peace.
2. Albers, S. (2009). *50 ways to soothe yourself without food.* New Harbinger Publications Inc.
3. Albom, M. (2018). *Five People You Meet In Heaven.* S.l.: Hachette Books.
4. Albom, M. (2009). *Have a Little Faith.* Detroit: Thorndike Press.
5. Albom, M. (2018). *The first phone call from heaven.* Leicester: Thorpe, Isis.
6. Albom, M. (1962). *The Timekeeper.* New York, NY: Hyperion.
7. Alexander, E. M.D. (2014) *The Map of Heaven.* New York. Simon and Schuster Paperbacks.
8. Altucher, J. (2013). *Choose yourself* (1st ed.). United States: Lioncrest Publishing.
9. Alvarez, M. (2012). *365 ways to raise your frequency: Simple tools to increase your spiritual energy for balance, purpose, and joy.* Woodbury, MN: Llewellyn Publications.

10. Andrews, A. (2009) *The Noticer* Sometimes, all a person needs is a little perspective. Nashville, Thomas Nelson.

11. Andrews, T. (2006). *Animal-speak: The spiritual & magical powers of creatures great & small.* Woodbury, MN: Llewellyn Publications.

12. Angelou, M. (2009). *Celebrations rituals of peace and prayer.* London: Virago.

13. Angelou, M. (2008). *Letter to my daughter.* New York: Random House.

14. Angelou, M. (1993) *Wouldn't Take Nothing For my Journey Now.* New York. Random house.

15. Berger, W. (2016). *A more beautiful question: The power of inquiry to spark breakthrough ideas.* New York: Bloomsbury.

16. Bernstein, G. (2015). *Spirit junkie: A radical road to self-love and miracles.* Retrieved May 2, 2018.

17. Blue Mountain Press. (2001). *Always follow your dreams, wherever they lead you.* Boulder, Colo.

18. Bolman, L. G., & Deal, T. E. (2011). *Leading with soul: An uncommon journey of spirit.* San Francisco, CA: Jossey-Bass.

19. Braden, G. (2008). *The spontaneous healing of belief: Shattering the paradigm of false limits.* Carlsbad, CA: Hay House.

20. Brown, B. (2018). *Braving the wilderness: The quest for true belonging and the courage to stand alone.* Retrieved April 7, 2018.

21. Brown, B. (2017). *Rising Strong How the Ability to Reset Transforms the Way We Live, Love, Parent, and Lead.* Retrieved April 19, 2018.

22. Brown, B., & Fortgang, L. (2015). *The gifts of imperfection.* Center City, Minnesota. Hazelden Publishing.

23. Brown, B. (2018). Listening to shame. Retrieved from https://www.ted.com/talks/brene_brown_listening_to_shame

24. Brown, B. (2018). The power of vulnerability. Retrieved from https://www.ted.com/talks/brene_brown_on_vulnerability?

25. Burchard, Brendon. (2008) *Life's Golden Ticket A Story About Second Chances.* New York, NY. Harper One.

26. Burpo, T. (2011). *Heaven is for real.* New York: Gale Cengage Learning.

27. Byrne, R. (2016). *The secret.* New York: Atria Books.

28. CAUDILL, M. A. (1995). *MANAGING PAIN BEFORE IT MANAGES YOU.* S.l.: GUILFORD.

29. Chopra, M. (2016). *Living with intent: My somewhat messy journey to purpose, peace, and joy.* New York: Harmony Books.

30. Coffin, W. (2005) *letters to a YOUNG DOUBTER,* Louisville, Kentucky; Westminister John Knox Press.

31. Cole, J. B., & Baer, H. (2017). *Good naked: Reflections on how to write more, write better, and be happier.* Hanover: University Press of New England.

32. Coyle, D. (2013). *The talent code.* New York: Bantam Books.

33. Courteney, H. (2010). *Countdown to coherence: A spiritual journey toward a scientific theory of everything.* London: Watkins.

34. Dale, C. (2010). *Everyday clairvoyant: Extraordinary answers to finding love, destiny, and balance in your life.* Woodbury, MN: Llewellyn Publications.

35. Daniel, C. (2016). *Bioenergy healing: Simple techniques for reducing pain and restoring health through energetic healing.* Retrieved December 15, 2017.

36. Dyer, W. W., & Hicks, E. (2017). *Co-creating at its best: A conversation between master teachers.* Retrieved May 18, 2016.

37. Dyer, W. (2010). *The Shift.* Hay House Publishing.

38. Farmer, S. (2006) *Animal Spirit Guides.* New York City. Hay House, Inc.

39. Frankl, V. (1959). *Man's Search for Meaning.* Boston. Beacon Press

40. Gillespie, D. (2008). *Sweet poison.* Penquin Books.

41. Grout, P. (2013). *E 2 Nine Do-it-Yourself energy experiments that prove your thoughts create your reality.* New York City, NY: Hay House.

42. Gracie, M. (2017). *EMPATH A Comprehensive Guide for Emotional Healing, Self-Protection and Survival for Empaths & Highly Sensitive People.* Retrieved July 9, 2018.

43. Hanson, R., PH.D., & Mendius, R., MD. (2009). *Buddha's Brain, the Practical neuroscience of happiness, love and wisdom.* Oakland, CA: New Harbinger Publications.

44. Hay, L. L., & Kramer, J. (2012). *Gratitude: A way of life.* Carlsbad, CA: Hay House.

45. Hay, Louise L. (1984) *You Can Heal Your Life.* Carlsbad, CA; Hay House, Inc.

46. Hicks, E & J. (2007) *The Astonishing Power of Emotions Let Your Feelings Be Your Guide.* Carlsbad, CA. Hay House, Inc.

47. Holland, J., & Pearlman, C. (2007). Born knowing: A mediums journey-- accepting and embracing my spiritual gifts. Carlsbad, CA: Hay House.

48. Holland, J. (2018). *Bridging two realms: Learn to communicate with your loved ones on the other-side.* Carlsbad, CA: Hay House.

49. Hunt, J. (2009) *Building Your Leadership Resume Developing the Legacy That Will Outlast You.* Nashville, TN. B & H Publishing Group

50. Hyatt, M. (2012). *Platform.* Nashville, Tenn.: Harper Collins Leadership.

51. Jones, R. (2013). *I am More Than Enough: Helping women Silence Their Critic and Celebrate Their Inner Voice.*

52. Junger, A., Greeven, A., & Witkowska, M. (2011). *Clean.* Warszawa: MT Biznes.

53. Knight, S. (2016). *The life-changing magic of not giving a f**k: How to stop spending time you dont have doing things you dont want to do with people you dont like.* London: Quercus.

54. Liptak, J. J. (2010). *2012--catalyst for your spiritual awakening: Using the Mayan tree of life to discover your higher purpose.* Woodbury, MN: Llewellyn Publications.

55. *Living sober.* (1975). New York: Alcoholics Anonymous World Services.

56. Macleod, A. (2010). *The Transformation Healing Your Past Lives to Realize Your Soul's Potential.* Boulder, CO: SoundsTrue.

57. Mass, W. (2010). *Every soul a star.* Retrieved December 1, 2013.

58. Mayer, E. A. (2018). *The mind-gut connection: How the hidden conversation within our bodies impacts our mood, our choices, and our overall health.* New York: Harper Wave.

59. Meyer, J. (2002). *Never lose heart: Encouragement for the journey.* New York, NY: Warner Books.

60. Moorjani, A. (2015). *Dying to be me: My journey from cancer, to near death, to true healing.* New Delhi, India: Hay House India.

61. MOORJANI, A. (2017). *WHAT IF THIS IS HEAVEN?: How our cultural myths prevent us from experiencing heaven on earth.* S.l.: HAY HOUSE.

62. Myss, C. (1997). *Why People Don't Heal and How They Can.* New York, NY: Three Rivers Press.

63. Niemeier, S., & Dirven, R. (1997). *The language of emotions: Conceptualization, expression, and theoretical foundation.* Amsterdam: J. Benjamins.

64. Northrup, C. (2018). *Dodging energy vampires: An empaths guide to evading relationships that drain you and restoring your health and power.* Retrieved May 2, 2018.

65. Northrup, C. (2012). *The wisdom of menopause: Creating physical and emotional health during the change.* New York: Bantam Books.

66. Notaras, K. (2018). *The book you were born to write* (1st ed.). Carlsbad, CA: Hay House, Inc.

67. Orloff, J. (2015). *The Power of Surrender.* Retrieved June 2, 2018.

68. Orloff, J. (2014). *The ecstasy of surrender: 12 surprising ways letting go can empower your life.* Retrieved June 2, 2018.

69. Orloff, J. (2005). *Positive energy: 10 extraordinary prescriptions for transforming fatigue, stress and fear into vibrance, strength and love.* Retrieved June 2, 2018.

70. Orloff, J., Dr. (n.d.). *Guide to Intuitive Healing 5 steps to physical, emotional, and sexual wellness.* Retrieved 2018.

71. Orloff, J. (2010). *Second sight: An intuitive psychiatrist tells her extraordinary story and shows you how to tap your own inner wisdom.* Retrieved May 30, 2018.

72. Osteen, J. (2017). *Become a better you: 7 keys to improving your life every day.* New York: Howard Books.

73. Osteen, J. (2006). *Scriptures and meditations for your best life now.* New York: Faith Words.

74. Peirce, P. (2011). *Frequency: The power of personal vibration.* New York: Atria Books.

75. Piper, D., & Murphey, C. (2015). *90 minutes in heaven: A true story of death & life.* Grand Rapids, MI: Revell.

76. Rothstein, D., & Santana, L. (2014). *Make just one change: Teach students to ask their own questions*. Cambridge, MA: Harvard Education Press.

77. Ruiz, M., & Wilton, N. (2012). *The four agreements: A practical guide to personal freedom*. San Rafael, CA: Amber-Allen.

78. Ruiz, M., Ruiz, J. L., & Mills, J. (2011). *The fifth agreement: A practical guide to self-mastery*. San Rafael, CA: Amber-Allen.

79. Rushnell, S. (2001) *when GOD winks How the Power of Coincidence Guides Your Life. New York. Atria Books*.

80. Sartori, P., & Walsh, K. (2017). *The transformative power of near-death experiences: How the messages of NDEs positively impact the world*. London: Watkins.

81. Schaub, E. O. (2014). *Year of no sugar: A memoir*. Naperville, IL: Sourcebooks.

82. Schwartzberg, L & MJRaval. (2014) *MINDFUL INTENTIONS. New York. Hay House, Inc.*

83. Segal, I. (2014). *The secret language of your body: The essential guide to health & wellness*. Glen Waverley, Victoria: Blue Angel Publishing.

84. Simon Sinek: Find Your Why | One of The Best Speeches Ever. (2018). Retrieved from https://www.youtube.com/watch?v=YnBs6YGPAu4

85. Sinek, S. (2018). *Leaders eat last*. Portfolio Penguin.

86. Sinek, S. (2016). *Together is Better A Little Book of Inspiration*. New York, NY. Portfolio/Penguin

87. Thielke, J. (n.d.). *The SLEEP Learning system Instant Pain Relief, Create Healing Energy*. Retrieved December 15, 2017.

88. Tolle, E., & Tolle, E. (2011). *Practicing the power of now: Essential teachings, meditations, and exercises from the power of now*. Sydney: Hachette Australia.

89. Tolle, E., & DiCarlo, R. E. (2016). *The power of now: A guide to spiritual enlightenment*. London: Yellow Kite.

90. Virtue, D. (2007). *How to hear your angels*. Carlsbad, CA: Hay House.

91. Virtue, D. (2011) *The Angel Therapy Handbook*. New York. Hay House Inc.

92. Virtue, D. (2010). *The crystal children*. London: Hay House.

93. Weiss, B. L., & Weiss, B. L. (2002). *Many lives, many masters ; Messages from the masters*. New York: One Spirit.

94. Weiss, B. L., & Weiss, A. E. (2013). *Miracles happen: The transformational healing power of past-life memories*. New York, NY: HarperOne, an imprint of HarperCollins.

95. Weiss, B. L. (2005). *Same Soul, Many Bodies: Discover the Healing Power of Future Lives through Progression Therapy*. Riverside: Free Press.

96. Wheeler, E. (2013). *Miss Maple's seeds*. Nancy Paulsen Books.

97. Zukav, G. (2010). *Spiritual partnership: The journey to authentic power*. New York: HarperOne.

Websites:

https://www.ask-angels.com/spiritual-guidance/angels-and-numbers/

https://aurainsightsauraphotography.wordpress.com/2011/08/17/aura-photos-of-before-and-after-reiki-1/

https://exemplore.com/paranormal/What-is-an-Empath-Traits-signs-solutions

https://hsperson.com/

https://www.huffingtonpost.com/tree-franklyn/youre-not-an-alien-youre-an-empath_b_7763702.html

https://www.carl-jung.net

https://www.reiki.org/faq/whatisreiki.html

https://aurainsightsauraphotography.wordpress.com/2011/08/17/aura-photos-of-before-and-after-reiki-1/

https://www.thebetterhealthstore.com/043011_top-ten-toxic-ingredients-in-processed-food_01.html

http://sensitive-theuntoldstory.vhx.tv/

More Dimes from Heaven A Journey to Self-Publishing

More Dimes from Heaven A Journey to Self-Publishing

Dedication

To both of my parents,
James and Deanna Palmer.
I know you are always with me now.
Thank you for your guidance
during this lifetime.

Acknowledgments

Thank you to my husband, Brian, who always encourages me to follow my dreams. Thank you to my Father-in-law and Mother-in-law, who taught me to have gratitude for everything in life.

Thank you to my two sons, Shamus and Patrick, for being who you are. I hope you always enjoy life to the fullest with Emily and Heather!

Thank you to my darling Grandsons, Lincoln James Morrissey and Jackson Douglas Morrissey. I love spending time with you both!

Thank you to my Sister, Debbie, for always being there for me.

Thank you to Merrilee and Don, who treat me like their daughter.

Thank you to my team- Chelsea and Tracy Collier. You both cheer me on and support me in ways that thank you just doesn't seem enough. I cherish our time together and so appreciate having you with me in this journey of life!

Thank you to my Editor in chief, Kim Knudson. Thank you for your support and your knowledge of the English Language.

In my first book, I wrote about building walls up to protect myself. I built a wall with my boss when I was 19 years old but am thankful that Barb Grant is back in my life now. I so appreciate our friendship and great conversations. Thank you for your advice on my book and in life!

Thank you to all of my Readers- I love to hear your stories about signs from your loved ones. Thank you for your continued support and I hope you enjoy Book #2!

A Note From the Author

Dimes From Heaven, How Coins and Coincidences Helped Me Discover My Life as an Empath came from my soul. It was a journey within myself that I hadn't planned to do. It was as much of a surprise to me as it was to many of my friends and family. I was honored that people enjoyed reading my story.

More Dimes From Heaven, A Journey to Self Publishing is a bit different than my first book. The one thing that will be the same is that there are many dimes within the story. There are also other messages from my Angels in Heaven that were sent during my writing journey. The reader will hear these stories along with some other topics to think about. Each chapter has questions to help you write your story or book. The last part of each chapter is my experience and knowledge about how to self publish. I hope to encourage you to share your story with the world!

Connect with me:
Facebook @monicalmorrissey
Website www.monicalmorrissey.com
Email monicalmorrissey@gmail.com

More Dimes From Heaven, A Journey to Self Publishing

Introduction- From Teacher to Author: Following My Soul's Journey

"The Secret is the law of attraction! Everything that's coming into your life you are attracting into your life. And it's attracted to you by virtue of the images you're holding in your mind. It's what you're thinking. Whatever is going on in your mind you are attracting to you." ~ Rhonda Byrne

On the night of my first book signing event, I saw a young woman, a friend of my son, and I shared with Renae that I was having my first book signing. The name of the event was Messages From Heaven, where the same Medium, Rebecca Anne LoCicero (https://www.re-beccaannelocicero.com/) that I wrote about in my first book would be doing a group event. I shared with her the story when the Medium said, "A dime a dozen." Sitting in the front row, I held up my dime necklace and Rebecca said, *"Is that a F*@king dime?"*. My father came through with a lot of messages for me. The dimes were my Dad's way to communicate because he had given me a special dime from his coin collection. Renae responded, *"You are so lucky!"* I would love to say that it is luck. I responded, *"It might be luck but it is because I am so open. I used to close* *down my heart because I was scared to be hurt. Now, I am open so these things tend to happen more often!"* She agreed and I walked away hoping that her heart would be a little more open because she felt it was safe. I also hoped that Renae would get messages from her Dad.

"What some people call luck and coincidence is the precise execution of an infinitely intelligent universe that works in amazing ways to fulfill exactly what we imagine ourselves to be, with conviction." ~ David Cameron Gikandi

My husband and I are back at the condo in Indian Shores, Florida, exactly one year after I began writing Dimes From Heaven. I get asked the question, "How long did it take you to write your book?" I began writing in early April of 2018 on our annual spring vacation in Florida, sent my manuscript into the publisher (I self-published through Balboa Press, a division of Hay House) on January 8th, 2019, and my book was released on February 27, 2019. It took me approximately nine months. I don't think this is the average, especially if you have a traditional publisher. My book seemed to literally appear out of nowhere from the beginning to the end, an unexpected blessing in my life.

Originally, I set out to write my dime story - nothing more than a neat short story. I started writing because I was in physical pain and the doctors couldn't figure out why my bladder felt like I had to urinate all the time. It was awful and I had been going from doctor to doctor with no relief. Somewhere along my travels I had heard that writing was therapeutic. I seriously rolled my eyes as I put pen to paper. *How would writing heal a physical pain? This was crazy! When I had physical pain, wasn't I supposed to go to the doctors? They would give me something that could heal me. If I had to look at my emotions to heal, how long would that take? Plus, that sounded way too difficult and time consuming.*

I kept writing because I wanted to share my dime story. I envisioned myself making photocopies for friends and family - imagining it would be like 10 pages total. Then, when I first started writing, my husband asked me if I was writing a book. I never thought I would have enough of a story to make it into a book. He had planted a seed that grew into an idea. Then that idea turned into a reality. Never in my entire 50 years had I EVER wanted to write a book!

Writing was for "other" people! As a teacher, I enjoyed teaching Math and actually hated to teach writing. I wanted my students to enjoy the creative free writing but the curriculum wanted me to direct them in not only how to write but also what to write about. I wanted them to write about whatever they were interested in. You have ducks for a pet? Tell me a story about your ducks! You have a horse? Tell me about your horse. You have a cool Grandpa? Write about your favorite day with him. Write about whatever you feel in your heart.

That's how you, too, can find out what you want to write about. Your husband had a stroke? Write about your story to help the next person who might be going through the same thing. You have cancer? Write about it to help the next person who has cancer. You adopted a child? Share your story - all of it - the good, the bad, and yes, the ugly. Be authentically *you* in every way. Be brave because not only is it possible that you help the next person in your shoes, you can also help yourself.

I was scared to share a lot of my story, but I also knew that I needed to share. I had faith that it would help someone, somewhere and it most definitely did!

In Dimes From Heaven, when my husband and I were chatting about my writing, he said that the wire cable near the pool area was there all along, even though I couldn't see it. The sun blinded me from being able to see the cable.

"Has my ability to write and listen to my intuition been within me all this time? Were the answers inside me all the time, but I wasn't looking the right way to be able to see them?" ~Monica L. Morrissey

I hadn't been able to see that I could listen to my intuition and write a book. I thought maybe my ability to write had been there all along but I hadn't been able to see it because I wasn't looking at it the right way; I was too busy being angry and feeling resentment.

This year, we swim in the pool and I say, "There's that wire, but there isn't one on this side of the pool. You know- the one I saw last year?"

He responds, "You have to be on the other side to see it. It's there." His words have a deeper meaning for me. I think of being on the other side of publishing my book. I am a different person now. I can't quite explain it but something in me has shifted.

"The unknown carries tremendous opportunities, knowledge, potential, and rewards. Step into it often." ~ David Cameron Gikandi

It all feels like a dream. Last year, on our way to the airport, I stopped at Barnes and Noble. I found a beautiful turquoise journal and wrote on the front cover, "More Than a Dime." My 'dime story' was so much more, but, even then, I had no road map as to where I was going with my writing. I listened to the voice inside; it was time to share my story.

I started writing the day we got to Florida. Once I started, I didn't want to stop. I was dumping a lot of emotional baggage onto the pages. In between those stories, the dime story began to appear. It would be transformed over the next several months, but the 'bones' of the story would be developed that first week.

It was like a secret portal connected to a universal intelligence opened up for me. One that I had not dared to go through for fear of someone not liking me. I was scared to be me. I was scared to share my story. When I allowed myself to be me and be present (at this point I was just learning mindfulness practices), the portal opened up even more and I was able to see the universe in a whole, new way. God, my Angels, and my Spirit Guides were all there ready to support me. They were there because I asked for their help. I spoke the words out loud instead of just thinking about them in my head. I felt the connection inside my body. That's the only way to open up the secret "portal" I began experiencing.

The portal opened up because I was feeling and not just thinking. The mindfulness training had brought me back into my body instead of always being in my head. I was paying attention to my thoughts and the sensations within myself. The portal connecting me to the universe was guiding me in a new direction and I was stepping into something that I felt was unplanned. This new access to the portal was the beginning of my spiritual awakening.

"You always have the choice to *pay attention* and take an unfamiliar and perhaps risky path. Likewise, you can choose to *not pay attention* and stay with the version of your life implanted in you by familial and cultural influences dictating precisely what your limitations and aspirations ought to be." ~ Dr. Wayne Dyer

Writing is a journey that opened my eyes to a whole other world; one I knew little about. It was a world I was, at first, scared to enter. I had to have faith that it was a work I was destined to be a part of. I was stepping into the unknown with a knowing that I was exactly where I was supposed to be at the exact time I was meant to be there.

I never once in my life thought I would actually write a book. Within the first two weeks of receiving feedback from my readers, one reader (whom I did not know) wrote an Amazon Review, *"To pour your heart out and tell your story was amazing to read. It is nice to know that I can relate to some of the stories. If you are looking for your next book, please consider this book. I had a hard time to put it down, once I started reading it.* ***Thank You for sharing and I look forward to reading more, if you continue to share."*** I looked at my husband and said, "Oh my goodness. I'm not ready for that! I don't know what I would write about!" He responded, in his usual supportive manner, *"You'll figure it out."*

Just like I hadn't thought of taking a different path when there was a rock blocking my path, I had absolutely no idea what to do next. I hadn't prepared myself for this. *Was there really any way to truly prepare for a book release?* For me, it was a wait and see what happens. I didn't know what to expect and now the readers wanted more!

I began to observe my life - like I was watching from the outside looking in. *What was happening? I listened to my readers. What were they asking about?* A lot of them seemed interested in writing their own story. My story gave them the courage to want to share their story. They asked questions like, *"Why did you write your book?"* or *"How did you get your book published?" When I listen to the universe, it seems to have the answer I was seeking. I would write a book about my writing journey-which, in and of itself, was pretty spectacular!*

In Dimes From Heaven, the readers heard my thoughts of how scared I was to write and tell my story to the world. What the readers didn't hear about were all the crazy signs from the universe when I started writing. Unbelievable things happened to show me I was taking a whole new path in life and everything was going to be ok. I listened to my own advice and believed that I was following my soul's journey in a whole new exciting way.

I kept track of all the mysterious synchronicities that were happening. Originally they were all included in the manuscript. They were cut when my publisher told me the cost of the book would be $58.99! *What? That's CRAZY! That price was way too high!* When I self-published, I didn't get a say in setting the book price. Even without this section, the price of the book was going to be $32.99. By cutting that part out, I realized that there was a reason for it. I would be able to share my story about becoming an author to help the next person write their story! I thought it was unplanned, but I think the universe had planned this.

Brené Brown states that the opposite of belonging is fitting in. I think what she means is that if I am fitting in, then I am trying to be like everyone else. But, if I truly belong, then others accept me as I am and I can be me without having to change to fit in.

I have spent most of my life trying to fit in. I have tried to be like other people instead of me. You are reading this today because my readers were willing to see me as my true self and did not ask me to "fit in". I first had to see myself and then allow you to see me.

I have been hiding for 50 years. **I have been within myself searching for a sense of belonging. What I didn't understand was that in order to belong, I had to accept myself first and the rest would happen automatically.** I had to understand that we all belong to the universe. We are all connected to something greater than ourselves. We are all exactly who we are supposed to be. *What does belonging mean to you now that you know to seek it through loving yourself versus fitting in?*

"The real benefit of looking back at all of those significant events of your life and seeing how that invisible hand of God was there for you at the time is not to rehash your entire past looking for the hidden meanings, but to awaken you to becoming a more conscious person now, today, in the present moments of your life."
~ Dr. Wayne Dyer

My Dad loved to have conversations about a bigger purpose in life. We had many conversations about coincidences or synchronicities when I was caring for him after my Mom transitioned to Spirit. I knew that he missed her a lot but we tried to feel connected to her through signs that we felt were from Heaven. Once my Dad transitioned to Spirit, I knew that he had figured out the Spirit Communication System I had told him about.

"Hey dad- there is this new communication system you haven't heard of yet. It's a new Spirit Communication system. It's where angels in Heaven can talk to humans on earth. It's awesome and works well. You won't really be away from us. We will be able to talk all the time. I can talk to you and you can talk to me. We will always know that you are here with us. It's kind of like a new telephone system (my dad was a mechanic and always had to understand the details of how things worked). It works so well you will be able to call me anytime and I can call you too! Mom has already tried the new system and she is excited for you to join her. Your Mom is there too! Your Mom is waiting for you. You can send messages anytime you want and we will all talk to you too." ~Monica L. Morrissey

My Dad had given me a special dime from his coin collection. It was called a Liberty Head Dime or a Mercury Dime. It symbolized Freedom of Thought and he had it made into a necklace for all of his children and grandchildren. Since my mother had passed away, she had been sending me pennies from Heaven. I knew when I started receiving dimes, they were my dad communicating with me.

There are more dime stories in this book, but they are sprinkled throughout my story. It isn't like the last book where you knew some of the dimes would be at the end. This time, you are going to be reading and then all of a sudden - there is a dime story! That is what life is like with unexpected surprises all along the way.

Note from the author: Each chapter is set up to encourage you to dig deep to uncover your story. You might journal along and answer the questions I propose or you might even write your own book! I hope you enjoy the stories along my journey to becoming an author.

"By taking the courageous step of sharing a story that is deeply true to you, that makes you feel vulnerable and has real emotion, you will experience a new feeling of personal power, and your audience will feel that power too." ~ Heather Box and Julian Mocine-McQueen

Chapter 1: My Career Path

"When you are working within your purpose, work is no longer a job; it becomes a pleasure, and it becomes life. The boundary between work and fun vanish." David Cameron Gikandi

I graduated High School in 1986 and went to college to become a teacher. At this point in time, most guidance counselors were encouraging students to attend college. The question wasn't, "What are you passionate about?" but more like, "What career path will provide you a safe, secure life?" I thought everyone was going to college so that's what I did too. It wasn't, "Should I go to college?" It was, "Where do I go to college?" After I figured out where to go, "What do I want to study to provide me with money?"

I applied and was accepted into two colleges - Johnson State College (ten minutes away from my childhood home) or The University of Vermont (about an hour away). I felt Johnson was a better fit for me; both financially and socially. Since my parents didn't allow me much freedom in high school, I couldn't imagine going to Burlington - which seemed like a big city to me at the time!

I had two career paths I was interested in. I loved working with numbers but I also loved babysitting children. I either wanted to be a Certified Public Accountant or a teacher. My mother went to Johnson State College in the 1950's to receive her Elementary Education teaching license. She only taught for a very short time before becoming a stay at home Mom and helping my Dad with the family business. Johnson State was known for their education program so that also contributed to my decision about where I decided to go to college.

If you read Dimes From Heaven, then you know my first year in college was pretty tough. I had no idea how to make friends and I was so insecure that I turned to alcohol for confidence. After that first year, I met my husband and was able to get more focused on studying.

Because I was young in my class, I graduated college at age 21 and began my first year teaching. It was 1990. I graduated college in May, got married in August and began teaching 6th grade in the fall. It was a whirlwind of a year and I grew up fast. I had a big class that year and I did not feel very confident in my teaching. I had no mentor to guide me and felt like I was thrown into a sink or swim situation.

I remember that year. My students and parents were a great group. I felt very supported by the families, my colleagues and the principal. I was making a few mistakes here and there, but everyone was very supportive. On the other hand, because I internalized all of my stress, I ended up getting very sick with shingles that year. Looking back now, I would imagine that if I had practiced self care as I do now I might have avoided this illness.

I loved my job as a teacher and at one point, I thought, "Wow. They are actually paying me to do the very thing that I love to do! How amazing is that?" I was having so much fun with my students and watching them grow that I sometimes forgot that this was a job.

"The surest way to enjoy your work is to work within your purpose in life. Work within whatever you determine is your purpose in life, not your job or obligation, but that which you feel called from within to do, that which you dream of doing- and joy at work will be easy to experience." ~ David Cameron Gikandi

The years as a teacher seemed to literally fly by. I was a busy working Mom of two boys. I worked as a teacher taking care of everyone else and then came home to take care of my family. Teaching offered me a lot of time to spend with my boys. We loved to spend time doing fun things outside, especially camping and going to the beach in the summer.

When my boys were teenagers and got their licenses, I had more free time for me. I don't do well with time on my hands; I like to be busy. I decided that I would work part-time as a Realtor. At the time, we were trying to sell our house and I thought it might be an interesting job.

Originally, I began working as a Realtor for extra money. The extra income would help our family be able to go on a vacation and help our boys with the insurance and vehicle costs of being a new driver. It took me some time to realize that for me, Real Estate isn't just about the money. It's about helping people. Buying a new home is a big decision. I had to reframe my thinking about Real Estate from a "I want this deal to go through for the money" to "I want to help people find their perfect home". I had to understand that the universe had a bigger purpose for me.

"Was being a realtor supposed to teach me to believe in letting the future unfold instead of trying to control it? Was it forcing me to feel out of control so that I could learn ultimately that God is in control?...I had to learn to let go of the outcome." ~Monica L. Morrissey

I can see clearly that the knowledge of how the real estate market worked was extremely useful information to have when I helped my parents sell their long time family business and when we sold their houses as part of their estate. I never could have known at the time, but the universe was giving me an opportunity to prepare myself for the events that would come later.

I promised myself when I was young that I would never be a grumpy, angry teacher. I started to become that person and knew that I had to do something different. I loved teaching but I was taking on everyone's energy (and didn't understand it at the time!). I was turning into the angry person I didn't want to be. I sometimes showed this side of myself in the classroom, but tried hard not to. Often times, I would react to things that happened to me at school in a very defensive way. Parent complaint? *Well, let me tell you what I think about them!* Administration problem? *Well, I can tell you what <u>they</u> should be doing.* I was becoming a defensive "know it all" anytime I felt threatened or attacked. Small things could send me into a tailspin of stories that would ultimately make me out to be the victim of injustices done to me. I didn't understand that this is how we are built as humans, but I knew that I had to do something different with my life.

While writing, I learned that I was an empath. This affected my teaching career and eventually, because I did not take care of myself, it caused me to be sick. As an empath and highly sensitive person, I physically and emotionally absorb other people's energy. This is wonderful if I am near a positive person, but with so much negativity in the world today, I was taking on too much negative energy. I also thought it was my job to fix everything. This was too much for me and I eventually got burned out being around people so much. Teaching was becoming a career that I couldn't do anymore because it was impossible to take care of myself and everyone else. My nervous system was overloaded and I had no strategies of how to care for myself.

I worked toward my Master's degree and thought I might want to be a Principal. When I was about to graduate, I interviewed and was a finalist for three Principal positions. I remember getting the phone call that I didn't get the job. I was runner up. I called my husband and I said, "I'm ok with not getting the job. I am upset because I know that I can't keep teaching. I HAVE to do something else with my life." I had no idea that the universe had a plan and I needed to be patient.

Weeks later, I got the perfect job. It wasn't a job as a Principal. The universe knew, even before I knew, that being a principal would be too physically and emotionally demanding for me. I needed a job where I would be able to take better care of myself. In this new job as a Curriculum Director, I would begin to love helping teachers, which in turn helped students. While doing this, I would be able to balance my work and home life better. I would slowly learn that I was more than my job.

"I was pushing, striving, and controlling, instead of listening, trusting, and allowing. It took my whole life to come tumbling down for me to realize that everything I was searching for was inside me all along." ~ Rebecca Campbell

In my book Dimes From Heaven, there is a chapter called **Come What May.** I tell the story of when I had bought a ring with this saying on it and at the time, I placed the words facing toward me so that I was able to read the words. Recently, I started wearing the ring again. This time, though, I placed the words facing the other direction. It might seem like an insignificant change, but inside me there has been a profound change since I first purchased that ring five years ago. Let me explain.

At the time that I purchased the ring, I felt like life was going to change because I had a feeling that my parents might not live through the winter and I was going to have to deal with everything this would entail. Life was going to give me some challenges and I was going to have to dig deep to get through this time period. Life was happening "to me". Things would be "coming at me". I felt inside that there wasn't going to be much I would be able to do about anything that happened. I wasn't in control. I would sit and wait to see what happened. Inside, I felt that life was going to be like a truck moving full throttle with a lot of momentum. There was no way that I could slow it down. I would just wait for it to hit me. One truck at a time. I would deal with whatever happened when it happened. I thought that life was going to throw some difficult things at me.

Fast forward to writing my first book. I was scared to share my story and I never would have guessed how it changed my life and my thinking. Tara, a friend, who read my book, sent me a copy of *The Untethered Soul The Journey Beyond Yourself* by Michael A. Singer. I had no idea how this one book would change my thinking, which prompted me to switch my ring facing outward instead of toward me.

"Come to know the one who watches the voice, and you will come to know one of the great mysteries of creation." ~ Michael A. Singer

The voice inside my head had taken over my life. I wanted to get away from this voice. I had many readers approach me and say, "I thought I was the only one who thought like that!" I also got questions from friends who wondered if I was ok now. I began questioning my entire thought process.

Here is one of my favorite sections from Michael's book,

"Basically, you're not alone in there. There are two distinct aspects of your inner being. The first is you, the awareness, the witness, the center of your willful intentions; and the other is that which you watch. The problem is, the part that you watch never shuts up. If you could get rid of that part, even for a moment, the peace and serenity would be the nicest vacation you've ever had." ~ Michael L. Singer

I had been busy thinking that life was happening "to me" and that I needed to respond to everything. I was in reaction mode and most of the time I felt like I needed to protect myself. This is a normal human component but sometimes in life it just isn't helpful. This was a way to run from my fears by trying to protect my psyche, as Michael calls it. I discovered I wanted out of this way of thinking.

Since Tara had recommended this book to me, I figured that I would also listen to his other book, The Surrender Experiment, at the same time I was reading the first book.

In his book *The Surrender Experiment,* Michael applies his work from *The Untethered Soul* and reflects on his life choices. He explains how he let life happen instead of forcing something arbitrarily. He walked us through life events where he was able to let go and let life happen. Never, in a million years, would he have guessed that life would lead him in the direction it did.

I saw many similarities in my own life. When I let life flow and wrote the book I felt called to write, it led me in a different career direction than I ever imagined!

"Sometimes it's just tricky to hear what is being said before your head comes in and doubts it all. To differentiate the crazy voice from the wholehearted, enlightened, centered voice of your soul." ~ Rebecca Campbell

The same is true for my career path. I never would have dreamed that I would use my training as a teacher to write a book. All of the writing courses that my principal had forced me to take (which I was very unhappy about at the time!), would give me the necessary skills to turn my dime story into a book.

The ring faces the other way now because I am open to whatever the universe brings my way. I seriously don't know what is next for me. As I enjoy my time as a Curriculum Director, I know that writing has led me in a different direction. I seek answers in a different way. I ask the universe for guidance and am curious to learn more. I am a certified Health and Life Coach (through www.healthcoachinstitute.com) and hope to be able to help others find their true soul calling and life path; one that might be different than they originally planned!

Last summer I went blueberry picking with a friend and her granddaughter. To get to the field, we had to drive on a path through the woods. There were two forks in the road and both times I went the wrong way. I had to turn around and go back. My friend and I said to each other, "Seems like they would have some signs for people to know where to go." Her granddaughter speaks up and says, "They did. Didn't you see the arrows?" Often, young children notice signs more than adults do. Honestly, I was too busy looking at the path and thinking about other things in my head. I didn't see the signs that were clearly marked.

Was life like that sometimes? We are so busy planning our path that we forget to look at the signs from the universe all around us? Was I so busy planning my career that I didn't listen to Spirit whispering in my ear? Did the universe have a different plan for me- one that I would have no way of knowing what would come next? Would I need to trust that the universe was working its magic and that if I was patient enough, it would guide me in the right direction?

At 51 years old, I feel like I am beginning my path toward a more passionate, fulfilling work as a Health and Life Coach, Speaker, Editor, Writer, and Educator.

"And if you want to build deeper personal or professional relationships and be a more effective change maker, you have to show up honestly and vulnerably in your life - for your colleagues, your kids, and everyone else in your world. Your story can influence and inspire someone - perhaps many people - and it can expand your understanding of your own experiences and values." ~ Heather Box and Julian Mocine-McQueen

<u>**Questions to Ponder**</u>

- What has your career path been like?
- Do you wake up each day excited to go to work? If yes, what excites you? If no, why not?
- What are you passionate about?
- What are your dreams?
- What job would you have that wouldn't feel like work?
- What has happened in your life that you might want to write about?
- How would your story help the next person?
- Try writing something (anything!) and see where it leads you.

"I allow my fingers to be taken over by the energy of what my heart most needs to hear." ~ Rebecca Campbell

Chapter 2: Weeds or Flowers?

Recently I was at a conference for work. It was summertime in Vermont and I was admiring all of the beautiful flowers at the resort. The gardener was there as I walked to the conference. I commented, "The flowers are so beautiful!" She replied, "Thank you." But then she added, "There are so many weeds though!" I stopped to look. I hadn't seen the weeds until she pointed them out to me. I know that that is her job but I couldn't help but wonder about weeds and flowers in life.

Trust me when I say that I had to work through a lot of weeds in my first book to get to any of the flowers that you saw in Dimes From Heaven. I started writing and it opened up a door that led to things I didn't really know or understand. Later on, I would form it into chapters and sections. At the beginning, I just wrote and wrote and wrote some more. I didn't stop to think or analyze any of it. I didn't spell words correctly. I didn't have paragraphs or any structure. It was a very cathartic experience for me. It came from deep within me and I let it flow.

"As Jesus said, 'It's the Spirit that gives life,' and words on a page appearing out of nowhere are a result of the dance of creation." ~ Dr. Wayne Dyer

Whenever I told my dime story, people were always amazed by it! My Dad had given me a unique dime from his coin collection. Because of this coin, I would always know that dimes were a sign from him. I could tell that most people believed in signs from heaven. *Would my story be better if they knew every conversation I had with my Dad?* I usually never had time to tell them the story about the minister on the mountain, but that was pretty spectacular too!

My goal was to share all of the pieces and parts of the dime story and weave in all of the learning from all of the different books I had read. I would be able to give the reader tips on how to change their lives for the better. My story had the power to transform and give people the information to live differently - better and happier lives.

Right from the moment I put pen to paper, my story was "More Than a Dime". I knew that I had more to share than "just" my dime story. I had been reading books about healing through emotional work for years and I knew that other people didn't have the time or the opportunity to read as much as I did. I saw so many people in pain and wanted them to feel better. **If only people knew that what they think in**

their head has such an impact on their physical health! This information could be transformational to millions! I wanted the people in my community to know and understand Louise Hay's messages about how our emotions affect our physical bodies. This was now a topic we were discussing in the educational world with the Adverse Childhood Experiences (ACE) study. My personal passion was meeting up with my professional world. More and more we were discussing emotional health in education- for the teachers, students and families. Now was the perfect time to use my dime story as a way to draw the reader in to learn more about how to heal in a very different way than the American medical system says we should heal.

I also wanted people to believe in signs from Heaven. I knew if they heard my dime story even the non-believers would most likely believe. I had a pretty clear vision of my message, but the process of writing took a lot of twists and turns. In this early phase of writing, I asked the universe for clarity and was given many messages. While I wrote about believing in Heaven, I began to feel sensations in my body as I wrote about events.

"Good morning, This is God. I will be handling all of your problems today. I will not need Your help, so have A miraculous day." ~ Dr. Wayne Dyer

Wayne Dyer speaks of writing first thing in the morning, because that is the time when we are close to Spirit, the place we visit while we are asleep. This is my best time to write. I get up at 3:00 or 4:00 in the morning and write for as long as possible. My mind is clear and fresh. I had no road map for my first book. Ideas would come when my mind was clear. To clear my mind, I exercise, do yoga and eat healthy, whole foods. Junk food equaled junk thoughts so it was important to cleanse my body from processed foods.

"I have been writing day and night for almost a year now. The words come fast and furious, flowing freely like water from a spigot that continues to flow because of a broken pipeline. I can't plug the leak - I've never known such intensity in my writing. It comes in the middle of the night, it comes in the afternoon, and it comes in the evening as well." ~ Dr. Wayne Dyer

My first draft was messy and I wrote in a journal instead of on a computer. I spilled lots and lots of weeds before my writing turned into the book. An example of a "weed" that I removed from my writing was the part about buying my Grandmother's house. I had originally added, "Looking back, I see now it was a way for my mother to control me." I filtered that "weed" out and realized I was blaming someone else for what I felt to be true. Judgments divide us and I didn't need to listen to that voice inside me that always judges each experience I have in life. This was me beginning to look within myself instead of judging my Mom.

For me, my writing was better if I wrote it out by hand and then transcribed it to the computer. That way, I could "weed" out some of the things that were important for me to write about to heal, but didn't necessarily need to be shared with the world!

Ideas would pop into my head in the middle of a run or when I was in a meditation. It was like as soon as my mind surrendered and quieted, messages were whispered to my soul. Ideas that I never could have come up with my conscious mind.

I've always wondered who determines which plants are weeds and which plants we call flowers. It seems as though we shouldn't have to sort them and instead be in awe of all of the beauty that surrounds us! When you are writing, there may be some weeds that you may leave behind in your final draft. But, for your first draft, let them sit there. Enjoy them. Don't worry about them. Sometimes your soul needs to express them!

Weeds or Flowers?

- I can see flowers instead of weeds in my life.
- I acknowledge the weeds but don't focus on them.
- I realize that both weeds and flowers are important in my life. They help balance my life and keep me humble.
- I understand that it is one's perceptions and judgments that determine which we see as weeds or flowers. It's always a choice.

"Some people could be given an entire field of roses and only see the thorns in it. Others could be given a single weed and only see the wildflower in it. Perception is a key component to gratitude. And gratitude is a key component to joy." ~ Amy Wentherly

<u>**Questions to Ponder**</u>

- What big message do you want the reader to gain from your book or story?
- What are the smaller messages within the big message?
- Sometimes people like to have outlines for their books. Decide if that feels right to you.
- When you begin writing, brainstorm around 20 different titles and subtitles. Then, don't get too attached to them. Put them aside until later.
- Write from beginning to end and don't worry about perfection. Just write and write and write some more. Don't worry if you don't know where you are going. It might appear at any moment!
- What "weeds" are you focusing on?
- What "flowers" do you see in your writing?

"We spend way too much time in filtered social media moments and not enough time in the sometimes prickly weeds of real life." ~ Heather Box and Julian Mcine-McQueen

My Self Publishing Journey

"Once you make a decision, the Universe conspires to make it happen." ~ Ralph Waldo Emerson

 April 14, 2018 - On our flight home the week I started writing my first book, I decide to finish reading a book I had started reading months earlier. Normally on vacation, I read instead of write. I had brought a few books on my trip. I like to finish things so I decided on the flight home, I would finish this particular book. I had a few chapters left. Timing is everything. The book ended with this, "**Kelley makes a resolution. He is going to write a novel.** And forget the Christmas letter! He's going to start right now, **this instant.** He doesn't have any time to waste!" (pg 243 Elin Hilderbrand's book, Winter Storms.) **Those were the very last words of the book. Talk about a sign? Really?**

As I wrote in Dimes From Heaven, I felt strongly that I wanted to be able to keep my story **my** story. I didn't want an editor or publisher to change the flow of my book. I knew this from when I started writing. A few weeks after my trip to Florida, I googled Hay House self-publishing. I knew I would be able to publish for free on Amazon, but I felt like I needed a little more support.

I discovered Balboa Press, a self publishing company that is a division of Hay House. I knew it! I knew Louise Hay would have a way for someone like me, a new author, to get published. Some other self-publishing companies are www.outskirtspress.com, www.lulu.com, https://kdp.amazon.com/en_US/ or www.bookbaby.com to name a few. The book you are now reading was done on Kindle Direct Publishing. The first person I speak with at Balboa Press has a bunch of 5's in his extension- *immediately I feel this is a sign!* The number 5 was the number my Dad sent to my son and I on our trip to a Red Sox game. I share this with the representative. He says, "*Well, you're with Balboa now. There will always be messages. There really aren't just coincidences.*"

The company asks how long it will take for me to finish my manuscript. I naively say, "*Oh, maybe a few months.*" I ask my friend how long it took her to publish her young adult fiction book. "*About 10 years,*" she says. I *think to myself, "Hell no! This will not take me 10 years!"* Honestly, it did take me longer than I originally anticipated, but I was on a mission. I was ready to share my story with the world!

June 2018 - I decide to buy Louise Hay's movie You Can Heal Your Life. Right at the beginning of the movie, Louise says "I worked in a **dime** store." *Do I think this sign to continue writing was directly from Louise Hay?* ***FOR SURE! A true God Wink!***

"Don't be practical. Don't think about making a living; think about doing something you love." ~ Brené Brown

Chapter 3: Seen or Unseen?

There are hidden messages everywhere and the only way to "see" them is to believe in them.

June 30, 2018

I chat with my friend, Tracy, on the phone. We talk about the title of my first book. We talk about my life as a teacher and how much passion and excitement I put into teaching Math. Kids and parents could feel my energy and they all start to love Math! After talking, I listen to a Hay House audio book. It is an interview with Deepak Chopra and Judith Orloff. Deepak begins by talking about how everything that God created is Mathematical and how all Mathematics come from nature. *How could this be? He was talking about Math after I finished talking with my friend. Was it a message from Deepak? For sure! Why does this happen? What does this mean? My linear, mathematical brain always wanted an explanation for everything to be proven. I didn't want any guesswork - only things that I could see would I believe in. That's the part in the story I was working on.*

 Along with books, I began to notice patterns and lessons in my life. *What were the people around me teaching me? How would I use this information in my book?*

"Faith is a place of mystery, where we find the courage to believe in what we cannot see and the strength to let go of our fear of uncertainty." ~ Brené Brown

I read the first three chapters of my first book to Eldon, my father's best friend. We talk about God and his beliefs throughout the time I read. Right before I read chapter three to him, he says, "Oh, that breeze feels so good." The end of chapter three is where I say, "Wait, is Faith like the wind? The wind blows but one cannot see it. We all know the wind is there because of the effects it has on other things, like leaves and flags...Is Faith like that?...Are they feeling faith blow onto them like the wind hitting their skin?" ~Monica L. Morrissey *Was there an unseen force from the universe at work here?*

Then, I tell him the name of the chapter - Faith. He says, well, what does the scripture say about faith? I smile and read the first quote from the Bible, "For we live by faith, not by sight." 2 Corinthians 5:7. He smiles and says - "You got it."

After reading some, Eldon says, "For a book about faith, you don't have much from the Bible, dear." I think - yup, he is right. I think back to the lawn sale I went to a couple of days ago. A friend told me to go because there were some really good baskets that are usually super expensive, but these were priced about half what one would normally pay. I go because she is insisting. I think maybe I'll find something for Christmas presents. I am looking around at the lawn sale. I find one basket for $10 and decide to get it. I glance down at a box of books. Inside is the book The Secret. I had read this book years ago but couldn't find my copy. I grab it up and then dig into the box some more. I find several books about God and notice one in particular. I think of this book as Eldon tells me I don't have enough information from the Bible. It is called Never Lose Heart by **Joyce Meyer.** *I also wonder if Eldon's wife,* ***Joyce,*** *was trying to send me a message. Was she one of my cheerleaders in Heaven; helping me believe that I was meant to publish my book? Only if I believe!*

"You are learning, growing, and discovering the tools you will need for the manifestation. The fun is walking on the path. When you go for a hike in the mountains, you don't ask to jump to the top, right? You walk each step of the trail and see the plants, animals, rocks, and enjoy being out in nature. The same applies to the steps we take toward our goals." ~ Maureen Scanlon

I continued to read books that were put in my path. *I felt like there was something missing. Something I was searching for and hadn't discovered yet.* I also began to gather quotes from a variety of authors. I re-read books to see if there were messages for me. I looked for evidence to back up some of my story. *What were other authors saying about our connection to Heaven or past life regression work?*

I decide that I want to go to a Brian Weiss event as part of my research.

"As a traditional psychotherapist, Dr. Brian Weiss was astonished and skeptical when one of his patients began recalling past-life traumas that seemed to hold the key to her recurring nightmares and anxiety attacks. His skepticism was eroded, however, when she began to channel messages from "the space between lives," which contained remarkable revelations about Dr. Weiss's family and his dead son. Using past-life therapy, he was able to cure the patient and embark on a new, more meaningful phase of his own career." www.brianwiess.com

Brian Weiss followed his internal guidance when presented with a different way of thinking about what our human experience is really about. He was willing to change his beliefs and ultimately change the course of millions of people. *How would it feel to be a traditional doctor now believing in things that some people think are nonsense?* I wanted to understand this concept more.

I buy a ticket and decide that it was my gift to myself for my 50th birthday! His book was the book that had inspired me after my nephew, Tyler, passed away suddenly. Tyler was only 21 years old when he transitioned to Spirit. He is my reminder that life is not promised and we need to cherish every single day. I know Tyler is always around during every baseball game where his good friend, David Price, is pitching. He is also around every time the number eight appears in my life.

Maybe I would get some insight if I went to see Brian Weiss in person. I knew there was another presenter who was also going to be there, but I had no idea who that was. I only cared about seeing Brian. Well, the universe sure knew that I needed to hear John Holland that day too!

John Holland is a medium with a lot of experience in the Spirit world. That day, I gained an understanding of what a medium was and was not. His presentation and books would help me describe how messages from Heaven are received.

On the way to Boston to see Brian Weiss, some friends and I stop to shop. Tracy and Chelsea, long time friends, decided to join me on my trip. They are now an integral part of my team and I am so thankful they are in my life.

"I feel as if a warm shower is running inside of me, which I often call 'the tinglies.' ~ Dr. Wayne Dyer

We all buy Converse sneakers and wear them while we shop. When we get to the hotel, Tracy takes a picture of the sneakers. She posts the picture on Facebook and asks me for a good quote to go with her post. I brought chapters 1-4 of my book for them to read. *I thought of my nephew Tyler's poem at the end of Chapter Four in Dimes From Heaven, but didn't want to spoil their reading for the night. Here is his poem:*

"His Road Not Taken
Going along the path,
There's a split in my way
Which way should I choose?
I will find out another day.
The two paths are different,
I don't know which one to choose.
One seems to be very new,
The other has been stomped on by shoes."
By Tyler Morrissey March 7, 2001

She posted the picture with something from Dr. Seuss about "Oh the Places You'll Go!" But in my head, I was thinking, "Which way should I choose?" or "The two paths are different, I don't know which one to choose?" from Tyler's poem. *After they read the chapters, I mention it to them - the significance of the shoes and the poem. That's "CRAZY", we say as we laugh, get goosebumps and tingle feelings all over our bodies!*

We are walking in Boston trying to find the venue for the "Journey of the Soul" day with Brian Weiss and John Holland. We happened upon James St. (my Dad's name was James) right after I see a gray squirrel running in the street. My Dad's bird feeder was for the gray squirrels too! I mention it and we all agree that street helped us find our way to the venue. *A message from my Dad?*

While we were waiting for the speaker to begin, Chelsea pulls up her memories on Facebook. We had recently joked about me telling her to write a book, but we couldn't remember when I had started to tell her that. She was my boomerang advice. Boomerang advice is advice that I give to others that really should be advice I give to myself. **It's what I need to hear!** *She opens up the comments on one of her posts from exactly one year ago. Here is her post:* **"Unf*@k yourself. Be who you were before all that stuff happened that dimmed your f*@king shine."** *And my comment was,* **"Is that the title to your new book you need to write? I'd buy it!"** *It was exactly one year ago that I told her to write a book!*

It was my birthday the day after the workshop. During the presentation Brian Weiss thanked Hay House for supporting this event. *I thought in my head, yes - thank God for Hay House and Louise Hay! Because of her and her dreams, I was going to be able to self publish my book! Then Brian said, "And it is Louise's birthday tomorrow!"* **Louise Hay and I have the same birth date!** *Well, let's be honest- different years but the SAME DAY! Did I take this as another sign? You bet! Louise was cheering me on to continue writing.*

July 2, 2018

I order a book from Amazon today. Just out of curiosity I track the item to see where it was shipping from (something I never usually do). It is shipping from **Goodyear,** Arizona. My Father ran a Goodyear dealership for years. *Really? I think. There is actually a town named* **Goodyear?** This message might not have been **seen** if I hadn't listened to my intuition when it said, "Hey, let's track this book!" It wasn't what I usually did but I decided to do it just for fun!

"Start before you feel ready. You don't need to know where it's all going. You'll work it out along the way." ~ Rebecca Campbell

Once I started writing, there seemed to be this unseen force where everything around me began to listen to what I was thinking or writing about. The signs would appear out of nowhere and although no one else would know, I knew that all of the coincidences and synchronicities were being coordinated by the universe to help me along my journey.

"I know when I am writing from my soul as my whole energy changes, my writing style shifts slightly and it feels like I am being pulled by a gentle current in a deep, warm ocean." ~ Rebecca Campbell

Seen or Unseen?

There can be hidden messages everywhere. I have to believe in them to see them.

I had to follow my intuition (unseen thoughts, feelings, and guidance) in order for the signs to be seen. I also had to ask my Angels, Spirit guides, and God for help. They are always there - we have to be willing to ask for help in order for them to support us!

Questions to Ponder

- Discover what other people say about your topic.
- What have other people written about? Many people most likely have written about the topic you are writing about. How will yours be different or unique?
- Are there any quotes that might help your writing? These should support either your smaller or bigger messages.
- Watch for signs from the universe - these can be anywhere! Something pops up on Facebook or a commercial on TV. Get curious and find the meaning in the messages.
- Meditate. Sometimes our research and guidance comes from deep within us - from our soul. It wants to help you!
- If stuck, talk to someone OR go to bed and ask your guides to help supply you with a direction. When you wake up, write about your dream - even if it doesn't make sense! It might make sense later on or if you think about your dreams as a metaphor or an analogy. What was the story in your dream trying to communicate?
- What is your intuition telling you?

My Self Publishing Journey
"Your job is to work out the what. The Universe's job is to work out the how."
~ Rebecca Campbell

A Stitch in Time by Daphne Kalmar was released in the town where I live. It was a young adult novel that takes place in Vermont in the early 1900's. I knew Daphne personally as we had worked together years ago. I went to her book release night and asked a few questions about the process. It took her 10 years to write her book! And, to get an agent or a publisher is next to impossible! This made me nervous about how long it would take me to finish writing my book. The one big piece of advice she said that night was she had to figure out that the book was really about grief. I went home and thought about that a lot. *Was my story about grief?* I didn't think it was, but, if it wasn't about grief, then what was it about? I decide that night I need to ask for guidance - I went to bed and asked out loud - *"What is the main theme of my book?"*

Answers can come in mysterious ways! The very next morning, my older sister, Debbie, sends me a picture of a cute puppy she wants to adopt. I reply, *"Awesome! What is her/his name?" Her response, "I'm thinking Faith, but not sure right now." Is this what my book is about? Do I need Faith in order to believe? And, exactly what do I believe? I had to be willing to "see" this as an answer to my question.* My sister did end up getting the puppy, but she didn't name it Faith. She had given me part of my answer to the theme of my book! When I zeroed in on that, it helped me with my entire book.

Turning a Story into a Book

Another part of the research phase was reading books by authors who had a style of writing that I liked. I had to figure out who I was as a writer, not just a storyteller. It helped me go from telling a story to having the person feel like they were a part of my story.

I had a good story to tell, but had no idea how to turn it into a book. An opportunity through Hay House for an online Writer's Workshop course appeared in my email. The cost was $699 but was valued at over $2,000! I was hesitant. I searched for other online writing classes and discovered that some of them were over $5,000. Since I loved Hay House and trusted them, I bought the course. I never once regretted that purchase. It led me to things I could never have imagined! I even met and spoke with Reid Tracy, the CEO of Hay House!

When I want to learn something new, I am curious and I'll do whatever it takes. I began watching all of the online videos for the Writer's Workshops while running on the treadmill. I would have my computer set up on top of the treadmill and keep clicking through them all! Through this course, I not only became a better writer, but I learned more about what it meant to be an author. From social media training to book releases to the publishing industry, Hay House was where I learned the most about the process. I learned how to turn my story into a book and how to build my marketing platform.

"When you follow what you love, the Universe will pick up on your expanded feelings and send you more things to match your newly found expansion." ~ Rebecca Campbell

Chapter 4: Connected or Disconnected?

"In my research, I found that what silences our intuitive voice is our need for certainty...And there it is. '*What does your gut say?*' We shake our head and say, 'I'm not sure' when the real answer is, '*I have no idea what my gut says; we haven't spoken in years.*'" ~ Brené Brown

I had no idea how disconnected I was from my physical body until I began to slow down. When I began to meditate, I realized that I avoided outwardly feeling emotions and was in my head much more than I realized. I was busy judging others and reacting to every little thing that happened. Life was easier this way because then I can numb any feelings I have. By doing this though, I was disconnected from everything in my life.

August 3, 2018

I had been reading Dr. Christian Northrup's book about menopause and aging. She cited several studies about positive thinking and how it affects your body as you age. *How would this information work its way into my book?*

"I wish that more women would realize the degree to which their musculo-skeletal problems - be they with shoulders, hips, neck, or back - have an emotional basis. Simply acknowledging this possibility opens up huge vistas of healing. ~ Dr. Christian Northrup

At some point, I had heard that hip pain is related to male and female energy, and possibly your parents. I was on a pretty challenging hike this day and was thinking negative thoughts. As I was heading down the mountain, with everyone way ahead of me, in the pouring rain, I was thinking things like, *"My knees hurt. My hip hurts. I am going to be so sore after this. My ankle feels weak. "* And many, many more negative thoughts. Then, I became aware of my negative self talk and I thought of Louise Hay and Dr. Christian Northrup - both of them turning negative thoughts into positive affirmations. My frame of mind changes to, *"My hips are strong and stable. I have strong muscles around my knees. I flow down the mountain with ease and strength."* I was trying to think of something similar to Dr. Northrup's "programming" her mind:

"My body is now radiantly healthy, beautiful, flexible, strong, and eternally youthful. The spirit of Divine Love and Power now manifests throughout my entire body as radiant health, radiant beauty, and radiant youth. I give thanks that my body, mind, spirit, and behavior now align to easily maintain my ideal size and weight." ~ Dr. Christian Northrup.

I'm hiking with my husband and another couple. It is raining and beginning to thunder. They are way ahead of me and I can't even see them. My shoes are extremely slippery and at times I need to slide on my bottom just to navigate the trail. I begin to get angry. The trail is difficult and, even though I don't want to admit it, I may need help and I wished that my husband was there with me. The old me would have been fuming the entire way and never would have admitted that I wanted or needed help. Instead, I stop and text him. *"Would you please wait up for me?"*

Within minutes, I see him stopped at the trail, waiting for me. Simple as that. All I had to do was ask and he was there. *How would he have known that I wanted his help if I never asked?* He proceeds to help me down the challenging parts of the trail.

This is when I begin my positive self talk. *"I am strong. I have strong hips. I will not be like my mother who did not stay active. I am changing my DNA footprint and creating a new, stronger one. I will succeed and be more active than my mother."* At one point, he offers me a hand as I am trying to place my foot on the next step off a high rock. He pauses and points. There is a penny in the middle of the trail on the same rock I am about to put my foot on.

For real? I believe pennies are a sign from my Mom. This is how my mother shows herself to me? In the middle of the trail? When I am in the middle of doing positive self talk and getting totally freaked out because I know there are more challenging parts in the trail coming up soon? We pick up the penny and I ask my husband to keep it for me. *He has absolutely NO idea what has just been going through my head.* That penny gave me the courage and strength to get through some steep parts of the trail when I was scared and nervous. I felt a tipping point - I knew that I needed to be exercising more and making sure to stay strong as my body ages. I also needed to get back to my writing. This was me practicing using some of the research I was reading about. *I knew that I would somehow have to work positive affirmations into the book and my life. And, I knew, my mother was helping me.*

Another "coincidence" happened when I watched Louise Hay's movie, "You Can Heal Your Life." Dr. Christian Northrup talks about "jumping in front of a car" because it would be "easier" than life. In Dimes From Heaven, I shared that during my first year of college I wanted to run my car head on into a tree. I thought life would be easier if I wasn't here. Dr. Northrup showed me another sign for me to continue writing my story and share some of my most intimate thoughts. I hoped that by sharing my story, people would see that everyone struggles for a sense of belonging. *Most people who look at me from the outside most likely believe that I am fine on the inside. I wanted people to be more understanding and treat people with more kindness because we don't know everyone's story. By sharing my story, it would make it a safe place for others to share their story. Dr. Christian Northrup helped give me the courage to share.*

I was still focused on the four main ideas of my book 1. Messages from Heaven (the dimes) 2. Loving myself (Anita Moorjani), 3. Healing with emotions (Louise Hay) and 4. Past Life Regressions (Brian Weiss). I had yet to discover anything about being an empath. I was curious and I was beginning to connect into something that I had been disconnected from for a long, long time - **my intuition, the universe's positive energy and the secret portal where there is an unseen force that we are all connected to.**

Connected or Disconnected?

- I know I was connected to Spirit while writing.
- I felt disconnected from my body.
- I began to learn to be connected to my body through meditation and practicing mindfulness.
- In the past, I disconnected from myself with food, alcohol, and avoiding my feelings.
- I was beginning to connect back to the light within myself.

<u>Questions to Ponder:</u>

- What part of your story resonates with you the most?
- How will you use this information to move your writing forward?
- What pieces (if any) are you missing?
- Continue to gather information and integrate it into your story.
- Connect with your gut. What does it say?
- Who can read your book/story for honest feedback? Make sure you tell them it is safe to share their honest opinion.

"By not addressing what's going on inside us, we often find ourselves stuck and feeling limited. But by simply rearranging our priorities, we can release the internal change needed to begin the external result." ~ Lisa Marie Runfola

My Self Publishing Journey

I run on the beach and reflect on my writing. A storm has come through during the night. It changed the look of the beach. Before, there was a red, slimy, thick seaweed all over the beach. Now, the waves are bigger and the wind from the storm has stayed a while longer. The sun glimmers on the new beachfront. The red seaweed is all gone. It is replaced with green, grasslike weeds. Writing my book was like a storm. I'm on the other side and I can reflect on my journey. I can see now that my years of teaching writing helped me become an author. I can see that I had to face my fears in order to share my story.

It's important to figure out what type of help you need in your writing. There are two types of editing services. One is for content and structure. The other is for grammar, usage and mechanics. Both are critical to the writing process. It's important to figure out which one you need and how to get it without spending a fortune. When I investigated into professional editing services, the cost was extreme. I had friends help me. I know that as I transition into being an author and coach full-time, I will most likely be providing some of these services. Because I taught writing for so many years, I have the necessary skills to help others and I look forward to helping the next person write their story!

Because I was a teacher, my editing process was most likely not the normal process. I read my drafts over and over and over again. Chapters began forming and when I thought I had it close to being done, I called a friend to help. Kim looked for spelling, verb tense, transitions, story elements, and clear, precise, descriptive language. We went over my manuscript several times.

Sharing with people is critical to the writing process. The first time I read part of my original manuscript to a friend, I was extremely nervous. Just before Vicki arrived, I was sitting outside on my front porch and my voice was born. I wrote the section where I found the dime on the mountain. The italicized writing and questions flowed like never before. I was becoming a writer instead of a storyteller. I had found my voice. The reader would hear my internal thoughts, a way for them to experience the story right along with me.

I heard feedback from several readers about that voice inside my head. My cousin texted me and said, "Your book was delivered a little over an hour ago and I haven't put it down!!! It's an incredible, courageous journey. So far, I LOVE it! So much is happening inside of me. I can't explain." Another friend said, "Somehow I feel lighter after reading your book." Someone else would send a "Thank you so much for writing your book. Somehow I feel different."

Using the internal voice and asking myself questions within the dime story was helping the readers activate their metacognition, requiring them to not only think about my story but apply the questions to their own life. They were thinking about their thinking as I shared my internal dialogue.

Toward the end of the process, I thought about who would want to read my book. I phoned a few close friends and asked them to read my book to see if they liked it. They were reading it for the content and storyline. The question would be, *"Did the story make you want to keep reading the book?"* That's the sign of a true good book! One where the reader doesn't want to stop reading!

I had to be open to constructive criticism but also listen to my intuition. I had to make decisions of whether or not to listen to their advice or stay with my ideas. While one friend didn't like all of the quotes; another friend told me she loved the quotes! I had to decide for myself what felt right to me.

"My creations uplift and inspire people all around the world. I serve the world by being me." ~ Rebecca Campbell

Sometimes we have to feel the disconnection before we learn how to truly connect. It was important for me to disconnect from the negative voice inside myself who was filled with fear. It was important for me to connect in a lot of different ways. I felt that pain in my body was a way for me to connect to my physical body. Pain brings a person into the present moment. I had to learn to connect with the environment around me to feel the power of the universe, especially in nature. Writing and sharing most definitely helped me connect more authentically with people in my life.

BY MONICA L MORRISSEY

"I write extensively on the specifics of moving from an ego-based identity with its focus on competition, fear, and outward appearances; to higher awareness such as peace, truth, love, and purity." ~ Dr. Wayne Dyer

Chapter 5: Subconscious or Conscious?

"Conscious thought is characterized by attempts to rationalize based on structure and logic and forced inhibitions because of social constraints."

"Subconscious thoughts flow freely, uninhibited, as in a dream, and usually reflect on the deeper feelings you have or emotions you feel biologically and physically."

retrieved from https://www.quora.com/What-is-the-difference-between-conscious-and-subconscious-mind-in-simple-terms

Our subconscious mind controls about 90% of our thoughts while our conscious mind controls only about 10%. In education, we talk about the "hidden or societal curriculum" --as defined by Cortes, 1981, "the massive, ongoing, informal curriculum of family, peer groups, neighborhoods, churches, organizations, occupations, mass media and other socializing forces that 'educate' all of us throughout our lives." I compare that to our subconscious programming. Our subconscious controls our beliefs, emotions, habits, values, protective reactions, long term memory, imagination, and intuition that we learned at a very young age, when the world was very different and we were so young that we didn't know we were absorbing the feelings of those around us. Some of the feelings and thoughts of past generations are no longer useful in our society. Our experiences in life determine all of these things. Our conscious mind is filled with will power, long term thinking, logical and critical thinking. We all have learned to navigate the "societal curriculum" of life in both our subconscious and conscious thinking.

While writing, my subconscious and conscious supported me along my journey. I would have dreams and wake up with messages. I had to figure out what the dream was trying to tell me. *What information did I want to include and what was extraneous information that didn't quite fit?* My conscious self began to hear messages from my subconscious and I began to form "sandwiches" of topics within each chapter. The beginning and the end of each chapter had a message that clearly gave the reader a topic or idea to think about. The name of the chapters came after I wrote them!

June 2018

I have two bunny rabbits that live near my house. I often see them, especially while driving down my long driveway. Last year whenever I saw them, I always thought to myself, *"Chase your dreams. Chase your dreams." Like the bunnies running away, I envisioned the next part of my life. At this time last year, I was interviewing for a new job and was trying to chase my dreams. This year, as I write, I am chasing my dream to publish my book!* **"Chase my dreams. Chase my dreams,"** *a voice whispers as I* **watch the bunnies jump away.** *My subconscious helping push my conscious mind.*

I let my writing sit. I walked away. I didn't look at my writing for weeks. I went swimming, hiking and enjoyed watching my son marry the woman of his dreams. I enjoyed my friends and family. I let my book "cook". I was worried about some of the things I had written about my parents. They weren't horrible; but they weren't good either.

At the time, I thought I was procrastinating. Mel Robbins, in her book *The Five Second Rule* explains there are two different types of procrastination. I thought I was doing it out of fear. Like Mel says in her book,

"Procrastination can easily become a habit. In the early stages of building my own company years ago, I used to procrastinate due to the fear of rejection." ~ Mel Robbins.

Then she goes on to explain that there is an intentional type of procrastination that is part of the creative process. Here is what she says:

"Use Productive Procrastination: Big projects at work or things *like writing your first book* **can take a lot of time and energy. Sometimes you need to step back and take a break from the problem to let the answer find you.**

Don't be afraid to use "productive procrastination" to help you solve a big problem. It might take a few days or even a few weeks but often times a break is just what you need to get clear and find a new solution." ~ Mel Robbins

Seriously, I didn't know I was doing this! I thought I was avoiding my writing because I was scared! I can see now that I was supposed to do this and I didn't need to feel guilty about it!

June 17, 2018

It's Father's Day. My sister posts a picture on Facebook of me, her and our father. I am about one and a half years old in the picture. I am lying on top of my father's chest on the floor. That same morning I take a walk with a friend and find a penny. The year on it is 1969, which would be about the time the picture was taken. *A message from both of my parents? My mother always sends pennies, but the picture was me and my dad!*

When I originally hired Balboa Press to publish my book, I told them I would have my manuscript ready in a few months. *What was I doing? I was letting my book just sit there. I needed to work night and day to get this done! My conscious brain trained for so long to finish whatever I start. A voice inside whispered, "Remember your action research - enjoy the journey and don't worry about 'finishing'." I listened but felt a stirring inside me, willing me to eventually get back to writing.* **"Time does change your perspective."** *~ Monica L. Morrissey I knew something wasn't quite right but didn't know how to fix it.*

Through meditation, I went deeper into my subconscious and more miracles began to happen. My mind was relaxed and stories came to me to support my ideas. Metaphors like the boots compared to relationships began to appear out of nowhere. I had to learn to relax and allow the thoughts to come. It wasn't my linear brain focused on completing my book project.

"No matter your family history or what you've been through, what you choose to do today has the greatest effect on your tomorrow." ~ Dr. Mike Dow

Every time I read something I had written about my mother, I got this sick feeling and felt ashamed that I was talking badly about her. I remember a phone call I had with a medium once. I said I was struggling with my mother. She responded something like, *"You feel bad because a lot of people seem to really like your Mom."* I was like, "Yes!" She understood. My Mom was super nice to my friends and the customers at our family business. *I knew I had to dig deep into this relationship and this could eventually be part of my healing process.*

When we got home from a camping trip the summer I was writing, I went to a friend's house. Their daughter had been taking care of our dog while we were away. I wanted to pay and thank her. While chatting with them, their four kids are all playing. I notice the woman's shirt, "Faith over Fear"- what I almost named my first book. Interesting... Then, the two boys are playing on the stairs. A coin mysteriously appears out of nowhere and gets knocked down the stairs. I immediately look to see what it is - you guessed it - a dime! Nobody noticed the dime, but I knew that I had seen a sign.

"Your soul is always calling you in the direction of your wholeness, flow, dreams and purpose (and everything else). But, you have to show up to it to hear it." ~ Rebecca Campbell

This is a reminder to get going on the "project" you told your friend, Jessie, about at the wedding last night. We were talking about following our inner guidance from our soul; the thing we feel passionate about. I told her that I had a "project" that I was working on because I didn't think I had the energy to become a principal. I expected that being a principal would take over my entire physical health, making me ill and I just didn't think that was what I wanted to do with my life. The demands that a principal faces nowadays are impossible for one person to be able to do. When I said I had a "project", but wasn't ready to share about it, her eyes lit up and she said, "That's it. That's what you are supposed to do. I don't have any idea what **that** *is, but* **that** *is what you are supposed to do. Do it. Tell people about it. That's your answer." The extra dime was a reminder for me to get doing* **that!**

I had taken a break from my writing, but all of these signs sent me back to working on my book!

I let go and let God help lead the way. I had to release my fears to the universe and trust that I was supposed to more forward to publish my book.

"You are the consciousness that is behind the mind and is aware of the thoughts." ~ Michael A. Singer

Subconscious vs Conscious

- My subconscious mind was rewiring and changing my internal belief system.
- My conscious mind was helping me accomplish the tasks needed in order to publish my book.
- My subconscious mind sent me messages in my dreams and thoughts and wanted to express my creativity.
- My conscious mind was worried about what others might think or say.
- My subconscious mind knew that I was being called to write a book.

"You are capable of ceasing the absurdity of listening to the perpetual problems of your psyche." ~ Micheal A. Singer

<u>**Questions to Ponder:**</u>

- Walk away from your writing. Run, plan, exercise, spend time with people. Whatever you do, just don't consciously think about your writing. Use productive procrastination.
- Connect with your gut about the material so far. It will guide you. Should you keep writing more or do you need to work on what you already have?
- Have you truly relayed to the reader what you set out to in the beginning?
- If your message is different than your original thoughts, what happened? What changed? How do you feel about this?
- Think of who your reader is and pretend your book is talking directly to them. What would they say?
- Who do you have that can read your book and give you feedback?
- Do you know anyone that will help you with editing?

Mantra: "My creations uplift and inspire people all around the world. I serve the world by being me." ~ Rebecca Campbell

My Self Publishing Journey

It's important to share your story with others to get honest feedback. If real people are in your book, make sure to get permission to use their name before you publish. Some people may request their name to be changed so they won't be identified.

Another coincidence happened during this phase. Since Merrilee was in the book so much, I wanted her to read the entire book. I knew she would be totally honest with me and since she knew my Dad so well, she would give me good advice. I went to her house and she was so excited! Her husband, Don, was there too. She begs me to read the first chapter to her.

Her husband mutes the TV and I proceed to read to both of them. At the end of the chapter, Don replies, "Hmmmm..... The guy on TV was just holding up a huge dime...." Merrilee and I gasp and say, "What do you mean?" We rewind the program and can't believe our eyes! I snap a quick picture on my phone that shows a big plastic dime about 10 inches in diameter. It is attached to a stick. My Dad was getting pretty clever with the messages now!

I submitted the 1st copy of my manuscript on Tuesday, January 8th, 2019. Most companies will want your manuscript as one document, preferably using Microsoft Word. Some writers use the program Scrivener to help organize their work. (https://www.literatureandlatte.com/scrivener/overview) I chose to first put all of my chapters on separate Google documents in one folder. When I felt they were all ready, I uploaded them into a Word document. In Scrivener, the program organizes your chapters and outline for you so you can easily transition and move things around.

I emailed my book consultant and asked what the timeline was now that they had my manuscript. She responded, "It will take our readers about 2-3 weeks to read your book. After that they will recommend what type of editing services you will need." From the Hay House Online writer's course, I knew that most writers don't think they need editing services, but they really do! I sat back and waited to hear from them.

The package I purchased from Balboa included the following: ISBN number, Copyright registration, Library of Congress registration, Book Sellers return program, and editorial assessment.

On Monday the very next week, the company sends me the book proof - a layout of the book with all of the pictures included. I was so confused! They had said 2-3 weeks and that I would have to have an editor of some kind. *This was 3 business days later and no discussion of an editor. I had no idea that this was not normal! Well, I guess I'll just go with it; what else was I supposed to do?*

I highly suggest Kelly Notaras's book The Book You Were Born to Write or Joni B. Cole's book Good Naked. Both have helpful techniques for writing a book!

"If the subconscious is your iPhone's cloud-based memory with limitless storage potential, the conscious is the small 8 GB memory on the phone itself, with a limited amount of videos, pictures, and apps it can hold at any one time. I wonder how the power of imagery, visualization, and rehearsal will empower you to take control of your life and take action." ~ Dr. Mike Dow

<h1 style="text-align:center">Chapter 6: Mindfulness or Mindfullness?</h1>

"And, when you want something, all the universe conspires in helping you to achieve it." ~ Paulo Coelho

"Quantum leaps come from your soul," Deepak Chopra speaks to me. "All creativity is based on quantum leaps and uncertainty." ~ Deepak Chopra.

This "in-spires" you to speak from spirit. As Wayne Dyer points out, Inspiration comes from Latin and means "In-spirit".

A Quantum leap is about to get real......

My mind had been so full. When I let myself relax, messages came and I gained a whole new perspective. A quantum leap is an abrupt change. For me, the abrupt change would be in how I viewed my life. *Had the events in my life offered me lessons to learn from?*

I make an appointment to have the woman who bought my parents' house give me a make-up lesson to prepare for a photo shoot for the book. I don't wear much make-up because of my sensitive skin. I go to her house (the house I grew up in) and we spent almost three hours chatting and doing make-up. She was amazing. It was great to see her family making our home their home. She shared with me how the first day they bought the house, she felt like she was "home". Her husband handed me a birthday card he found- It was to my Mother, from her brother (my uncle). The title was, "From ribbons to wrinkles". How funny that he had never given this to me before and, on this particular day, brings it to me. It even had a picture of my mother when she was young. *It makes me realize that I don't know my mother's young life. What made her the way she was? I was beginning to see my Mom in a different light - my book was about to change and I would make a huge quantum leap!* The card was significant to me because much of what I was going through was accepting this next part of my life - over 50 and loving life. *I wanted ribbons with my wrinkles!*

"I define *calm* as *creating perspective and mindfulness while managing emotional reactivity." ~* Brené Brown

The summer I was writing my book, I felt very alone. I had plenty of family and friends around, but I felt like I was on a journey down a new path. I was searching for my center through writing. In the body, the third chakra is located at your solar plexus (just above your belly button). Along with writing, I was adjusting my body to be more confident. The third chakra has to do with self confidence, self motivation and a strong sense of purpose. While at a conference, a woman who I met in one of the workshops says to me, "When are you expecting?" I said, "What did you just say?" She repeated the question and it took me a minute to wrap my brain about what she was asking. *She thought I was pregnant! Am I really that fat? I immediately suck in my gut and am worried about my physical appearance. I thought this dress was flattering! Does it make me look fat? Obviously, if she thought I was pregnant! I respond to her, "Um, I'm not expecting. Thanks," and quickly change the subject.* I thought about that a lot over the next few months. I sort of was pregnant - just with a book, not a baby! And, I think she was actually sensing the energy I was giving to my third chakra.

I began thinking about what it would be like to release my book to the universe. *How could I write those things about my mother?* I read Dr. Christiane Northrup's books, The Wisdom of Menopause and Mother Daughters. She says that we take on our ancestor's stories - they are built into our DNA! They are built into our subconscious mind from childhood. *Had I taken on some insecurities or other things from my mother? Which she had taken on her Mother? Yes, but* every time I re-read something that I had written about my mother, I felt a twinge in the pit in my stomach. I learned during this lifetime, insecurities was something I needed to heal. I was willing to heal myself and then this lesson ends with me. I don't have to pass it on to my children.

At some point, I stumbled upon some books about empaths. I had remembered my friend, Michelle, telling me I was an empath but hadn't really thought a lot about it. I had organized a training for teachers about compassion fatigue. During the presentation, they were talking about Highly Sensitive People. *Yikes! She is describing me. I don't even want to take the assessment to know my score. I'm sure it will be a high score. I decide that I won't focus on myself; I'll focus on the teachers. It's so much easier to help other people instead of looking within myself. I didn't want other people to know anything about this part of me.*

After this initial training, I read more about Dr. Elaine Aron's research about the highly sensitive person. Her work is based on Carl Jung's work and is most definitely helpful for anyone who thinks they might be highly sensitive or an empath.

Later, when I discovered Dr. Judith Orloff's books about being an empath, I was ready to hear the information. Or should I say - the books found me? After a good friend sent me a few audio books about surviving as an empath, *Amazon "suggested" more books about empaths to me - a sign from the universe? The one I had been searching for? The key to my understanding?*

This was the time for what Deepak Chopra calls a "Quantum leap" and I had no idea that I was actually doing it. It happened naturally, as if the universe was helping me. I was willing to look at myself as a highly sensitive person.

"Stillness is not about focusing on nothingness; it's about creating a clearing. It's opening up an emotionally clutter-free space and allowing ourselves to feel and think and dream and question." ~ Brené Brown.

This is when I began to look inside myself instead of blaming others. I changed my anger and judgments to compassion. That's when the real story began to unfold. The abrupt turn in my thoughts changed my entire story. I would begin my story showing the reader what it felt like as a child who didn't understand how being an empath affected my life. As a child, I regulated my body by being outside, swimming, and playing. I held onto words inside my body. It was the way I was born and I had to accept who I was instead of running or blaming. It was time to stop blaming my mother and discover **who I am, a highly sensitive person.**

"When I change the way I look at things, the things I look at change." ~ Wayne Dyer

<u>Mindfulness or Mindfullness?</u>

- <u>I am mindful when I am in the moment.</u>
- <u>I am mind**full** when I am thinking about the past or the future.</u>
- <u>I am mindful when I pay attention to my surroundings - sights, sounds, and feelings.</u>
- <u>I am mind**full** when I am thinking about too many things.</u>
- <u>I am mindful when I let go and let God.</u>
- <u>I am mindful when I observe instead of judge. Nothing is good nor bad. It just is.</u>

<u>Questions to Ponder:</u>

- What, in your research, has given you new insight or a whole different way to look at things? Do you want to share these details with your readers?
- What do you know now that you didn't know when you began your writing journey?
- What information will the reader need in order to understand the new information?
- What have you learned from your research or new insight that you will use when editing your writing?
- Do you need to go back to the research phase to learn more about this new information?
- What is the main message you want your reader to take away?
- To connect with your body, put your hand over your heart, take a few deep breaths. How do you feel about this?

• How do you connect to your subconscious using mindfulness practices?

"Your message is the moral of your story. And there are people waiting to hear it. A story left unsaid is the saddest story of them all. Share yours now." ~ Rebecca Campbell

My Self Publishing Journey

It's important to have photos done professionally if you choose the path to publishing. You will need them for your website, blog, book and any social media that you use.

I hire a friend to do a photo shoot for the book and my website. We were going to a few different spots for the scenery. As we walk by a house toward the fence, I look up at the house and see the numbers **1188.** *Was this a sign? I had walked by that house several times and never once noticed those numbers. It was a house that had accumulated so much junk on the porch, the exterior and in the field next to it, that the distraction of the "stuff" was so overwhelming that I never saw the numbers. I was clearing away the clutter in my life to see things more clearly- that's why I could see the sign. Those were my repeating numbers which I feel are signs from my Angels-* **11 and 88-** *Signs to me that the photo shoot was a necessary part of writing this book.*

*"**Angel number 11 is a message from the angels concerning your soul mission or greater life purpose. When the angels send you messages containing Master Number 11 they are sending you inspiration and encouragement to develop your abilities in ways that will help all of humanity."** retrieved from, https://thesecretofthetarot.com/ angel-number-11/*

And the number 8 was my nephew, Tyler's favorite number. I was walking on the new shiny path. Although the path was shiny and new, I had angels walking with me as I wrote my first book.

I tried to shut off the negative voice inside my head saying that having a photo shoot was a dumb idea. Seeing those numbers immediately changed my thinking to positive thoughts. It went something like this, *"Sam (my photographer) knows me so well that these pictures are going to be amazing. How lucky am I that she is in my life? Nobody else would be able to capture "ME" in these photos. She knows me and is so excited about this project. Enjoy it. Love myself as she takes my picture. I know that I am more than my physical body. She will see inside my soul when she takes my picture. Other people will see my soul too. When they read the book, it will help them to be in touch with their soul, too."* I am uplifted by my thoughts and I begin to enjoy the photo shoot.

Book Release Date

With self publishing companies, it's difficult to determine the exact date of release and when it will be available for purchase. With a traditional publisher, it takes longer (at least 12-18 months) and you can pre-order the books.

When my book was available on Amazon, I was not notified. I began watching every day. One day - there it was! I overnight shipped it and it arrived the next day. I had my husband videotape me opening my book and posted it on social media. It was approximately nine months since I first put pen to paper and began my writing journey.

At Balboa, when the book goes live (meaning it is available for purchase), my contacts at Balboa change from production to a Marketing and Editorial Consultant. *You'll never believe what happened during the first phone call! As the people at Balboa will say, "There are no coincidences at Balboa or Hay House. The universe will give plenty of signs."*

After speaking with my Marketing and Editorial Consultant for over an hour about my book, I said, "I'm sorry. I didn't catch your name." She responds, "DeeAnna." This was my Mother's name!!! - spelled a little differently, but at the time I did not know this! If I was looking for my Mother's approval - I think I got it!

DeeAnna then helped me plan how to get my book out to the world. She talked to me about my Platform (my online presence through social media, website, etc) and what I was planning on doing for outreach. She suggested different services from Balboa and guided me in the right direction. She calls and checks in to see where I am with marketing my book.

DeeAnna even told me her dime story! She told me about hiking a mountain with her boyfriend and along the hike she found two dimes. She said she immediately thought of me and thought the dimes were like bread crumbs up the mountain. Then, when she got to the top, her boyfriend proposed to her! She said the dimes made it even more special!

"To be free, to truly experience life, you must come out. You have to let go and pass through the cleansing process that frees you from your psyche." ~
Michael A. Singer

Chapter 7: Planned or Unplanned?

"Who is 'turning the knobs'? To make everything happen." ~James H. Palmer
"The day unfolds and the mind doesn't say anything. You simply interact with the day with a peaceful, fully inspired heart. " ~ Michael A. Singer

I like to plan my day, my life, my everything. When I decide I want to do something, it's like my body thinks I'm already there, doing it instead of being present in the moment. It's hard for me to let life happen and enjoy it as it comes. But, when I do, miracles happen!

While writing my first book, my husband and I are traveling from Vermont to Delaware to visit friends. We randomly pull into a rest stop along our way. I am driving and have lots and lots of choices of where to park. I almost park in one spot, then decide at the last second to park in a different space. My husband looks up and notices a man standing next to his car- directly in front of us. He says, "I think that is Roger". We haven't seen him in years. As we get out of the car, my husband says, "Hey there!"

Our friend, Roger, is moving to live with his son. *Was I guided to park in that particular spot? There are several other rest areas we could have stopped at. There are 100's if not 1,000's of people at this particular rest area and we park **directly next to someone we know from Vermont?** What are the chances? God brought us together for one last good bye. Most likely we will never see him again in person. I am always amazed at how the universe works- sort of like my Dad suggests, "Who is 'turning the knobs'? To make everything happen."*

Our psyche likes to feel safe. We feel safe when we plan and try to control what is going to happen. It is a constant battle inside. When things don't go as planned, it can be easy to feel upset or emotional. I lived like this for a long time. Writing my first book was most definitely not something I planned and I wouldn't be able to control what happened after it was published. I had to learn to trust that this unplanned surprise in my life was planned by something greater than me.

October 13, 2018

I was in a store where a TV was on. I am not sure what the show was as I couldn't actually see the TV. *They were about to take a commercial break and all I heard was,* **"And, when we get back, we will learn how one single coin can change your life."**

Ha! A sign? No doubt! I left the store so I have no idea what it was all about, but I knew that **one single coin** *had seriously changed my life! Was the unplanned coin a part of a bigger plan?*

November 16, 2018

I am working from home on a snow day and an email comes through about a class I will be teaching to adults in the Southern New Hampshire University Master's program, the same program I went through to get my Master's degree. *The class is called "Dimensions in Curriculum and Management" but there isn't room for the entire title. All that shows up is, "(name of person) has invited you to join Dime".*

December 23, 2018

Today is my Mom's birthday. I am baking for Christmas and go to the store to get a few things. The store is very busy and has all the registers open. I get in line. The woman in front of me bends over to pick something up. She says really loudly, almost like she is making a big announcement to everyone in the store, *"I just found a DIME!!! I found one yesterday too!"* I thought she had won the lottery; she was so excited! I look at her and say, *"That is very interesting because I am writing a book called Dimes From Heaven and am about to send it to the publisher!"* She looks at her arms and says, *"Oh my. I have such goosebumps right now. I don't understand. Are the Spirits trying to contact me?"* I laugh and remind her that spirits are not scary like ghosts you might see in the movies. She asks me for my name and really wants to read my book. Thank you Pat McAllister! I hope you get to read my book someday!

January 8, 2019

My son is in a Vermont Public Service TV commercial about being safe when driving near plow trucks. The series is called, "Don't Crowd the Plow" and is sponsored by the Vermont Agency of Transportation. The first quote on one video says, "These trucks cannot stop on a dime." My father is getting pretty clever now!

Synchronicities seemed to be taking over my life.

"What is Synchronicity? The term is coined by Carl Jung to express a concept that belongs to him: *the acausal connection of two or more psychic and physical phenomena."* **~retrieved from** *https://www.carl-jung.net/synchronicity.html*

Planned vs Unplanned

- I planned to publish my book.
- The universe understands the plan more than I do.
- I could plan what the book would look like.
- I wouldn't be able to plan for what would happen after my story was shared.
- Sometimes when we let go of the plan, the unplanned is so much better!

<u>Questions to Ponder:</u>

- Have you discovered your voice? Your own, unique style of writing?
- How will your story inspire others?
- Has the reader felt inspired through your story?
- Discover your WHY. Why do you want to write? What is pushing you to do this? Research Simon Sinek if you need help discovering your why.
- Be you and be proud of it.
- Address any lingering fears that might be lurking around in the background. Bring them to the surface and face them.

"You don't need to pretend or prove that you have it together, rather, just share what you have figured out so far. We are all in this school of life together. There is no final destination, no end point, just increased consciousness and a deeper understanding." ~ Rebecca Campbell

My Self Publishing Journey

There is so much that needs to go into the business aspect of writing a book. I had my website designed by a professional and then I needed some physical printing completed; things like business cards, book marks, fliers for my book launch and a poster to display for events. I asked around for advice on options and had at least five different businesses to choose from. I chose a place in a town about forty-five minutes away to have my business cards printed.

I stop by to pick up the business cards. As I am chatting with the owner and the sales person, they ask about my book. *"Is it something about dimes?"* I reply with a yeah - it's a pretty cool story. **Then they proceed to tell me that they have a DIME glued to the floor in their office!** *FOR REAL!* It was put there as a joke to a previous employee. The employee always had holes in his pockets so change was constantly falling on the floor. They thought it would be funny to glue a dime to the floor to see if he would try to pick it up! *Out of all the places I could have chosen to print my business cards, I chose the place that has a dime glued to the floor? Seriously?*

Becoming an author is very similar to starting a business. For me, I enjoyed the writing part of creating a book. The business part used a different part of my brain. I read the book Platform, Get Noticed in a Noisy World by Michael Hyatt, as was suggested in the Hay House Online Writing Course. In this book are all of the ins and outs, do's and don'ts that a person would need in order to "get noticed." Along with the website and the materials being printed, I needed a game plan of where to market my book. I would do a mixture of in-person events and online targeting. Read the book for the nitty gritty how-to details!

"Intuition is not a single way of knowing - it's our ability to hold space for uncertainty and our willingness to trust the many ways we've developed knowledge and insight, including instinct, experience, faith and reason." ~ Brené Brown

Chapter 8: Inside or Outside?

"We exist largely in theta brainwaves state for our first six to seven years of life, absorbing the world like a sponge and forming beliefs about self, others, and the world." ~ Nikki Gresham-Record

Writing Prompt- "Yes, I lied." Here is my response:

For sure. Without a doubt. I didn't know how to speak the truth. I didn't think anyone would believe me. I thought people would be angry if they heard the truth.

I didn't think it was safe to say it out loud. I thought that people weren't ready to hear it. I thought if I lied, then they would believe the lie. But, in truth, they all knew the truth. They could not only feel it but they could see it in my eyes. They knew I was lying even though I didn't want them to know.

It was the elephant in the room that I wasn't ready to talk about. It would mean I would have to face the truth.

How would I ever be able to do that? What would help me be able to face it?

I can't believe this is happening. Especially now, of all the times in my life. *Why couldn't it happen next week, after I have been able to talk about it and accept it?*

I can't lie. I don't know how to do it. Internally, I am sick and my body listens to everything my mind thinks. *Why did I ever think I would be able to do this?*

I couldn't do it even when I tried. I ended up blurting the truth and apologizing. Lying is not something I can do. I think because it hurts so much when it happens to me. It cuts into my heart and I can't seem to cut into someone else's heart. It's not how I am built. It isn't inside me to do that.

Do you see how much changed in that short writing? This is an example of taking a topic and journaling on it for about 7-10 minutes. When I started writing, I wasn't sure where my writing would take me. This is the power of writing by hand, without worrying about a polished final draft. I let go of the outcome and enjoyed the writing process.

I wrote this at a weekend writing retreat led by Joni B. Cole, a Vermont author and professor of writing (https://www.jonibcole.com/). I learned several things that weekend that helped me in my writing.

There is a rhythm to the writing I like to do. I like to share stories. She explained that we first show the reader something, tell more about it and then reflect. The "back story" means so much more when you have a "front" story. Writers show emotions with scenes. There is a "Rule of 3". 1. Bring it up 2. Repeat it 3. Resonate the why

- the symbolism. Most people remember some of the stories in Dimes From Heaven. One of the best examples of this was regarding my favorite pair of boots that I didn't take care of (front story). I compared these to relationships in my life (back story - reflection). By not taking care of my boots, they were ruined. I couldn't go back in time to care for them. Relationships can be like that. I don't get to go back in time and re-do it. I can only change my actions from now on. The boots represented mistakes I made in my life.

Most of my internal messages about life were buried within me from years of my insides not matching my outside world. I stopped listening to my gut when I was young because people around me told me my gut wasn't right. When people told me lies, I was told to believe them, even though inside I felt something different. I learned to shut off and disconnect from my body and I didn't know how to listen anymore. I had to relearn this and it took a long time!

I learned from a young age to be alert for danger. I have always had extreme anxiety and I wasn't aware of it. I learned that it was super important to listen carefully because if I didn't, there might be consequences. If I missed a cue like, "Clean up your room," I might be reminded again in a harsher tone of voice. Maybe not screaming, but in my mind it felt like I should be ashamed of myself for not listening the first time. I learned to read body language. Any little fluctuation in someone's eyes, mouth or facial expression could mean serious danger to me. By looking at the outside (their slight body movements), I thought I knew what was happening on the inside.

Often times, we make stories in our heads and add to them to make them great. Brené Brown calls these, "Shitty first drafts." Some aspects may be true and whatever we tell ourselves we seem to believe. But, the story is only true based on our perspective and it is our psyche (subconscious) talking to us. Someone else may believe something totally different. At the beginning of Dimes From Heaven, I put in a disclaimer. "I have tried to recreate events, locales and conversations from my memories of them. These memories are from my perspective only. Others may or may not remember them as I do."

I re-read parts about my Mom or Dad and the passages didn't "sit right" in my gut. Things like "My mother was insecure" changed to "I sensed my mother might be insecure" or *"Was my mother insecure?"* I took ownership of the feelings and stated everything from my point of view. *I was only looking into the "windows" of my mother.*

I really couldn't tell how she felt inside and I had no business writing it as a fact. I sorted through the "lies" I was telling myself in order to protect my ego. This was Spirit guiding me, nudging me to help myself heal with my words. I was facing my truth even though it didn't feel good inside. I wasn't going to listen to the voice inside my head anymore.

August 5, 2018

We stop off at a lake on our way home from camping. My husband was kayaking and I was on my paddle board. We are enjoying the day and I am swimming near my paddle board. A dragonfly lands on my paddle board. I remember when I was a kid I would always brush them away because I was scared of them. As an adult, I know that some people view them as a sign from a loved one. *I stare at the dragonfly on my paddle board and in my head ask, "Who are you?" This one felt new and different. I decide that I think too much and let it go.*

We get back to the boat launch, load up and head home. I decide to check Facebook and the first status I see is a post from one of my husband's cousins. *One of their beloved cousins transitioned to spirit after battling brain cancer for a year and a half. I begin to cry. I know that the dragonfly was David in his new spirit form.*

I first started studying Louise Hay in 1996 and Brian Weiss in 2008. When I talked with people about certain things in life, I began pointing them to books. I'll never forget one woman saying to me, "You always have a good book to mention about everything. I wish I had that much time to read!" I realized that Dimes From Heaven was actually my thesis about life. I was summarizing a bunch of different authors I had read over the years and how their work related to my life. I discovered I was actually writing a memoir. *But, it wasn't a regular memoir; I learned I was writing a **teaching memoir.***

I stop by the library at one of the schools where I work. I am chatting with the librarian about the new books for kids. I explain how I used to read a lot of the young adult books when I was teaching 5th and 6th grade, but now I am enjoying reading other books. . She says she tries to keep up on the latest kid books too. I share that my favorite books are based on true stories. She replies, "Ooooooo, I **LOVE** memoirs!" I think, *"Ooooooo, maybe you'll **LOVE** my memoir!!" I feel tingles throughout my entire body as I imagine all the people who would read my book.*

Inside or Outside?

- I felt uncomfortable on the inside when I tried to blame things on the outside.
- I had to look inside to connect to my true self.
- I had to understand that nothing on the outside would be able to hurt me.
- I understood that due to my sensitive nature, I might misread body cues. I wouldn't be able to tell what someone was thinking on the inside by looking at the outside of their physical body.
- I had to feel God on the inside.
- I had to realize that what I felt on the inside would help me attract things on the outside.

<u>**Questions to Ponder:**</u>

- What do you feel on the inside?

- What signs are you seeing on the outside?
- How will the outside help you inside?
- What inside of you needs to be healed?

"**When you follow what you love, the Universe will pick up on your expanded feelings and send you more things to match your newly found expansion.**" ~ Rebecca Campbell

My Self-Publishing Journey

Because I was writing a memoir with real people and real lives, I needed to make sure that everyone was okay with the material I was writing about. It didn't make sense to me to change the names of people to protect them. At times, this might be valuable for non-fiction. I decided to have people read over the manuscript to make sure they were okay with what I wrote.

As part of my Balboa publishing package, their editors would also look for content in which they thought either someone might get upset about or laws about using other people's materials. I learned that it is okay to quote a few sentences here or there from another author, but not too much. Whole pages of content were not allowed. Songs and poems are also a place where you need the writer's permission to use their content. Originally, I had some of the words to songs in my writing but learned that was not something I could use in my book.

Although I wrote my material inside during the quiet moments of solitude, it was now time to share my story with the outside world.

"**We don't discover our soul calling, we uncover it by following the trail of things that light us up and then lose ourselves in the doing.**" ~ Rebecca Campbell

Chapter 9: Comfortable or Uncomfortable?

"I didn't *want* to think about stuff that made me uncomfortable. And I certainly didn't want to feel any of it." ~Seane Corn

When writing, I had some of the worst anxiety EVER! Sharing my story was scary! It made me very uncomfortable on a physical level. My body didn't like me sharing "inside" information. *How would I ever dare to share my story?* The signs kept coming that this "project" was worth it! As a Southern New Hampshire University student told me, "I had to learn to be comfortable with being uncomfortable." *I seriously didn't like the sound of that! Luckily, the universe was supporting me every step of the way.*

One of the books Reid Tracy recommended in the Hay House Writer's workshop was Choose Yourself, Be Happy, Make Millions, Live the Dream by James Altucher. James references dimes throughout his entire book. *First sentence of the book, "I don't need to make a dime off of this book." For real? I guess I am reading the book I am meant to read! Some of the other sentences throughout his book are: "I never raised a dime for that business." "But more important is to build relationships than to kill everyone and take every last dime in a negotiation." "At the drop of a dime, I would show up for dinner wherever and whenever he asked me to." "Ideas are a dime a dozen." Thank you, James Altucher - I think I'll choose myself!*

This book gave me the strength to accept myself as an empath and highly sensitive person. I had to accept myself first and then own my story. I had to believe that sharing my story about being an empath would help others. I began to revise by looking at my life through the lens of being an empath. I believe every high school student should read *Choose Yourself Be Happy, Make Millions, Live the Dream.* In this book, James explains that not everyone has to go to college and follow that path. We all have options and we should choose what we are passionate about. It really made me think about my choices for my career. Did I have to stay in the same career path that I had decided when I was 17 years old or was there something more for me to do in this lifetime? How would I ever leave the job that provided me with security and safety? How would I step into the unknown and be able to trust that this was what I was supposed to do? One step at a time...One day at a time....

Now that I had discovered I was an empath, I had to integrate that into my story. This one key piece of information transformed my entire viewpoint. Admitting this to the world would be difficult but I felt the need to share this information. *I believed by admitting this, it would help others. Some people might be able to relate and some would not. I felt that by having the words to explain how I felt, it helped me accept myself and understand I wasn't alone.*

"To end suffering, you must first realize that your psyche is not okay. You must then acknowledge that it does not have to be that way. It can be healthy...You don't have to constantly be mulling over what you said or what this person thinks of you." ~ Michael A. Singer

I didn't want to teach about being an empath in the middle of my story. I was trying to think of a way for the reader to learn but not be preachy. That's when I decided to explain further in Dimes From Heaven, Section Two is called Who am I and Why am I like This? It would give the reader information about how being an empath affects my everyday life. It would also explain tools and strategies for highly sensitive people or empaths.

I am going to be totally honest about using the quotes throughout my book. They were my security blanket. I worried about people thinking I was making this stuff up. I thought that if I quoted other authors talking about our connection to heaven, it would help make my story valid. I also hoped that the reader might want to read more about the topics. I secretly wanted people to be curious about Brené Brown, Judith Orloff, or other authors. I was planting seeds of information to get the readers curious. Even if they didn't, they were getting some of the main topics throughout my memoir!

I imagined different "threads" of thought throughout my book and asked myself questions like the following:

- Where does the idea of an empath begin and where does it go?
- How will the reader understand about past lives?
- What will the reader learn about food choices?
- How will I address the non-believer? That's where the chapter starts with "The living can't speak to the dead." ~ Mitch Albom and ends with "You're not a jack-ass whisperer." ~ Scott Straten.
- How will I incorporate the suspense of the dimes? Leading up to finding the dimes? Make sure to sprinkle a little hint in each chapter!
- How could I use italicized writing to put emphasis on some things?
- How would I transition the reader when I jumped from Florida and then back to the dime story?

By asking myself questions, I was able to integrate my ideas better.

Messages can come from anywhere. Here are a few more that I felt were signs during my writing journey.

July 5, 2018

While waiting to get an oil change on my car, the TV is playing a news show about "Veterans Helping Veterans". The thought behind the program is to change the PTSD negative thinking to be more positive thoughts about growth and change. They explain that we hold our emotions in our cells and our body remembers. If you fail to deal with your feelings, then they will get stuck inside your body. It's important to rewrite the story you are telling yourself inside your head.

Wait, is that a coin around his wife's neck? Could it be? I'll have to check again after the commercial.

I watch more of the segment, not quite able to hear everything. I'm reading the book, *The First Phone Call from Heaven* by Mitch Albom. In the book, it is talking about how Alexander Graham Bell almost didn't go to the convention where his phone was being displayed. He jumped on the train at the last minute because of love. His wife didn't want to be away from him. That moment in time would change history. The telephone would become a way to communicate with people. This didn't have anything to do with the Vet's story, but a quick segment came on about how to make homemade speakers for your cell phone- out of two paper cups and a piece of cardboard! *How would that ever work?* Ha! Was this a sign? You bet! I was writing about the "new" spirit communication system I had explained to my father. I described how the spirit communication system was like a telephone - a new way to communicate with people in Heaven.

I might not have watched the segment if the woman's necklace hadn't caught my eye. *In another 10 years, would people be talking about how the spirit connection system works like a telephone? How everyone would have the ability to access it as easily as a cell phone? I felt the positivity of the news article about changing trauma into something positive in my bones. Imagine if all news was only positive? Would everyone be happier? 10 years ago we would never have imagined talking to someone on top of a mountain with a little black box (a cell phone). Will we be able to phone Heaven easily in another 10 years?*

The next day, I write all morning and then take a break to enjoy the sunshine and pick apples. On my way home, I am thinking of the last few chapters and some things I want to add. As I am about to go up my driveway on my way home, I look at the time. 11:55 and the temperature on the car thermometer is 55. Guess my angels are telling me it is time to work on my book!

When I get home there is a small snake next to my front step. I decide to look up the meaning of snake in the *Animal Spirit Guides* book by Steven Farmer to see what sign the snake means.

"You're about to go through some significant personal changes, so intense and dramatic that an old self will metaphorically die as a new self emerges. You're

going to feel a surge of energy that will sharpen your senses, alert your mental faculties, and open up new channels of awareness. You're about to resolve a long-standing issue, one that has required a great deal of your attention, by seeing things in a new light. It would be a good time for you to start doing either tantric or kundalini yoga. You'll experience a dramatic and unexpected physical or emotional healing very soon, coming from an unexpected source." ~ Steven Farmer

This was shortly after I had gone back to the parts about my Mom and made sure that I wrote that this was how I "felt", not trying to guess what her internal feelings were. **Sentences like, "My Mom was insecure" turned into "I sensed that my Mom was insecure."** *I had no idea what was happening within my mother and made sure to mention how I felt instead. I had spent a lot of years judging my mother because it was easier than admitting I was different than others. At times, I didn't want this gift of being an empath. I had to learn to accept the gift and learn how to deal with the challenges. I was most definitely going through a huge transformation!*

A lot of people loved my Mom and I wanted to make sure that I took responsibility for my feelings. She was a wonderful person who enjoyed people.

Comfortable vs Uncomfortable

- I was comfortable in my life as an educator.
- I was uncomfortable thinking about a new career in writing. I wouldn't be able to plan what would happen.
- I was comfortable with blaming and judging other people. By judging them, I realized, I also judged myself and this is what caused some of my anxiety!
- I was uncomfortable looking within myself for the answers.
- I was comfortable hiding my story.
- I was uncomfortable sharing my belief in God and being an empath.
- I had to learn to be comfortable being uncomfortable because I knew that my soul was growing through a process of self-acceptance.

"Contentment arrives when our wholeness comes from within. If we define ourselves by how much money we make, how many friends we have, or how many things we own, we can never be satisfied. There's never enough out there to fill the emptiness inside because what we're actually lacking is a sense of our own goodness, a sense that yes, we *are* enough." ~ Seane Corn

<u>Questions to Ponder:</u>

- Have you integrated your main message with all of your smaller messages?
- How does your writing flow?

- Do you have a clear beginning, middle and end?
- What voice makes the most sense?
- Is your voice consistent throughout the entire book?
- Who have you asked to read your book and give you feedback?
- Are you using the feedback to make your writing better?
- Do your readers understand the main messages?
- What messages from the universe did you integrate into your book?
- Is there more information you need? Do you need to go back to the research phase?
- Quiet your mind and be open to the answer coming from Spirit or your intuition.

"The world is filled with people who, no matter what you do, will point blank not like you. But it is filled with those who will love you fiercely. They are your people. You are not for everyone and that's OK. Talk to the people who can hear you." ~ Rebecca Campbell

My Self Publishing Journey THE FINAL TOUCHES
November 21, 2018

*I am filing my bills and receipts. I pick up a receipt from one of the herbal supplements I purchased to help me heal. Normally, I would just file the receipt but I decide to look at the receipt and notice the address for the company includes **Palmer St**. Palmer is my maiden name!*

Some other parts to a book that you might want to think about are:

- **Note from the author** - Do you have something to say to the reader before they begin reading?
- **Foreword** - Is there someone who would be willing to write this for you? Someone who knows you and is connected to the topic you are writing about.
- **Resources** - If you use any quotes, make sure to include the books, websites, etc. in your resources/bibliography.
- **Cover** - Hire a professional to do your cover. Some publishing companies will help you with this.
- **Epilogue** - Does the reader need to know something else that will help them understand the story? Something that might be after the main story?

I call the photographer who did my Senior photos and wedding pictures. He has lots of pictures of Elmore Mountain, where I found one of the first dimes from my Dad. When I asked him for a photo, he says most of his photos are of sunsets. If I want a daytime photo of the mountain, I should call someone else. I refuse; explaining that I want him to be a part of my book. He took photos of my wedding and I want him, not some other photographer. He thinks and then says, "Well, is your book Spiritual at all?" *Huh? Is he like the minister on the mountain - asking me if I have Faith?* "Oh my Gosh! Yes - my book is very spiritual! What are you thinking?" I ask. He responds, *"I have the perfect picture for you. I just have to find it..."* Months later, after digging through ten or more hard drives, he would send me the photo that is on the front cover. It was the perfect picture for my book cover.

What makes a good title?

Write down several titles while writing and don't worry about the final choice until the very end. Choose several titles and ask friends or other writers which ones make them curious about your book.

The entire time that I was writing, my book was called "More Than a Dime." I couldn't see it any other way. Then, I realized that the reader wouldn't understand what the book was about if it had that title. My dimes were from my father, who was in the spirit world or Heaven. The reader needed to know this from the start.

The subtitle gives the reader more information and may be longer than the title. After I discovered I was an empath, I knew this had to be a part of the subtitle. I wanted people to learn what the word meant. It was also the most scary part because even if people didn't read my book, I was admitting that I was different! I wouldn't "fit in" but I would belong! It wasn't until one of the last edits where I was sitting with my friend, Tracy, that the final title was born. While discussing my writing, she said, "I LOVE the part where you say 'the beginning of the word coincidence is **coin.**" We both say "that's the second part of the title!" at the same time! It was magical and we both got goosebumps!

A new title was born. It changed from Dimes from Heaven How a Few Dimes from Heaven Helped Me Discover My Life as an Empath to Dimes from Heaven How Coins and Coincidences helped Me Discover My Life as an Empath. It was the final step I needed before sending my manuscript to the editor!

Online Presence- Building my Platform

Because I was a public educator writing a spiritual based book, I was VERY uncomfortable about sharing. I began my author Facebook page right before my book was released. Honestly, it was so frightening for me! I did two free drawings to try to get people to share, like, and comment on a post on Facebook. Within the first few weeks, I had almost 400 likes to my page. Then it began to slow down. Facebook was the platform I was most comfortable with and where I spent most of my time. Putting myself "out there" in the world was risky and scary, but I had faith that it was important for me to share.

It is incredible how you can target an audience in a Facebook Advertisement. From interests, to age, or location, your sponsored ad will bring in the audience you are looking for.

I named everything Monica L. Morrissey. My Facebook, Instagram, email and website would all match. The reader would just type in monicalmorrissey.com and instantly they would be able to find me. At first, I thought I would brand my sites with dimesfromheaven.com, but I learned that my followers would be following me, not just my first book. Dimes From Heaven would be my first book, but what about after that? Was this book going to be the end? Or, was it actually just the beginning of my new adventure? Would every book, blog, post, etc always be about Dimes? Maybe, maybe not. I had to leave that door open by naming everything with my name.

I immediately loved connecting with my readers about my book! It filled up the cup of love inside me. I imagined my book had wings and the love inside helped make it fly all over the world. It was up to me to give it a little push here and there.

I imagined that every book I sold or gave away, it produced a sale of at least ten more books. "What is the the way most people find out about a good book? One that your friends or family recommends!" ~ Reid Tracy, CEO of Hay House. One by one, I was producing more love and happiness in the world. Some would choose to read it and some would not be ready to read it. It wasn't up to me to decide- I let go of the outcome and knew inside that the book would continue each and every day to make a difference.

Nick Ortnor (The Tapping Solution by Hay House Publishers) says that if you don't have a one star review, not enough people have read your book. I braced myself for the negative feedback. It came sooner than I suspected and from people I didn't expect. Some of my good friends never said a word about my book when it was first released. *Did they know about my book? Why wouldn't they support me? Aren't we supposed to encourage our friends to follow their dreams?* It was confusing for sure! Then, acquaintances contacted me telling me how much my book changed their life! While one person said, "There's a lot about God in it. It surprised me. I didn't know you were so religious," the next person said, "I loved how you talked about spirituality not having to be about religion." A song came on the radio about this time. It was "Jesus Freak". I asked the first person if she read where I explain about the difference between Spirit and Religion. She did but I felt she was still stuck in the subconscious programming of our society's view of God in a structured religion. I had to learn how to let go of what some people thought about my book. At times, the publishing world and book stores were overwhelming. *How would I be able to get my book on a book shelf in a bookstore?* I was a lone, self-published author with no help from a publishing company. I decided to go through some back doors to get my book on a shelf.

While on trips to Oregon and Florida in 2019, I got my book on a bookshelf in two used bookstores. I sold my book for $2-$3. I secretly imagined someone finding this gem on the used bookshelf and then telling all their friends about it! This was, of course, after the person at the counter of the used book store had perused it!

No matter if you are a self-published or a traditional published author, marketing is your responsibility. I imagined my book sprinkled all over the world like confetti. There would be one sprinkle that turned into many sprinkles. It was one book at a time!

Locally, I posted on Facebook that I had books if anyone wanted a signed copy. I loved hand delivering them, especially to people I hadn't seen in years. Online, I reached out to other self-published authors. I read their books and, in return, they read mine. I was slowly gaining momentum as a published author.

I was initially shocked when Balboa told me the price of my book would be $32.99. This was strictly based on word count, color pictures, and the layout. I cringed. Would people really pay that much for a book? *I had to believe they would.*

I worked with local bookstores to try to get my book on their book shelves. It was an interesting experience as a first time, self-published author. I had purchased a lot of books at bookstores throughout the years and I walked in naively thinking that they would support authors, especially a local author! Their words said they wanted to support me, but some of their actions didn't feel supportive.

There is most definitely an interesting dynamic with the internet world of Amazon and local, Indie bookstores. Amazon was out of my control as far as the price for my book. The price would change daily at times and the lowest it went was about $24.00. My eBook was originally priced at $9.99 but that also fluctuated. I advertised a mixture of ideas of where people could get my book. If people were local, please go to the local bookstore. But, I was meeting people from all around the world! I had a person in Australia want my book but it was going to cost $60 just to ship it! The e-book would be a way to reach people on the other side of the world. I most definitely listened to the voice inside at first and reacted with anger and frustration. Then, I dug a little deeper into the publishing world. I was "different" than a "real" author because I "self-published". I felt like I was a second class citizen. I wondered about this a lot. I began to realize that the publishing world was really controlling what we, as Americans, read. I heard stories from Hay House authors that they were turned down by seventeen different publishing companies! *What was going on in the publishing world that I didn't know or understand?* I realized that book store owners want to make sure their inventory is going to sell. I believe they stock famous authors and books that get a lot of attention. This is how the publishing companies control what we read and who has a voice to share their story. I wondered where I fit into this puzzle. I was not famous and I didn't have a traditional publishing company to support my work.

This is how the nitty gritty works when you are an unknown, first time, self-published author eager to get your book on a bookshelf. My publishing company would sell me my book at a discounted rate, depending on how many books I bought. Most of the time, I purchased 100 books at 60% of the full price. All publishers are different - this was the rate I was given for the number of books I was able to purchase at one time. Then, I would ask a bookstore to stock my book. They would sell my book on consignment. The split? They would give me 60% and they would keep 40%. Basically, I would make nothing. I don't get my royalties on books that I purchase directly from my publishing company. I chose to do this and believe that it was worth it. I felt I had a bigger purpose. I wanted to share my book with the world! If this was what I had to do, then I was willing to do it.

On the other hand, a larger bookstore like Barnes and Noble was different. I walked into our Vermont based Barnes and Noble and explained that I was a Vermont author. I asked if they would be willing to stock my book on their shelf. They immediately agreed and ordered my book on the spot. They placed it in a key location near the register and for months, whenever I stopped by to check, if the book had sold, they would happily order another. I realized that with as many books as they had on their shelves, it was up to me to make sure that they restocked my book.

Amazon has most definitely opened up the world to a self-published author like myself. I met all kinds of other writers through online Facebook Writing groups - mostly through Hay House. I met people from all over the world who read my book and I read their book.

One author I met even had a story about a dime in her book!

"I have experienced some very profound events that are signs from Rick...He sends me dimes to remind me that with time all will be well. Time on a dime."
~ Lisa Marie Runfola from her book A Limitless Life in a Powerless World

I felt that although we want to support our local businesses, it would be very difficult for me to continue the path of approaching every single bookstore - *all over the world?!?* - to get my book on shelves. It just wasn't possible. I would need to use Amazon. I wouldn't be able to solve the digital world problem of purchasing vs. supporting local businesses. I was on a mission to share my book and the internet allowed me to do that.

I learned that publishing companies have controlled what we have been reading for years. I had read Brendan Bouchard's book The Golden Ticket. I loved the book! The character was doing a life review and then realized that we only get one ticket for our life. We have to use it properly because there isn't another one. It seriously changed my life and now I appreciate each and every day. But, the interesting thing that I learned while writing my book? Seventeen publishers said, "No" to Brendan's book proposal. He finally found a publisher that would publish his book. Imagine if he had given up? I never would have read his book and I never would have thought about life in a very different way. I know publishers most likely get a lot of book proposals for books, but it is time for everyone to have a voice and be able to write their own book without relying on approval from big publishing companies.

Through Balboa Publishing, I hired a Publicist. They knew more about how to get my book to the places it needed to get to in order to be noticed by the book world. This was not a world that I was familiar with. They knew where to send the press release and how to get my book noticed. This process can be at anytime after the book is released. For me, I waited about 4 months after my book was released. I had some Amazon reviews and the book was gaining momentum. This process would give it a whole new wave of sales! Through this publicist, I was able to get media coverage all over the United States and they even secured some interviews for me!

Book Launch Party

I began studying about book launch parties. (check out https://www.authorlearningcenter.com/) In my head, this coincided with the book release, but that wasn't the case. Book launches can be big parties - almost like a birthday party - or quiet, intimate book signings at a local book store.

When I began to plan my book launch party, I actually began with questions like, "Why did I want people to read my book?" The answer to the question guided me in my planning. I wanted people to be happier, learn to care for themselves in a different way and I wanted people to understand that Heaven wasn't as far away as they thought.

The plan began to unfold. I would ask the many healers in the area to provide a sample treatment for 1 hour, paying them with a free book. Then the author of the Foreword would speak. A local documentary about the Adverse Childhood Experience (ACE) study would also be shown, highlighting how emotions affect our physical health- my most passionate subject! Kim Pierce was following her soul's calling and created a Vermont based film called, "The Faces of Aces". It would highlight her work at the local health center to help her patients understand the connection of emotions to their physical health. She was changing the world with sharing her passion!

We planned it for a Sunday afternoon. I worked with the local bookstore so that people would be able to purchase books through them. We gave away door prizes and had dime necklaces and dime jars for sale. It was a sunny afternoon and I had a team who helped me.

We started with an hour of mingling and people were able to have acupuncture, massage therapy, sound therapy, Reiki, essential oils and much more! People tried alternative ways to heal and won gift certificates to continue that work. I heard many stories of healing and signs from their loved ones. I spoke at the end and read the first part of this book that you are reading right now. It was truly a magical afternoon.

"Yes, the Universe has got you covered. It wants to support you. We just need to leap in order for it to catch us. Once landed, our life can become one big stream of flow." ~ Rebecca Campbell

Chapter 10: The End or The Beginning?

"There's so much pressure on us to be perfect but that perfect person is just an illusion of our own mind and wanting a perfect life- and comparing our lives to others' so called perfect lives- is a pattern that just creates unnecessary stress and pressure." ~ Anshu Singh

I grew up always worried about money. I realized that I had watched my parents work hard to create a thriving family business. I thought the only answer in life was to go to college, work long hours every day and get as much money as possible. Nobody actually said,

"I want my children to be wealthy, to be better than anyone else, to win at everything they do, to get a good job, to get the best grades, to get into the right schools, to look good to their peers. Yet, this seems to be how they're raising their children." ~ Dr. Wayne Dyer.

This idea was what I internalized at a young age and thought I was supposed to do.

America is obsessed with the thinking mind instead of the spiritual experience in life. We encourage our high school students to think that they need to make a life decision about what they will do for work for the rest of their lives. Most youngsters think that they have to have a traditional job working for a company. I was never encouraged to think of my own idea or create a business idea based on my passion. I was taught to use my rational mind to create a life where I would work in a job to save for my retirement and then I would be able to enjoy my life. I wasn't taught to follow my dreams or my interests.

I realize now that I was experiencing secondary trauma from my teaching job. The symptoms of secondary trauma are: Inability to listen, anger and cynicism, sleeplessness, fear, chronic exhaustion, physical ailments and guilt. I was unable to stop the hamster wheel in my head because I worked all the time and never slowed down. I wasn't taking care of myself. I was busy taking care of everyone else. I had to learn how to slow down and take care of myself. (for more information, read Cheryl Richardson's book Extreme Self-Care) I thought self-care was selfish. It's not. It is so important. I was so busy doing that I was not being.

Nowadays, it seems that we are talking more about finding our own internal strength and valuing each moment we are alive. I can most definitely say that I tried to raise my own children differently. I encouraged them to find out what they wanted to do every day. I wanted them to find a job where they were happy. I knew they would need to be able to make money but I didn't want it to be at the cost of their happiness.

"I want my children to enjoy life, to value themselves, to be risk takers, to become self-reliant, to be free from stress and anxiety, to have peaceful lives, to celebrate their present moments, to experience a lifetime of wellness, to be creative, and above all to fulfill their highest needs and to feel a sense of purpose." ~ Dr. Wayne Dyer

These things are so much more than what money can give us. I can see clearly now that I was meant to be a teacher for most of my life but now I know that writing and sharing my story is helping me take a risk and fulfill a sense of purpose. I thought when I finished writing my first book, I was at the "end" but, in reality, it was only the beginning. The beginning of more writing, more sharing, and helping others write their book!

It's the second to last day of our vacation in Florida. During this week, I've written the first draft for this book. All week I had been thinking about how I had looked furiously in the sand for a dime when writing my first book. I saw lots and lots of seashells, but no dimes.

My phone rings while sitting on the deck at the condo. It's a loud ring and people by the pool turn to look. I answer it. It's another telemarketer with no voice on the other end. I sit and listen to nothing. I hang up and decide on my attitude. Do I get super angry that I seem to get these type of phone calls daily now? I hang up and look at the time 11:55 on April 11th. Just in case the dime didn't fully give you a message, here are some numbers. There are no mistakes in the universe, not even telemarketers. That phone call helped to send me a message from Spirit, but only if I was willing to see it.

"I now pay much closer attention to what shows up for me, and I'm willing to listen carefully to any inclination I might have and act accordingly, even if it leads me into unknown territory. I urge you to do the same." ~ Dr. Wayne Dyer

My mind remembers the phrase, "That isn't how it works. Faith is believing even when you can't see any proof." I'm also thinking about giving up meat for my health because of the messages from the universe telling me my system was too sensitive to be able to process meat. I again don't want to accept this message, wanting to be "normal" and eat whatever I want. I still think belonging means to fit into society's norms.

"Begin to pay close attention and view every event and every circumstance - in particular, those that result in dramatic shifts - as guidance from this Divine organizing intelligence." ~ Dr. Wayne Dyer

Then, as we are walking back from the beach, out of nowhere, appears a dime in the sand! I say to my husband, as I bend down to pick it up, "Guess what this is?" He responds, "Is it a Liberty Head?" He knows it is a dime, but wouldn't that be a BIG miracle if it was a Liberty Head dime? *It wasn't but my message is clear. I have my answer. "Your system is sensitive and my body feels better by cutting down on my meat intake." I begin to heal even more.*

I imagine my father grinning yet again. A voice, like the one on the mountain, whispers to me, **"This is such a fun game! Can we keep playing?"** *I also hear him say,* **"Write that second book. I know you can do it!"**

I look at the year of the dime - **2013.** The year often signals a message. *Any significance? Well, this morning when I opened up my memories on my Timehop APP, a picture of my Dad and my son, Patrick, popped up. It was the family business's 80th year anniversary. The year?* **2013.**

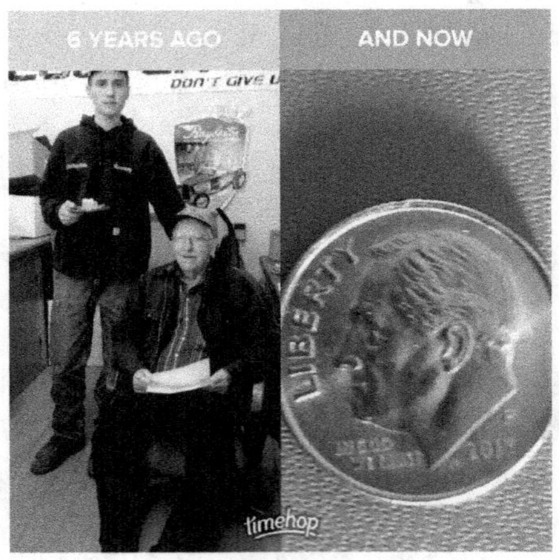

Many people have found dimes since they have heard my story. When they find a dime, they automatically think of me. The same thing happens when a person shares their signs from heaven - dragonflies, butterflies, cardinals, and rainbows. I begin to see their signs and think of them. In this way, I feel connected to people and feel a sense of belonging to something bigger than our human journey. These people believe and understand that our souls continue on after we leave our human bodies.

"There are things working on a different level that are impossible to see, but can be felt...Regardless of whether you had a wonderful childhood or a terrible one, it was the perfect playground for your soul's growth." ~ Rebecca Campbell

As I work on the manuscript and am excited to publish my second book, three birds hit my window. *Could they feel my excitement?* It wasn't like one hit, then a half hour later another one hits the window. They all hit the window within about 60 seconds. Boom. Boom. Boom. I smile as I know it is some sort of sign. (poor little birdies!) I decide to look up to see what a chickadee represents. "..chickadee symbolizes positivity, cheerful natures, flexibility, courage and social behavior." retrieved from https://dreamingandsleeping.com/chickadee-spirit-animal-symbolism-and-meaning/

I realize I will need all of those characteristics in order to be able to publish my second book.

"Find someone who believes that he is alone, and convince him that he's not."
~ Dr. Wayn Dyer

Signs can be anything. Now that I am on this path to accepting myself, I know that I will most likely explore more about my connection to spirit. This connection is available to anyone. Even you. I encourage you to trust your own intuitive abilities. When you think you see a sign, think in your head, '*Who is this and what is their message?*' Whatever your next thought is, that is your message from your loved one. Trust it. You don't need validation from anyone else. Let your soul express itself and speak to you. Let your subconscious mind speak to your linear mind. Don't let your conscious mind analyze it too much!

There were times when I was writing that I listened to my intuition and not to other people. I would receive advice, think about it and stay strong in my belief for some things in my book. I remember thinking about the part in the book where I write, **"I guess having four children to deal with, there wasn't much time to help me deal with my insecurities, or other such silly things, like not making the soft-ball team." ~Monica L. Morrissey** For some reason, I felt that this particular memory was important. I didn't explain it anymore but I knew that it had to be included. The reason it needed to be included would come almost a year after my book was published.

I am now an instructor for Southern New Hampshire University. I teach Master's classes to teachers in the same program that I received my Master's degree. A few weeks before the Spring 2020 class begins, I start finding feathers all over my house. I know that some people believe this is a sign from a loved one in Heaven. I have no idea who would be sending me feathers. I've never had so many feathers!

 I receive the roster for a new class starting and I notice a familiar name. It is the name of one of my softball coaches; the coach who helped make the decision that I would not make the team. I immediately remember that part in my book.

During the first class, I share a lot about my career path and how I have grown as a person. Jean shakes her head as I share how sensitive and shy I was as a child. I explain that curriculum is important in education but so is the relationship between the teacher and the student. Every child deserves love and each child is more than a test score. As I share, I begin to pick up on an energy in the room. One that goes beyond our five senses.

Jean laughs about how much difficulty she has with technology. All of the students receive the email I sent to them. Jean's is lost in the cyber world of technology. She grins as she tells stories about her first graders going down the hall to get help from the IT department. She says that the same is true for her husband. They have difficulties with electronics at home too. I ask her if she understands that this might be a sign *from Heaven. She says that she has never heard of that before. She then shares that her daughter usually sends her feathers.*

I realize the energy in the room is her daughter, who transitioned to Spirit too early in life. Her daughter is laughing at her Mom. She thinks the funniest part of the whole thing is that her Mom doesn't realize it is her daughter playing with the electronics. Now I understand why I needed to include the part of not making the softball team and I understand where the feathers were coming from. It was because Jean and I were meant to connect in a very different way than I would have ever imagined. On the outside, I would be her instructor during her Master's program. But, on the inside, I knew that I was here to help connect her with her daughter in Heaven; the universe had a plan all along.

I'm home from Florida and it's Sunday. I have been writing since I woke - stopping for a short break. My husband goes for a hike up a mountain. I found a dime on Thursday. It was in the sand, exactly on the path I was walking to go back into the condo. Now, as I write, my husband sends me a video. He was on top of Mount Pisgah and in the video he says, "I'm on top of Mount Pisgah and you'll never believe what I just found.....a dime. A Canadian dime but a dime no less." I crumble just like I did when the minister on the mountain asked if I have faith. The dime story will never be done. The dimes will continue on and on forever. I wonder why Dad sent a dime from Canada?

The End or The Beginning?

I thought when I finished writing, I was done. I didn't realize the work was just beginning. My brain knew what to do but I didn't feel it in my heart - my "other" brain. I hadn't felt it inside. The information I was reading about over the years was only knowledge, not yet born to internal guidance.

For my whole life I had followed the path "that had been stomped on by shoes." It was the place I felt safe. I followed the crowd by going to college and then having a career in teaching. Writing is taking me on a whole new shiny path. One where I needed to discover for myself where it might lead. *Is a new path in life calling you?*

Questions to Ponder:

- What social media platform feels best to you? Twitter? Facebook? Instagram?
- What will be important information to put on your website?
- Where will your book be located? Online? Book stores?
- How will you get your book out into the world?

- What can you do yourself and what will you need help with? Ex. creating a website, accounting information, photos, etc.
- How are you accepting advice and/or criticism? Are you using the information to help you grow?
- What will your book launch entail? Where, When, Who, and What? Make sure to market it so lots of people come!

"This book demanded vulnerability and raw honesty in a way I hadn't expected and frankly, I wasn't so sure I wanted to comply, at least not publicly. But I quickly realized that I couldn't ask you to do the brave, messy inner work of transformative change and opt out myself." ~Seane Corn

My Self Publishing Journey
Audio book

I remember the day that I first started taping my audiobook. I had tried to do it myself based on the Do-it-Yourself information at https://www.acx.com/. I sent my audio recordings to the Amazon and they reported the files were not good enough. I didn't understand all of the language around sound bits, etc. I think about who I would be able to ask to record my audiobook. The answer came from an unexpected source. A guy that I went to high school messages me on Facebook. He is looking for a copy of my book. He decides to go to the local bookstore in town. He sends me a message that our Grandfathers used to be friends. I had no idea! He said he has pictures of our Grandfathers at the family camp. It dawns on me that Corey has created musical recordings. I ask him if he knows the name of anyone who might help me record my book. He did! Corey was brought to me right at the moment when I needed to be willing to ask for help. Thank you Corey! Colin McCaffery did an amazing job! (http://www.colinmccaffrey.com/)

On the day of my first appointment, I received a text from my son and daughter-in-law. They are on their way to the hospital to have their first child. *Should I cancel my appointment? Should I go to the hospital? Such a difficult decision!* I wanted to get my audiobook tape completed. I had so many people waiting for the audio version! I decided to go to my appointment and stop to text my son every so often. *Can you believe that as I was reading about souls and lessons here on earth, we were welcoming our first grandchild into the world? Only divine intervention can control such a synchronicity.*

Audiobooks cost a lot due to the time it takes to create them. I negotiated with my publishing company because I wanted to be the one to read my book. I didn't want to hire a professional reader - which costs even more money! I felt strongly that this was my story and my readers wanted to hear me read it. I purchased a package through Balboa where I would send the recordings to them and they would do all of the final edits to then put the audio version on a few different platforms. The whole process from start to finish took about seven months.

By this point in my writing journey, I realized that I was taking a leap of faith in everything I was doing. Just like my life as a Realtor, I had to know inside that this journey my book was taking me on was more about helping the world be a better place to live. I turned my ring around and welcomed every new experience and was happy when I thought, "Come What May."

Book Signings

I did several local book signings at local craft shows. I also sold my books at The Beyond Center Expo and Messages From Heaven, a local event. (https://www.thebeyondcenter.com/) I donated books for charities.

My Publisher offered a book signing opportunity in Toronto. It was going to cost me a lot of money, but it might help get my book get some attention in the Canadian market. I decided to do it and was so thankful that I did! Right before the event, I targeted the Toronto area with a Facebook Advertisement. Balboa Press refers clients to Authors Press (a Marketing agency) and this is the company I would work with. For one hour, I would give books away (this is why it cost so much - I personally bought all of the books!) and sign them for all of the readers who were there. It was amazing connecting with people. Some people would look at the title and turn away. When they looked back at me, they were crying. I heard all kinds of stories from people. "My Mother always sends me dimes." "My Uncle sends me dimes." My story validated for them what they always felt in their heart. While others were interested in the dimes, some were interested in the information about being an empath. I was helping them and it felt wonderful to share my story.

On the way home from Toronto, I phoned Merrilee (she is a very good friend of mine who helped care for my Dad). She said - "I can't wait to tell you a dime story!" She explained that she was getting out of her car and she found a dime. It wasn't a regular dime. It was a **Canadian** dime! She knew I was in Canada this very weekend! She couldn't believe it! *I wonder about the other Canadian dime that my husband had found on the mountain. Was my Dad trying to send me a message that the Toronto book signing was a good choice?*

Blog/MailChimp

At all of my in person signings and on Facebook, I collected emails. I used Mailchimp to be able to send out letters and my blog. I published my blog on my website, Facebook and Instagram accounts. People didn't always purchase my book at the event, but my story made them curious. When I sent out a follow up letter after an event or sent my blog in an email or Facebook, it reminded them and they might purchase the book.

I didn't think at first that I wanted to write a blog. I changed my mind as time went on. I wrote about one blog post a month and hope to be able to write more soon. I encourage you to begin this as well. I published them on Facebook and people enjoyed the short articles and updates about my second book and my audio book. It was a great way to connect with my readers.

Chapter 11: 180 or 360?

"It's only in looking back that the dots begin to connect." ~ Steve Jobs

"If there are aspects of yourself you can't accept, it'll be near impossible to accept the same qualities in others. By learning to love fully your own humanity and journey- seeing it all as holy- you can learn to connect, in love, with the souls around you." ~ Seane Corn

I recently read Gabby Berstein's book, *Judgement Detox.* I realized how much time I spent judging other people. Constantly. Like all day long! I wanted to step away from this part of me. It was hard. One day I was about to tell someone, "You are so impatient!" I didn't. I thought about it but realized that anything that the universe is giving me is a reflection of what needs to be healed within myself; a lesson my soul needs to learn. I asked myself, "Where in my life am I being impatient?" In my book, Dimes From Heaven, I call this "Boomerang advice". The advice that I give to others is actually the advice I need to listen to! Anytime I have advice or a feeling about someone else, it is a time to look within myself and heal that part of me.

"In fact, being truthful feels lighter, freer, and, in the end, more liberating." ~ Seane Corn

Here is my story about being impatient:

I was training to be a Health and Life Coach. I was terrified to share this with people because I wasn't sure what people would think. I posted an opportunity on Facebook as I needed two people to be my first clients to help me complete my certification. I posted it and got a little interest. One person committed, but I needed two. I waited a day and kept thinking that I either needed to post again or re-post my original post. I was most definitely worrying about what others were thinking and wondering how I was going to get another client. Within minutes of healing the impatient part of myself - facing it head on and admitting that I don't like waiting, someone messaged me asking about my post. The universe was sending me a positive experience when I was able to look within myself at my own judgments and took the time to reevaluate myself instead of pointing the finger toward someone else. The secret portal opening up.

It seems like the universe is like one big scavenger hunt. The universe leaves clues and if we are paying attention, we can follow them like bread crumbs. Sometimes it takes time to see how the clues fit together but looking back I can see now the signs supporting me were there along the way.

"The first step is to remember that this kind of self-awareness requires no makeovers or do-overs; instead, it pulls back the veil of doubt, anxiety, insecurity, fear, blame, and shame, and reveals our true nature- which is basic goodness and, of course, love." ~ Seane Corn

Now, when I am trying to understand life, I use the 180^0 or 360^0 rule. If I come upon energy that feels good, I go forward toward this experience. Like a line - 180^0. If I come upon something that doesn't feel good, I turn around my thoughts back onto myself. Like a circle - 360^0. I look within myself for the answers. When that happens, I need to heal the part inside myself that needs to be healed because every experience in life is here to teach me something. By listening to my gut, I know when to move forward or turn around and look inward. When I feel resistance, I know I need to go 360^0 back to myself. Like a boomerang that, if thrown correctly, always comes back to you.

"I had to run to a solution, not away from a problem, and I'm glad I did." ~ TJ Menhennitt from his book Taking the War out of the Warrior

Gary Zukav and Linda Francis talk about the "earth school" in their book, The Heart of the Soul. They explain that we are all here to learn our lessons. In this earth school, it is important for us to turn inward (3600) to heal. If we don't the same lesson will be given to us over and over again. If I didn't face my fear and realize I was being impatient, more of those lessons would keep appearing in my life in different situations and different people. We need to look for patterns in our life - situations that are very similar. Jealousy? Anxiety? Fear? What is life trying to teach you? Use the 3600 rule to look within instead of complaining or judging other people or situations. The universe will support you more and more when you are willing to learn your life lessons. Otherwise, the same lessons will repeat over and over again until you learn how to solve them a different way. These lessons will be passed down from generation to generation until they are healed.

If you began your career when you were young, do a 360^0 turn-around and see what your heart is interested in doing. Maybe you might go in a different direction than you ever imagined!

Whatever you send out to the universe will be returned to you, just like a boomerang traveling back to its owner.

Here are some 360⁰ turn-arounds to think about:

If you look at a plant and think it is a weed, do a 360⁰ turn-around and look at it from a different perspective. Does the plant have a medicinal property that helps people heal? Well then, that "weed" is actually something to be grateful for. Why not call it a flower?

If you think you "see" what is happening in your life, do a 360⁰ turn-around and be willing to look at the unseen forces in your life that brought you to where you are. Where can you find the universe working to support you?

If your conscious self is telling you one thing, do a 360⁰ turn-around and be willing to examine your subconscious to see if your "programming" is actually controlling your thoughts. *What do you believe at a subconscious level that is controlling your thinking?*

If you feel disconnected in your life, do a 360⁰ turn-around and look for places where you are able to connect. Maybe this is connecting with people, nature or God.

If your mind has been full, do a 360⁰ turn-around and look for places where you can clear the clutter in your mind. This is where the magic happens and Spirit speaks to you. Take time to quiet your mind every single day. It will change your life. *I know it changed my life.*

If you are busy planning every single part of your life, do a 360⁰ turn-around and try letting the day unfold without any planning. Ask the universe to help guide you. Then watch the miracles start appearing.

If you think things are happening "to you on the outside", do a 360⁰ turn-around and look within yourself to see what needs to be healed within you. *What life lesson is the universe giving you?*

If you are uncomfortable, do a 360⁰ turn-around and be willing to discover what might make you more comfortable. What's happening that is making you uncomfortable? Get curious about where this originates and be willing to let it go.

Just when you think something might be ending, do a 360⁰ turn-around and realize that you are only beginning. Beginning a new life; free of thoughts and open to new possibilities.

BY MONICA L MORRISSEY

> Every opportunity in life that is given to you is an opportunity for you to learn.

In my first book, I spoke a lot about how our emotions affect our body. My father was a mechanic and he thought the doctors could fix his body just like a car. This is true for some things, but our emotions affect our bodies also. If we don't learn to face our emotions, our bodies will become ill. Medicine will only heal part of our illness. We will keep getting the illness back in our bodies if we aren't willing to face our emotions. These can be from long ago or more recently. Either way, it is important to move through them and release them. This is what will heal everyone. *Check out Louise Hay's book, You Can Heal Your Life to find the link between a physical ailment and an emotion. Hurt knee? Maybe you are going through a transition in your life.*

Changing ourselves is both difficult and scary, but it is also the only way to free ourselves from our own thinking. Our human brains have a built in alert system for signs of danger, especially anything that feels like a change to what we are used to; that which feels safe. The alert system is controlled by our Vagus nerve and it is responsible for our ability to fight, flight or freeze during an emergency situation. This nerve connects our brains to the rest of our body, controlling both the parasympathetic and sympathetic nervous system. It sends messages to and from our gut and to and from our hearts and other parts of our body. When we sense danger, the vagus nerve will tell the heart to pump faster; we won't be in control. Humans needed this nerve to find food, build shelter, be part of a tribe and basically stay alive.

Nowadays, the Vagus nerve is responding to every little thing; sensing danger when there actually is no danger. In Malik Chopra's book, Just Breathe, she explains that the fight, flight or freeze was made to run away from animals who were chasing us. She explains that kids are activating this nerve and the fight, flight or freeze response can come from a Science or Math problem or when they struggle learning how to read. In adults, this is activated by misread text messages or during meetings where someone says something that activates a past hurt within the person. *Where is your vagus nerve being activated in your life?*

"This road led to a place my soul had been missing: Peace. It was exactly at that moment that everything was so clear that I knew the war had finally been taken out of the warrior." ~ TJ Menhennitt

When I was writing, I turned toward the people who supported me and, when I came upon someone who didn't, I looked within myself for the answers. That was how my first book was written- from my soul. Looking inside is a long journey but it is so worth it. Learning how to shine our light brightly in the world will always be the true way to internal freedom. When I looked within to learn my life lesson, the universe was ready to support me.

"Sharing your story is giving back to the world." ~ Christina Goetz

Christina wrote a book called *Truth Be Told How to Overcome the Fear of Sharing your Truth and Unleash your True Potential from Within*. I want to encourage you to tell your truth. Write about it. Share with others. When we share our authentic selves, we feel connected. I hope this book has sparked something within you that needs to be shared.

"When we heal the fractured parts of ourselves and learn to love who we are and the journey we've embarked upon, we will see that same tender humanity in all souls. This is the revolution of the soul." ~ Seane Corn

I know now that everything is perfect within the Divine Timing. The door to the secret portal was open to me as soon as I started writing my first book. Writing has most definitely helped me heal from the inside. As humans, we don't always know the bigger picture of how everything works. It's like one gigantic puzzle piece and it is up to me to do my part. I want people to be healthy and feel a sense of belonging. Writing has given me the opportunity to share my story and begin a whole new career in life; something that I never dreamed would happen.

I continue to work on rewiring my brain and change the way I think. I am grateful for so many things in my life. I am grateful for the people I have connected with through my book and I am grateful for the opportunities that writing has given me. I am grateful for my family and wholesome food. I am grateful for understanding how important it is to appreciate every moment of my life. I am grateful that I feel the support from Spirit, God, My Angels and the Universe.

One of the ways that I worked to reprogram my brain is to write in a gratitude journal. There is a suggested abundance programming activity and I highly recommend it! For 40 days, write in a journal for 15 minutes everything you are grateful for. If you skip a day, you need to start again. It has to be 40 consecutive days and it has to be for at least 15 minutes. You'll be amazed at how your life will change! The thoughts will creep into your subconscious and all of a sudden you will be thankful for each small thing in your life. From paper clips to an apple - everything in life will be grand!

I am still wondering about this concept of subconscious vs conscious. In my first book, I shared the story about my father waking up from his nap, where he had quieted his mind, and said, "Hey- would it be possible to have those Liberty Head dimes from my collection made into a necklace?" *Did my father dream about necklaces? Was Spirit speaking through my father? Did he remember something from his childhood - something that he had seen but never talked about? Something that we would have no way of knowing or understanding at the time...*

"The soul speaks in feelings, in longings, in yearnings, in deep knowing, in vibration, in signs, in nature, in people. It centers itself in the heart, and carries

within it a blueprint for your life. You can't hear the calling of your soul if you don't create space in your day to listen to it." ~ Rebecca Campbell

The reason I am wondering if someone sent him a message is because you will never, ever believe what I found the other day.

I had bought some toothpicks at the store. I hadn't planned to buy toothpicks. The universe led me to the toothpicks, which would then led me to something else. I went to the store looking for a lighter. When I went to the aisle where I thought they might be, I saw toothpicks. I knew that we were almost out of toothpicks so I bought some. When I returned home, I went to put the toothpicks into a special glass container that was from my father's house. The old toothpicks in there were broken so I decided I was going to chuck the old ones into the garbage. As I almost dumped the entire container, I realized there was something in the bottom. I reached in to grab it and this is what I found:

"Believe. Believe in Heaven. Believe in signs. Believe in the unknown. Believe in a bigger purpose. Believe in miracles. Believe that there is good in the world. Believe in yourself. Believe that I am always with you. Just Believe." ~ Monica L. Morrissey

Resources and references:

1. Box, H., & Mocine-McQueen, J. (2019). *How your story sets you free.* San Francisco, CA: Chronicle Books.
2. Brown Brené. (2019). *Dare to lead: brave work, tough conversations, whole hearts.* Place of publication not identified: Random House Large Print Publishing.
3. Byrne, R. (2018). *The secret.* New York: Atria Books.
4. Campbell, R. (2016). *Light is the new black: a guide to answering your souls calling and working your light.* Carlsbad, CA: Hay House Inc.
5. Corn, S. (2019). *Revolution of the soul: awaken to love through raw truth, radical healing, and conscious action.* Boulder, CO: Sounds True, Inc.
6. Dyer, W. W. (2015). *I can see clearly now.* Carlsbad, CA: Hay House.
7. Gikandi, D. C., & Doyle, B. (2015). *A happy pocket full of money: infinite wealth and abundance in the here and now.* Charlottesville, VA: Hampton Roads.
8. Menhennitt, T. J. (2019). *Taking The War Out Of The Warrior: an inspirational journey through divorce & healing... into empowerment, self-discovery & spirituality.* S.l.: Balboa Press.
9. Morrissey, Monica L., (2019). *Dimes From Heaven: how coins and coincidences helped me discover my life as an empath.* S.l.: Balboa Press.
10. Northrup, C. (2012). *The wisdom of menopause: creating physical and emotional health during the change.* New York: Bantam Books.
11. Richardson, Cheryl. *The Art of Extreme Self-Care: 12 Practical and Inspiring Ways to Love Yourself More.* Hay House, Inc., 2019.
12. Runfola, Lisa Marie, (2019). *Limitless Life In A Powerless World.* S.l.: Balboa Press.
13. Scanlon, Maureen, (2019). *My Dog Is More Enlightened Than I Am.* S.l.: Outskirts Press.
14. Singer, M. A. (2013). *The untethered soul: the journey beyond yourself.* Oakland, CA: Noetic Books, Institute of Noetic Sciences, New Harbinger Publications, Inc.
15. https://www.quora.com/What-is-the-difference-between-conscious-and-subconscious-mind-in-simple-terms

16. https://www.elephantjournal.com/2019/07/what-if-all-i-want-is-a-simple-life-
on-a-farm-amanda-
whitworth/?fbclid=IwAR1ZNpUcDY1Kq_U1p_Vjvs68a7lWLN-
_13IADhX7QEKUcJ4BTR6RWLHBcAQ

Once Upon a Dime

Once Upon a Dime
Heaven is Talking to Us, Do You Know How to Listen?
When Proof of the After-life Activates the Secret Signs from the Universe
By Monica L. Morrissey

What readers are saying about *Once Upon a Dime*

Once Upon a Dime by Monica Morrisey was a beautiful, moving and evidential (of an afterlife) story.

This is a sequel to her first book on the topic, Dimes from Heaven, with of which share how and why dimes became a sign from her dad after he passed away. Monica not only shares some pretty mind-blowing times she got dimes, how other people got dimes (or other signs), but also helps guide us how to notice signs and communications from our discarnates (what I refer to as our loved ones who have passed away). She has some interactions with other people with some unexpected twists that are a little hard to dismiss as coincidence.

Monica also openheartedly shares about grief, loss and learning to be honest with our emotions and that all of our relationships with those who we love are not perfect - they can be far from it, but we love them anyway. She is very open about herself, her loved ones, who she is and her life's ups and downs in a brave and relatable way. Whatever you think about an afterlife, you will come away from reading this thinking that these are some remarkable "signs" that are hard to just dismiss.

Liz Entin: Entrepreneur, Author of WTF Just Happened?!: A sciencey-skeptic explores grief, healing, and evidence of and afterlife, Podcast Host: WTF Just Happened?!: All about the afterlife. No woo. www.wtfjusthappened.net

PS

I want you to know the following - I've been planning and saving today to finish the write up. Sorry to be a little behind. But...

1 - I never use cash. Ever.

2 - I never take coins on the VERY rare occasion I use cash

3 - I went to sweep my floor and clean a bit before getting to work so place is comfy And.... I found A DIME!!!!

4 - also note bc I'm sciencey I asked as an experiment to get a dime in some way when I finish the book - I didn't think I would! In fact I forgot I had even asked over a week ago

"Losing my mom at the age of 29, I found myself angry because I had so much left to say to her. I always kept thinking, if only I could tell her this one last thing. Then I got

the privilege to read, "Once Upon a Dime" by the amazing Monica Morrissey. This book helped me realize that I can talk to her and the signs I received confirmed just that.

The sign from my mom is a Cardinals. Before my mom passed, she gave me a little cardinal luck charm with a prayer to hold on to for my speaking events. I used to be deathly afraid of public speaking. While reading "Once Upon a Dime", I noticed that anytime I have a moment of question, a Cardinal comes to my window. Then I notice I started to see them everywhere from tablecloths to pictures to the outside.

Receiving signs from Heaven can be powerful and has changed my life. In this book, Monica provides insightful guidance on the process of recognizing and interpreting these signs. Drawing on both personal experiences and expert knowledge, Monica offers practical exercises to help readers develop their intuition and cultivate a deeper connection. Whether you're seeking comfort, guidance, or looking for confirmation, this book is a must-read, highly recommended!"

Darcey Elizabeth, Founder of Claim Your Network, www.claimyournetwork.com

<h1 style="text-align: right;">Foreword</h1>

You are about to be connected to the Heavens above through your own human experiences. If you were looking for a way to move forward on your soul light journey, then you have the right book in your hands. My name is Rebecca Anne LoCicero, and I am right beside you on this adventure. I have always been aligned to spirit and have joyfully and willingly been bringing everyone I know toward those connections. This book guides you and connects you naturally by the words of the author. A gift, this book is the forward motion we all need to get that feeling of *really receiving* a gift from our loved ones in Heaven.

I have been working as a psychic medium in the public eye since 1994. I have been able to travel and present my trademark presentation Messages from Heaven™ to many audiences. These galleries are part of my work. I love to bring the reality that Heaven is real to as many people as I can. I do that by bringing through validating and accurate messages directly from the true personality of the loved one's soul they have lost. I do tend to be a bit brassy; it comes with the confidence I have in the truths in the messages they share with me. Once such gallery in Vermont happens to have had a woman right up front and I had to ask her if that was"a f'n dime she was wearing on her necklace', which at the time was a sign through me for her that she was getting a hello' from her dad in spirit. Little did I know then that her dime would become my dime too, and now, your dime as well.

I have been connected to Monica Morrissey, your author, since that first group. I was overjoyed when she presented her first book, *Dimes from Heaven*, where she clearly embraced all the empathic energy that was already within her. I have seen many people enter the metaphysical realms and find themselves seeking teachers whilst becoming one themselves. Monica has now found herself on this journey. I have seen her start to present at seminars and conventions as she put her second book out, *More Dimes from Heaven.*

Once Upon a Dime.... Will leave you with an endless amount of amazing resources to continue your learning and expanding into your own 'Conquest for Dimes'. This third book takes you through the feelings of grief balanced by the stories of survival. You'll feel the pain of finding and losing signs while you gain the confidence to clearly ask for more signs. As a medium, I find that the most important part of living without your loved ones is to clearly see the signs as a hello and an 'I love you' from those we are missing. If you can find a way to bring yourself a touch of the peace they feel in Heaven, you can feel a calmness withing that grieving process. As human beings, we need that. Monica expands the basics of grief steps while allowing you to accept your human emotions. Moving forward, this book allows you to believe in miracles. You'll feel as if you are walking with her and taking deep breaths alongside her as she climbs mountains to find signs. You'll see how a sign from your loved one can be more than just a 'hello', it can be a full-on validation of a moment in your life! Through a barrage of characters, family and friends of Monica's you are able to vicariously relate to each encounter. Let her change your perceptions, choose love, meet your light body.

By Psychic Medium/Author, Rebecca AnneLoCicero www.RebeccaAnneLoCicero.com May 2023

Once Upon a Dime Poem

Once Upon a Dime
Once upon a time, there was a woman who was showered with dimes.
She knew these dimes were the keys to connect each time.
When she was a little girl,
She knew there was more to life than the eyes could see,
More than the ears could hear,
More than the nose could smell,
Most of all she knew that she was connected to something in her heart.
She didn't have the words to explain it to others.
She didn't have the knowledge she needed yet to connect to this place.
She knew that what she was feeling was so real.
She went on with her life but seemed lost.
She tried to fit in to what society seemed to communicate to her.
She was told to keep reaching for more.
That was the only way to happiness.
The search seemed like a never ending to do list.
She was told that fear was more real than love.
One dime at a time, they guided her back home.
Heaven is near, not far.
Heaven is a feeling, not a place.
Heaven is all around us, not above us.
Heaven is a way to be, not a place to go.
Heaven is right here right now.
Supported, alive, guided,
she now
Smelled the memories.
Saw the lights.
Heard the guidance.
Felt the love from within.
No longer lost, she began a new relationship with life,
She now knew the roses she smelled,

Were her Grandmother nearby.
She now knew the lights flickering were her guardian angels.
She felt the messages in her heart and
Knew the garden of life was the key to happiness.
She listened to the messages from the Divine,
With each found Dime.
She felt connected to this mystical, invisible dimension that she knew as a child.
Most of all, her heart felt the love she had longed for.
No longer chasing happiness, she was able to live life in gratitude.
No longer living in fear, she knew love was all that was needed.
Each dime was filled with unending love,
Connecting our souls forever.
Thank you, Dad, for the Dimes from Heaven.

Chapter 1: My First Dimes

"So many different synchronicities have taken place in my life over the last few years that confirm for me again and again how connected we actually are. For me, a synchronicity is when a connection is made between myself and someone else that is so utterly beyond chance, so stunningly transparent and unlikely, that the idea of a simple coincidence is way too far-fetched even to consider." ~Anita Moorjani

Tears flowed freely down my cheeks with each step I took. My eyes burned, making it challenging to see. This had to be one of the hardest hikes I had ever done. The trail up the mountain was easy and it was a warm sunny day. I was out of breath but that wasn't why the hike was difficult. The difficulty was in my mind, and I could not imagine the intense pain I would feel when I reached the top of the mountain. Each step up the gravelly path brought more stabbing pain to my heart. As I came upon the steep moss-covered rocks and saw the white birch trees, I was getting closer to my favorite spot to call my dad. My friend, Peggy, had told me, "You will know what to do when you get there."

Questions spun in my mind like a fast-moving merry-go-round. How would I know what to do? What did she mean? How would I ever get through this? As I sat on the bumpy rock and looked out to see the sun forming diamonds on the lake, I remembered the last time I called my father from this very spot. Our family camp, a rustic, modified 1930's cabin with wood paneling, sat at the northeastern point on the lake below. It was partially covered by a tree, but that didn't matter. I knew exactly where it was. When I called my dad, he would be sitting inside the living room as he peered out the cathedral ceiling windows toward the mountain when he said, "Can you see us waving?"

Growing up in the 70's, who would have thought that a person would be able to call another person from on top of a mountain? When I was young, the phone was always connected to the wall. Heck, when my family purchased our first cordless phone, it was like we had won the lottery. How would anyone in the 80's ever believe that voices would be able to travel through time and space through a little black box? My understanding of the possibilities of communication was only just beginning.

I would laugh and say, "Yes! I can see you," even though it was too far to see anyone from on top of a mountain even if peering through a set of binoculars. It would be like looking at ants while on top of a hundred foot ladder.

grief, I wondered if it might just be possible to connect one last time. I had no idea how to do this and no idea if it would be able to happen. Can we really communicate to people who no longer have a physical body? And, can they really send us messages? Could I believe in something that I couldn't see and might not be able to prove? Could it be possible for this invisible communication system to work like a cell phone-traveling through time and space with no wires or anything physical to connect us?

Shortly before his death, I had explained to my father what I believed to be true. Illness had taken over his body and his eyes were closed, but I was hopeful that he heard me say, "Hey Dad, there is this new communication system you haven't heard about yet. It's where people who don't have a body anymore are able to talk to people still on earth. You won't really be away from us. We are able to talk all the time because your soul is in spirit form and is always here with us. We are always connected."

My father might have thought I was telling a fairytale bedtime story like he might have done when I was a little girl. Hours later, his soul left his body and went to the spirit world. If my father was able to whisper to me, I think he would have given me the key to understanding death. He would have told me, "The end is not the end. Be aware and not only will you be able to hear me, but I'll send you physical signs that show I am near." This is what happens when people arrive in Heaven and I now know that he understood this.

Trembling, my eyes still stinging from the tears, I sat on the rock and looked out over the rolling hills and lush green mountains of Vermont. My body was tense with grief and pain at the thought of never seeing or talking with my dad again.

I suddenly realized there were two couples behind me now, exploring the cement foundation of the old wooden cabin that burned years ago. I quickly wiped my tears and tried to pull myself together.

I began explaining my disheveled state to them. "I'm sorry, I must look like a wreck. My father died last week. I always used to call him when I got to this particular spot on the mountain."

The older woman responded, "I'm so sorry. Would it be alright with you if we gave you a hug?"

I was dripping in sweat and tears and I'm sure my aroma wasn't the sweetest, but these people didn't seem to mind. I kept talking and one by one, I received hugs from each and every one of those strangers on top of that mountain.

"My family has a camp on that side of the lake. Growing up, I spent every summer there. Even my great grandparents owned the Elmore Store on the other end of the lake," I explained, wondering why I felt the need to keep talking to these people.

I could just walk away and go back down the mountain. I could stay in my own little world, filled with grief and despair. I didn't. I chose to connect with these people.

"Wow, that is so neat," I can't remember who said it but they responded politely and looked where I pointed. "This is such a beautiful spot."

"I'm so sorry. I feel like I am ruining your hike with my sadness," I apologized again.

The younger gentleman walked over closer to me, looked deep into my eyes and asked, "Do you have faith?"

Tears ran down my cheeks like fast dripping raindrops and my body shook more as I grasped the dime on my necklace between my thumb and forefinger. A few months ago, my father had given me a 1919 Liberty head dime from his antique coin collection. That dime reminded me of my father, but I felt the special powers infusing my heart with love and faith.

Faith and love for me are like the wind blowing; they are all invisible but you know the wind is there when it cools your skin. Faith blows goosebumps on me reminding me that there is an invisible force of life, an energy in the air that one senses without physical proof. All are invisible but powerful. Was this invisible connection really possible? Could our thoughts travel through time and space like a cell phone? The communication is between souls- even without a physical body. Is there some sort of soul consciousness that continues after death?

I had shared with my dad how much the dime meant to me.

"Do you know how special those dimes are that you gave to all of us kids?" I asked him. We were riding in his light blue mini van heading back from his camp on the lake to his home just ten minutes away. As we drove down the hill toward town, I said "A dime is just a dime unless it is a dime from your father. Then it is a *dime*!" This would be my dad's last car ride and one of our last conversations.

He didn't respond but looked down as he shook his head in agreement. His cough seemed to increase the flow of tears. His body seemed to be betraying his will to live and at seventy-nine, heart disease was taking over his physical body. He was scared; not knowing what the next part of his soul journey would be like.

"Yes, my faith is very strong," I replied and smiled at this man who dared to ask me such a personal question. His next words would surprise me even more as my tears changed to happy, joyful tears. I was still shaking and crying, but it was different. I was filled with love even with my broken heart.

"I am a minister. Would you like to say a prayer from your father?" he asked me.

Could this minister on the mountain really be the phone call from my father that I had requested? Could this coincidence really be the communication that other people talk about and I thought might only be a silly fantasy?

As I stood face to face, holding sweaty hands with a stranger on top of my favorite mountain, I knew my father was somehow able to arrange this to prove to me that the invisible spirit communication system worked. He was able to call me without wires or cell service, just like I had explained to him. Death did not end our relationship. His soul traveled on without his physical body and his energy form was now near. A new relationship with my father was beginning to develop; one that was very different than when my father was here on earth. My father was able to show me unconditional love from where his soul lived on.

The next week I hiked the mountain again. It didn't seem quite as difficult as the week before. I was out of breath again but there were no tears. Some say time heals grief but I'm not sure it really does. Mostly, time changes my grief and as life moved on, I felt more at peace. I was at peace on this hike because I truly felt that my father had "called" me, exactly one week ago.

"Hey Merrilee, I'm on top of the mountain. Remember when you and dad used to pretend to wave to me?" I laughed into my cell phone as I paced near that same rock. I couldn't sit down this time. I was all alone and the fall air cooled my sweaty skin, sending shivers through my entire body.

Merrilee was there each and every day to care for my father during his last summer on the lake. She laughed as she corrected me, "We weren't pretending! We were actually waving to you. Your father and I would laugh and say, 'Do you think she can see us?'"

I laughed, imagining the fun Merrilee brought to my Dad's life. "I sure do miss his sense of humor."

"Me too. I am so happy that I got to know him. He was such a good, kind man." As I walked and talked with Merrilee, I gazed into the horizon filled with trees beginning their transformation from green to a splattering of yellow, red and orange. I wondered about my father and what it was like for him now, after his transition to spirit form. My imagination seemed to be running wild as I felt like my dad was right there with me.

I wasn't looking at my immediate surroundings, but I knew the wild rose bushes were on the far side of the clearing and the pine trees were behind me. They were as familiar to me as my own home. As I walked and talked, I remembered to look down so I wouldn't trip on the uneven ground near the rock.

When I looked down, I couldn't believe what my eyes saw in the dirt right near the tip of my hiking boot.

I gasped into the phone. "Oh my gosh, Merrilee. You are never going to believe what I just found." As my mind wondered about the reality of this, I moved as if in slow motion bending down to pick it up.

"I don't know. What is it?" her curiosity peaked by my comment about finding something on top of a mountain. A moment in time to share with another person is what makes memories in our hearts. This one is forever with me.

It glistened in the sunshine showing me the invisible communication system was working yet again. I felt like the princess in the story and my prince sent me the love that filled my broken heart. Smiling from ear to ear I exclaimed, "A dime! Merrilee, there is a dime right here in the dirt!"

How could this be? How does a coin, this particular coin, land on top of the mountain exactly in this spot? Was my father grinning like this was some sort of game to him? Could he really do things like this without his physical body? It was a sign that could only mean one thing. For the second week in a row, he was sending me a message that even in his death he was always with me.

Time stopped as Merrilee and I processed the chances of me finding a dime on the top of a mountain exactly in this spot.

"I can't believe it. How could that happen? Do you think your father did this? I have goosebumps!" Merrilee talked as I looked at the coin.

"The year on the dime is 1995 and there is a P just above the year," I told her.

"What year was your son, Patrick, born?"

My smile grew as big as an upside-down rainbow. "1995."

We laughed and the tears squirted onto my cheeks. They were the same happy tears when the minister asked if I had faith. My whole body was alive with energy, electrical currents running through my blood. Even though it had been a few short weeks since my father's death, suddenly this coincidence helped me transform my intense grief into pure love and happiness. My immense gratitude for this moment was difficult to explain as love poured into my heart like a full cup of red wine.

My father's sideways grin and the twinkle in his eye revealed to me that he still had his sense of humor. His voice was clear in my head when he said, "Yes! It is me! I figured out that spirit communication system. Isn't it great? We really can connect from here. You told me my 'engine' would still be running, this engine is so different! I'm not in any pain and my engine will run forever!"

I had no idea that this first dime would lead me to write three books! Pennies seemed to pop out of the concrete wherever I walked ever since my mother died. When she was alive, she would have rolled her eyes at me while explaining, "When you are dead, you're dead. It's the end."

I didn't want to believe that and these events gave me the verification to believe our souls are like a car engine that never stops. Our physical body was just the frame of the car that the engine traveled in during our earthly life. The engine traveled on and through many coincidences and synchronicities, my father's and my mother's engines were alive and well. And, the invisible communication system worked as slick as calling from a cell phone. We didn't need wires. We needed faith to believe that our loved ones' souls are right here with us - mostly invisible to the naked eye, but palpable in our heart.

The dime on the mountain wouldn't prompt me to write my first book, *Dimes From Heaven*. It would be two years later and another coincidence.

Anxiety about my son purchasing a new house at the age of twenty-two consumed my thoughts. As I helped clean the entire kitchen, scrubbing the black moldy grime hiding under the fridge, I wondered if this was the right decision for him.

Dog and cat hair seemed to cling to every part of the house. As I vacuumed the bedroom, a penny ricocheted off the baseboard heater near the wall. I smiled as I thought of my mom. As I crawled into the bedroom closet to vacuum up all of the accumulated pet hair, a dime popped out of the closet door jamb. I smiled as I felt a deep connection to my dad.

Our Realtor, who was a good friend of ours, had predicted that we would find a dime and she was right! Since my friends had heard my story about the dime on the mountain, I posted a picture of the dime on Facebook. I felt as if my parents were here with my son in his new home.

That wasn't why I ran out of the house screaming like I was announcing a fire to my son and husband who were up on the roof checking out the broken chimney. Instead of a warning, I was confirming my belief that I received another clear message from my father.

"You cannot call me crazy anymore!" Of course, they had no idea what I was holding in my hand or how strongly I believed that this coincidence was a form of communication from what I call the "other side"- where our souls live after they leave the physical body.

The filthy green rug in the small spare bedroom was so dirty that it was going to need to be either shampooed or replaced.

I was dead tired. We had been cleaning all day. At the last minute, I spotted a nickel caught in between the wires that were shooting through the wooden floorboards. Something urged me to get that coin. I sort of almost freaked out when I thought the vacuum almost ate it up. I wish I had the fingers the size of a two year old as I could barely squeeze my thumb and forefinger into the hole trying to grab the edge of it. My fingers slipped. I felt I was playing a game of tug of war. Who would win? And why did I feel like I needed to get this nickel? I mean, it was only worth five cents!

It wasn't a nickel.

It was a 1936 Liberty head dime; the exact type of dime that I wore in my necklace from my father. My anxiety disappeared as quickly as a bubble could pop. My son was meant to buy this house and my father gave his approval with that special dime. This coincidence didn't seem random. It felt like a magical dime confirming again this invisible connection to my father.

I could tell dime stories all day long. When we believe in this mysterious connection to the Spirit world, it seems to activate the communication system even more. I wrote my first book, *Dimes From Heaven,* to share my inspiring dime story and help people believe in signs from our loved ones. I had no idea that sharing my story would create a series of events that were too incredible not to share!

For example, when I went to pick up my business cards, the store employees asked me about my book. Then, to my surprise, they shared they had a dime glued to their floor as a joke on an employee! Can you believe it? The business I decided to use to print my business cars has a dime glued to the floor of their building! What are the chances? Then, on the day my second book, *More Dimes From Heaven*, was published, a dime literally popped out of the grass as I raked my lawn. I said to my husband, "Can you believe this?" As he shook his head and smiled, he responded with a simple, "Yes, of course. It always happens just when you need it." Even though I now understand how this all works, I am still surprised when coincidences happen!

I didn't always believe that our souls traveled on after death. In fact, I took life for granted most of the time and thought most people would be able to live into their seventies, eighties, or even nineties. It wasn't until I experienced the shocking death of a loved one that I began to wonder not only about death but about life as well.

Ever since I was young, I wondered about death. I had not grown up with this knowledge or belief system and I was curious as to whether or not it was really possible to connect with our loved ones who were gone. They say that when the student is ready, the teacher shall appear. Even though my job at the time was as a public school teacher, I was a student learning about life and death in a whole new way.

What happens when we die? Why do young people have to die? How does a parent go on living after the death of a child? Are mediums real? Can a butterfly really be a sign from someone's mother? Where do our souls go when they leave the physical body? What would happen to me if something happened to my child? What would my children do if something happened to me?

I had a few friends who thought that butterflies were messages but I often doubted it. I mean, really? How many butterflies do I see every summer? How could that possibly be a sign? The thing about signs from Heaven is that a person might not believe until something happens to them that is so crazy, like my dime on the mountain or in my son's house, that the coincidences convince them that it must be true.

On April 24, 2008, the fast track education about life after death began for me.

"Tyler was in an accident," my sister-in-law told me as I held the cordless landline to my ear. When she called me on April 25th, I imagined a minor accident for my twenty-one-year-old nephew. Maybe his car hit a tree or went into the ditch. My kids were only twelve and fourteen at the time which meant I had no idea what it was like to have a child who could drive.

"He's okay. Banged up and in the hospital but he will be fine." These are the words I imagined her saying next. They are the words I didn't hear.

Her voice was difficult to understand but in between her sobs she explained, "He's gone. He died."

Speechless, I handed the phone to my husband, who was glaring at me, as if he already knew something was seriously wrong. The fear was in the air and my children sensed it. You could almost smell the shock like a gas leak warning us of danger.

Except, the shocking news of death wasn't a smell; it was an invisible feeling radiating from our bodies.

In moments like this, our hearts beat faster and time slows down. It's probably the same feeling that I felt as a baby inside my mother's womb when she received the shocking news that her father died suddenly of a heart attack. It was just a few short weeks before I was born. My soul knows about losing a loved one quickly and unexpectedly. The adrenaline that traveled like a river in her blood would travel in my blood too. It wasn't a feeling in the air like the phone call; it was an emotion traveling in the blood we shared. My DNA footprint was established and as a soul not even born yet, I forever would be affected by the sudden death of my mother's father.

My children experienced the unforeseen grief of losing one of their beloved cousins and how they managed it would depend on how I handled the news. This would be a hard lesson for me to learn as a mother, and I didn't feel ready. I could barely keep myself together as tears sprang into my eyes and dribbled down my cheeks. Soon, the water spigot would open up on their cheeks too. And, at this time, I had no knowledge of there even being a possibility to be able to connect with someone after they were gone.

Tyler died immediately on impact when the car, driven by a friend of his, hit a large brick mailbox in Tennessee. Tyler's death forever sent me searching for answers to questions I had never discussed with anyone.

Grief is so different when it is a young person or a sudden death. This was many years before my parents died and this sudden shock to our family was the first time my children experienced such a deep, transformative loss. As a mother, I wanted my children to be able to talk about their cousin who they missed dearly and I wanted them to appreciate how precious life really is.

Our family talked about Tyler and anytime the number eight appeared, we thought of him.

We began to feel the energy of Tyler thanks to his best friend, David Price. David knew that Tyler was with him when he pitched his first game on a major league baseball field.

"No one enjoyed David Price's performance in Tuesday night's All-Star Game as much as Tyler Morrissey did. He was in the upper deck. He was behind the dugout. He was behind the plate. He was even on the mound with Price. After all, as far as Price is concerned, he always is. Almost three months after Tyler's death, David felt Tyler's presence- helping David as he began his MLB career as a pitcher. This was something that Tyler always believed would happen to David and David knew that Tyler's spirit was right there with him every step of the way."

~Gary Shelton St. Petersburg Time July 13, 2010

Our family loves to watch David pitch. Do you ever notice how he looks up? Or taps his heart? If David believed, could we also believe Tyler was still here with us?

Would I be able to guide my children to believe in something different than how I was raised?

I went searching for answers about the afterlife and what I found surprised me. A friend recommended I read Brian Weiss's book, *Many Lives Many Masters.* Brian was a psychiatrist and a skeptic about anything that science couldn't prove or anything we couldn't sense with our five human senses. After losing his son as a baby, he had no intention of understanding anything about the after life. Death changes our lives in ways we may never have imagined. During hypnosis, one of Brian's psychiatric patients remembered many past lives. One life she shared was when she was killed. She knew the name of the person and other facts about the person's life. She had no way of knowing the information she spoke about during the hypnosis but Brian was able to verify every piece of information she said during the sessions. He went on to write about how souls return to earth to experience many lifetimes and how important it is to turn to love instead of fear.

In my research, I discovered that our soul, which is the spiritual part of our physical body, chooses our life plan to learn and grow. We choose the best time for our growth to come to earth to learn the lessons we need to learn as we are each on a different path. Each event in our life has something to teach us. Some souls stay for a short time and others stay longer. Tyler's time here wasn't nearly long enough.

I helped care for my father-in-law during the last few days of his life. His death wasn't a shock as he lived eighty-eight wonderful years. He had seven beautiful children and a wife of sixty-three years whom he loved dearly. Even in the last few days while confined to his bed, he cherished his bride.

His transition brought back so many memories of my own father. Each day, as we navigated the Hospice care, we were reminded of how heart disease slowly takes over until there is no life left.

My in-laws' faith carried us through the week, accepting that Jack would be with God soon. We knew his time was near. Since I was at the house around the clock to help the family care for him, the chances of me finding a dime were slim.

I found a penny on the bathroom floor one morning. It hadn't been there all week and then all of a sudden, there it was! My mom was sending love to me and my husband's family.

I placed the penny in the pocket of my shorts. I was reading in the formal living room while the family spent time in the small den where their father's hospital bed crowded the small space. Later that day, I reached into my pocket and the penny was gone. I retraced my steps back to the blue armchair. As I sat down, and pushed the cushion to the side just a bit, I found the penny.

In the exact spot where the penny was, there was a dime right next to it. Can you believe it? The penny led me to the dime, almost like the universe creating a scavenger hunt! I felt both my mom and dad were with me helping us say goodbye to Jack. They would soon be welcoming Jack to the spirit world.

A few hours later, my dear father-in-law transitioned. I imagined my father telling Jack all about the spirit communication system and I'm sure they both will send some more dimes. (While working on this chapter, my niece, Madeleine and Mother-in-law found two dimes! 7/27/21)

Jack passed away quietly in his home with his bride holding his hand. This loss wasn't like the experience the family had years ago when my nephew died at the young age of twenty-one. It doesn't matter how our loved ones transition to the spirit world, they want to connect with us. They are right there waiting for us to ask and to have faith that it works!

Some people are uncomfortable talking about death, regardless of whether it is their own death or the death of someone else. When I was growing up we most definitely weren't encouraged to talk about any kind of "weird" signs from people who were gone.

I grew up thinking that "those" type of people were a bit on the crazy side. After Tyler's death, a few of my close friends wanted to go see a medium. We weren't really sure about it and wondered if they could really receive messages from dead people. Over the years, I slowly reframed my beliefs about the possibility of an after life- one where our souls are somehow still intact, even though our bodies are gone. It wasn't until both of my parents died that I was able to put into practice everything I had learned about the spirit world.

I never intended to be a writer but felt that my dime stories might help others experiencing grief. I was surprised by the number of people, even in my small town in Vermont, who believed in signs from those who had passed. I guess that before I shared my story, people might not have talked about signs from dead people because people might think they were a bit on the crazy side. Nowadays, it seems so much more acceptable than it did years ago. The more people reached out to me, the more stories that seemed to unfold in my life made me realize that we don't need to be a medium to be able to connect to the spirit world. We are born with this ability. We just need to know how to access it.

These days, I am one of "those" people my mother would have brushed off as non-sense. She understands now because when a soul transforms back to the spirit world, there is an immediate understanding about their soul lessons. They leave behind all other human emotions because in the Spirit world there is only love and light. My mother even showed me her approval and love when I published my first book. (keep reading- you'll find out about this story in chapter three!)

We all experience grief in a different way. Within the sadness, there is also a certain amount of love in our hearts when we know that our souls continue on and are able to communicate. We are all connected and there is another dimension to this life to explore.

The more that I wrote about these coincidences, the more synchronicities happened to me and those around me. These experiences altered my life, enlightening me to live in a more spiritual way.

Something happens when we decide to share these stories about how people communicate in the after-life. Other people "catch" the signs, just like a cold is contagious. People start finding dimes or coincidences happen where people stop and wonder, "Could this really be true?"

Story by story the evidence and the strategies help to understand:

- The possibilities of an after-life
- Popular signs from Heaven
- That coincidences and synchronicities have meaning
- How to request and receive a sign from your loved one
- How understanding death helps us to be grateful for the life we have been given
- How to listen to your intuition using your natural born spiritual abilities

Since ancient times, cultures around the world have told stories. Our brains love the full circle loop that comes from a story. Each story is filled with deep pain and sorrow for the ones we miss but also filled with love when the key opens the door to the communication system.

Chapter by chapter the stories about communication from what I call "the other side," in which souls who have passed on are free to visit in energy form may transform some of your pain so you feel unending love. Somehow our loved ones create coincidences that can only mean one thing, "The end is not the end." Like a cell phone with no wires, our souls are forever connected with unending love. These incredible stories empower you to use intentional thoughts to connect with your loved ones in the Spirit world and learn to live in a more spiritual way, where the things we cannot see inspire us all.

Chapter 2: Experiencing Grief- Beyond the Five Stages

Chapter 2 Experiencing Grief- Beyond the Five Stages

"Sometimes I forget how rich I am. My hot water works on a dime, my a/c works when I need it to. I can go to any grocery store and purchase what I please to eat. I have a clean kitchen to cook in. I have a clean shower to bathe in...sometimes I forget I'm beyond blessed." ~Author unknown

If there is one thing in life people can be sure of is that they are going to die. Eventually, the body we were given at birth will fade away and many will wonder, "Does this mean I am gone forever?" I've wondered about why I am here on earth for so long that now I don't know what it would be like to not wonder about my life.

When I was growing up and a person died, the person was erased like hitting the delete button on a computer. They were gone and there was nothing else to discuss. We did not celebrate their life and we didn't even express how sad we were that they were gone. My family didn't discuss death before it happened and we definitely didn't talk about the possibility of someone else dying. I barely heard stories about my Grandfather who died two weeks before my birth.

The most well-known stages of grief in America were developed by Kubler Ross in 1969 (I was one year old!) and these would become so ingrained into our society that fifty years later they are still accepted (in America) as the only way to grieve. Some are guided to "heal" by "moving through" the stages. Why are we using such an outdated system? I'm not still using the telephone system from the sixties, why would I use an outdated psychological process for dealing with a major life event?

What most people might not know is that Kubler-Ross and David Kessler designed the five stages to be used for people who were facing their own death. They didn't create them to use after a person died.

The five stages developed by Kubler-Ross & Kessler are the following: 1. denial 2. anger 3. bargaining 4. depression 5. acceptance. A person who lost a loved one is made to feel that if you dealt with these feelings, eventually you would feel better. As anyone who has experienced the deep loss of their loved ones knows, grief is not something that goes away. Losing someone affects us for the rest of our lives.

I remember when my mother died. I definitely wasn't in (1)denial- she was gone. How could I deny that? I was (2)angry. I was angry that she wouldn't go get help when she knew she was sick. How was anger going to help me feel better? It wouldn't bring her back so it was pointless to be angry. (3)Bargaining? What was I to bargain for? She was gone and there was nothing to do but live without her. The (4)depression didn't catch up to me for years after her death. My father most definitely experienced depression and wondered why he was left behind. He was ready to go be with her. My depression hit later on when I realized that I never had the relationship with my mother that I wanted. (5)Acceptance seemed to be difficult at first but with time, there was nothing else to do but create a new life without my mother.

David Kessler added two new stages to the five stages - shock and finding meaning. The shock felt by an unexpected death can rock us to our core. When this happens to me I feel like time stops and nothing else in life matters anymore. It's like I'm watching a movie and I am one of the characters. I get angry easily and can't seem to focus on anything. Nothing else seems important. After the initial paralyzed feeling, then it's time to create a new way to live without the physical presence of the person.

It is difficult to describe but there is this overwhelming, unbearable feeling, especially if the death is a surprise. Brene Brown nails the emotion in her new book, *Atlas of the Heart*. She calls it anguish and this is her description," Anguish is an almost unbearable and traumatic swirl of shock, incredulity, grief, and powerlessness." It feels like life is so out of my control that there is no way to get through the experience. Since we all do get through it, I wonder what the lasting effects are of those moments when we first learn about a death. The trauma stays in our bones and radiates within our bodies. It's what I felt as a baby inside my mother's womb, but as a child I didn't have the resources to process the grief.

One thing that I believe is missing from the stages is anxiety. When someone dies, I immediately think, "Oh no, what if I die? What if someone close to me dies?" I go to this place where everything is scary. What if I have cancer? What if I have heart disease? What if someone I love gets into a car accident? Everyday becomes scarier and scarier. I have to remind myself that each day is not promised. I have to remind myself of the value in being alive and that our time on earth is determined by a greater power than me. I am able to take steps to create a healthy life but, ultimately, when it is time to go, we all leave this earth and transition back to our spirit form.

What if there was another way to experience grief? What if there weren't linear stages to work through like we were attending school and trying to graduate? What if through our loss we found strength and a deep connection to something beyond human explanation- like universal spirit or our own soul? What if we allowed our grief to express itself every single time it appeared? And then, we took time to remember the love of the person who was gone. What if we found meaning through the experience or decided to find meaning in our loved ones' life? And decided to embrace that part of them in our own life?

I've noticed a difference in how people experience death depending on their belief in God. When I speak of God, I'm not talking necessarily about a specific religion or a man up in the sky controlling everything. What I mean is there is a universal, invisible connection to "something" and that "something" is "out there" and "in here". "Out there" includes many mysteries like nature, the solar system and all of life. How else are we able to explain how a tree grows or how animals live or how the moon circles the earth? The "in here" is a feeling within us that feels love and connection. Our hearts are alive and connected to "something". This connection with God or universal intelligence or whatever we want to call it is so much more than we are able to put into words and it requires trust; which I call faith. If we allow this connection to "something", then our life experiences are filled with awe and wonder.

There are two other models of grief that may help more than the original stages. J. William Worden's four tasks of grieving (from his book *Grief Counseling and Grief Therapy*) and Thomas Attig's grief process (from his book *How We Grieve: Relearning the World)* introduce us to a different perspective.

Worden's tasks are not linear in fashion and may be done for the rest of your life. There is no graduation in your grief and it is acceptable to continue your journey using these. The four tasks are 1. Accept the Reality of the Loss 2. Process Your Grief and Pain 3. Adjust to the World Without Your Loved One 4. Find a Way to Maintain a Connection to Your Loved One. These tasks allow for a lot of emotions during the process. And, personally speaking, I love number four as that is what has helped me the most. Grief and death have changed my life in such incredible ways that I never would have imagined.

Thomas Attig's process includes some of the similar tasks to Worden's. Thomas suggests the following: 1. Changes in the Physical World 2. Changes in Relationships with Others Still Living 3. Changes in Perspective on Time 4. Changes in Spiritual Grounding 5. Changes in Relationship with the Deceased 6. Changes in Identity.

Both of these models allow you to stay connected to your loved one. This is the key to experiencing life after loss. Without this connection, the pain and suffering can be overwhelming. As David Kessler states in his book, *Finding Meaning,* "Pain is inevitable. Suffering is optional." David also wrote, "When we move through pain and we release it, we fear there will be nothing, but the truth is, when the pain is gone, we are connected only in love. "

Recently, I was chatting with a co-worker who found meaning in her friend's death. Tracy shared with me that her lifetime friend, Missy, passed away due to cancer and because of this, Tracy had a whole new outlook on life. Tracy said that the family was not having a "funeral" but they were going to have a Celebration of Life instead. She explained that Missy was full of life and that, along with their tears, they were going to remember all the great things about Missy. Tracy wasn't going to wear black or a dark color; her outfit would be bright and colorful - just like Missy's personality. This would remind her of the love she had for her dear friend.

Then, Tracy went on to explain how she had changed her thoughts after the death of her friend. She realized that we aren't promised to live forever and that life is very short. Tracy was going to think about food differently. Instead of filling her body with junk, she made the decision to treat her body better so that she might live a long life! She was going to be grateful for each day that she was alive.

I felt Missy's presence in the room with us. Tracy's love for her friend helped Missy in the Spirit world be able to share her energy. Tracy's goosebumps were all I needed to know that her friend appreciated everything about Tracy. Missy's legacy lived on in Tracy; forever changing the way Tracy viewed her life.

I, just like Tracy, have learned to live life differently now that I understand that this life is not guaranteed. Before we journey on together, let me preface the remainder of this book by saying that I am not a grief expert. If you need help from a professional, please get help. What I am going to share with you is what I learned about life and the possibility of an afterlife while I experienced grief. This book may not be the book for you to deal with deep pain. What this book does do is give the reader a different way to look at death and learn how to connect to a spiritual world - one that I discovered while searching for answers about death. It's a different way to live and I hope you enjoy the stories.

The magic of connecting with our loved ones seemed impossible to me at first. It's in my gratitude practice and belief in "something" that allowed me to live my life each day as though everything is a miracle. I sort of believed in signs before my parents died, but through my grief, I learned how deep this connection is. I also experienced the magic of connecting where my relationships (with my mother especially!) were healed and I let go of the pain and emotions of anything that didn't serve me.

Loss and grief show up in our life in many ways, not only death. It showed up in my life when my kids moved out, when I switched jobs or even when letting go of physical objects. My grief for my mother was very different from losing my father. With my mother, my grief was for never having a strong mother-daughter relationship. For my father, my grief was more about both of my parents gone. I was too busy making plans and taking care of their estate. These feelings of grief appeared years later and I didn't exactly know how to handle all of my feelings.

In this book, you are going to hear stories about people connecting with their loved ones in the spirit world- which I think is magical. Through my search for understanding grief and the signs of after-life, I am forever grateful to know these people and for them sharing their stories of deep connections to their loved ones. They are magical and most definitely show a connection to "something" more than we may ever fully comprehend. They guide us along this journey of life and most likely may spark changes in your life that you may not have expected. When we look beyond our physical world into this invisible layer of love, our hearts feel better and our lives are richer.

Chapter 3: The Power of a Name

Chapter 3 The Power of a Name

Since the day I was born, it seemed my mother and I did not see eye to eye on a lot of things. I worried so much when I was about to share my book with the world; even though she wasn't technically here on earth in a physical body. I felt her around me but in a very different way. She had told me years ago not to write down anything "embarrassing" so I never dared to express my feelings on paper. My first book came from my soul and as I poured out my story onto the page, the fear of what I shared glowed within me like a small fire.

As humans, we at times seek our worthiness from outside ourselves. We look to our parents as young children and then we turn to our jobs, constantly looking for acceptance and validation that we are important. I was no exception. My mother never once said to me, "Congratulations! I'm so proud of you!" I stored this disappointment and memory inside my subconscious for many years.

I believe that when people arrive in what I call "the other side"- where the soul/consciousness lives without a body, they understand some of their mistakes. Each person does a life review to see what their soul learned during this lifetime. This information helped change my relationship with my Mom after she transitioned to spirit.

I wasn't sure if I would be able to connect with my Mom because I'm pretty sure she didn't believe in people who were gone communicating with the people left here on earth. Boy, was I ever wrong!

As a past life regression therapist, I have had clients that when guided to their in utero time and asked what they sense emotionally from their mother, they respond with things like, "She is anxious. I can see that she wasn't sure about having another child. That would make four children and she was nervous about having so many kids to take care of." or "She is excited to meet me but also nervous about being a mom for the first time." or "She is anxious and overwhelmed."

Since my mother had experienced such a traumatic experience with me in utero, my mother passed on some of her emotional trauma from that moment of deep grief- her anguish was floating within my blood.

What's scary about love is that we may get hurt. My mother loved her father so much that the pain she felt at his sudden death was very overwhelming. The pain of losing our loved ones changes our lives in ways we may never understand. I believe my mother changed the day her father died and then again on the day my father almost died of a heart attack- about 13 years after she lost her father to the same disease.

Subconsciously, when we are in pain, we reach for safety. Our hearts hurt and we search for a life without despair or grief. Brene Brown describes what my mother felt and the internal vibrational energy I had carried with me for so many years when she describes anguish- the "unbearable and traumatic swirl of shock..."

My mother didn't have the tools or resources to understand all of the emotions our hearts and bodies feel. The tools in my toolkit now have helped my body heal and be able to experience joy each and every day instead of keeping those same stories in my bones and cells.

I didn't understand why I couldn't be happy on Mother's Day. I loved being a mom and I loved watching my new daughter-in-laws become mothers. I got curious about my thoughts and discovered grief was hiding inside me. I didn't recognize it until I was ready to release my shield of protection.

As picture after picture appeared in my Facebook feed, I realized something. Someone posted, "I miss my Mom in Heaven." or "I love my Mom so much." Along with pictures of mothers and daughters together, getting pedicures or just being together, it finally hit me.

I was jealous and still in grief- a different type of grief. The grief I had was that I never had the kind of relationship with my mom that I wanted and I never would because she was gone. And, the even worse thought- if I was to be totally honest- which I never wanted to share my true self- was I did not miss my mom. This feeling was filled with shame and guilt. Did this mean that I didn't love my Mom? Was I a bad person because of this? Wasn't a child supposed to love their parents?

The shame that I felt was overwhelming. Brene Brown states that shame can't survive if we share it and bring it out into the open. When we do this, we are being our true selves and allowing others to see us. It's like it dissolves because it isn't hidden anymore.

Shame focuses on who I am as a person- "I am bad". I felt like I was a bad person because I didn't miss my mom. Guilt is the judgment I gave on myself. I was a bad person because maybe I failed in my relationship with my mother.

The key to shame and guilt is self-compassion. Could I forgive myself for having these feelings and thoughts? Could I let them go as they were no longer necessary or serving me? Was I worried what others would think of me if I shared these deep seeded feelings?

After I wrote my first book, my mother began to connect with me in ways we never did when she was here in physical form. Since the after-life is all about love, that is what I began to feel.

I was so excited to discuss the marketing side of my book release. My book had been born like a baby and, after writing for exactly nine months, it was ready to meet the world. I ordered copies through my publisher but I wanted a copy ASAP. I overnight shipped it on Amazon and waited patiently for the package to arrive. What a feeling of accomplishment! My hope was that my story would help someone somewhere understand that signs from Heaven are really possible.

The same day that I received a copy of my book, my new marketing agent called to learn more about me and my book. The marketing agent and I talked about my book and my wishes for distribution and marketing. At the very end of our hour-long conversation I felt bad because I had forgotten her name.

"I'm so sorry," I said. "I forgot your name." I knew she had said it quickly in her voice message the day before. "What is your name again?"

"Deanna," she replied. I gasped into the phone. My mother's name was Deanna. This simple coincidence for me meant that I received my mother's approval, the thing that had eluded me when she was living. My marketing agent spelled her name differently than my mom, but I did not know it at the time. Love and light surrounded me and I felt my mom said to me the words I had longed for when she was alive. "Congratulations! I'm so proud of you!"

DeeAnna was even "dimed" after she learned about my story.

"I have to tell you this story," she wrote in an email. When I phoned her, she was so excited.

"I went for a hike with my boyfriend. It was so weird. I found these two random dimes on the trail in the middle of the woods. I thought of you finding your dime on the mountain after your Dad passed. Anyways, I sort of forgot about it until my boyfriend proposed on top of the mountain! Finding the dimes on the trail made the day extra special. I felt like someone was there with me that day."

I was so happy for DeeAnna and felt such a deep connection with her. When looking for signs, always pay attention to names! They are a great way for Spirit to connect!

When you see your loved ones' name on a street sign, on the TV, or anywhere, know they are there with you. One time, I was watching TV and the name of the reporter was James Palmer. What are the chances? I knew my father was with me.

My friend Barb's husband transitioned to spirit after a long battle with multiple sclerosis. Barb cared for Ric during his last few years and missed him dearly after he left his physical body. Although she thought she felt his presence, she never seemed sure of any true signs from Ric. About a year after Ric's death, she read my book and our friendship was rekindled.

I visited Barb a few years prior to writing my book. Since I hadn't seen Barb for years, I actually didn't know Ric was ill. After chatting in the kitchen, Barb directed me toward the sunroom to say hi to Ric. I wondered at the time why Ric couldn't just come into the kitchen to say hi, but I walked over to see him anyways. Ric was propped up in a wheelchair and could only move his head. Covering my initial shock, I put on my cheery face as I talked to Ric.

"Hey Ric. How are you?" I asked, which I immediately regretted. Anyone looking at him could tell that he wasn't well.

"Good, and you?" He responded with a more positive attitude than I imagined. When I walked into the room, there was a different energy in the air. There was nothing to see but the feeling in the air was there. I wondered if Ric would transition soon.

I quickly wrapped up our short conversation and returned to the safety of the living room where the other women were gathering for our women's group. Ric passed away but not for several months after my visit.

About a year after Ric's death, Barb and I reconnected, and she welcomed me into her home to talk about the things she learned in my book, *Dimes from Heaven*. When I walked into her house, the energy in the air was palpable. Was she aware that Ric was right here with her? For a person who doesn't feel things the way I do, it's difficult to explain. It's like a vibrating energy within my body where I feel such happiness and love. I'm never quite sure how people will respond and I don't want to diminish their grief by saying something like, " Ric is right here!" I understand that not everyone feels as connected to this other dimension as I do. Some people envision it as a "haunted" house- one where the spirit of the deceased might do bad things. Reframing our vision of the after life takes time. One has to let go of the ideas presented to us in mainstream media. The other side is filled with unending love.

One day when I called Barb, she explained that today was difficult because it was Ric's birthday. She always missed him a bit more on this day. Don't we all miss our loved ones on special days? Christmas? Thanksgiving? Anniversaries? The empty chair sits there to remind us they are no longer here with us.

"Did he send you any signs?" I asked.

"Not that I know of," she laughed. " I didn't find any dimes." That's not the only way signs appear, I thought as I listened to Barb tell me all about her new car. She really wanted to make sure that I knew that she loved the color of it.

I knew he would give her a sign if she allowed herself to "see." When we look for signs, we have to open up our own energy to have faith and believe. We might not know how or when the sign will appear.

"I just love my new car because of the particular color red," she explained.

As the conversation moved on to talk about other things, I let go of the need to find a sign for Barb. It's not my job. Barb will either see it or not and I have no idea what the sign might be. She didn't ask for anything specific so it may be more difficult for her to recognize a sign.

A few days later, we were talking again and Barb said, "My son, Adam, looked up the name of the red color for my new car. You know, he has access to all of the specific colors for his car detailing business."

Why would Barb feel the need to have the exact name of the color? Why couldn't the color just simply be "red"?

"The color is grant maroon," Barb told me, not yet "seeing" the sign.

Barb's last name is Grant; which she took when she married her husband. Her three sons would always carry on the Grant name.

"That's it! That's your sign from Ric! You took the Grant name when you married Ric. The car color is a sign from him!" I explained to Barb, excited that she got a sign from her husband. Her seemingly innocent curiosity was spirit guiding her. She followed her intuition and her son just happened to be in the car business to have access to the exact color name for her new car and, of course, she was connected to me who would help her understand this was a sign, proving her continued connection with her husband.

"I never thought of it like that. Maybe you are right!" Barb sounded surprised. Barb's wish for a sign from her beloved husband was "Granted" through the power of a name, just like my mother "granting" her approval of my book.

Chapter 4 Have you been "Dimed"?

"It doesn't mean that we're sad the rest of our lives, it means that 'grief finds a place' in our lives. Imagine a world in which we honor that place in ourselves and others rather than hiding it, ignoring it or pretending it doesn't exist because of fear or shame." ~Brene Brown.

"Dimed" is a phrase I coined to explain when a person either receives a dime or a different sign from spirit. You can be "dimed" with a dime or "dimed" with a butterfly or "dimed" with a heart-shaped rock. A lot of times, after someone hears my story, their loved ones send them a dime because now Spirit knows they might believe in the invisible communication system. When we believe, our stories spread faith and can start a chain reaction with signs from Heaven.

It took me five years to be able to have the courage and strength to stop by the family camp on the lake that we sold after both of my parents passed away.

My grief was still raw. It was right there on the surface; ready to pop open like a water balloon being sliced open with a knife. I was longing for days gone by and felt like a lost child without my parents. The tears burst out as I remembered our times at camp. I always felt I let my Dad down by selling the camp. The camp was his pride and joy; handed down through three generations.

I hadn't planned to stop. I was doing my normal drive by when I threw my car into park and jumped out of the car. I love to drive the camp road; flashbacks of swimming and barbeques remind me how lucky I was to live on a small Vermont lake in the summer. It's time. I gather my courage and wonder if the new owners would remember me.

Dean is standing next to his truck and he immediately recognizes me after I introduce myself. He and his grandson are working on the dock today. As we walked down the hill toward camp, I was grateful for Nancy's warm welcome as she stepped out the back door.

Why did it take me so long to stop by? Why was I so worried? The answer- grief; a sense of loss and guilt for selling the property had consumed me. They had torn down the old camp to build something new. Change is hard and camp reminded me that my parents were no longer with me here on earth. My life changed so much the day they both left their physical bodies and returned to the spirit world.

My heart feels the pull of memories. Grief arriving like a tidal wave crashing over my whole body. It hits you when you least expect it and when you think you have it under control, something happens that either breaks your heart or fills your heart with incredible love. Walking on the land that I grew up on filled my heart with great sorrow but when I allowed love to flow freely, the tears seemed to sooth my aching heart.

I envisioned the camp the way it was when I last walked inside. I can hear the creaks in the floor and the porch door slam shut behind me. I can see the unfinished wall in the bathroom. There was no sheetrock; just two by fours standing as if waiting for the hammer and nails. I can see the "WOMEN" sign on the bathroom door that confused many people. If this bathroom is only for women, where do the men go to the bathroom? We would laugh as we said in unison, "Outside!"

Nancy and Dean shared how much they enjoy this spot on the lake. Nancy said that the camp was on "the right side of the lake." On the other side of the lake, the mountain blocked the sun in the afternoon and one couldn't see the beautiful sunsets that they see from this side of the lake. I smiled as my father would agree with them. Was my father there with us enjoying this conversation? I know I couldn't see his physical body but I seemed to sense something in the air.

When they tore the camp down, a lot of the wood was rotten. Yes, I think. We always suspected this but of course my father never wanted to look within. Sometimes when we look within, we find old, outdated things that are no longer needed; metaphorically speaking.

At some point there was a fire within the wall near the fireplace. I suspected such a thing but I honestly had no way of knowing this. They understood my surprise at this information and I felt any worries melt away. A smoldering fire inside the wall that by some miracle had not burned down my father's pride and joy. I secretly send a thank you to the Divine for stopping what could have been a very painful loss for my father.

Nancy wanted to show me the beautiful new house they built. I hesitated; unsure if I was ready to take this next step. It is actually a physical movement walking but it feels like I have to let go of the past as I walk into this new reality. The new world is built on the foundation that my father built. Family values are always within me and, even without our old family camp, I feel my roots steady and secure. As I walk and talk, I feel a new life opening up; one where I am able to explore a new way to live.

I imagined the old brown picnic table where our family crowded around with paper plates piled high with hotdogs and potato salad. Each year we would sing happy birthday to my boys as I tried to light the candles with the breeze from the lake blowing them out one by one. July birthday celebrations always included a party at camp with boat rides and swimming with their friends in the lake. I let go of the past to walk into the present, opening up a new chapter in my life. One where I transformed my heartache to feel love.

Before we walked toward the camp, I shared with Dean and Nancy about my books. I handed them a copy of both books and they felt honored to accept them. I turned to the page in the book and showed the oldest picture of camp from the 1940's when my Great Grandmother purchased the camp. They loved the books and looked forward to reading my story about the dimes.

As we stepped into the new front door and took a few steps in, I imagined my parents' bedroom to the left; where their new bedroom is now located. I can see the new blue rug my parents put in the room in the 1980's but my mind is in two worlds. One is the new room where new people live, but my mind travels to a distant memory; a part of me that never forgets. The antique claw bathtub is long gone and new flooring and sheetrocked walls create a beautiful new space.

Grief likes to do this. It's difficult to be in the moment because my mind wants to go back to the past, where my heart reminds me of the good times we had together.

The 1970's yellow refrigerator and stove would have been about where my feet were. The marshmallows were always in the white metal cabinet above the stove. Nancy directed me to the large bathroom but my brain remembers the red countertop and big sink where we used to spend time washing and drying dishes by hand. There was no dishwasher at camp. As I remember this, I realized that was part of the magic of camp. It slowed us down in our busy lives. It taught us to be together and to be present in the moment. Memories continued to pull at my heart strings creating a sense of nostalgia for times gone by.

My grief changed as we toured the newly built camp. My heart feels full and my eyes do not leak the tears that I thought might appear. Nancy's excitement makes me feel such positivity that I don't seem to have the sadness I thought I might. I sense love all around me. Gratitude surrounds me as the sun glistens through the many windows where the lake and mountain appear in perfect view. The gratitude is for both the past and the present. The memories of the past are always within me and now I can enjoy being with the new owners in this time and place. It's truly magnificent to see and I am overwhelmed by the beauty. The outside world transforms my insides from dark to light. I have to imagine a better feeling within myself. In Heaven there is no anger. This tour helps me release my guilt and feel my father's forgiveness within me.

We walk upstairs and as we do, I imagine Nancy's grandchildren enjoying sleepovers at the lake. There is a loft with many beds. It brings back memories of spending the night at camp with friends or with my own children. The loft is peaceful and inviting with the new bedding and slanted ceiling. At camp we imagine that the world is far away and it gives us time to spend with each other. My roots continue to feel strong as these memories are always a part of me.

I know enough about the afterlife now that my father is with me during the tour. He is not angry with me at all. He never was. The anger I felt was on a human level and I worried way too much! It was time to let this worry go. I believe that as soon as our soul transforms back to a spiritual essence, there are no judgements or regrets and all of our problems when we were here on earth are gone. All is well and our loved ones want us to know and feel the love from within.

As I descended the stairs to the basement, I realized that even though the ceiling racks where the kayaks hung and the old red white and blue striped waterskis from my youth are gone, they are always a part of me. Good memories solidified in my mind like a good movie. They are replaced with Nancy and Dean's new couches, pine walls and a wood stove to keep the room toasty warm.

Another bedroom to the back of the house and a full bathroom with laundry. Can you imagine? A washer and dryer at camp! I imagine my Mom carrying the dirty laundry in the cream colored plastic laundry basket back home to wash and then the clean clothes neatly stacked when we returned to camp.

I was completely filled with love as Nancy and I continued chatting in the kitchen. She was thankful for the books; I was thankful for the love and care for the land and camp they purchased from our family. I envisioned her family enjoying their time here; happy that they are making memories for generations to come.

Nancy invited me to stop by anytime - even if I want to sit on the lawn and just look at the mountain. She understood that I was still missing my Mom and Dad. Maybe more than I wanted to admit.

Fear inside me bubbles up at her offer. If I do sit on the lawn and look at the mountain, I might open up that grief bubble I have so carefully buried within me. What if I open it up? Will it ever stop? Will the tears overflow and I may be unable to stop the rush of water? I built a beautiful damn for my grief that keeps it safe and secure inside of me.

I've been trained to bury my grief. At times, I even put up a wall to protect myself from more pain. When I used to do this, I was not able to connect with the Spirit world. Acceptance lingers as I adjust to a new life without my parents. It's pulling me in a new direction. What if I believed that life is everlasting and my parents are always with me? What if I choose to cry but then feel amazing because they have sent me so many signs?

I thought of the dimes as I walked away from my tour. I felt an unseen force of energy as if my parents along with my Grandparents and Great Grandmother were there with me during this visit to the land I remember as a child. My grief shifted from sadness to love during that visit.

There seems to be something magical that happens after someone hears my dime stories. After my visit to camp, it sets in motion a series of coincidences for Nancy and Dean.

Nancy sent me a private message a few days after my visit. "You'll never believe what happened after your visit!"

Nancy and her daughter were "dimed". When they went to get their cart at the grocery store, a dime was stuck in the top part of the cart! How does a coin get stuck in the top of a metal grocery cart? Wouldn't it fall down in between the bars? How was it in the particular cart that Nancy and her daughter chose? Right after they learned about my dime story?

It's one thing to find a dime on the ground or near some other coins. This coin seemed to be carefully placed for them to find. I envisioned my father saying, "I'm glad you went to see the new owners. Make sure to forgive yourself. It's important to move on."

I always enjoy hearing stories when people are "dimed". Positive energy is contagious and when I shared my story with others, the energy spread like the wind blowing all around the world. I learned to connect to a totally different energy than ever before. One that is filled with love and does not focus on regrets. Every lesson in life is perfect and as the universe unfolds its plans, I allow myself to see beyond this physical world and look at life as a more mystical, spiritual journey.

Months later, Nancy would be "dimed" again. I wouldn't hear the story directly through Nancy though. The story would come through a mutual friend; someone who knows that souls who have crossed over show us signs every single day.

My friend, Ellen, sent me the following message, "So, I have this client that I've been doing his hair for years...he was telling me about his father-in-law passing away last week...we chit chatted about signs,etc and we both were like ya, we totally believe in that... 'the family that we bought the camp from...Monica...' I stopped him and said, 'Oh my God, Monica Morrissey??!!' I have been hearing about the renovations they have been doing in this camp they bought on Elmore since day one and I never knew it was your family's!!!!! So how we got started on this was that at the grave site...he saw something silver and shiny but didn't get a chance to look...he and his wife were talking about it later so they decided to go back....and sure as heck...it was a dime!! I love how the universe works!! And, he was going to tell me that you wrote a book about dimes from heaven. ..but I already knew!!!"

Ellen's story validated even more what Ellen and I already knew. Ellen and I had attended many of Rebecca Locicero's events called Messages from Heaven™. Rebecca Anne LeCicero is a talented and well-known medium featured in the Netflix movie series *Surviving Death.* She volunteers for the Forever Family Foundation. (https://www.foreverfamilyfoundation.org/) and has her own local TV show in Connecticut. During the evening event, Rebecca delivered messages from loved ones who have crossed into the Spirit world to help those of us left behind. Often it is exactly the message the loved one needed to hear to move forward with their life on earth. Rebecca uses all of her senses to help her understand the messages from Spirit. She asks for the audience to respond with only a yes or no as she does not want any extra information from the audience which might create doubt. Rebecca offers names, dates, numbers, significant objects, and even messages about the way the person died.

Ellen lost her dear sweet niece at the age of twenty-seven and her father at the age of seventy-two. (interesting as I write this, I noticed the numbers are reversed - a message right now from both of them?) One time, Ellen's father came through at an event. Rebecca kept looking between Ellen and myself. She was confused. Spirit kept telling her we were family but we said we actually were not related. We weren't family but our families were so connected that Ellen's father wanted us to know that he cared about all of our families. Ellen's niece, Samantha, was our next door neighbor.

Many people send me dime stories. The random dime makes them think of me. I try to explain that the dime isn't necessarily from my father. It is a way for their loved one to get their attention. It's like the first key they get and the door to Heaven cracks open. In time, the door can be unlocked with their own signs. Nancy's father was reaching out to her to say, "Hey, here is a dime to help you believe that I am still here." Then, he may use other signs after that to show that he is able to communicate with her. Nancy can try to figure out what her key is. It may be something other than a dime. It should be something that is meaningful to her and her father. This has the power to transform the pain of her loss to love and connection.

I worried so much that my father would be angry with me because I sold the camp but this meant that I missed out on enjoying peace throughout my day. Here are some suggested things to do to bring your loved ones closer to you.

- Do you have regrets with a loved one? Write about it and let it go. You are forgiven. Your loved one wants you to know this. The energy of your writing will bring your loved ones closer to you.
- Visit a place that reminds you of your loved one. Remember the love and the good memories like my friend Tracy. Think of a favorite memory.

Recently, my Uncle was dimed. It was the day before it would have been his dear wife's eightieth birthday. We lost Aunt Jean to cancer nine months before. When my Uncle found the dime, he said, " Jimmy sent me a dime." It may have been from my dad but it may have been sent from his wife! She knew that my Uncle would recognize that the dime was a key to Heaven!

The keys to Heaven are available to everyone. Your energy, your beliefs, and your thoughts are the keys to opening the invisible door to another dimension.

Chapter 5: Numbers and Intuition

Chapter 5 Numbers and Intuition

"Love and life remain within us, and the potential for meaning is always there." ~David Kesslar

Threes had never been my number, but threes were about to teach me a lesson about my intuition and the clairaudience whisper I hear from Spirit.

It was the summer of 2020 and repeating threes kept showing up for me. I would wake up in the night and the clock read 3:33 or I would check the time during the day and it would be 3:33. Threes would appear on license plates or on addresses. Threes seemed to be appearing out of nowhere, surprising me like a shooting star. I asked the universe, "What is the message?" I didn't hear or feel any message, so I sort of forgot about it.

My husband, my son, my son's wife (who was his girlfriend at the time) and I rented a camp on a lake for a week. I love the water and remember all the years I lived on the lake in the summertime. I felt like I needed a break and some time away. I absolutely love to swim and be out on our boat. Summers are short where I live in Vermont and I wanted to enjoy the sunshine and fresh air. It would be fun to be together on the lake. My son moved out of our house about three years prior and we all were looking forward to spending time together.

Soon after we arrived at the camp, my son's dog introduced us to the neighbors. Dogs aren't afraid of going over to say hi to strangers. My son began chatting with one of the neighbors. My heart was filled with pure joy as I watched my twenty-four year old engage in a conversation with a stranger.

I overheard parts of their conversation. Joel, the neighbor, shared about how they remodeled the camp when they bought it a few years ago. Since my son is a lineman, he was interested in hearing about the electricity and Joel shared all about the updates. They discuss things that I don't know anything about.

There is peace as I watch my son interact with Joel. Patrick is respectful, kind, and caring. There is something about the far away look in Joel too but I can't quite put my finger on the feeling I seem to be picking up on. He seemed so kind to my son but also had this distant look in his eyes.

As we talked, we discovered we have a mutual friend. His wife is a hairdresser and she is friends with my friend, Ellen. (yes! The same Ellen from earlier!) I heard this little voice inside my head, "Tell them about your books." My analytical part of my brain responded to the whisper, "Just because these people knew Ellen, and Ellen likes my books, doesn't mean they are interested in my dime story! Why would I tell complete strangers about my books?" I kept wondering if this idea came from their connection with Ellen or if there was another reason.

The week goes on and we chatted here and there with Tammy and Joel. The dog enjoys playing fetch on their lawn. They fed him a few treats when walking down to the water. We enjoyed our week on the lake and our time away from work.

Learning how to tune in to my intuition and turn away from my ego is a big lesson for me. Intuition comes from a feeling and a different voice within. For me, it's repeated whispers like when I was given the message to go find the lost penny in the armchair on the day of my father-in-law's passing. Intuition gently guides me in my life. Ego comes from a place to make me feel important or better than another person. I use the following messages to figure out if the message is from my intuition or my ego.

Is the message positive? Spiritual guidance is never negative or punishing.

Is the message given in a spirit of love and kindness? Does the message guide myself or others to live differently? With more peace and gratitude?

I thought my intuitive guidance to share my book was coming from a sense of bragging, which is my ego wanting notoriety for being an author. What if they thought I was being pushy about my book? All week long the whisper would not stop.

Joel finished his yoga routine on the grass near the edge of the lake. As I packed a cooler into the car, Joel stopped to chat on his walk back to his house.

"I wanted to live on the water. That's why we bought this place. We turned a very old camp into our new home," he shared and I thought about my old family camp being turned into a new home.

"I grew up on the water in the summer. I wanted to come stay on the lake so that I could relax during all this COVID craziness. I needed to shut off technology and just get centered," I explained. Then I said something that still sounds weird when I say it. I said, "I am a writer and I needed a reset to shut off from work. I wanted to sit by the water and decide what to write about next."

"What do you write about?" Joel asked me and I felt a sense of relief that he is interested. This released that voice as the pressure had been building all week long. My head seriously felt like Old Faithful about to erupt. For some reason, I felt the need to share this information with Joel and I had no idea why.

"Well, I wrote two books. The first one is called *Dimes From Heaven*. It's a cool story about some dimes that my father sent to me after he died. One dime I even found on top of a mountain! I can't tell you where the other dime was found because

I don't want to ruin the ending of the book," I focused on the dime story, not about being an empath.

"Oh wow. That's pretty cool," Joel responded as his eyes looked beyond me toward the calm, smooth lake.

I'm never quite sure how people will react to my story. Will Joel be interested in my story? Mostly I connect with women. Do men believe in signs from Heaven too?

Joel then surprised me when he shared that he receives signs but his signs aren't dimes. "I lost my son a few years ago. He was twenty-one years old when he was in an accident. My son showed me the number 333. He died at 3:33 in the morning. I read it on his death certificate. The address to this property is 333."

I can't believe it. I ignored the whisper telling me to share my book all week long. Now, I understood why I was being guided to tell Joel about my dime story.

"Oh my gosh. I have been seeing threes all week! I had no idea why. Well, that explains it!" I am astonished but sad as he shared about his son's death. The pain of losing a child crushes my heart. Joel's grief floats through the air.

"Would you like a copy of my book?" I spontaneously offered him a free copy.

"Yes, I would love a copy of your book. I truly believe in the signs," Joel said.

Joel believed that Jared was with him always and forever. I wrote "Believe" in the book I gave to Joel, but Joel truly believed it already. I hope he enjoyed my story. His son is with him always and forever.

I shared with my son the story of Joel's son. We do the math. Joel's son would be the same age as my son. Was that what I was seeing when Joel and my son were talking? Was Joel wondering what his son would have been like had he still been alive?

It took me almost a week to listen to that little voice inside me telling me to share about my books. When I did, I figured out why I had been seeing 3's for weeks. His son knew I was coming to that camp and he knew that his father believed. I believe it was Joel's son whispering in my ear, "Tell my dad about your books."

When events, numbers or signs repeat over and over again, it is a way for spirit to get our attention. Divine guidance can be about anything, not just numbers or messages from Spirit. If you are having health issues and you happen upon three different articles about cutting out caffeine, that might be the answer you were searching for. One time, I had three different people tell me about a book they just read. I took that as a sign that I was supposed to read that book! I wasn't sure why but it didn't matter. Spirit was sending me a message and I needed to be willing to listen.

I'm glad Joel knows that his son is with him all the time. I enjoy listening to these stories but also feel the heartbreak when we lose our loved ones. It's comforting to be able to feel the love in the midst of missing his physical body.

On the day we were packing to leave, Joel and his wife were driving by the camp. They stopped to say hi and then Joel said with a big grin on his face, "Monica, I thought of you this afternoon. I looked at the clock and it was 3:33."

Joel and I had connected in such a powerful way. I still think of him often but especially whenever I see repeating threes.

This experience helped me to learn how to distinguish between my critical, problem-solving mind and my intuition. There are a few ways to tell the difference.

Our intuitive guidance comes from both our minds and our bodies. Close your eyes and take a few deep breaths. As you relax your body, begin to relax your mind. When your mind is quiet, think of some time where "you just knew something". When you have that feeling, where in your body do you feel it? In your gut? In your heart? throat? A lot of people feel it in their gut but I feel it in my heart. Then figure out where the voice is coming from. Usually, there is a pattern to this voice. It may be coming from the right, left, or center of your mind. Start to tune into this like you are receiving a signal from a radio. If the guidance comes from a place of love, listen. It is guiding you in your life.

I learned how to be in touch with this positive spiritual part of myself through my connection with my father. We are all here to learn our soul lessons. Sometimes the lessons seem so difficult that we don't know how to keep on living. When a loved one is taken away from us, life seems unbearable. It was through the pain of losing someone I loved dearly that I was able to learn to live my life differently.

When I first met Joel, I had no idea the pain he lives with each and every day. I'm sure he misses his son. I believe we choose our parents when our soul enters earth school. Lessons are learned for everyone when we lose a young person. It reminds us that tomorrow is never promised so we need to enjoy each moment for what it is: "a present". Each day is a gift. I think of this when I go places. I sometimes let people go in front of me in line at the grocery store. You would be surprised at how this little gesture means so much to people. Another thing that I love to do is give compliments to people. This simple thing changes a person's day and makes my day better.

Since meeting Joel, I have had three - three penny days! And they all have to do with following my intuition while parking my car. A simple daily task that helps me feel connected to Heaven.

I used to choose my parking spot in a very different way than I do now.

I used to try to find the closest parking spot to wherever I was going. Then, my insurance agent explained that most accidents happen when backing up, especially from a parking spot. He suggested always parking in a spot where I would be able to drive out without backing up and to park further away from other cars. Then, I became thoughtful about more movement throughout my day so I decided to park further from the destination to be able to take a short walk. Now, I think of these things, but sometimes at the last minute I decide to switch my choice of where to park. This little change in the way I live has had such a profound effect on my life; showing me how to let my intuition guide me each and every day.

On this particular day, I picked a spot further away from the other cars. As I was getting out of the car, I noticed two people who attended one of my book events. I had known them for years and the gentlemen even won a dime necklace at my book launch party! I thought it was fitting that a minister won the dime necklace - truly a message from my Father as to how important Faith was to him. I said hi and then I looked down. My friends were about 20 feet away and this was during the beginning of COVID so we were keeping our distance. I told them I just found 3 pennies! I think there must be one for each of us! I picked them up and began to look at the years. They choose their pennies based on the meaning of the year. The two they picked were very significant to them - I can't remember if they were birth years or their anniversary. We were all so happy! We believed that these pennies were truly, "Pennies from Heaven!"

Later that fall, my sister, Merrilee and I went to visit my Aunt and Uncle, my Mother's brother. For me, pennies are always a sign from my Mom. We met at a local grocery store and I drove everyone to see my Aunt and Uncle. I parked on the right side of my sister Debbie's car and she hopped in the back seat. We had a great visit and then we headed back to drop Debbie off at her car. Instead of parking on the right side of the car, like I did earlier, at the last minute, I decided to park on the left side. I put the car in park and my sister proceeded to step out of the car. Debbie went to put her foot down and said, "Merillee, look at what is near my foot!" It was a penny! That was a sign from my Mom!

Instantly I thought, "well, she got a penny. Maybe I can find one too!" I jumped out of my car so fast that I didn't have time to rationalize my thoughts. Why would I think I would get a penny just because she found one? In less than two seconds, I listened to my intuition and didn't analyze anything.

I proceeded to open my door and guess what? There was a penny on my side of the car too! Mom gave us BOTH a penny! Then, in less than a millisecond, I decided that Merrilee needs a penny too....I opened my door again and looked really closely at the pavement. My penny was brand new so I saw it easily when the sun was shining on it. I looked harder this time. Sure enough, I found ANOTHER PENNY! I gave it to Merrilee and she said, "I never met your Mom!" I explained that it didn't matter. My Mom knew she was here with us now and she was sending love to all of us!

My Mom wanted all of us to know that she was sending support to her brother that day. I felt it, my Sister felt it and Merrilee felt it. We knew she was close to us.

I went home feeling good but also worrying about my Aunt, who was very ill. I prayed for her and her family. That night I had a dream. In the dream, I called my Grandmother, my Mother and Uncle's mother. I don't remember talking to her much about anything. I told my Grandmother I just called to say "Hi" Grandma. Dreams are a way for our loved ones to visit. When I woke up, I wondered what the message was. Instantly, I thought, my Grandmother wanted to let us all know that she, like my Mom, was with us to support us during this time and would take care of Aunt Jean when she transitioned to Spirit.

A few days later, Merrilee was worried about going on a trip. Her car was making a funny noise and she was worried something might happen. She called to tell me that she found a penny, thought of my Mom and she felt it was going to be ok to go on her trip. Her worry and anxiety melted away. They went on the trip and everything was fine, just like Merrilee's intuition had told her.

While working on this book, I had my third three penny day. I found my first penny at the chiropractor's office, where both of the chiropractors had graduated from 'Palmer' College. Palmer is my maiden name so I knew this was a sure sign from both of my parents! Then when I stopped for gas at a local store, I found a penny next to my car. As I walked toward the store, I saw what I thought might be another coin. It was so dirty that I thought it might be a dime or just a piece of trash. I almost didn't pick it up but decided it would be number three for the day. I picked it up and sure enough, it was another penny! I felt my Mom was supporting me while writing this book!

As I finished writing this chapter, I was filling out a form to send in the mail. The address was 333. Then, I opened up a piece of mail. There was a bill for $333.35. I will forever think of Joel and Jared whenever I see threes. And, I have learned how to listen to the guiding intuitive whispers from my soul.

Chapter 6 Heart Shaped Rocks and Four Leaf Clovers

Chapter 6 Heart Shaped Rocks and Four Leaf Clovers

One time I cut open a hard boiled egg and the shape of the yolk was a heart! Hearts had never really been my sign. I wouldn't always understand the meaning of different signs that began appearing in my life, until I learned to listen to my intuition and follow its guidance system like a GPS directing me to my destination.

I went for a hike up Elmore Mountain with a woman who went to my high school but we hadn't seen each other in years. She loved my book and wanted to connect about the topics I wrote about.

It was a beautiful day in Vermont. The greenery filled every part of the forest and the sixty degree weather was perfect for a hike. We chatted along the way and I enjoyed the time spent talking about what it is like to be an empath. We feel so deeply that at times it can be a challenge. The most important thing about being an empath is sharing our love; which we both do as we hike. As I hiked, an unusual thing happened on this particular day. It seemed that everywhere I looked, there was a rock shaped like a heart. I took a few pictures but then stopped. Hearts were sprinkled on that mountain like confetti sent from God.

I didn't think much about it until following my intuition guided me to a coincidence that was difficult to ignore, sending me a direct key to heaven's messages.

My husband's cousin had shared a dime story with me a week before my hike. It went something like this:

"I got your book a few weeks ago. Something interesting happened on the first day I got your book! I brought it in my car to the hospital where my husband was about to have surgery. I grabbed the book, stepped out of the car and, I kid you not, there was a dime on the ground. I thought that was kind of cool. Then I was about to get on the elevator, but it was so full, I decided to take the stairs. I couldn't believe it when I saw another dime- on the stairs! Then, after my husband's surgery, I was getting back into my car and~ you guessed it! Another DIME! It was a **THREE DIME DAY!** I actually didn't get to read much of your book that day, but I thought how coincidental it was that I find these dimes today! I had a feeling my husband was going to be okay for his surgery."

My intuitive whisper kept sending me a message over and over again. "Tell Molly that it is going to be okay." Until I send the message, the whisper seriously won't shut up. It keeps replaying like a stuck record- over and over, again and again. Finally, I sent her this message:

"Good Morning! So, when you were sharing your dime story, your Father kept popping up in my mind. All I kept hearing from him was, "It's going to be okay" every time you talked about being in the hospital and another dime. I have no idea how this all works, but I felt the need to share this with you! Luv ya! And hope everything goes okay today!" Now the voice inside my head was able to stop replaying the message.

On the day of my hike, Molly responded.

"Thanks Monica. There is so much of your book that rings true for me. My father usually sends me heart shaped rocks. We never talked about them as far as I can remember but I just know they are from him. He was always picking up interesting rocks and handing them to me. He also visited me in a dream once. After his death I was a mess. And I was a mess for years! I could not talk about him without crying and I was just so sad. So finally he came to me and said, 'Hey! I'm okay. I'm happy and you have got to get a hold of yourself and be happy too!' I woke up from that dream so relieved and so much more at peace."

Did she just write about heart shaped rocks?

"Oh my goodness! I went on a hike today and I saw so many heart shaped rocks! That is so cool. Now I know it was Uncle Doug. Check out these pictures. I did not know who was trying to get my attention!" I replied, excited that we discovered this connection.

She responds, "Oh my goodness. Yes. And don't even get me started on four-leaf clovers. I practically trip over them!"

A few days later, I hiked Elmore again. I saw a lot of heart shaped rocks. I knew that Uncle Doug was welcoming my dear Father-in-law to Heaven.

Molly's dream was very clear. Her dad was sending a message to her. When we sleep, we are able to let go of our rational mind and allow our subconscious, along with spirit, to send us messages. His message was clear. Our loved ones in Heaven want us to live our lives and be happy. They want the best for us. They don't want to see us be in so much pain. The more we turn toward love, the more they are able to connect with us.

I shared this heart-shaped rock story on my blog and the love would return to me with two boomerang events. I believe that when a person sends positive energy into the world, it comes back to them like a boomerang. The old saying, "You get what you give." is true with all things. Positivity was about to come right back at me.

Lynn was a teacher at one of the schools I worked at. She and I both had been in education for over thirty years and we knew that taking care of everyone's social and mental health was, at times, more important than math or reading. It is just as important to learn how to connect with nature, eat in a healthy way and take care of ourselves. We brought this passion to our work each and every day.

Lynn read my books and connected to many topics. In the summer, Lynn lives on an island on Lake Champlain, the biggest lake in Vermont. Lynn enjoyed taking care of the animals in the barn and caretaking for the rental property. The wind can howl during a storm but the calm of the lake at night is enough to quiet even the most active mind. The paths Lynn walked on the island connect her small log cabin to the beach shore, the barn and the rental house.

As Lynn walked the rocky trail from the log cabin through the woods to the barn, her mind was on other things. She had her phone with her and decided to check Facebook. That's exactly when it happened. As she opened up my blog post about heart-shaped rocks, she looked down and saw right in front of her a rock carefully placed on her path. There were many rocks on the path but one seemed to stand out in the pile. The rock wasn't the shape of a heart, but a heart seemed to be carved into the rock. A magical transformation made many years ago when the water swirled over and over through the rock to form the heart, showing the true beauty and power of nature.

I received this rock in the mail from Lynn and I knew the power of connection. I understood that the more I shared these amazing stories, the more love was in the world. Love was beginning to return to me like a boomerang more and more.

Another teacher I knew would then connect with me. Carrie and I taught at the same small elementary school in northern Vermont for twenty-four years. She retired during the pandemic, and, unfortunately, we were not able to have a retirement party for her. She always said that she wanted to write a book, so I thought *More Dimes From Heaven, A Journey to Self-Publishing* would be the perfect retirement gift for her. I hope she writes the book she always dreamed of writing.

We sat on her front porch and talked about life, work, school and memories of our own children growing up together. We talked about how life is such a gift and how important it is to enjoy every moment. It was so nice to sit and have time to talk with a friend, who was truly a role model for me throughout my years teaching.

"Life is so precious. You just never know what might happen tomorrow," I say and remember her dear sweet niece, Sam. Ellen and Carrie are sisters and they both felt such a big loss when Samantha transitioned to Spirit so young. I know how they feel because we lost Tyler so young.

As I was leaving and walking back to my car, I looked down and spotted a four-leaf clover. I debated about picking it and then decided I probably should. This is a critical moment when following my intuition. My first thought was to pick it but then my brain tried to convince me to do something different. When we let our intuition guide us, it is usually our first thought that is the better thought.

We are all connected in this world in ways that are surprisingly shocking and at times seem so incredible one may struggle to try to explain it using our linear thinking brains. We try to rationalize the unexplainable events that occur that just don't seem to make any sense to us. When Spirit is involved, there is no explanation other than we are connected with an invisible energy field, just like cell phones. There is no cord connecting us but we are connected to this mysterious and invisible communication system. Molly had set in motion some more signs from Spirit when she shared the words, "And don't even get me started on four-leaf clovers. I practically trip over them!"

As I gave it to Carrie, I wondered if the four-leaf clover was a sign for something. I suggested she put it in the book I gave her and walked away. I think it might be good luck for her book.

I hopped in my car and was ready to leave. My cell phone sat in my car while we chatted so that I wouldn't be distracted while we visited. I took a quick peek to see if I had any messages before I drove away. The message I received got me so excited that I ran back out to show Carrie.

"Carrie, you are never going to believe this message I just got!" She might have thought I won a million dollar lottery. It wasn't the lottery, but that's how excited I get when someone makes a connection to Heaven.

When I shared the message, she and I both knew that this was a sign from Heaven.

"Hi there- so I'm feeling like I need to write about my dad. I keep finding 4 leaf clovers... I know probs sound crazy... is this a real thing? I found the first one on the day he passed- a few hours before... but I keep finding them. Monica- life is so crazy right now... my world is turned upside down. I'm trying to stay positive but it's so hard..." ~Heather

This was within minutes of me finding the four-leaf clover that I gave to Carrie. We both smiled and I went on my way. We both felt Heather's pain deeply as Carrie and I have both lost our fathers. Within that pain and heartache, we knew that Heather felt her father was with her. It was beautiful that Heather now understands love from Heaven can be a simple coincidence.

Heather's family grew up on the lake right next door to our camp. She and I swam and played together during the summer months. I'm sure Lake Elmore is a part of her like it is me.

I explained to Heather that if she thinks it is a sign, then it is. We don't need verification or validation from anyone. It's our choice to believe in the signs.

Heather has since found 14 four-leaf clovers, 2 five-leaf clovers and 4 feathers. I know her heart is hurting because her dear father is no longer a physical part of her family. Her father is reaching out to her in such a different way. I know she can feel him in her heart. He is always with her.

This is how positivity spreads. One person at a time. One penny or dime at a time. When I shared the four leaf clover story to my sister she shared with me that some of her co-workers found four leaf clovers the very same day that I found the one at Carrie's house. These four leaf clovers were so big that she took a picture of them next to a dime. The dime looked miniature next to them! Spirit was having fun by making it such a big event to find gigantic four leaf clovers so that my sister and I would connect at the same time Heather was messaging me about her four leaf clovers.

Dimes are always my sign but Spirit kept showing me more and more signs; my heart expanding and guided towards love. Heather and Molly reached out to me for help in believing in signs from Heaven. All of these helping me understand the Spirit world more and more.

Chapter 7 Does the Other Side Watch Everything we do?

Chapter 7 Does the Other Side Watch Everything we do?

Angie moved from France to begin a new life in Canada. She was starting life fresh after she lost her husband to suicide. Friends helped her when life seemed unbearable and her heart was shattered.

I met Angie after writing my first two books and about the time I began doing Intuitive Angel Card readings. Since it had been years since her husband had passed, Angie wanted a new relationship with a man. I met her during COVID so it was a challenge to meet people. She also knew that something was holding her back but she didn't know what or why. She was struggling to move on even though she knew she wanted to.

I asked Angie if she would like an Angel card reading and maybe we might tap into some messages from her deceased husband. She was receptive and we set a date to work with James Van Praagh's card deck, *Talking to Heaven.*

The first card brought deep tears. "It was not your fault." Angie might have thought that maybe she could have done more for him. The woulda, coulda shoulda's filled her mind. Unconsciously, she might have thought she could do more for him but ultimately, she knew that she had done all that she could have for him. Forgiveness is a powerful message and Angie felt it deep within her. It was time for her life to move on.

The next card, "There is no such thing as death" revealed another incredible message. My mind instantly thought of a story to help Angie with this idea.

"Well, let's think about this for a minute. I want to tell you a story. When I was first married, my husband and I bought my Grandmother's house. I felt her all the time and worried about what she would think or say. I mean, we were newly-wed, if you get what I'm saying," I hinted at what I didn't want my Grandmother to see.

Angie and I both laughed as our minds wondered if Heaven watched everything we did.

"You need to understand that Heaven feels but doesn't see. It's their essence that is here but not their physical body with eyes watching everything we do. Your husband wants you to find someone to be with and wants you to know he promises not to watch," I explained to her.

Rivers of tears ran down her cheeks as she hadn't been aware that this may have been blocking her ability to have a new relationship with a man. She shared her worries that she would hurt her husband if she was with another man.

"I never thought about it but you're right. I feel him and know he is here with me. I am better able to understand this now and let go of this worry. I am so grateful for this authentic conversation about things like this that most people don't want to talk about. Thank you, Monica," Angie was filled with gratitude as we spoke the unspoken feelings we have after someone dies.

The last card was "Tears cleanse the soul" and the picture was a heart made with water droplets. Angie's tears created space within her to allow love to flow again. She had released an invisible block by tapping into her worries and letting go even more.

Another client who I met with had lost her father and she struggled a lot since his death. She buried her grief deep within her. The card "It's not your fault" is powerful in many situations. This woman had been holding on to blame for years. When I read the card, she immediately started crying and said, "I thought it was my fault that my baby died." The woman had a miscarriage and, in her grief, had kept this deep feeling to herself for many years. By releasing this guilt, I could tell she was ready to let it go. We never know what types of emotions we hold onto until we hear everyone's stories. Heaven wants us to let these feelings go and be able to enjoy living.

Grief hides out in ways that are difficult to understand. Once we share our true feelings with someone, it's like the shame and guilt dissolve, releasing the block we need to let go in order to connect to our loved ones.

<h1 style="text-align:right">Chapter 8 Remembering
the Love</h1>

Chapter 8 Remembering the Love

As I got closer to publishing, I called Jay to help with the cover of my book.

"Hey Jay, It's Monica. I'm writing this book and I really need a picture of Elmore Mountain. I was hoping you might have one I could use for the cover," I explained.

"Well, you can look at my Facebook page. I have a lot posted," he responded.

"Well, I was thinking of a daytime picture, not a sunset picture. I've seen lots of sunsets. Do you have any daytime pictures?" I asked, hoping he would say yes.

"No. I do mostly sunsets," he surprised me with his answer. "I think you should call this other photographer that I know." He gave me the name but it was meaningless to me. I knew I wanted a photograph of Elmore Mountain from Jay. Jay had done my High School senior pictures, my wedding pictures and we stayed connected through the years.

"No Jay. I want a picture from you. Each part of my book means so much to me. The cover is a piece that I would love for you to be a part of," I pleaded.

"Okay, Well. Is your book Spiritual at all?" he asked. If we had been in person, he would have seen my jaw drop and my eyes open wide as I smiled.

"Oh my....Yes! You have no idea how spiritual!" I said.

"Then I have the perfect picture for you. I just need to find it," he explained.

Relief washed over me and my happiness traveled through the phone line.

"Great! I can't wait to see this picture."

What could the picture be? What would make the picture spiritual?

For weeks and weeks I waited patiently. As Jay looked through hard drive after hard drive, he knew what he was searching for. He was determined to find this one picture his mind remembered.

When Jay finally found the picture, I thought he had altered it. Was that cross in the sky really in the original photograph? He assured me that the photo had not been altered. I needed more help though. The picture was great but I didn't have the necessary computer skills to create a book cover. Jay sent me some ideas and I absolutely loved them! It was the perfect cover for the book I never ever expected to write.

When it came time for my second book, I sent Jay another message.

"Any ideas?" I asked without even explaining what my book was about. I sent him some title ideas and he responded, "Let me sleep on it. I'll let you know."

A few days later, he said, "What about dimes floating around in the solar system?"

I couldn't believe it. It was exactly what the theme of my book was- being guided by the universe to write my books. Jay had no idea how perfect this was.

Jay died while I was writing this book. It was one of those deaths that shocked our community to our core. It was a homicide-suicide. Jay first shot his wife and then himself. I heard about it while at work and couldn't shake this agitated feeling. Since I was working, I didn't take the time to process my feelings and buried them like I had done for years. I watched myself process this and as I tried to stuff the sadness down, it suddenly appeared as anger. How could he do that? What was he thinking?

"Death by suicide is not a selfish act or even a choice. It's a sign of a mind that needs help." ~David Kessler

Suicide wasn't new to me. I remember wanting to run away when my mother told me my high school friend, Donna, had died by suicide. I was sixteen years old and had never had someone close to me die. I didn't even know she was suicidal. I didn't want to hear that news. I didn't want my friend to be gone forever. My mother's tight grip on my arm brought me to the reality that Donna was so bothered by life she felt she needed to leave.

All kinds of woulda, coulda, shoulda's came to me. If I woulda done this, maybe Donna wouldn't have done it. I coulda helped her if I only knew. I shoulda spent more time with Donna. These all came flooding back to me as I processed Jay's death.

"Such thoughts are a product of guilt, but they are also the mind's way of trying to assert control in an uncontrollable situation that has already happened." ~David Kessler

I personally knew what it felt like to be so depressed that I wasn't sure I wanted to live. Several times in my life, I experienced such depression that I thought about suicide. I'm grateful that I had people in my life who helped me dig myself out of my depths of sadness and that I had made a conscious decision that I wanted to live.

I shared my first book with a friend and she returned the gift by gifting me the book *The Untethered Soul* by Michael Singer. This book helped me understand how my brain worked. The negative voice inside my head was loud and clear in my first book- I was so scared to share my story and share my spiritual side with the world. I was a public school teacher and the rules of this responsibility to my profession were inferred- I didn't feel that I would be allowed to show my true self because I wasn't allowed to teach anything that might be considered religious or spiritual. When I began to understand how that voice inside my head worked, I began to understand a key to living a more loving and accepting life.

Our brains were built to look for patterns in order to keep us safe. Years and years ago, the only way to survive was to remember that the tiger was dangerous. Nowadays, it is important that we understand how the amygdala is constantly working to try to keep us safe but also be able to access the prefrontal cortex to calm the amygdala down.

Since we are human and there are dangers here on earth, we were pre-programmed like a computer to survive the elements. So much so that the negative things that happen are like velcro in our brains and all of the positive things are like a teflon pan- they slip right off! The problem with this internal programming is that it has become dysfunctional, leading people to be in such a rut that they might not understand why their mind thinks like that. It's like the wires in our brains have become tangled so much that the system needs a spiritual re-boot. We aren't in survival mode but our brains are still functioning like we are.

We are hardwired for fight, flight or freeze so that we are able to stay alive. If a bear or a tiger chased us, we would be able to take action in order to survive. Now, our stresses are so different. Modern society has created a space where we are safe inside shelters and the food system has grown so much that most are able to shop for the food they need. The stress is now in the form of a student not understanding a math problem or being able to read. Teachers can go into fight or flight when an angry parent calls them. The worker at any business struggles with the daily stress of emails, phone calls or working long hours. And, when someone isn't nice to us, we think we are being rejected by the tribe- which could signal to our bodies that we wouldn't survive the situation. Our bodies know how important being a part of the tribe is for survival.

Our minds begin to create stories to help us combat the stress, creating a theory-evidence loop. The story is based on the evidence we have seen and then those stories begin to guide us in our life.

Our brains were built to look for patterns in order to keep us safe and they love to create stories- a full circle loop, beginning, middle and end. Years and years ago, the only way to survive was to remember that the tiger was dangerous. It is important that we understand how the amygdala is functioning in a different way in modern society-so much so that people are getting caught up in the stories their brains create.

I get caught up in what I call a "negative evidence loop". My brain was trained at a young age to see people as threats so I began searching for the evidence that would prove my theory correct. Of course, none of this was done consciously. It's the sub-conscious family programming that I grew up in. In order to retrain my brain, I had to do a lot of conscious work.

This is how my mind was programmed. Since my mother didn't trust people and spoke poorly about her friends, that's what I learned. I know it wasn't her fault and that is how generational trauma is passed down. The more I looked for problems, the more problems I created in my mind- creating stories to prove my theories. My mind didn't know how to search for the good things because I wasn't programmed for this.

Looking for good things takes practice- just like a soccer player practices their shot on goal. The first kick might be a fail but with practice, the shots get better and better.

My gratitude practice started out small. I remember the first night that I wrote my first gratitude. I seriously hadn't even remembered what I had done that day. The positive thoughts did not come easy. I had to search and search for them. How would I ever get positive thoughts to stick like velcro and the negative thoughts to slide away?

Practice. I had to practice looking for the good. I had to practice saying positive things when I was around other people. My practice shifted my evidence loop and grew more and more each day. Suddenly, I was thankful for the blue sky or the birds chirping. By writing ten things I was grateful for and ending my day with the one best part of my day, this helped velcro the good parts of my life into my subconscious.

I tried to grow broccoli one time in my garden. It grew but the harvesting totally creeped me out. I'm not a fan of worms or snakes and when you harvest broccoli, there are these big, green worms that are hiding out in the plants- similar to our thoughts hiding in our brains. These are the thoughts that we don't tell anyone.

I heard from a friend how important it was to put fresh broccoli into salt water. The reason to do this is to remove the hidden worms from the plants as they don't like the salt. As I looked over my plants, I wondered if my friend meant that *sometimes* there are worms. It seemed as though I didn't have any on my broccoli.

To be on the safe side, I decided to fill the bowl with salt water and see if any worms might wiggle away from the broccoli. I watched and nothing happened. I walked away and almost fifteen minutes later, there were several worms floating in the water. The worms had to be summoned off the broccoli. They were hidden and tricked me into thinking they weren't there.

This is how trauma is stored in our subconscious and how our negative thoughts need to be brought to the surface. We do this by allowing them to move out into the open with "salt". We face them by listening to them, maybe even sharing them with someone safe and then moving beyond the negative voice.

Emotions are only supposed to last for ninety seconds. Think about that. Think of a negative emotion that you are holding onto right now. What's that emotion about? Most likely it is about something that happened days, months or even years ago or it is worrying about something in the future. Ditch it. Throw it away. Stop engaging with it. Then, look around you and bring your body and mind into the present moment. If it is something big, get help releasing it.

Our bodies get programmed to remember what to do based on past experiences. Depending on whether those memories are happy or stressful, our bodies take the messages from our brains and turn them into chemicals in our bodies. Happy memories create oxytocin and the feel good hormone dopamine. Stressed, scary emotions create cortisol, the stress hormone. Once the experiences are over, our bodies remember that feeling and take the cues from our brain. It gets used to whatever our thoughts are and wants more of it- even if it is a stressful, negative experience!

It doesn't make sense that our bodies would be programmed to want more of the negative hormones, but if that is what we feed our bodies, it is exactly what happens.

Our bodies like routine and patterns so therefore it is looking for more of what it already knows. If we try to change that from a negative to a positive experience, our body doesn't know what to do. It actually "feels" weird and might even feel like a bit of anxiety! Your body doesn't know what to do with this new energy and your brain might try to tell you to be worried.

I was raised with a negative mindset. Actually, I was in a toxic environment when I was young but I was being told "everything was fine". It's taken me years to move out of this. I realized that I didn't know how to be happy and I was scared of happy people. Immediately, my mind would tell me (this was an unconscious act) that I couldn't trust this person and that I better figure out what was wrong. My brain would look for evidence and wouldn't even know how to engage with happy people. Sounds crazy to those who know me, but it was true. I would put on a pretend happy face around the people and then go home and worry that I couldn't trust them.

When people are raised always looking for the good, it changes their brain and body chemistry. Since our brains are constantly searching for danger, a person who grows up in a negative environment has to retrain their brain so that life is viewed through a different lens-one that is searching for good things.

The problem is we hold onto our emotions for way too long and keep reliving the past experiences by talking about them over and over again. We stay stuck in those same emotions that were only supposed to last for ninety seconds!

Understanding our emotions is a complicated task- one that has to involve both our mind and our body. In Brene Brown's new book, *Atlas of the Heart,* she captures the complexity of understanding where our emotions come from, how our environment shapes our emotions and gives us the tools to move through our emotions, instead of burying them within ourselves. As Brown shares, "I want this book to be an atlas for all of us, because I believe that, with an adventurous heart and the right maps, we can travel anywhere and never fear losing ourselves."

We feel with our hearts, then our brains receive the messages and then we respond or act. At heartmath.org, it is noted that actually it is our heart sending messages to our brain. "Our heart rhythms affect the brain's ability to process information. The heart has 40,000 sensory neurons involved in relaying ascending information to the brain." If we think about this, then it is actually our emotional response that is cueing our brains to function. It is important to understand how our hearts can turn to love instead of fear. This then sends different messages to our brains!

This invisible world of energy connects us at a cellular level that is difficult to understand. When we stay stuck in victim mode and complain about how awful the world is, more of that appears because our body is accustomed to the feelings and the chemicals floating around in our blood stream.

Our brains are like a security system, constantly looking for danger. We theorize about this and then look for evidence to support our ideas. There are so many invisible inputs of information that go into this experience. Beyond what the physical eyes see, or our ears hear, our intuitive self is receiving messages to inform us about any and all events. For years, I shut this part of me off because I didn't understand how to listen to these signals. My brain was constantly looking for evidence instead of listening to messages from my body.

The only way out of negativity is to work on our body system- to make it feel good from within, an energetic feeling that is done with body regulation techniques like EFT (emotional freedom technique), yoga, breathing exercises, cold showers, exercise, EMDR (eye movement desensitization reprogramming), and many others. The list is endless but important to practice everyday.

I have many things on my bathroom sink. I went to reach for the tube of toothpaste and imagined grabbing the wrong tube. Hair gel wouldn't work so well on my teeth! That's what it is like to get up in the morning with the wrong feelings in the morning. It's like brushing your teeth with hair gel. We have to choose the right feeling to feel good each and every day. We have to do the work to relax our minds in order to prepare for the day.

The other thing that I wish Jay, Donna and anyone else thinking about suicide knew was that you are not the thinking part of your brain. It's important to first observe that part of your brain, disconnect from it and then tell it to shut up! You may thank it kindly for trying to protect you and then rewrite the story that your mind might have created based on love and kindness.

I sort of remember my mother's voice as she shared, "Well, you know her son committed suicide." It wasn't in a caring way but had a more judgmental tone to her words. At the time, I would have no idea that years later, I would connect with this woman who was from my small hometown. We were both writing about death and our connection to Heaven.

Cathleen was always kind when I saw her around town. I was a bit younger than her so I wouldn't really know her. I definitely didn't know her son but I would hear about her through a mutual friend while working on this book.

Her son's suicide shattered her beyond belief. It was through his death that she began to learn how to allow herself to grieve and discover a different way to live. She first received the help she needed with therapists and a variety of modalities to help not only her mind heal but her body too. She is grateful now to help others. She still experiences deep sadness but also the magical connection she has with her son now is such a gift to her. She shared her journey in her book, *Shattered Together: A Mother's Journey From Grief to Belief. A Guide to Help You Through Sudden Loss.* Her story encompasses David Kessler's Sixth Stage of Grief- Finding Meaning, where they both agree that "Pain is inevitable but suffering is optional." ~David Kessler

Through her loss, she discovered living life a different way. She quit her corporate job and followed her trail of grief to help others, creating a program called Stepping Stone to Grief (https://cathleenelle.com/shattered-together/). Her life was shattered but within that space, she discovered a whole new way to live with her loss. Her program helps not only the person's mind but she uses specialized techniques to help the person's body to heal as we hold our grief within our bones.

When she needs guidance in her life, she reaches out to her son and asks for a sign. She is able to receive her sign almost immediately because she understands the many ways Heaven is able to communicate with us. Using a variety of intuitive, spiritual abilities, she sees numbers, hears messages and even feels her son nearby. Her willingness to share her story has helped hundreds of people who have experienced loss.

Cathleen reminds me of my Grandmother. My Grandmother was full of laughter, kindness and love. I'm not sure when my parents shared with me the story of my Great Grandfather, but when they did, I never forgot it. It made me wonder if this event changed my grandmother's life in such a way that it actually changed who she was at her core, just like Cathleen.

It was 1918. My Grandmother was about to graduate from Peoples Academy High School. She was valedictorian in a class of about twenty students. I don't know what she said in that speech, but her courage and strength are an inspiration to me. Her father killed himself the very day of her graduation speech. Yet, she stood in front of a small crowd of family and friends and spoke anyway. Is this why my Grandmother was never negative to anyone? Is this why she was full of life? Had she seen what negative thinking could do to a person? Did she know and understand the secrets that I was discovering now? Was she grateful to be alive? Did her pain change her in a way that only some understand?

I never spoke to my Grandmother about her father's death. Even though nobody stated it, in my family talking about death was a social taboo that I learned at a very young age. I'm sure that her father's death changed her life forever. Maybe her father's death taught her to live each day more alive than the previous, to think of others and appreciate everything she had.

I couldn't write a book in 2022-2023 without acknowledging the pandemic. It is forcing every single person to face and talk about death. The fears are constantly being shown on TV and we all have a choice to choose love or fear. The fear of the virus and other stresses have caused more overdose deaths than Covid deaths in our little state. This pandemic has affected everyone's mental health in ways that we may never understand.

With death knocking on everyone's front door through the fear of the pandemic, it's time to re-evaluate how we live.

It's Christmas morning and I have a choice to make today. It's a choice most likely my Grandmother made when she was only seventeen years old. My choice is to be present with the ones I love and to be filled with gratitude.

Do I miss past Christmas's when my children were young and the excitement of Santa was in the air? You bet. Now I sit by the Christmas tree enjoying my cup of coffee, I notice a few of the lights on the Christmas tree aren't working. It is odd that it is only a part of a string. As I think of my Grandmother, they suddenly turn on. Was this my Grandmother with me as I write? Yes, I believe so therefore it is true. I don't need validation from others and I feel my Grandmother's presence helping me make my choice today.

I do hope my Grandmother cried for the loss of her father. I do hope they honored him at a service. I know nothing about him other than this one fact. I imagine that whatever was bothering him was just too much for him at the time. I do believe that when someone leaves this world in this way, they may regret their decision. At the time, they felt there may not be another way. This is their soul lesson.

When I dusted off the images from when I was young, I saw my Grandmother happy every time I visited. She lived next door so it was an easy run across the field to her back door. As she opened the door to the kitchen, I would either be interested in the built-in toy drawer under her china cabinet or would look to see if she had any of my favorite cookies with the raspberry jelly in the middle. The bible next to her chair was filled with notes and her diary sat there ready for her pen. I didn't really pay any attention to them when I was young; but we would find them years later. Her smile when I walked into her house was like a laser beam of light shining right into my heart.

My choice today is the choice I imagine my Grandmother chose all those years ago. I choose to be filled with love and kindness. I choose to embrace the memory of my Grandmother through being like her. I feel that is the best way to honor her memory, her legacy living on within me.

It can be easy during the holidays to miss the people who used to be here with us. When I am stuck in my grief, I have learned to turn toward Heaven and ask for help. I like to talk about the people who have passed and share stories about them. When I'm struggling in my life with a decision, I ask my Grandmother or my father for their help. I wonder what they might have done. I live my life encompassing the best qualities of who they were, allowing their legacy to continue on.

Also while working on this book, I had two friends who phoned me to reach out for help. Their exact words were, "I'm having dark thoughts of ending my life." (Please, if you or anyone you know are having these thoughts, reach out for help at https://suicidepreventionlifeline.org/) I know as a trained educator, the first question to ask someone who states this is, "Do you have a plan?" Then the next step is to make sure they get professional help, immediately if they do have a plan. They called me because they knew they didn't want to end their life. Neither of them were even close to developing a plan but just said they felt, "off". The first thing I told them was, "You are loved." I wanted both of them to feel love from deep within their hearts.

I can relate to this feeling of wanting to leave earth because throughout different periods of my life I have thought those same things myself. I used to beat myself up about the mistakes I made in my life and had difficulty letting go of the past. When these two people called me, they explained over and over all of the things wrong with their life. I listened and continued to say, "You are loved by many."

Then, when they were done sharing, I slowly guided them to think about what they did want. They were very caught up in what they didn't want, but what exactly did they want in their life? They were doing what anyone should do when having these thoughts, they reached out for help and for that I am grateful. This can be a difficult thing for many of us, but they did it. There was a deep trust and love with these two friends and although I am not a counselor, we worked through some of their negative thinking in a very different way than what they were used to.

Love from God/Universe/Spirit (whatever word you might use for something beyond what the eyes can see) is always there and loves each and every one of us. They slowly began to feel it and started to move their way of living toward a different style- one where they were able to feel joy and happiness instead of all anger and sadness. They were able to move past their mistakes in their life and understand that it was the behavior that was the mistake, not them. They were not a mistake. They were human and humans make mistakes. They didn't internalize the mistake and say, "I am bad". Instead they said, "I made a poor choice." They also stopped listening to that other voice inside their head- the one that is looking at life through a negative lens to keep us safe.

Did they heal overnight? Absolutely not. They began to slowly see that asking for help and then showing gratitude began producing small signs of magic all around them. Both were going through a breakup and this brought up feelings of deep pain and loneliness. They both were eager to move away from this deep pain to experience life fully.

Once they were able to feel the love, I asked them what they wanted in their life. They were so focused on complaining about how awful their life was it was actually creating more of those events. And, since their brain and body were used to that, it was a comfortable feeling for them. They were moulding their reality with their thoughts so more negative things kept showing up because that is what they were focused on.

Both of them shared about the anger and arguments they had with their significant other. I asked them if there was any grief within that anger. Anger is the easiest emotion because it hides all of the other emotions. Were they sad? Were they losing something they didn't want to lose? This was a turning point in their understanding of living differently. Both of them started reorganizing their thoughts with love and began to see the blessings each and every day; even though they were still losing their partners. It was grief in a whole different way. It was like a part of them was dying.

I received a text message that said, "I am finding at least about three coins a day. What does that mean?"

My response was, "You are loved and supported. Check the years. When you find them, ask the coins what you need to know right now. Trust your intuition. The answers are within you."

Finding the coins was more than just being a tiny bit richer. The coin was connecting them to a positive energy. The coins were my sign so that is what the universe used to give them a sign. It would be a way to get their attention.

"I keep seeing repeating numbers all day long. What does that mean?" Again I repeated, "You are loved and it is important for you to love yourself first." I encouraged him to google the different numbers to see what they meant. Each number was filled with more and more guidance towards a positive way to live.

"Monica, you are never going to believe this! I started my day with a mediation and gratitude practice. I felt so happy inside. I realized that I wasn't used to this feeling. I realized that there is nothing I can do about the past. I can apologize but I'm not going to stay in that bad feeling. It is so incredibly good to feel free! I have a different understanding of God now. I know he wants me to be happy and that it is okay to be happy. Even though I'm having a few bad days here and there, I'm not getting so upset about it. I'm observing my life like I'm watching a movie. I'm not attaching my self worth to the events that happen. I realize now I was so caught up in the negative and I talked about it all of the time- no wonder I kept manifesting more negative! I now want to talk about love and how the mind processes information and events. I want to meditate and clear my body to experience more love and I know that if anything shows up that is negative, it is like a test in school. I have to reorganize my thoughts back to love! This is so much fun! I am so thankful to have learned to live this way! I can't believe that I had no idea how to do this before. It would be great for everyone to know about this! Oh my goodness. I just feel so good inside! I am so excited to learn more about how to feel good. Thank you, Monica, for our connection and not judging me," Darcie's energy had seriously moved up the scale of vibrational energy and she was toward the top- with such gratitude that it bubbled up inside her. She had reached out for help, experienced deep gratitude and now was experiencing the life that is available to everyone.

It is through our pain where we find meaning in our life. Through their pain and darkness, they were both realizing that they had control of their thoughts. Our brains love patterns and even though it doesn't make sense that it would create more negative when we think negative, that's exactly what happens. Patterns make us feel comfortable. When they tried a different way, it was actually more difficult than staying the same. They were able to step back and observe the pattern and then change their thoughts. They "watched" their brain instead of "being" their brain. They were able to begin slow bits of gratitude and when their mind went to a bad place, they turned it around and remembered love. They both got new jobs with more pay. Talk about changing their life! They attracted exactly what they wanted with this new feeling.

A patterned belief was uncovered when I was talking with these two friends. We grew up in the 1980's, where college was pushed onto students. It was considered the only way to success. Is this still being taught in schools today?

Darcie was fifty-three and never felt that she had the career she dreamed of as a high school student. She felt like a failure so she kept pushing herself and wanted to enroll in classes to be a psychologist. I always encourage people to follow their dreams, but this dream seemed like it would put Darcie further into debt and wasn't really the best option for her at this time in her life. I got the feeling she would never feel complete until she finished the dream that began when she was young. By doing this, would she only be able to feel success based on society's definition of success?

"All I do is clean houses. I never really had a career," her voice oozed with regret.

"Why is cleaning houses a bad job? Why do you need a 'career'?" I asked. I suggested something different. People love to have someone clean their house and it is a good paying job. If she was good at it, why shouldn't she do it? Could she find joy within the job she has now? As I had often done, Darcie was living the life with the ideas of happiness being something that we chase, "We will be happy when... fill in the blank." I wanted Darcie to experience joy and love right now.

Darcie slowly let go of the expectations she had placed on herself so many years ago and re-imagined her life. She began listening to online trainings while cleaning and she began to find incredible magic in each day. She learned to love and accept herself just as she is right now. She sees joy in each day. Her thoughts about death taught her how to live differently and she was so grateful for the changes she made in her life.

Did both of them get the love of their life back? Well, that depends. They might not have gotten their romantic love but they sure as hell know how to love themself more. That is the most important soul lesson we can all learn. Self-love can cure anything.

"Be the best me that I can be." is my new motto and they both embraced it. I hope they always know how much they are loved.

I spoke at my Grandmother and my father's funerals. It was an honor for me to share memories and my love for them. My memories fill my heart with love and their legacy continues on.

Now, I live each day thinking about what people might say at my funeral. What do I want to be remembered for? What do I do each and every day that would be nice? I'm not talking about my job- although teaching was such a big part of my life. I'm not talking about the books I have written. Who am I each and every day? What am I like when things go well? What am I like when things don't go so well? How do I support other people? What do I truly care about?

When we are willing to zoom out the camera lens and look at our life from a different perspective, we get a clearer picture of who we are. When we don't get caught up in the stories and drama of life, that's when we see the real person in the mirror. From the outside looking in, I am able to give myself better advice each and every day.

My Grandmother ended every prayer at the dinner table with, "And let us be ever mindful of the needs of others." As a child, I had no idea what she meant by this. I'm sure she had seen a lot happen in her ninety-eight years. Now, even at fifty-four, I understand the importance of this.

Complaining about the pile of shoes in the mudroom? I'm glad the shoes are there because that means my kids are home. I think of the parents who have lost their children or the woman who wanted to be a Mom but was never able to conceive.

Complaining about taking the garbage out? I'm glad that I get to go for a walk outside. I'm happy that I have a garbage man who comes to pick up the trash each week.

Worried about money? I'm happy that I had the money to pay the bills or buy a coffee or buy gas for my car. I've got clothes that I am wearing and a house to live in.

Worried about tomorrow? I'll pray for a good outcome for wherever the road leads me.

Got stuck at a red light and running late? Maybe God was slowing me down or helping me avoid a car crash up ahead on the road.

Missing my Grandmother on Christmas day? I'll be a smiling and a happy Grandma to my own Grandchildren, filling their hearts with love just like my Grandmother did for me.

It's only through the pain that I am able to reframe my life. It's only through the pain of watching a mother lose her child that I view those shoes in the mudroom through different eyes. It's only through the pain of watching my own brother addicted to drugs and penniless that I feel rich when I am able to buy a cup of coffee. It's only through the pain of watching a car accident and seeing the person dead that I can pray for a safe trip every time my family and I travel. It's only through the pain of losing so many people in my life that I am able to find joy in each day that I am alive.

I'll be that person with an open heart who cares for everyone, just like my Grandmother because that is what this world needs. Because I didn't know that Donna and Jay were in pain, I'll be that person that brings light to others. It might only take one person's love to help someone feel better and change their life to be full of gratitude. I choose love.

Our hearts and minds are powerful things. What we feel, think and perceive determine our thoughts and the universe responds exactly to this.

Recently I was at a brunch where there were waffles with fruit and home- made whipped cream. Due to my medical diagnosis, gluten was a no-no for me. I knew that I couldn't eat the waffle, but I absolutely love whipped cream and blueberries. My heart, and stomach, really, really wanted them. My brain told me that people would think it was weird to just get the blueberries and cream. I spoke to my mind like I was talking with an old friend. I said it didn't matter what others thought- I was perfectly able to eat the blueberries and cream! It was like my brain was trying to convince me it wasn't a "safe" thing to do. I did it. I loaded the edge of my plate with berries and cream. As the whipped cream melted on my tongue and the berries burst open, a woman across the table said, "Are you eating just berries and cream?" I nodded and mumbled a "mm..hmm".

She then went on, "That is so awesome!" I then explained that I couldn't have the waffle but that I loved berries and cream. She was so excited for me and didn't judge me at all. She accepted me and I had made a conscious choice to do what I wanted. Life is like that- I choose to determine what I want and need and then do it. And, I was able to tell my brain that was riddled with fear to shut the hell up.

How we live is our choice. Understanding brain science helps us to make sure we are choosing our thoughts carefully. The invisible energy system that is running our subconscious is so powerful. It's important to tap into good energy each and every day. The universe is listening!

I choose to focus on the love that I had for the people who thought suicide was the only way out. I choose to acknowledge how they left this world, but not focus exclusively on the moment of their death. I want to also embrace who they were and continue their legacy. Their life was worth more than just that one moment.

"Here's the hard truth: people who die by suicide don't die because of anything we did or didn't go. They died because they were mentally compromised, and their suffering mind told them that was the only way to escape excruciating pain. We can live our life in a way that honors them and brings hope to their struggle. All life has meaning, no matter how it comes to an end." ~David Kessler

<h1 style="text-align:center">Chapter 9: Requesting a Sign
from H(e)aven</h1>

Chapter 9: Requesting a Sign from H(e)aven

"Open yourself to an encounter with heaven, be as a little child. Release your desire to the winds of the universe. Trust your angels to catch your wish and bring it to you in a delightfully surprising way." - Doreen Virtue

Haven was on her way home from college when she transitioned to the spirit world in a tragic car accident totaling the car and ending her life on earth instantly. Hannah, Haven's sister, would never see her again. It was Christmas break and her family couldn't wait for her to return from college. Penny, Haven's mother, shared with her closest friends that she had a sense that something was off that day. She wanted to pay for Haven's ride to the airport.

"I'm all set," Haven insisted. "My friend said she can drive me." Those words would replay in Penny's mind forever. I'm sure she always wonders- what if I had done something different? Was Haven's destiny pre-determined yet we think we have more control over our life and when we die?

 Hannah became so distraught over the death of her sister, but when introduced to the idea of requesting a sign from Haven, she would forever transform her beliefs about signs from H(e)aven.

Haven's family lived in my husband's hometown, and she and Hannah were about the same age as my kids. I had never met Hannah, Penny, or Haven but heard the news of Haven's death through my husband. Even though I didn't know them, I felt the pit in my stomach and pain in my heart thinking about how sad this Christmas and every other day would be for their family.

Haven started getting my attention the week I began writing my first book, while I was vacationing on the gulf coast of Florida. Or, should I say, I started noticing more signs because I was more aware of this connection. My husband and I were driving to dinner when I spotted a hotel called "Beach Haven." Even though I had driven by it many times I had never noticed the name before and even when I noticed it this time, I had no idea that Hannah and Penny would eventually become a part of my life.

Just a month after noticing the hotel "Beach Haven," I met Penny at another of Rebecca's Messages from Heaven™ event. I attended the event with my sister who was close friends with one of Penny's friends. Penny seemed to have a whole team there to support her. She was sitting in front of me, a little to the left. When Rebecca walked over toward us, she was describing someone dying in a bad car accident. I knew Haven had transitioned in an accident, but so had my nephew, Tyler. More than one hundred eyes watched Rebecca to see what would happen next and who the message would be for.

Yes, I hoped with all my heart, Penny is going to get a message from Haven. I could feel her pain. Her grief, and everyone else's, was sitting in the room with us. It was in the air, invisible to the eyes but felt in everyone's heart. My best claire is clairsentience- being able to sense how people are feeling, especially if spirit is involved. It looked as if Penny might speak up. As she watched Rebecca moved closer, translating the messages from spirit. As she walked through the crowd to determine who the message was for. I wondered if Penny felt doubt creep into her mind. Was this woman who opened the night with the F word and had multiple tattoos really able to receive messages from dead people? I had been to many of Rebecca's events so I knew 100% that this lady was the real deal.

I felt jittery and excited and I was hoping Penny would make a motion to signal to Rebecca that the information she was receiving was connected to her daughter, Haven. Even a simple nod of her head would be enough for Rebecca to walk toward Penny. Penny was close to me but just far enough away so I couldn't give her a gentle elbow or kick her chair to encourage her to speak up.

Then Rebecca looked at me. When she asked me if I had a relative pass away in a car accident, I reluctantly nodded my head. My energy is so open that often Spirit brings messages to me. I could feel the audience's excitement as Rebecca asked me more questions. The energy in the room is such a mixed up feeling. There is sadness in missing our loved ones but also the room is so filled with love from everyone- both in Spirit form and those sitting waiting to connect to Heaven.

"Was it a relative who passed in the car crash?" Rebecca inquired.

"Yes," I replied, following the rules of not giving any more information.

"Was it a male figure?" My heart pounded and I started to tremble as tears filled my eyes remembering back to the shock of losing my dear nephew.

"Yes," I nodded my head, validating the information she gave.

"Are your families close? I get the feeling that you aren't that close to his family." Rebecca stated the information as if it was a fact, even though at first she asked me a question.

"True," I responded. "He lived in Tennessee so we didn't see them much." Tyler's death forever changed my life and the shock of his death sent me searching for purpose and meaning in my own life. I wouldn't even have been at this event if Tyler hadn't died so suddenly. Through processing my grief, I learned about signs that prove there is an after-life, and that coincidences and synchronicities are planned by Spirit to guide us each and every day.

"He was young," she stated, not needing verification from me, but I shook my head anyway for her and the rest of the audience to know that I agreed. Twenty one years old is way too young to die. Tyler and Haven's time on earth was so short.

"You understand that his soul was taken from his body just before the crash, right? He didn't feel the pain of the impact. That's how it works when someone is in a car crash," she added the answer to her own question. "You see, we have a soul that lives in our physical body. When it is our time, the universe or God or whatever you want to call it, takes our soul back to the Spirit world so that we don't experience pain and suffering. He did not suffer. I want you to understand that." This was Tyler's message for me but I felt it was a dual message for Penny also.

I hoped it brought at least a little comfort to her.

"Are the two of you related?" Rebecca pointed to my sister sitting next to me. My clairsentience felt the shift in the energy in the room and I understood that another spirit was about to come through. The room was so quiet one would imagine that the people watching weren't even breathing. We were all anxiously waiting to see what Rebecca would say next.

"Yes, she is my sister, Debbie" I replied.

"She isn't related to the man who died in the crash. I feel like someone else is trying to come through now. This person is related to your sister too. Is your father in the spirit world?"

"Yes," I again went back to the yes or no response, not revealing any more information than needed for Rebecca to do her work.

"I'm seeing rose colored glasses. Did your father not have a sense of what was really happening in the family? Was he always thinking everything would be fine?"

There was no holding back our chuckle as Debbie and I responded in unison, "Yes." We both loved him dearly but sometimes he liked to view the world as always fine even if there was conflict.

Rebecca looked directly at me when she relayed the next message. "Okay, your father is sending a message that he loved you both very much. I don't want to hurt your feelings when I say the next thing. It wasn't that he didn't love you," she began, directing the comment at me, "but," she continued as she walked closer to my sister, "you were your dad's favorite. There was something about you that he especially liked. Did you work together? Was it like a family business?"

My heart was not crushed by her words as some might think. I know enough about Spirit to understand that there is only love and not any negative energy. Others might not react with the same human emotion that I did. I was thrilled for my sister. Debbie needed to hear that. Her relationship with our father during the last few years was strained and difficult. I thought maybe my sister wondered if he still loved her after all of those events.

My sister laughed through her happy tears and said, "Yes."

I'm sure the audience felt the love my father was sending to my sister through Rebecca and maybe even worried about my feelings. I wished I could explain that there is only love from the Spirit world. Nobody needed to worry about my feelings. Only love shines through to us all.

I wondered about Penny that night. Did Penny need to see this reading to open herself up to messages? I didn't speak to her that night and wouldn't for at least another year, after I shared my original dime story.

When people come into my life, I always know there is a lesson to learn. Sometimes it can be challenging lessons and other times it can be such an incredible positive connection that I am forever thankful to have them in my life. I believe each person teaches me something new. The more I shared my stories and felt the gratitude within me, the more Spirit began to connect with me. This would be true for Haven, even though I never knew her when she was alive.

Months after the event, Hannah and I would slowly begin to connect. My youngest son had started dating Hannah's best friend and Hannah married one of my sons' friends. Hannah moved to our small town about forty minutes away from her hometown. As our connection grew, Haven started showing up in my life more and more. A lot of times, her name showed up in books I read. Haven even showed up in a video about Major League Baseball pitcher David Price. In an interview with NESN that included a story about his friendship with Tyler, David said that baseball was always his "safe haven." The synchronistic events that connected the family and friends of two young people whose parents were from the same small town in Vermont dying in different car crashes seemed almost impossible to explain. Was Haven connecting with me so I would somehow be able to share my dime story with Penny and Hannah? Could my story help them believe in connecting with Haven?

When Spirit wants to get a message to someone, they will continually send messages over and over again. It's up to us to decipher the code with our intuition and our various spiritual senses.

While we were renting the camp on Lake Champlain, my son's girlfriend, Heather, noticed a book on the shelf. She said to me, "Check out this book. The author's name is Haven. I didn't know Haven, but sometimes it feels like she shows up. Do you think this could be a sign from her?"

"Yes! You are one of Hannah's best friends. Of course Haven would reach out to you! Especially since you are connected to me," I explained, so excited because my son's girlfriend believed in what my mother would have called "crazy" when I was Heather's age.

Recently, when I went in for a color and a cut, Hannah shared a story about a coincidence from H(e)aven. Someone suggested to her that she should do an experiment and ask for a sign from her sister. She didn't ask for just anything. She asked for something very specific. She didn't tell many people about her experiment but the results would surprise even a non-believer!

"I decided I would ask for the numbers 924. My sister Haven's birthday was on September 24th," Hannah explained.

I got all tingly inside my body just thinking about it. I felt such gratitude and love for Hannah sharing her story with me. The excitement of her story raised my energy level. My energy felt good even though the sadness of her loss was sitting like a thick, dark cloud in the room with us. I love sharing stories because it seemed to dissolve that sad cloud. Hannah would never be sharing this with me if I hadn't shared my dime story. I sat on the edge of my seat as I asked, "Did you see the number?" I knew numbers are a fun way to connect and they could show up on a sign, in a book or even the amount of a grocery bill.

"I wondered if it would be on a car license plate or the time on a clock or the number of something. I looked and looked for days everywhere I went. Then nothing happened. I wondered if this experiment was a bust. I mean, does this stuff really work?" Hannah laughed and maybe felt a bit silly because she already knew my answer to her question. She stopped cutting my hair; scissors and a comb in her hand. As our eyes locked in the mirror in front of me, I imagined both of us pausing wondering about how the Spirit world works. We both knew that sometimes there is no explanation for how coincidences and synchronicities happened and some have difficulty believing in such "weird" or "crazy" things. That is, until it happens to them.

There was this sense of peace as she continued on in her story and I reassured her that I obviously believe in signs. It's not like a ghost or a haunted spirit like some people might imagine. Signs from Spirit are like rays of sunshine filled with warmth, love and goodness.

"Well, I could tell you a lot of stories about dimes, numbers and other signs. Have you read my book yet? You are talking to the right person!" I laughed as she continued her story.

"I sort of forgot about it because nothing happened. Then one day I was cutting this young girl's hair. Her mother was sitting in the chair by the window. She looked like she was ready to give birth any day so I casually asked her when her baby was due. I couldn't even believe it and didn't know what to say. She told me she was due on September 24th. This woman was due on my sister's birthday. I couldn't say anything because she had no idea about my experiment. Isn't that crazy?" Hannah again stopped cutting my hair; absolute shock in her face while she was trying to rationalize how this coincidence could really happen.

"Oh my gosh. That is amazing!" I said almost as if speaking to Haven instead of Hannah. Her sense of humor shined down from Heaven. Over the last few months, Haven had been showing up in my life more and more. This was why. Haven tried to get me to talk to her sister. This was only the second time Hannah had cut my hair. The choice to switch hairdressers felt like a pull from a magnet inside me. My intuition guided me to Hannah but I knew Haven brought us together.

The thing about signs is that we can ask our loved ones for a sign but spirit decides how and when the sign will appear. Hannah received her sign from her sister but she wasn't done. There was more. I couldn't imagine what could top that story but I could hear in her voice that whatever happened next was going to be even more unbelievable and even crazier than the woman due on her sister's birthday. As I waited patiently for her to finish like a grand finale at the fourth of July, I felt like I was on top of the mountain when I found my first dime. Hannah was being "dimed" but it wasn't with a dime; it was a clear message through her requested birthday numbers.

"Then, days later," Hannah continued on, "I was so surprised that I was telling this story to another client of mine. When I did, the woman said suddenly, 'Wait, what did you just say? September 24th? My birthday is on September 24th.'"

"That's crazy!" I said, "Not only the number but two birthdays on the same day as your sister! That was her. Loud and clear. I hope you believe now!"

This message was an amazing synchronicity from her sister and Hannah knew it. The coincidence proved Hannah and Haven's connection was continuing on even after Haven's death. It was a different relationship but Haven was there anytime Hannah wanted to reach out to her.

I wrote my first book for people like Hannah. She and her family grieve every single day for their beloved Haven. They miss her so much it hurts. When Hannah shared her story with me, she glowed. Her sister's energy filled the room with love and light.

Hannah is listening to her intuition like never before and understanding how to live in a whole new way. This will forever change how she lives, how her family lives, and she will pass this on to the next generation. She won't have to wait to talk about signs from Heaven until she is fifty like me!

As I waited in the chair for my hair to dry, Hannah walked over toward the desk area. She laughed and said, "Well, guess what I just found?"

I turned my head and watched her bend down to pick something off the wood floor.

"What?" I asked.

"A dime," she answered. "It wasn't there when you walked in, was it?"

"Nope, I didn't see it and I have a pretty good eye for spotting dimes." I chuckled because we both knew if there was a dime to be found, I would be the one to find it. The dime was like icing on the cake after Hannah's story.

My haircut was finished and I met Hannah at the counter to pay. As I handed her my debit card, I spotted a ceramic container on the left side of the dark wooden counter. It had the words "change is good" written in black lettering. It was a place to leave a coin for others or take a coin if you needed one. There was a lonely dime sitting in it. Hannah was changing her reality and changing the way she lived her life. Change is most definitely good.

I hoped Hannah would always know that her sister, Haven, is with her every single day. Then, now, and forever, she is smiling down on Hannah's children. Haven is always with her mom and dad, too. It's a different way to be, but she is always there in the rainbow they see, the dragonfly that lands on their picnic table, or in the penny or dime they find.

Since sharing this story, I have connected with Penny and I am amazed at how these stories help all of us heal and feel closer to our loved ones. My grief for my parents was vastly different than losing a child. Dimes aren't necessarily their sign from Haven. Penny believes that Haven shows up in pennies because of her name, Penny! What a beautiful thing. Penny forever misses her lovely daughter. I hope she always talks about her. Their love forever connects them to Haven.

I am so grateful to Hannah and Penny for allowing me to share their story. I offered both of them a free Angel card reading as a thank you. When I did Penny's reading, the card she received was, "It had to happen this way." That was a very difficult card for me to share with her and I wasn't sure how she would respond. Life doesn't seem fair when we lose a young person. Some people believe that our death, just like our birth, is predetermined by a universal intelligence. Some souls are only here for a short time and many lessons are learned by the ones left behind. Through the pain, we all learn to live differently. Penny accepted the card with tears flowing and a knowing that this was true.

After I posted a blog about this incredible story, a friend posted on Facebook, "Haven is going to be a great plase to be." Kevin has difficulty spelling words correctly and his misspelling of the word Heaven meant the world to Penny, Hannah, and me. Haven seemed happy to send all of us a message. After I shared the screenshot of Kevin's comment, Penny shared a picture of the words written in the sandy beach, "Haven is in Heaven."

Hannah tried her first experiment with the spirit communication system. She wanted to see if her thoughts would actually create an experience that would show her that her sister was able to send messages. Finding success meant Hannah could begin to connect to her intuition and understand how her thoughts create her reality. The truth is, our reality is shaped by our thoughts and we are able to affect some of the outcomes through focus and intention. This can be applied to all areas of our life, not just spiritual connections with Heaven. Hannah was only beginning to understand how powerful this can be in our daily life.

Are you ready to conduct your experiment like Hannah? What will you ask for? Be specific. Choose something meaningful to you and the person you want to connect with. Dimes were significant to me because my dad gave me a special dime from his antique coin collection. Would you want a butterfly? A dragonfly? Another animal? What about a special number? Did you and your loved one have an inside joke that only you two would understand? Did they like the circus? Maybe ask for a clown or a circus tent. I've heard stories of people asking for oranges, nickels or even a certain car. It doesn't matter what you choose as long as you are specific.

I compare asking for a sign from Spirit to a filter when you are looking for something online. When I go shopping online for clothes, I don't just say, "I want some clothes." What exactly do I want? Do I want pants? A skirt? A shirt? What color do I want? What style do I want? Don't just ask for any sign because then you might not really be sure or believe. You might doubt the synchronicity if it is too general.

The more specific the request, the better you are able to believe the sign because it will be such an incredible coincidence if you receive it. If you want a butterfly, what color butterfly do you want? Hannah didn't just ask for numbers, she specifically asked for her sister's birthday. Just like a filter on a computer, filter your request so that Spirit is able to show you without a doubt that it is a sign from your loved one.

The comfort that we find in signs and synchronicities helps us see another way to view simple coincidences. Learning to recognize when Spirit may be sending you messages is like taking a key and opening a new door- except it is invisible and we can't see it.

Recently, Penny held a "Compassionate friends global candle lighting" on the anniversary of Haven's passing. I read it and wondered about Haven. A few hours later, I felt Haven's presence through a Facebook advertisement showing a picture of six colorfully striped birthday candles. Underneath the picture, the following message was written: "34 cozy gifts that turn homes into havens all under $50." Haven is such a cool name because the word is also used as a noun to mean a place of safety. Whenever I see the word Haven, it reminds me that H(e)aven is a safe place.

I sent the candle picture to Penny and asked her, "Did you post something about candles?"

"Yes! Always here with us!" she responded. Penny and Hannah's dear sweet Haven is right here.

Directions to request a sign:

1. Think of something that directly connects you and your loved one. Be specific.

2. Think about it for a long time and write it down somewhere. Feel the love in your heart for your loved one.

3. Look everywhere for the item. If you are looking for a number, it might be on a license plate or on the odometer of your car. If you are looking for an item like a butterfly and it is the middle of winter, look on your computer or decorations wherever you go.

4. Let go and allow the universe to be in charge. Awareness is the key to discover the magic of this type of communication. When you have faith that it works, miraculous coincidences and synchronicities happen!

BY MONICA L MORRISSEY

When I began this journey of learning and writing about death, I didn't know just how powerful our thoughts could be. We are able to connect to Heaven with our thoughts- what a gift from H(e)aven.

Chapter 10: Invisible Energy

"Some people could be given an entire field of roses and only see the thorns in it. Others could be given a single weed and only see the wildflower in it. Perception is a key component to gratitude. And gratitude is a key component to joy." ~Amy Weatherly

What do you think of when you hear the word dandelions? Some consider it a weed while others think dandelions are beautiful. Imagine a field of yellow dandelions in a green bed of fresh spring grass. A young child views it as a pretty flower because they haven't learned yet what other people might tell them. That's what reframing is like. We view something totally different than the way we may have been taught. To many, picking up a dime meant they had an extra ten cents. My dimes are priceless to me because they connect me to a world we cannot see, hear, touch or smell. It's our perception that determines our view of life and death and whether or not we believe in an afterlife.

"And the dandelion does not stop growing, because it is told it is a weed. The dandelion does not care what others see. It says, 'One day, they'll be making wishes upon me." ~B. Atkinson

When my mother died, I went into caretaker mode. My father took a bad fall the very next day and since we had always been worried about my Dad's health, it was even worse now that he was grieving for his wife of almost sixty years. My father had little knowledge of the afterlife at the time of my mother's death so this time was a very challenging time for him.

I can still hear the musical tune to the show Grey's Anatomy replay like a broken record in my head, over and over and over again. It's a sound that brings me back in time. When I cared for my dad, I envisioned I would be able to function like I always had. Even though I had taken a family medical leave of absence from my new teaching job, I thought I would be able to plan my lessons for when I returned to school in April. Between all of the paperwork from my mother's death, caring twenty-four/ seven for my father and dealing with my emotions, I could barely function. Instead, I watched episode after episode of Grey's Anatomy and Private Practice. So many episodes that I went through all of the seasons of each show. My brain was trying to escape from the reality of losing my mom and eventually it wouldn't be long until my dad was gone too.

My battery was empty because I didn't take care of my needs. I only thought about my dad. I couldn't focus on anything else and didn't really care much about my job or what was happening in the world. My world revolved around being with my father and trying to make sure his needs were met and to prepare his estate for when he transitioned to spirit.

Eventually I went back to work but still had to manage my father's care. I hadn't even truly processed my mother's death because I was too busy. The connection to my mother was basically nonexistent because I didn't have the energy to tune into the love in Heaven. It wasn't until my father died eight months later that my grief for both of them was so intense that I felt like a train had hit me square in the chest. The tears I cried for losing both of them came hard and fast. The monumental grief was deep and filled with a love for both of them. Even though I am about to tell you about positive energy within your body, know that I believe it is critical to allow deep grief to flow though your body and out your eyes. It's within that pain that I was able to remind myself of the love that I had for both of my parents and everything they had given me.

It's in our perception that we are able to find the key to opening a door to connect us to this other invisible world. A world that I felt as a child but now have come to understand more and more.

"When you want something different for yourself, you have to start moving differently. Old keys don't unlock new doors." Unknown author

I have found so many random dimes throughout the years. I wish I had started to count them. There have been so many! Some of these are so crazy that at times I wonder how these ever could have happened! In the show *BlackList*, there was a special coin that would be the "key" to the mystery. The coin was a Liberty Head dime. This particular day had been a rather difficult day at work and I know that this coincidence was a sign to hang in there.

It's only in looking back that now I am able to see that the universe was supporting me in ways that I would have no idea or that would have no explanation.

Now, there are so many dimes, numbers, heart shaped rocks and other signs that it is a challenge to keep track of them all. I am extremely grateful for each one and they have changed the way I live my life.

The universe is so amazing and powerful- more than we can even imagine. When we write down our dreams and goals, the universe listens but makes it even better than we could ever imagine.

There are seemingly small changes to the way I learned how to mold my reality with my thoughts.

Let's follow the thought process through an example. Wording is the key to unlock the doors to Heaven and living a more spiritual life.

Let's go back to the example of a sign from my father and walk through some of the blocks that might be blocking a person's connection. Let's say that I tried this phrase when I sent my request for a sign:

- I really really hope that I will receive a sign from my Dad.

Do you hear the desperation in this? I hear people say all the time, "I've never gotten a sign." I reply, "Yup, and you won't until you stop saying that." This is actually sending the wrong signal to the universe. This is created out of a lack of something. The universe hears lack of abundance and the absence of something, so it sends more of that.

This intention also comes from the sign being in the future. Since today is the only thing we are able to experience, then writing something that happens in the future never comes because tomorrow is going to turn into today and then the next day is going to be tomorrow. Today is the present, both literally and figuratively-as a gift.

It is important to reword the request to be in the present moment- as if it has already happened. I felt it from within myself and didn't just think about it in my head.

- I am grateful for my signs from Heaven.

I felt it within my body and imagined that it already happened. Because I had experienced the feeling of the dime on the mountain, my body was in tune with this super excited feeling of connecting with Heaven. The universe is better able to deliver if we "fake it until we make it!" Sometimes when we try too hard we are trying to control the outcome. We have to let go and believe that it is happening right now.

The key to creating our reality with our thoughts is to open up the door to a much wider option. That way, the universe is able to make it even better than we ever imagined. Now, when I envision my life and the future, this is how I write:

- I am so very grateful and thankful for all of the dime signs because I love how my dad connects with me. I know he is here with me helping me write. I can hear his laugh as he chuckles every time he tells a story. I'm so thankful that he is still a big part of my life, even though he is no longer here physically- his legacy lives on within me.

Think of molding your reality like searching for something on Google. Google and Facebook track your actions (thoughts) by what you are clicking on. Then, it gives you more of what you want. The universe is the same way. What we think about then becomes true and the universe sends us more because it thinks we want more! For the person who keeps saying, "I never get signs," they will continue to never receive a sign.

For the person who remembers the love of the person in Heaven and feels the love, then it is going to be easier to connect and receive signs.

Dimes and other signs from Heaven keep appearing in my life because I know what it feels like to receive them. I believe at a very deep level in this connection to where we have the ability to connect to this invisible world with all of our natural intuitive abilities. We all have this natural ability. We just have to spend time in a quiet space to access it.

I'm very grateful for all the people who are here today and for the people who passed. Now, when I think of my parents, I try to remember a good time that I had when they were alive. I love to remember their legacy and embody that in my life.

Signs can be sent in a variety of ways. The most common signs from loved ones include butterflies, coins, dragonflies, deer, ladybugs, repeating numbers, rainbows, feathers, electrical problems, or music. The sign might be on the license plate of a car, a street sign, a computer, or a sign on a wall. Your sign might be found on the total of a bill or the change from a purchase, or a cloud in the sky. It's a mystery how coincidences and synchronicities happen, but they certainly show us we are a part of something beyond the physical world and our human thoughts. Our loved ones want to show us they are still with us.

In order for the communication system to work, it is important for us to work on our bodily energy. This is why it is so important to process your grief in whatever way works for you and then to find gratitude each and every day. There are so many emotions when someone dies that it is impossible to understand them all. Whatever you feel, allow that feeling in. Acknowledge it and then work to release it. Thank the emotion for being there and then ask yourself what you need in that moment. Cry, scream, reach out to a friend, watch a movie, eat ice cream. Whatever you need to do, do it and be okay with it. Ask for help if you need it! When we allow ourselves to move through the feeling, then it is better able to release.

We have emotions to help us survive and learn. Since I never learned how to move through my emotions instead of getting stuck in them, I used to hold onto my emotions like a baby's security blanket. Each time we retell stories where we were hurt, our body and mind think the event is happening again. It's important to share the story but then let it go. It's in the past and when we keep bringing it into the present, our bodies respond with the same emotion over and over again. Emotions were only meant to last about ninety seconds to help us learn to survive. I learned how to move through the emotion and then be in the present moment- which is filled with amazing new moments.

Since our emotions are what drive our energy system, it is important to understand how our mind, body and soul are connected. Think of our energy system like a battery. Negative emotions drain the battery but positive emotions charge our battery. Gratitude is the highest form of emotion for charging our battery. Sadness and anger drain our battery. When a loved one dies, our energy system (or battery) may seem so low that we can't imagine life where it would ever be recharged. That's what happened to me all those months I sat watching episode after episode. I seemed to be stuck and had no idea how to move out of my emotions. I had not started a gratitude practice and didn't understand how that might help me. Our internal energy sends a vibrational frequency to the other side that either helps or hinders Spirits' ability to connect.

When a soul returns to Spirit form after leaving the physical body, his/her battery is fully charged and vibrating at a very high speed. We, in our human form, have to try to match that energy level. The more positive our thoughts are, the more we are able to connect. This is challenging to experience during a time of grief, but it is the only way to help the communication system work properly. Remembering the good times we had with our loved ones helps charge our battery, making it easier for them to connect. Even though I cried on top of that mountain the day I found that first dime, I was able to feel the love within my heart. My connection with my father was strong and he was there with me.

Positive and negative emotional charges are exactly what you need to know and understand if you want to receive messages. Think of a time when you were so excited that you were able to feel it inside of you. Whenever I told my dime story, it seemed like my bones were plugged into an outlet because my body was so excited. Others reported feeling a "buzzing" in their body or like water trickling through their body. This is the energy to connect with. Now, remember a time when you were upset, sad or angry. For me, because I hate being lied to, when someone tells me something that I know is not true, I get triggered and inside I feel very angry. Feel both of the positive and negative feelings and then make a commitment to focus on the good feelings, especially love. That perspective helps to connect and open the door.

How do you do that? Think of the good times you had with your loved one. Remember who they were as a person. Maybe even write a letter to them. Pretend you are talking to them. What would they say to you? How would they want you to live? All of these help bring them closer to you.

Especially notice how the good feeling feels. I realized that because of past traumatic events that happened in my life, I was actually scared of this happy feeling. Anytime I felt happy, I worried that something bad was about to happen. I had intense anxiety anytime something happened or I traveled. I was afraid of everything! I had to train my mind to tell my body that everything was okay and it was good to have this feeling. Our bodies were built to remember negative events to keep us safe. Originally, humans needed to make sure to run away from lions and tigers and bears. Nowadays, we don't need this as much, but it is still a part of our human system. Our minds worry constantly that something bad might happen again. It's up to us to repattern our minds to live in gratitude and tell ourselves that we are safe and okay.

The chakras are invisible energetic centers in your body that affect our emotional and physical well-being. The ideas about chakras date back to 1500 BC and originated in India. Nowadays, the understanding of chakras has spread to the Western world, especially in Yoga and Reiki healing.

There are seven chakras and they go from the root chakra (base of your spine) all the way to your crown chakra (the top of your head). Each one is responsible for different emotions, which, in turn, affect our physical body. When chakras are aligned, the physical body is well and healthy. When a chakra is blocked or out of balance, this may lead to health or emotional issues.

Ancient scriptures relay that the chakras are like a sphere or ball. We have to use our imagination to sense the energy. During a Reiki session, the practitioner may envision the chakra of the client to help remove blockages and re-align the client's energy. Many yoga sessions are focused on aligning chakras.

Each of the seven chakra centers of the body correlate to a color, an element, a variety of emotions, a specific area of the physical body and specific areas of physical health. Here is a quick reference:

Chakra	color	element	location	emotions	Physical manifestation
Root	red	Earth	Base of spine	Survival, stability, self-sufficiency, security, fear, confidence, finances	Arthritis, constipation, bladder, colon
Sacral	orange	Water	Lower abdomen	Sexuality, creativity, self-worth, compassion, intuition	UTI's, low back pain

Solar Plexus	yellow	Fire	Between navel and rib cage	Ego, anger, aggression, self-esteem, confidence, focus	Digestion, liver, diabetes
Heart	green	air	Heart region	Love, attachment, compassion, trust, passion caring optimism	Heart problems, asthma, weight
Throat	blue	space	Base of throat	Inspiration, self-expression, creativity, communicating, faith	Sore throat,
Third eye	Indigo	none	In-between eyebrows	Intuition, spiritual connection, self-knowledge	Headaches, blurry vision, eye strain
Crown	violet/ white	none	Top of head	Spirituality, enlightenment, dynamic thought and energy	Depression, anxiety

Now, when your battery is fully charged, your chakras are aligned and you are grounded, it is time to get in touch with your intuitive gifts. These gifts were given to everyone at birth and they help us connect to the spiritual world. In Kindergarten, everyone learns about the five senses: hearing, sight, taste, smell and touch. What we don't learn in public school is the spiritual senses. These are called our "Claire" abilities and they mimic the senses but they are invisible and are part of our spiritual being, where our intuition is able to send us messages.

There are five main claires; clairvoyance, clairsentience, clairaudience, clairtancy and clairgustance. Each one taps into a different energetic way to receive messages from invisible thoughts, actions and coincidences. A person uses their five senses to tap into this energetic system to increase their intuitive abilities. Just like a cell phone works on top of a mountain; your senses are able to receive messages like radio waves traveling across time and space.

We are born with these heightened senses but as we grow older we tend to forget them, especially if they are not encouraged. Each person is gifted with at least one or more and some work better than others. It's through these senses that our loved ones are able to send messages.

Clairvoyance is clear seeing. When I was a young child, I had the ability to see entities floating around. They were like bubbles of white light. Some people actually see the shapes of people. Sometimes instead of seeing it in physical form, a person sees the vision in their mind. They may receive intuitive guidance about what is going to happen or may feel like they had a deja vu experience, where they feel like they have been here before. Dreams are another way to receive messages through clairvoyance abilities.

Clairsalience is receiving messages through a scent. Even though there seems to be no physical evidence, the person may smell roses that might remind a person of their Grandmother or even cigar smoke to remind them of an Uncle or Grandfather. Nobody else in the room smells what the person smells but the person knows they are able to smell it.

Clairaudience is the ability to hear even when it seems nobody is talking. For me, it is someone whispering to me but other people may hear voices or sounds that seem real. At times, people may think they are going crazy if they don't understand their gift because nobody else hears what they are hearing.

Clairtancy is when people receive intuitive guidance through touch. They don't need to have a physical object near them but they sense how the object feels to understand the message.

Clairgustance is receiving intuitive guidance through your sense of taste. A particular flavor may remind a person of an event that happened. Or, a person may get the taste of alcohol or medicine. Alcohol could be a clue the person liked to drink and medicine could be a sign of sickness.

So, like the senses we learned in Kindergarten, there are the following Spiritual senses that relate to the five senses.

Sight- Clairvoyance
Smell- Clairsentience
Hearing- Clairaudience

Touch- Clairtancy

Taste- Clairgustance

Beyond these claires, there are two more that have more to do with emotions. They are claircognizance and clairsentience and are related to the third chakra (solar plexus) and the fifth chakra (heart chakra).

Claircognizance is the gut feeling deep in your soul, where "You know". It isn't your brain rationalizing and convincing you of something. It is your whole body sending you a message. It can come from your gut or your heart and it is often this deep knowing that you have difficulty explaining to others. For instance, someone might know that something is going to happen in the future; either good or bad. My friend Kevin has the ability to guess when someone is about to have a baby. He even told my son, "You are having a baby." Kevin had no real reason for knowing this but said it matter of factly. It was true but my son and his girlfriend had just found out and hadn't told anyone yet. My son shared this with me and said, "How the heck did he know? We hadn't told anyone yet!" My son was so shocked he didn't know how to respond because Kevin was right.

Clairsentience is the ability to feel the emotions of others and it is by far my best claire. I am able to sense energy in the air. Obviously, we can't "see" an argument in the air floating between people, but if I walk into a room where there has been an argument, my senses alert me that there is tension. The same is true for when love is in the air!

Just like I wanted a sign from my father the universe heard and created that experience. Did my inspiration come from some sort of inner knowing that this was possible? The thought appeared out of nowhere. Could my intuitive self guided me during that moment and I wouldn't know it until I found the coins? The invisible world of communication is one of the greatest mysteries of our world.

All of these claires are our guidance system and our loved ones use these types of communication. We have to learn to decipher the messages. When I was young, I didn't understand how this worked and I tried to cover up my gifts. I had no way of knowing or understanding because I was born into a family system who didn't understand how any of this worked. For years, I either drank alcohol or ate food because it helped to dull these senses.

When I embraced my gifts and started writing, I began to understand how to live a more Spiritual life. Since we are souls with a body and not a body with a soul, it's important to connect back to our true selves. The events that transpired in my life were so amazing that I wanted to share them. When we allow the universe to work its magic, we may be surprised at how amazing this human journey can really be.

Within each story you hear how myself and others connect to someone who no longer has a physical body. Just by reading this book, your energy may be recharged and you may experience life in a whole new way - one in which you feel better and know how to turn to love instead of other emotions. For when we do this, our energy is ready with a fully charged battery and the universe is ready to shower us with blessings from Heaven.

Chapter 11: Help from Spirit

"Sometimes you get what you want. Other times, you get a lesson in patience, timing, alignment, empathy, compassion, faith, perseverance, resilience, humility, trust, meaning, awareness, resistance, purpose, clarity, grief, beauty, and life. Either way, you win." ~Brianna Wiest

My life changed the day my father died. Not in the way one might think. Yes, I was now without both of my parents. Yes, I had to deal with the estate and all the things that go with it. Yes, we needed to plan a funeral or a celebration of life- whatever we wanted to call it. Yes, we would never celebrate another holiday with them. Yes, I wouldn't be able to call my parents to see how they were doing. All of these things were true and they did change my life. The morning my father died, I changed one habit of mine to remind myself that I have the power to control my life and my thoughts.

On that day, I decided to drink my coffee without eating anything first. This may not seem like some big, major revelation, but for me it is always a reminder that I choose my thoughts and beliefs. I also have the power within me to change my life with my thoughts.

I tried to sleep for a few hours the last night when my father was alive. It was the third night I had been up all night helping to care for him. At 3:00AM, I got up to see how he was doing. I wanted coffee but I wasn't hungry. I decided to change a long time habit.

I love coffee but always told myself that I needed to have something in my stomach before I drank that first cup. Since that day, I start every morning with a cup of coffee and no food. I do this to prove a point and it has turned out to be the best part of my day. While drinking the coffee, I remind myself of all of the memories that are a part of me and I write ten gratitudes and five aspirations to start my day. Then, I either write or read for at least another half hour. This time to me is precious and I love to start my day like this. Each day that cup of coffee reminds me that I have the ability to change and reminds me how grateful I am to be alive.

Here are some of my gratitudes:

- I am grateful for the phone call from my friend because I value our friendship.

- I am grateful for the groceries I bought yesterday because we have food in the fridge and cupboards.
- I am grateful for a reader sending me a dime story because I know they are connecting with their loved ones.
- I am grateful for sliding with my Grandsons because we had so much fun making memories.

When I wrote my first book, the publicist focused on my "deep grief" of losing my father. This bothered me and I couldn't figure out why. When writing this book, I realized it is because when people think of grief, they immediately might be sad. The problem or disconnect I felt was that I was happy that I had this new relationship with my parents. I felt my parents supported me each and every day, more so than when they were here on earth. It was such a different experience for everyone else because they didn't have this deep connection with Heaven that I have. Yes, I was sad that my parents were no longer with us but they had a wonderful life and it felt like a normal part of life to say goodbye to them. I cried, asked for help and thanked God for the signs.

Life can throw us curve balls when we aren't paying attention or appreciating all that we have. This is true for me even though I've been doing this work for years. I wasn't ready for this next event in my life but it sure did teach me more about the quantum world that was so mysterious and elusive to me before. The invisible connection proved to me that we are all loved and supported in ways that are difficult to understand.

I lost the dime necklace my dad gave me. I felt more lost than when he died. Grief appeared suddenly and I wasn't sure how to handle it. It was grief for my missing necklace but it showed up like my Dad was dying all over again. I couldn't talk about this to anyone.

When I lost my dime and I was at a book event, I wasn't able to say, "My Dad gave me this dime from his coin collection," because I had to wear a decoy around my neck. The words were not true so I was unable to speak them. I replaced the dime I wore around my neck with one I bought at a coin store. It wasn't "the one" but it was a prop I could use when I wanted to talk about my books.

"My Dad gave me a special liberty head dime from his coin collection," I reworded my sentence to make it true as I grabbed the necklace around my neck. That's the best I could do right now. I couldn't lie and each time I said it I winced because inside I knew that I had actually misplaced the dime from my father. It was the dime that had started my entire spiritual journey.

How could a person who wrote two books about this special dime lose it? My energy was off and I felt like an imposter playing a role I wasn't fit to play. I felt I was a failure. I had not taken good care of my dime and now it was gone.

I know I put it "someplace special" where "I would always remember." I didn't want to talk about it to anyone and didn't for months. I kept praying that by some miracle I would find my dime. I believed in prayer and I knew this was a key part of my learning and growing. My prayers were very different than in the past. They included a feeling instead of begging for something. It wasn't, "God- please return my dime." It was more, "I'd love you to return my dime." I asked for the what and the when and how were up to Spirit.

Finally, I decided to share this news with a few people. I was lost and needed help. Maybe I just misplaced it or the cat had decided it was a great toy. I rummaged through clothes in my dresser drawers and looked under books, furniture or anything that might be covering it up. I wondered if I would ever find it. I checked a lot of "special spots" where I might have placed the dime. A drawer. Inside my father's antique clock. A special wooden bowl. Each place I looked, I seriously found a dime because I sprinkled my dimes in different places throughout my house. Just like the heart shaped rocks sprinkled all over the mountain, my house is filled with dimes and pennies.

I gave up but this weighed on me like I was carrying a fifty pound bag of rocks. I beat myself up about it. I had to face the fact that I lost it and I wasn't sure it was coming back. My grief came back and I missed my father. I remembered the good times with my parents. I remembered the moment my father said, as he woke up from his nap, "Hey. You know those dimes that were in that collection? Those different dimes? Could we have those made into necklaces?"

On March 14, 2021, I decided to write a request in my journal for my dime to be returned. This is what I wrote:

"I have a request. I would like you to return the dime you gave me from your coin collection. I understand that there was a deep lesson for me to learn when I lost it. I have been working on being more grounded and in the present moment. I also realize that although I am able to manifest some things in my life, ultimately Spirit helps guide me. I allow life to flow naturally. I am open to receiving abundance and I know that I am exactly where I need to be in life."

Organizing and cleaning my house helps me move my internal energy. Some people say that what our environment looks like is a reflection of our insides. As I redesigned myself, I redesigned my environment. I decided that I was going to redesign my work from home office to grow my card reading, Reiki and coaching business. My husband built me beautiful pine bookshelves to display all of my books. I love to read and my personal library grew each month to the point that I really needed a way to organize them.

As I was putting the books on my new shelves, I decided to open this one particular book. It was the book *The Astonishing Power of Emotions, Let Your Feelings Be Your Guide* by Esther and Jerry Hicks. Esther and Jerry write about how we create our world with our thoughts. They speak of our vibrational energy being alive and how to reprogram any negativity into positive affirmations.

My intuition guided me to open that book. I didn't open any other books that day.

The entire dime necklace fell out of that book. Tears came and I felt the weight on my shoulders release the guilt I had felt about losing my dime. When we let go of guilt, shame or other feelings that weigh us down, we offer a space in our hearts for love and connection.

That necklace then lived on my neck for weeks. My intuition told me, "Don't wear the necklace. You might lose it again." I didn't listen. I felt like I had my Superpower back and if I didn't have it on my neck, I wouldn't feel whole again. I decided to ignore that little voice warning me.

My head was looking down as I went to get up from my chiropractic adjustment. My necklace caught on the metal bars of the table but I released it quickly.

On my way home, I grabbed my necklace from beneath my sweater. Instead of being a closed circular rope around my neck, it was one long, unclasped string. At the moment my necklace was stuck in the table at the chiropractic office, it had broken the hook. This meant the dime didn't have anything to hang on to. I panicked. My dime was gone yet again. I started searching for the dime in my sweater, in my seat and all around me in the car.

I phoned the chiropractor and explained the situation to them. Would they mind looking for my dime? Would they please check the table, the room and the parking lot? I hated to call and ask them but also was desperate to find my dime. I asked for help but they might not really understand the significance of this particular dime. It was worth way more than ten cents.

How could I let this happen? Why was this happening? Would the dime be lost forever this time?

My thoughts had come true. I had lost my dime yet again. Did I actually create my reality with my thoughts? I felt that it was my fault. I had only had the dime back for a few short weeks and this time, I wasn't sure if it would ever return.

I was devastated and my heart was broken. This time, I felt like I hadn't appreciated the dime enough. I had assumed that now that I had found it, I would always have it. And, I hadn't realized how much that the universe really listens to all of our thoughts.

When I shared this with my friend, Tracy, she laughed as she said, "Spirit gives and Spirit takes. It controls the dime. It knows when you need it." What? Is it possible that my father, who had technically "died", was able to somehow control events like this in my life? I had to be willing to think that something powerful was happening.

I felt it deep within me and was willing to learn some lessons with my loss. This is what I discovered when I lost my dime for the second time.

1. Appreciate everything you have each and every day. Even simple things like your morning coffee or your bed. Imagine life without these things and you are able to realize just how abundant your life truly is.

2. Slow down. I moved so fast when the necklace got stuck that I didn't notice it broke. If I had gone slower, I might have noticed the necklace was broken and found the dime right then and there.

3. Let go of attachment to physical objects. I won't find peace and happiness with the amount of things I have. Even though I had lost my superpower necklace, I actually had the superpower within me all the time. I let go of the need for a physical object to remind me that Divine energy is within me.

4. Watch my thoughts. Because I had kept worrying about losing the dime, that is exactly what happened. I had seriously created my reality with my thoughts but not in a way that I wanted!

5. Spirit is in charge, not me. I had to let go and know that I am not able to control everything in my life. It's my job to have sincere gratitude for everything in my life and to know that God's plan for
me is way better than I can even imagine.

6. It is okay to be okay where I am and not always searching for happiness in the next thing.

For days, which turned into weeks, which turned into months, I asked Spirit for my dime back. I scoured the parking lot every time I went to the chiropractor. I cleaned my car often, never daring to vacuum my car because I was afraid the vacuum would eat my dime and I would never get it back.

My faith was being tested. I prayed often and it went something like this: "Would you please send my dime back to me? I would really, really, really like it back. Thank you! Thank you! Thank you!"

I felt it deep within me that Spirit would eventually return my dime to me. As the months rolled on, my faith began to diminish.

That same summer, I attended the Psychic and Beyond Event in Connecticut hosted by Rebecca Ann Locicero. The weekend was spent doing intuitive readings, selling my books and speaking to a small crowd how my ideas about death changed since my father had died. I truly believe that when we die, our souls stay here on earth-invisible to the naked eye. Their souls are without their physical bodies- not like in the movies haunting people. They are here to love and support us. I believe we are able to connect with those who have transitioned to this other invisible dimension.

I then went on to explain how to ask for a sign and shared a story about my signs. During this session, there was a woman in the audience who I thought had grief radiating from her body. I could feel it in the air. I decided to end my speech a little earlier and ask if there were any questions. She raised her hand and began to tell me her story.

"My husband told me before he died that he would show signs to me in a water-fall," she shared and her anger poured out of her aura and spilled into the room. "I have been several times to the waterfall where he asked me to marry him. I get nothing every time I go there." Her words were filled with frustration, disappointment and disbelief that she would ever be able to receive a sign. I know what that felt like because I doubted this connection for so many years.

I felt that she was trying too hard and trying to control exactly when the sign would happen. I explained this to her and she seemed even angrier at me. I could tell she deeply missed her beloved husband. I wasn't sure there was anything that I could do for her other than share my own experiences so that maybe, if she was able to let go of the need to control, a sign may appear out of nowhere.

That's when it happened. A thought appeared in my head. I put my books down on the table nearby. I looked at her as I formed a heart with my hands. I told her that for some reason I keep hearing, "Show her a heart. Show her a heart."

"I keep seeing a big heart and he wants you to know that he loves you so much and that he is always with you," I said.

Instantaneously, the woman began crying. "I can't believe you just said that," she whispered through her tears. I knew there was more so I stayed quiet as our eyes locked. This gave her the space to share her story and for me to honor her grief.

"I was recently at the ocean with a friend of mine. I searched and searched for either a rock or a seashell in the shape of a heart. I didn't find any. I was so sad I couldn't even think straight. I kept thinking, 'Why won't he send me a sign?'. When my friend and I got back to our towels to sit down, she said, 'Look.' When I looked to where my friend was pointing, there was a heart shaped seashell right next to my towel."

The crowd responded with "oh my God" and "wow". I have no idea where the heart idea came from but I do know that the message was perfect timing for this woman. Spirit spoke to her when she let go of the need to control the outcome. She knew her husband was there and now she believed even more. May she always feel him near her.

I knew I had to let go of the need to control so that my dime would come back to me exactly when it was supposed to come back to me. Letting go is one of the most difficult things to do in this earthly life. I had to have faith and pray.

This book was partially written, but I didn't have a solid ending. My books are not something that I am able to plan ahead and write an outline for. This is a prescriptive writing process that does not work for me but since I was entering a contest to try to win a book contract with a large publishing agency, I tried to use the outline form suggested by my writing coach.

When trying to work with a publishing agency, an author writes a book proposal. For nonfiction, the book doesn't even need to be written. This writing process is great for some writers but I knew in my gut that I wasn't able to do it because my books are filled with stories from my life. My book proposal needs to be written after I write the book!

I worked with a writing coach to prepare that book proposal and am so grateful for the opportunity but inside I knew something was missing. I was writing to try to impress someone and it wasn't coming from my heart. Also, I couldn't figure out the ending. I had a lot of stories, but was missing a key part of understanding how this all works.

Anyone who has ever experienced grief knows that grief is not like a cold that you eventually get over. Grief is always present. It ebbs and flows like the waves in the ocean. Sometimes it is calm and other times it is stormy. It is always sitting inside your heart and walking right beside you everyday. Through losing my dime, I was again experiencing deep grief for my loss. The loss wasn't about the dime, it was about losing both of my parents. The dime was just the physical reminder.

What if there was a different way to experience grief? What if life was everlasting? What if the person wasn't actually gone? What if we were able to sense our loved ones all around us?

I wrote the book proposal with a theme about reframing grief. Honestly, it was a flop. It was a flop because I was writing to impress someone and I lost myself as a writer.

After finishing the book proposal, I walked away from my writing. I needed some time to just "be" instead of being busy all of the time. I let go of the outcome but inside my heart I knew that the book didn't have a good frame. I didn't even know the ending of the book. This was in March of 2021; exactly a month after I lost my dime for the second time.

Eldon, my father's best friend, passed away on June 18, 2021. His death inspired me to pick up my pen again. I wasn't able to plan the ending in my outline because the ending hadn't happened yet!

On July 13th of 2021, I decided it was time to write again. I was ready to write this book. I printed off the material I had so far and planned to work on it two days later.

That's when it happened. I changed my thinking. I decided to just be me and write however I wanted to write. I wanted this to come from my heart, not some prescribed writing outline. My stories are based on Spirit and energy, not the analytical part of my brain. I hadn't realized it before but trying to please others is what was blocking my writing. I let go and let Spirit help me.

My mailbox is located a quarter of a mile away from my house, at the bottom of a long, dirt driveway. As I drove a few feet past my mailbox on my way home from work, I parked my car. The radio blared Spiritual music as I left the car door open. I sang as I half danced, half walked to the mailbox. It was the day after I worked on my manuscript, I returned home from work to discover something so preposterous that I struggled to make sense of it.

There, amidst the stones and gravel, was my long lost dime.

Spirit sent me my dime at the exact time that I needed a gentle push to get back to my writing. I had learned yet another lesson; one that keeps showing up in my life. It was important to "Be the best me that I can be."

When I worked on my manuscript this time I was able to write in a different way. One where I wasn't trying to impress anyone and I was being authentic. I believe that my father knew and returned my dime to me as a sign of encouragement.

Spirit knows when the timing is right and when we need a sign. I had requested the what- "I would like my dime back" but the how and when had to be so unexpected that I would recognize the sign and receive the message.

For those who live in the country, they might understand why this was such a miracle because they know what happens to our dirt roads. For those who don't, I'll try to explain why finding this dime on my short path to my mailbox was such an improbable event.

When I lost my dime in February, it was the middle of winter in Vermont. This means that the road and driveway are plowed several times a week. The snow, along with the dirt are pushed around in every direction to clear the roads to drive.

Then, during March and April, the snow melts and the frost underneath the dirt pushes from beneath to cause up to one foot deep ruts in the mud that only a truck or an SUV are able to drive through. As the frost disappears, the water then soaks into the ground and the dirt is smooth again. Mud season is Vermont's extra season in between winter and spring.

Then, in the summer months, the rain travels down the hill of our driveway washing away little rivers of gravel and the puddles create potholes. The dirt then has to be pushed around to smooth it back out.

Why is all of this important? Because I lost my dime in February and found my dime in July. Between the plow, the dirt work and the rain, it doesn't seem possible that I would ever find my dime amidst all the moved dirt.

I believe Spirit sent my dime back to me to remind me of who I am and to write from my heart.

Here are the things I was reminded of when I found my dime.

1. Asking for help from Spirit works. I had asked for my dime to be returned for months. I didn't know why it was gone but I knew there would be a lesson for me.

2. In order to shine my light, I have to embrace being myself. When I do things to try to please others, it doesn't work. My writing flowed better when I did it my way instead of a prescriptive writing plan to impress a publisher.

3. Being grounded is important. Know where your feet are planted each and every moment. I can still see the dime in the dirt like it was a gift from Mother Earth. This work is continuous each and every day. It's important to not ruminate over the past or worry about the future. Be in the now.

4. Gratitude is an incredible gift to yourself. It truly changes how you think and it helps to raise your vibrational energy. Life is truly a miracle. We are meant to live each day with joy.

5. My emotions have a direct connection to the health of my physical body and how my life flows each day.
6. In order to heal, I had to feel healed within me. I took the supplements and did the treatments, but I believed my body was healing and this eventually became my reality.

I'm still learning to embrace who I am and live an authentic life; one where I turn to love instead of fear. A life where I believe in the possibility of an after-life right here on earth. A life where through sharing my journey, I am able to "help my peeps" and in return my peeps help me.

May you believe that coincidences truly are signs from the souls of our loved ones who left their physical bodies.

Chapter 12: Frames and Cars

"Decide. You are the only one in charge of your destiny. Unfair things may happen to you, unfortunate times may come to you, but you *always* get to choose how you respond. You can live in frustration and bitterness, or you can be the bigger person and just play the hell out of the cards you are dealt. Because the truth is in this world, not a single person chooses the cards they receive, but every single person chooses how to play them." ~Walk the Earth

"Livin' the dream!" has been my response throughout the pandemic whenever someone asks me, "How are you?" I've gotten many different reactions from people. "That's awesome!" to "I hear the sarcasm" to "Is it a nightmare?" When I recently said it after eating a delicious breakfast at our local diner, Lynn, the owner said, "I love it! That's what my shirt says!" Her smile was wide and I knew she meant it. There was no doubt in my mind that Lynn was truly embracing each day.

I first met Lynn in my twenties. I was a young mother about to have another baby. My mind wasn't worried about death and I hadn't developed my sincere gratitude for the many wonderful things in my life. I had severe back pain chasing around a toddler who never wanted to take a nap. To say I was exhausted was an understatement.

Lynn was quiet but kind and I was too busy to really be able to chat with her as I was swimming with my toddler and then racing home to get dinner on the table before falling on the couch, waiting for my next baby to come into this world.

I did have a sense of gratitude for this new baby because I had a miscarriage before this pregnancy. This caused me to worry during my entire pregnancy. The empty, hollow feeling I had when I lost my other baby still left a whole in my heart that may never be filled. A mother's love for a child is so monumental that those who have not felt it may never understand. Being connected to another human being who is growing inside of you is the best and most scary thing a person can live through. It's through the love that we experience such deep pain when we lose someone. I had experienced that and was extremely happy to be a Mom again to another human soul.

Years later Lynn would come back into my life and I watched her embrace each day with such gratitude and kindness. I thought about it some more and realized that none of us are promised a tomorrow. That's why right now is called the "present".

Nobody really knows exactly when death is going to happen but we all know that our time here on earth is limited. I know people who have been told they have months to live. Some died and others did not. That happened to Anita Moorjani. She was on death's door with cancer and she had a near death experience (NDE). The doctors told her family she wouldn't make it through the night. She entered another dimension during her illness, saw her beloved father and best friend in Heaven. Then she returned to her body and within five days the cancer was gone. She asked the doctors to stop all treatment. She knew she would be okay because she knew how to live her life now. Her book *Dying to Be Me* explains that her internal struggles were what were making her sick. She needed to be proud of who she was and embrace life. Now, she speaks and writes about being an empath and her NDE where she spontaneously healed her cancer, inspiring millions of people all over the world.

Lynn shared with me that she now has a journal in which she records her dimes because she has found so many since reading my first book. Her excitement and sadness all rolled into one as she then shared her most recent dime story.

"I was so distraught. I had lost my other dog awhile back and now I wouldn't have any dogs left in the house. It was heartbreaking and I had difficulty even discussing it with anyone. I had a friend dig a hole where we were going to bury him. I went out to the hole to take a look and, there in the dirt, was a dime. It was in the middle of the field. I thought that was cool."

Her story went on like my dime stories- a continuous, never-ending collection of miracles.

"Then, when I went to the vet, I found a dime on the sidewalk. Finding each dime gave me a sense of peace and I really felt like my dog was right there with me. I would turn and even though my eyes didn't see anything, I knew he was there. I couldn't let go of the feeling. Then, you'll never believe this- I found another dime in my driveway when I got home. I seriously was like- okay, three dimes! My heart felt better and I still feel like he is right near my legs every time I walk into the house!"

Lynn glowed a happy light as she shared about her love for her dog and the connection to this invisible world.

We use frames to decorate and hang up pictures. The frame makes the picture look nice and it reminds us of a past moment to cherish. We never frame our worst moments in life. We try to capture the best moments like weddings, kids growing up or special places we visit. The truth is not all moments are picture perfect and would fit in a frame. We also frame our stories about how we view events in our life and this is based on our past experiences, which gives a different perspective for every event. Each event is different for the people experiencing it because they take in the experience based on their perspective.

How we choose to frame our stories is so important, especially when we are dealing with grief. This doesn't mean that we bury our grief. We are able to move through it in whatever way it shows up. We are able to have no expectations about the experience and we don't need to "heal" or feel like there's an end goal post to reach. Each day is different and different emotions are going to show up. It's okay to value and honor your feelings. Emotions come and go and most likely they won't be easy.

When you frame the story in a way where you are willing to feel your loved ones nearby and the possibility of an after-life, it may change your life forever. Framing your grief in a way that honors the past and begins to create more memories with those still here is a way to move through the new experiences without your loved ones.

Recently I was reading a post on social media. This mother lost her daughter to suicide. She wrote about crying when she looked at the laundry basket. She had used the basket many times since her daughter's death, but on this particular day, it seemed to bring up sadness. Maybe it was the extreme love for her daughter. She shared that she wasn't sure why she cried. Later on that day, she was able to laugh about the moment. Her story frame might have been I am going to allow myself to cry over this laundry basket and allow myself time to grieve. Then, she was able to look back at her grief, and take a moment to laugh.

Another woman, who had just lost her mother, shared another story about grief. She wrote, "Grief is a strange companion. At any moment an overwhelming sadness can creep up from behind to take you down unawares. Something seen or something thought. Which, it doesn't matter. After a while, it becomes expected. And, you cautiously sit and wait for it. As if you can best it. But wholly unexpected is the hilarity. Such as when my sister texts me from her walk telling me she can now "step on the sidewalk cracks". And I laugh. I even laugh a little too much. As if it's the funniest thing I've ever heard. But, there is this benefit after all, cracks" ~Angela Ogle

It's impossible to know and understand just how our minds work with memories. Every single time I pick up a spoon out of my drawer, I am reminded of our neighbor, Samantha. She transitioned so young. To everyone else, it might not make sense, but to me the memory rewinds in my head like a favorite song.

"This is the prettiest spoon I have ever seen in my life. Look at how beautiful this is! It is my favorite spoon and I like to use it each and every time I need a spoon," Samantha's happy go lucky voice was so incredibly excited over a simple spoon. As she showed me the spoon, I realized that it was from my silverware collection. I wish I could go back to that moment. I would have said this, "I'm so happy you like that spoon. It is one of my spoons but please keep it because it brings you such joy! I'm so happy to see you happy. If a spoon can do that, then you have at it!"

I didn't do that. Instead I laughed as I told her, "That is from my house." When I did that, Samantha felt that it belonged to me and gave it back to me. Looking back, she had such joy for that one spoon. Instead of beating myself up about it now, every time I pick up a spoon, I glory in the beauty of this particular spoon. Who would ever guess that every time I pick up that spoon I am reminded that life is sometimes cut short for some. Every time I pick up that spoon, I think of Sam and her family. They miss her bubbly energy each and every day.

Lynn's frame for her story includes "Livin' the Dream" because she is.

I like to compare life to driving a car. This analogy helps me frame my stories in a way where I am able to let go and enjoy life a bit more.

When I am driving a car, I feel like I have control and my anxiety is a bit less. Although I am able to control where the car is going, I can't control the other people driving near me. When someone else is driving, my anxiety kicks in because I feel like I don't have control over everything. I can't control where we go and I can't control what happens if another car comes near. I want to be able to stop the car or slow down if I think the person is going too fast.

Learning to live where we are working with the invisible divine energy and quantum physics requires us to drive our car (our life), but also to let go of the steering wheel once in a while. I used to drive with a tight grip and wanted control each and every day. Now, I choose the path to drive but allow the universe to guide me in a different way to my destination. When I grip so tight to the steering wheel, I get caught up in trying to control each and every part of my day. I have expectations for myself and others. I get caught up in being busy. This is how I spent most of my life. I thought the only way to live was to do, do, do and make sure I was in control of as many things as possible.

When I wrote my first book, I began to let go of the steering wheel. It was a slow process of learning to trust that the universe was helping me drive my car. It was sort of like when Hannah asked for a sign from her sister and allowed the most unexpected events to occur. When I let go, I choose the direction I want to go in life (writing, sharing my stories), but I let go of the steering wheel to allow the universe to drive me down a path I might not even know or understand yet. Like Lynn, I am now living my dream in a very different way. It's because of the faith I had in the universe and the gratitude for all the good and bad in my life.

There are going to be bumps along our journey. That is a given. It is how we frame those events that decides how the rest of the ride goes.

"Death takes the body. God takes the soul. Our mind holds the memories. Our heart keeps the love. Our faith lets us know we will meet again." ~Nishan Panwar

During our human journey, it is okay to be both sad and happy. It is okay to be both anxious and hopeful. You can be angry and excited. You can be lonely and grateful. You can miss your loved one and feel like they are right beside you.

Lori's first message to me said, "I wish I could see spirits!" Well, she can but she just doesn't know how to yet.

Lori lost her husband soon after she read *Dimes from Heaven*. She read my book as her husband slowly slipped back to his Spirit form. She wrote to me after and said, "I really thank God that I read your book before." After his death, she sent me several messages about signs from her dear, sweet husband.

"I wanted to share with you what happened at Dennis' service. The priest raised his glass and said do this in memory of me. Total silence and outside a jake brake came on. It couldn't have been more perfect! I believe that Dennis was saying ' I'm okay.' "

Dennis was a truck driver and even though Lori missed him, she felt so much love in her heart at that moment, just knowing that she was able to connect with him in a way she may never have imagined before.

Her next share melted my heart because she was teaching the next generation (her grandchildren) that we really can connect to Heaven and remember the love we have for family and friends.

"Dennis and I would always take the grandkids for a walk and they love throwing rocks in the pond and this is the outlet on the other side. This picture is the first time we went for a walk without him."

In the picture, there was a perfectly shaped heart in the grass. It was her next share that would show the deep connection Dennis still had with his family..

"They miss their Papa so much. Ryker was praying the other night and asked his mom if it was okay to thank papa for the heart rocks he sends him. He is three years old!"

Lori knows how to connect with Heaven now and is teaching the next generation that it is okay to feel this connection and know that it is true. She and her family have found many dimes, hearts and trucks. They feel Dennis nearby but also feel their sadness. It was her intention and belief in this connection that allowed the coincidences to happen.

"One day, you are going to hug your last hug, kiss your last kiss, and hear someone's voice for the last time, but you never know when the last time will be. Live every day as if it were the last time you will be with the person you love."
~Anonymous

When we frame our stories or drive our car, there are important questions to ask ourselves.

- Will this matter tomorrow?
- Will this matter in five years?
- What if I died tomorrow?

Framing the story with these questions may help put each event into perspective and allow you to let go of the steering wheel a bit to enjoy the ride. It's our memories that fill our hearts with love. We keep the old and create new at the same time.

Grief is not about letting go of those memories. It's about honoring those memories and connecting to those we love in Spirit form. When I think about my Grandmother and the memories inside of me, I feel such love surround me. Because of his Grandmother, Ryker is always able to feel his Papa's love in his heart.

When I visit my own grandchildren, I imagine my grandmother and bring that love with me. As each generation grows and then dies, we pass on this gift. I hope my own children and grandchildren always feel my unconditional love. It's the same love that we are able to receive from the universe or God or the Divine or whatever you want to call it.

I was so grateful when my friend, Ellen, sent me a dime bracelet. Immediately, I looked at the year as I believe that usually holds a clue as to the message from Heaven. It was the year my Grandmother passed away-1997. Instantly, I felt her presence and love.

I started writing because I was in physical pain. If it wasn't for the pain, I never would have started my new career as an author, Reiki Master and spiritual/intuitive coach and Angel card reader. I had no idea where this road would lead me all those years ago. I am thankful that I started this journey, and let go of the steering wheel a bit. Now I am able to connect with the Divine guidance that is available to everyone. When we are willing to acknowledge our pain by moving through it, this life may lead us to destinations we never could have imagined.

Most of my life, I have been a person who is always cold. Anything below seventy degrees and I would be bundled up like I was ready for a trip up Mt. Everest. Well, I may be exaggerating a bit, but this is important knowledge to show the point that when a friend shared that she was taking "cold" showers, my response was, "Good luck with that. I would never, ever do that." I could seriously not even understand why someone would ever want to take a cold shower. Then I learned more about body regulation and cold therapy, including the Wim Hof method. I got curious to see why anyone would do something that seemed so outrageous to me.

Cold showers help with the following: make you more alert, help you breathe deeper-increasing the oxygen level in your body, increases your white blood cell count (which increases your immunity to fight off diseases!), strengthens your will power and helps you maintain a healthy body weight. I never even had a clue about any of this.

Once I learned about it, it made more sense why a person might want to take a cold shower. First, you might take a hot shower. Then, you turn the water to cold and slowly adjust your body to the new temperature. You can put your arms and legs under the water and then move on to the rest of your body.

Cold showers changed my life. They taught me that I needed to learn more about something before I made a judgment about it. Sometimes my frames were wrong- the stories I had told myself for years were being reframed into something different. They taught me that I didn't really understand the why and how until I tried it myself. They taught me that I needed to connect my mind to my body. They taught me the answers I seek are actually within me.

My childhood version of Heaven was like my vision of a cold shower. I wasn't exposed to signs from Heaven so I didn't really understand. Now that I've experimented, just like the cold shower, I have come to understand more about how energy works and our connection to all souls.

The more that I connected to this lifestyle, the more I was able to access it and create a new reality. Our thoughts, both good and bad, are so powerful and once you realize this, you'll begin to see, hear, smell and feel differently than ever before.

Lynn shared with me recently that she finds dimes all the time now. She said that she checks the year and just asks what the message is for the dime. Sometimes it takes her a few days and then all of a sudden she has this thought. She said it feels like it is the right meaning and is glad she solved her own puzzle. Then she said, "I don't know if I am just making it all up or not, but whatever! I don't even know where these thoughts come from. It has meaning to me and that's good enough for me." Lynn is listening to and trusting her intuition and I am so happy for her. I'm glad that my books opened up this door for her.

Another time that I stopped into the diner, one of Lynn's waitresses wanted to give me a dime that she had received as a tip. It wasn't a usual dime. It was a gold dime. Abby explained that she found it in a weird spot. She had a tip with a bunch of change on a table that she was clearing. When she lifted up the salt and pepper holder, the dime was under that. Immediately, I knew that this dime was not actually meant for me. I felt a very strong intuitive sense that this dime was from Abby's grandfather, who had recently passed away. She still wanted me to have it but I knew the only way she was able to get the message was to share it with me. She was overwhelmed with love and her smile showed me she knew her grandfather would always be with her.

When I went for breakfast a few weeks later, Lynn spotted me at the table. She went behind the counter, grabbed something and came back to me. She shared that she recently found a dime in an unusual spot. She went to pick it up and it was tucked into a button. When she turned over the button, it said, "Never Let the Assholes Ruin Your Day".

My first two blog posts were about being grateful for garbage and toilet paper. If you had told me five years ago that I would be writing about these topics, I would have laughed. Who is grateful for garbage? I wasn't grateful for much of anything. I was living the American dream-house, family and job, but I wasn't really living each day with awe and wonder. It was through my experiences with grief and loss that I learned to look at life through a different frame and learn to drive my car in a very different way.

The universe likes to have fun with me now. I wrote a blog post about "Why I buy Toilet Paper in Bulk" in January 2020, two months before the nationwide shortage of toilet paper because people decided that if they had to be home, the one big thing they would need was toilet paper. When I set out to write, I had no idea the impact I might have on other people. Did my thoughts create this toilet paper coincidence? I'll never know but I knew inside that the universe was telling me to keep writing because I may be able to help others with my ideas. The coincidence was like a huge billboard sign flashing to me saying, "keep sharing!"

When I was first learning to drive, I remember my mother telling me that wearing mittens while I drove was dangerous. I could lose my grip on the steering wheel and that might cause an accident. She wanted me to wear gloves so that my hands wouldn't slip. I liked mittens better because they kept my hands warmer than gloves did. I recently bought these new mittens and went to drive my car. I could literally hear my mother's voice reprimanding me for wearing mittens. I also thought of the analogy of "driving safe." Yes, I wanted to be safe in this life, but I also want to let go of controlling each and every part of my life.

Chapter 13: Receiving More Keys to the After-Life

"I change my life when I change my thinking. I am Light. I am Spirit. I am a wonderful, capable being. And it is time for me to acknowledge that I create my own reality with my thoughts. If I want to change my reality, then it is time for me to change my mind." ~Louise L. Hay

Education (about the Spirit world) + Intuition (using your natural born abilities) + Invisible energy= transformation, the keys to understanding how our thoughts create our life.

Living a spiritual life is a journey that only some dare to travel. Some never do. It is a sweet dance between heaven and earth. Too much earth and we are disconnected from our spiritual self. Too much heaven and we are not enjoying our human journey on earth.

Living a more spiritual life has to do with letting go of the need to control everything and learning to work with the universe in a very different way than what we may have thought. It's reprogramming our subconscious so that we allow good in our lives. It's releasing the pain and hurt that lives within us so that we are able to love more and hurt less. We realize that our human body is just the car we are traveling in during this lifetime and that our engine is our soul that continues on after our death.

Before I published my book *Dimes From Heaven,* I read it to my father's best friend, Eldon. His approval was almost as good as receiving an approval from my own father. Eldon was someone who would be honest and give me the feedback I needed even if it might challenge me.

Eldon transitioned to Spirit while I was working on this book. The last time I spoke with him was on his birthday and the heavy breathing signaled to me that heart disease was affecting his "engine". I thought he might be transitioning soon.

I was standing at the edge of the paved street when I stared at the woman in the black jeep. She had stopped and I thought she was stopping to let me cross the road to the small bakery in town. She was but then she asked me, "Do you know where Jamison Road is?" It was exactly an hour and a half after I learned that Eldon had transitioned.

I froze right there in the middle of the road. I had no idea where "Jamison" road was but the name she said was just too close to my father's name, James, for me to not recognize it as a sign. I wasn't looking for a sign but here was my father letting me know that he and Eldon were reunited in Heaven. I thanked God when a woman behind me said, "Yeah- I know where Jamison road is." I couldn't even speak and these people had no idea this seemingly simple coincidence asking for directions was actually a sign from my dead father.

Later that same day, as my niece asked the waiter what mixed drinks were available, the waiter said, "Well, we also have a Mr. Palmer." As all of us chuckled, I explained to the waiter that my Dad's name was Mr. Palmer and we all think he might be here with us right now. He understood and apologized to us for our loss. It has been almost eight years but I still feel my Dad close by, especially when these things happen.

After these two signs from my Dad on the day Eldon died, I decided to request a specific sign from Eldon. I thought about my writing and wondered if I am able to follow my own advice about how to request a sign. Do I really have the power within me to create my reality? With either a sign from Heaven or something else? Like the first step of my directions stated earlier in this book- "Think of something that directly connects you and your loved one. Be specific." What would I ask for that would help me connect with Eldon?

Years ago Eldon shared a story with me about meeting his wife in the 1950's. Her and her mother were stranded on main street because they had locked the keys in their car. Eldon, wanting to be the hero, suggested that since he had the same car maybe his key would work. Like magic, Eldon opened the door to their car which in turn opened the door to Joyce's heart.

Thinking about this key story helped me figure out what sign I should ask for. "Send me something to do with a key please. I'm not sure if it is actually going to be a key but please send me a sign that involves a key of some sort. Thank you! Thank you! Thank you!" I thought about this in my head and didn't tell a single soul.

I let go and let God. I was super aware of everything in my environment. I was looking at my life like I was watching a movie. I felt like I was testing the universe. Was this what people mean when they talk about the power of quantum physics or manifesting? Can we really tap into this creative force of the universe to create a life filled with love? Do we have to feel the light within us for it to work? Do we need to change our energy inside of us to tap into this invisible field of energy? Am I really able to "order" what I want just like ordering a shirt or sweater on the internet?

This isn't like a child asking for a new toy for Christmas. It's such a deeper feeling from within, like the love I felt when I found the dime on top of the mountain.

The next day, nothing happened. I felt like Hannah must have felt when she didn't receive the sign from her sister. I mean, does this really work?

As I slammed the drawer of the antique wooden desk, I heard the clink on the floor and wondered if my Great Grandfather's spectacles, which were carefully placed on top of the desk, had fallen. I looked around and then spotted the guilty party. As I picked up the metal ornamental decoration that came unglued from the drawer, I looked deep into the keyhole and said, "Got it Eldon!" I had requested "something to do with a key" so this was good enough for me!

I felt shivers inside me like bubbles rising up in a fish tank as I stood alone in my house. I believed this was the sign I had requested and I didn't need anyone else to believe. I had created an event that was a message from Heaven with only my thoughts.

I went to bed a little earlier than usual that night. Still thinking about the sign from Eldon, I wondered if any more keys would appear.

It wasn't until the last sentence of the chapter that I realized Eldon was still going to help with that he used to call "God Moments"- which he had many throughout his life. I was reading the book *If I Die Before I Wake* by Eli Shaw. Eli's book was about the many ways he cared for people throughout his life. I was thinking of Eldon as I read this book because I remember him telling me that it would be difficult to take care of my father full time. He told me that I would get burned out being a full time care-giver. As caregivers, we forget to take care of ourselves. We get too busy with the needs of others.

He was right but I also treasured every moment that I was able to spend with my dad during his last days on earth. It was this burnout that caused me to ask for help. I couldn't work full time and care for my father. We were lucky to be able to hire full time around the clock care for my father. I transitioned from full time care seven days a week to monitoring my Dad's care through visits and periodic overnights with him.

I had been slow to read this particular book. Most books I whiz through and can read up to three or four books in a week. Looking back now, I see the reason for the timing of this particular chapter on this particular night. Eli shared about enjoying a sunset and slowing life down while caretaking for his friend who was dying. He compares life to a garden where everything is as beautiful as that sunset they watched that night. Gratitude became a way of life when he was faced with the upcoming expected death of a loved one.

Eli explains more about gratitude for all the things throughout the day. The miracle of the sun rising and setting each day. The glorious things like fresh water or coffee or the comfortable bed we sleep in. He compared life to a garden. What do we want in our garden of life? Do we want to take care of others? Do we want to paint or teach? What is it that we want in our garden? It's up to us to open the gate to our garden of life. First, we need to find the key to open the gate to our garden.

"I hope you find your key," was the very last sentence of the chapter. It didn't hit me until the last sentence that I was reading all about a key to life! I felt like a brand new door was opening and, just like the dime on the mountain, Eldon was showing me how "God Moments" would appear in my life. Eldon shared many God moments with me where the coincidence was so incredible that it helped solidify his faith, knowing that God was helping. Little did I know, Eldon was just beginning to play the key game like the dime game my dad liked to play. I can hear them laughing now as they plan each event over the next few weeks!

When I was a child, Eldon's family and my family went on many vacations to Florida where we always went to Disney World. The memories of walking into a restaurant and the look of shock when we told the hostess we needed a table for thirteen people still stays with me today. We had four kids in our family and Eldon had five kids. We were a wild, fun bunch.

As I walked down to the beach from the hotel, I saw a young boy getting his sandy feet washed off by his mom.

"I found a treasure!" he said to me as I peeked at the gold coins in his purple pail.

"Wow! Good for you!" I responded as I stepped down the next stair. "And, I found the key to Mickey Mouse's house!" he said. Was it just me or did this little boy just emphasize the word found and the word key? Was this random or was this heaven talking to me? I smiled as his mother explained that they are going to Disney tomorrow.

This woman and child have no idea what just happened. I know deep within me that Eldon was proving the magic of connecting to heaven, yet again, when I least expected it. I had decided the what- a key and Spirit decided the when and how!

I continued my walk toward the beach to catch up to my husband and babbled on about Eldon sending me another key. He smiled and knew how much this simple event meant to me.

As we walked near the ocean waves, I began to wonder about where life is leading me next. I'm close to retirement from my job in education but not exactly retirement age. I want to change my career and write full time, enjoy being a Reiki Master along with my coaching and intuitive angel card readings. How will I know if this is the right path to take? Was this book my key?

We walked and started talking about our newest Grandbaby who will be arriving soon. We have two sons and their sons will both have July birthdays too! We feel blessed to have four Morrissey boys all celebrating their birth within five days of each other!

I see the name "James" written in the sand and, I kid you not, the word "dad" right above it. Again, another crazy coincidence that happened just when I needed some reassurance and when I wasn't expecting it.

Just when we were about to turn around to walk back to the hotel, the most surprising sign gave me the answer I was searching for earlier, What do I do for this next part of my life?

There, written in the sand are the words, *"Once Upon a Time I helped my peeps."* I knew the title of this book was Once Upon a Dime and the theme was helping others understand how to use the communication system with our loved ones in Heaven and live in a more spiritual way. Death was again teaching me to live a very different life than I ever imagined. Writing was not a part of my life plan but here I was doing just that.

The next day before we left to fly home from Florida, I sat on the beach for as long as I possibly could. I wanted to absorb as much vitamin D as possible, listen to the ocean and sit in the sand. As I packed up my book and towel, I felt refreshed and ready to enjoy the day.

Dimes and keys also now show up in movies, in books and when people are talking to me. I don't necessarily always find an actual dime or key now. So, when I got into the elevator, I was shocked when the gentleman spoke the words three times like Dorothy in the Wizard of Oz clicking her shoes three times to take her home.

"Just when you think you have packed everything you need for your vacation but then realize you forgot something. You go to the store and you just can't believe how much they charge you for something. They just seem to nickel and dime you, nickel and dime you, nickel and dime you." Seriously, he had to repeat it three times? Well, honestly, had he not I might not have taken the sign as a message.

The key to my garden is writing and sharing my dime stories. I hope it helps my peeps to live a more spiritual life where we are connected to a universal energy where we know and understand how precious life truly is and that Heaven is right here with us each and every day.

When I first started writing about my grief, I had no idea where I was headed. Looking back now, I see how much I have learned about life through the lens of death.

Since our souls never die, when we leave our physical body, the soul is still communicating with those left behind. The energy of the person is always with us. We can tap into this with our thoughts- just like I did with the keys.

It was a quick hello but little did I know it would be a goodbye, the last time we ever would be able to communicate the way all humans know how- by being physically present. We almost ran into each other at the end of the grocery aisle. She was in a hurry and so was I- a reflection of how I was letting life pass by without appreciating my life. Forever, this memory of seeing Samantha helps me remember that tomorrow is never promised- a saying that is common but not really embraced for what it truly means. The very next day, Sam didn't wake up. I would never see her again. Now, whenever I see people, I always make sure to appreciate the moment and I play a little game when I go to the store.

I am always curious about how God is able to create such coincidences to help us learn during this lifetime. When I go to the store now, I ask myself, "Who am I going to see today?" It helps me imagine that God is supporting me. When I see people, I stop to chat and at least say hi. I appreciate that they were brought into my life. One time, on my way to the store, I happened to think of someone and wondered how her children were doing. Seriusly, when I got to the store, she was there! Did I manifest seeing her? Or, was my intuition guiding me to the energy of this person? I'll never know but it was very interesting to have this experience.

I believed there was a way to communicate with those who had transitioned to Spirit, but I had no idea that this invisible communication system was so much bigger than just messages from our loved ones in Spirit. There is an invisible way to communicate and it is important to remember that our thoughts affect our external world.

I began applying this invisible communication system to other areas of my life and I realized that the message my mind sent to my body affected my health. I realized that I sent messages to other people using energy instead of words. It was these thoughts that would determine my inner and outer world.

My father thought his body was like a car he could fix. As a mechanic, he solved all types of car engine difficulties. It was his life's work. He thought the doctors were mechanics of the body. You might have a leaking engine. Let's fix it! What he didn't understand was that his body was carrying his soul and, if he lost control of listening to his soul, it wouldn't matter what a doctor could do.

Our bodies respond to our thoughts in both positive and negative ways. I have no idea what my father's thoughts were that affected his heart so much so that he spent thirty three years fighting heart disease. I know he must have been stressed out owning his own business and providing for his family. My Dad believed in the doctor's superpowers but our bodies aren't like cars that can be easily fixed with a mechanic or doctor.

Since the heart represents love, security and joy, I am able to see how my father's love for his family made him want to work hard to provide financial security for all of us. When he did this, he may have lost his sense of joy.

He worked hard, ate Snickers bars for lunch and lived on cortisol in his veins like bad oil in a car engine. Even with his smiles and his sense of humor, his body couldn't hold up. When I was about to make a change in my career, I thought a lot about my dad's fight for survival. I myself had been in a cortisol storm for the past ten years and my cholesterol level showed it. The stress was getting to me and my soul wanted me to listen. I was juggling a lot at work and knew that in order to enjoy my life, I had to make some big changes.

I used to live my life in the thought pattern of "I'll be happy when...." Here are a few of my favorites over my lifetime:

- I'll be happy when I get married.
- I'll be happy when I have a baby.
- I'll be happy when I get a teaching job.
- I'll be happy when I get a different job.
- I'll be happy when I move out of my house.
- I'll be happy when I receive a sign from my friend, mother, father, grandmother, daughter, son or whoever I am missing.
- I'll be happy...well, you get the idea, right?

My happiness was based on the "next best thing in my life." I was always chasing happiness. It wasn't yet a part of my daily life.

Now, I've stopped thinking that I'll be happy when....I'm happy right now. My gratitudes each and every day are many. I'm happy writing and sharing my story with all who want to read it and I'm grateful and blessed for each day that I am alive. Life is too short to keep chasing happiness. We truly never know how much time we all have here and I've decided that I am going to be at peace with whatever happens in my life.

I asked Spirit for help and was amazed when the messages were clear. My father came to me in a dream and said, "Don't make the same mistake I made. If I could go back, I'd do it all differently. I wouldn't work so much and I wouldn't have stressed out so much. I realize now that by stressing myself with my thoughts, it affected my body in ways that were invisible. These invisible worries created chaos inside my body and then eventually showed up in the form of heart attacks."

My Dad was forty-six when he almost died of a heart attack. I was turning fifty-four this year and with my cholesterol over two hundred fifty, it was time for me to listen to his guidance. I used what I knew about asking for signs from the other side to help guide me in my life.

Here are the adapted directions to change your thoughts from worry to something positive.

Step 1: Think of something that you are worried about. Be specific

Step 2: Write down why this worries you.

Step 3: Change the belief to something positive and believe it has already happened.

Step 4: Ask and allow the universe and your spirit guides to support you and help you with a positive outcome.

Example

1. I'm worried about selling my house.
2. I'm worried that it is not the right decision.
3. I sold my house and all is well. I have the resources to be able to move forward in my life.
4. I am grateful for my Spirit Guides supporting me during this transition in my life.

This connection to something bigger and the invisible communication system wasn't something that I could see. I needed to tap into this in order to create the life I wanted- one filled with love, peace, forgiveness and joy. At first, it was like a game I was trying to learn how to play.

The trick is that it's not only what we think about but how our bodies are feeling. We are vibrational, energetic beings meant to live joyful lives. We are meant to experience Heaven on Earth during our time here. Instead (myself included), we have gotten caught up in the stress of what society, our ancestors and our linear brains told us we were here for. We get stressed out with our jobs and that affects our energy.

Some religions dictate that our behavior is going to determine whether we go to Heaven- putting pressure on perfectionism and sets in motion the negative voice of worry.

Some schools send the message that we aren't good enough unless we go to college and get a high paying job.

Some of us try to make our parents proud by trying to meet the unwritten expectations parents place on us.

Some of us get so caught up in our mistakes that we can't seem to move forward in our lives.

I have a whole new perspective of life and death. When I step back from all of the demands placed on us and the beliefs that society has told us, what is there?

There is love.

There is peace.

There is joy.

If I was to write advice to my Younger Me, here is what I would tell her:

- Life is a gift and tomorrow is seriously not promised. Our life could end at any time. Enjoy each day so if something happened to you or someone else, you would have no regrets.
- Love your body and stop worrying. Appreciate every part of your body because your body needs to know that you love it.
- See others' souls and love them because if you love yourself, then you have the ability to love and accept others.
- Listen to your body and take care of it. You only get one and it's important to make it last a long, long time!
- Nature resets your natural body rhythm. No matter what, get outside each day for at least 20-30 minutes. An hour is even better.
- Remember the legacy of the people who have passed and embrace that core value that they were able to give you. Think of it as a gift from their spirit.
- Appreciating abundance is okay to do.
- Being confident is a good thing.
- Stop comparing yourself to others.
- There is enough and more for everyone. Abundance comes from within and believing that you deserve greatness.
- Notice how your brain tries to keep you safe by telling you lies- it automatically turns to fear. Tell it to shut up and feel love within yourself.
- Feel soul connection with yourself first and then with others.

- We are all one in an ocean of love.

"Just as harnessing electricity changed the outer world, when we learn how to harness the true power and intelligence of the heart, everything will change about how we think and feel, and how we relate to one another." ~ Heart Math Institute

I have a necklace with two hearts on it. Recently, my grandson said, "Grandma, you have two hearts on your necklace!" He was in the moment and noticed something so simple yet so wonderful. I felt and thought, "Yes, darling. They are your heart and my heart connected. You are loved." I try to feel the connection to everyone around me with this necklace. It helps me turn to love instead of fear.

My friend, Carrie, shared recently that she finds four-leaf clovers all the time now. She often finds them while walking her grandson on the road that I live on. I am so happy to see her spending time with her grandson and that she is aware and looking for miracles. When we begin to look for small miracles, oftentimes we begin to feel so incredibly grateful for our lives. She treasures her time with her grandson and knows that the four leaf clovers are most likely a sign from her loved ones.

I experienced asking and receiving something recently that showed how we can use this practice to attract or manifest other things in our life. It wasn't a message from Spirit but I was able to mold my reality with my thoughts. I was organizing and cleaning my basement for weeks. The energy felt clean and fresh after I painted and vacuumed my new work from home office. I had new pine bookshelves, a beautiful wooden desk and my Grandmother's coffee table set up with a salt lamp and an essential oil diffuser. I was clearing out the clutter in my life and making space for new opportunities; both literally and figuratively.

At the same time, I started doing intuitive angel card readings as part of my health and life coaching business and it allowed me to release old fears about sharing my stories about the afterlife. The energy inside me was like a spring flower blossoming.

Soon after, an absurd idea popped into my head. As I was getting dressed after my massage, I noticed a spider plant on the coffee table at my massage therapist's office. Like a lonely cloud drifting across a clear blue sky, a thought blew into my mind that I seriously wanted a spider plant for my new office space. I remembered reading somewhere that a spider plant helps clean the air in a room. This idea was absurd because I have never been able to keep any household plant alive for more than a few weeks. I never knew which plants wanted more or less water, or whether or not they wanted more or less sunshine. It was almost like the plant could sense my stress. I had given up years ago on having any plants inside my house.

Once, my sister gave me a plant that was from my great grandparents' house. She didn't understand that there was no way this plant would survive when entrusted to my care. Sure enough, months later I gave her back the yellow ceramic pot filled with what looked like only dirt and no sign of any plant life. Luckily, my niece was able to bring it back to life. Because I almost killed that plant, it was ludicrous that this idea of a spider plant popped into my mind.

Then this stronger feeling came through. It was persistent. "No, I really, really, really want a spider plant." The thought was no longer a cloud; it was like a magnet sticking to my mind. I tried to let the idea go again but since it wouldn't, I resolved it with the thought, "Well, if a spider plant appears in my life, maybe I'll try again."

I forgot all about the silly idea about a spider plant and did not talk to anyone about it. I was technically "ordering" a spider plant from the universe, just like ordering a package from Amazon. I wasn't sure the how or the when but I had put the energy out that I would accept a spider plant for my new office, if one came along.

This is where the spirituality part of being human appears and surprises even those of us who know and understand how the universe works. Other people are able to hear our thoughts even without being connected by a telephone or even speaking the words. It can sometimes creep people out if you have ever had this happen. Have you ever thought of someone and then they text or call you? This way of communication seems so unbelievable at times but it is most definitely real.

In a town about forty-five minutes away, at about the time I was thinking those thoughts, one of my Southern New Hampshire University students was preparing to mail a thank you card to me. He not only mailed me that card, but he carefully placed something inside the card.

I had "ordered" a spider plant and I received it in Neil's thank you card! I was so shocked that it took me two days to reach out to Neil to share this crazy coincidence.

Neil read my book and was inspired by my story. He was an educator and understood how our thoughts create our reality. It wasn't always something we were able to talk about when working in public education. My story changed his life and he was changing mine. He was proof that universal intelligence or God or whatever this energy was could hear our thoughts and respond to create our reality. This is true for receiving signs from Spirit but can also be applied to other areas in our life. That's why it's important to filter your thoughts because what you think may come true. What appears in your life is exactly what you think about.

Think negative thoughts and more negativity appears in your life. Think positive thoughts and more positive things appear in your life. My daily gratitude practice includes starting and ending my day with being thankful. I begin each day with ten or eleven gratitudes. I write in a notebook and add an explanation as to why I am grateful. Some examples are "I am grateful for my morning cup of coffee because I love the taste of coffee and it wakes me up." or "I am grateful for my house because it is a wonderful place to live." At the end of the day, I hold a rose quartz rock to my heart and think of the one best thing that happened during my day. This trains my brain to remember all of the good things. From driving home from work safely or watching the sun set or dinner with family, I always find several things I am grateful for.

Grief is inside each and every one of us. It sits like a rain cloud ready to burst open at the mere memories that live in our minds. Whether we stuff it down or let it rise up, we are able to feel deep love within.

I was born in 1968. The telephone had been around for a while but at that time many would have thought the concepts on the Jetson's animated cartoon were make believe. Video calls and microwaves seemed like an impossible idea. It was only for the imagination. Nowadays, people Facetime easily and most homes have a microwave that creates invisible heat! We also store information on an invisible "i-cloud". Just because we can't see it, doesn't mean it doesn't work.

At a crossroads for understanding, there are now many scientists proving this idea of an invisible connection to what they term consciousness. They describe this consciousness continuing on after the physical body has died and there are many studies proving both Mediums and Psychic abilities for some people.

Liz Enton notes the scientific researchers in her new book, *WTF Just Happened*. Liz was very science minded but found comfort during her journey with grief by the verified studies completed by both The Forever Family Foundation and the other scientists around the world. Now, Liz believes that there is a strong possibility that consciousness survives our bodily death.

If I had been five minutes later or earlier, I would have missed it. If I had not forgotten my purse in my husband's truck, I would have missed it. If my radio had been set to Sirius XM instead of the local radio station, I would have missed it. If I hadn't asked a friend to come thirty minutes later, I would have missed it. If I hadn't unpacked the groceries first, I would have missed it. If I hadn't taken part of the day off for a doctor's appointment, I would have missed it. The list could go on and on. The fact is: I didn't miss it and the title of this book was sent to me by Spirit because I let go of the steering wheel.

I let go and didn't worry about leaving my purse somewhere. I let go and didn't worry about asking my friend to come a little later. I let go and didn't worry about making another trip downtown. I let go and took care of myself by going to get the medicine to help me feel better. I let go of the day to go exactly how I planned it to go.

I had been thinking about the title of my book all day. I was meeting with someone about my book and I couldn't figure it out. I had a list about a page long and had asked a few friends what they thought of all of the different possible titles.

"Kim, would you mind coming at 1:30 instead of 1:00? I need to run to the store and get some medication before we meet about my book."

"Of course. I'll see you at 1:30," Kim graciously agreed.

I felt bad. I hate being late and I hate not showing up to something I had agreed to prior. I was asking for something that I needed, which was so hard for me. Why do I struggle asking for something so simple? I know the answer. I have spent most of my life caring for everyone else instead of myself. My frame was to take care of others before I took care of myself- something I had done my whole life to try to make others happy.

I needed the medication to help me feel better and because I had forgotten my purse in my husband's truck, I had to come home to get an extra insurance card. That meant I had to make an extra trip back downtown.

"Come on down to our Once Upon a Dime sale. Live Happily Ever After in a Nicer, Newer Car for just one dime down!" The Shelburne Mitsubishi ad on the local radio show came on the radio as soon as I started my car.

"Thank you Dad," was all I thought as I was dreaming of a life happily ever after where I live in a more spiritual, connected way. I hope *Once Upon a Dime* helps you to connect to your intuition, your natural born gifts and that you are able to feel your loved ones right beside you.

"One day she woke up different. Done with who was with her, who was against her, or walking down the middle because they didn't have the guts to decide. She was done with anything that didn't bring her peace. She realized that opinions were a dime a dozen, that validation was for parking, and loyalty wasn't a word, but a lifestyle. It was this day that her life changed. And not because of a man, or a job, but because she realized that life is way too short to leave the key to your happiness in someone else's pocket." ~Anonymous

While looking up to see who wrote this quote, I found the quote on a site that said, **"Relationship Rules. A Safe Haven for emotional human beings."**

You have everything you need within you and your loved ones keep showing you they are still here with you. Believe in this connection.

The keys to life are always inside me like my keys to my car being in my pocket.

When I walk away from my car with the keys in my pocket, my car beeps. I imagine my father and Eldon telling me,

"The answers are within you. Take your keys wherever you travel. Notice the signs. Believe in more. Get rid of outdated subconscious belief systems that no longer serve you. Connect to your intuition and know that we are always with you."

Heaven is trying to get our attention through dreams and synchronicities. Now, you know how to listen.

Monica Morrissey lives in Northern Vermont with her husband and two cats. She loves hiking, swimming and being with her grandkids.

Monica has been an educator for over thirty years. Her experience teaching others helped her gain the knowledge she would need for the unexpected career change; becoming an author. At the age of fifty, she published her inspiring *Dimes from Heaven* story to help others understand our connection to loved ones who are in the spirit world.

Following her intuition like never before, she began sharing stories about synchronistic events revealing that our souls never die. As an empath and natural-born teacher, her faith is guiding her to help people experience life and death in a whole new way.

Monica was careful to leave spirituality out of the classroom. Since the tragic death of her nephew in 2008, she secretly began reading and studying about mediums, death, grief, and how our body (and life) are affected by our thoughts. She now has a better knowledge about the afterlife to share with others. Her retirement from the public school system allowed her to follow her true passion; helping people who want to learn more about everlasting life and who want to live healthier and happier lives. Monica is a Reiki Master and Instructor, Intuitive Card Reader, Past Life Regression practitioner, and loves to analyze dreams. While others encourage self-care, Monica is dedicated to helping clients with soul-care.

When she started writing her stories she knew they were powerful and they would and will continue to help readers experiencing loss. She wants everyone to be able to experience this feeling.

Dimes from Heaven was a finalist for the International Indie Book Awards in the category of death and dying and was an Amazon #1 Top New Release in Supernaturalism.

Monica knows how powerful these stories of coincidences are from another dimension. Dimes are her signature sign from heaven and people love listening to her stories. The synchronicities reveal a soul's life is eternal. Each of her books gives us the tools to open the door to heaven so we are able to feel the deep love for those no longer with us.

www.ingramcontent.com/pod-product-compliance
Lightning Source LLC
Chambersburg PA
CBHW071727150726
47998CB00005B/1533